AVATAR AND NATURE SPIRITUALITY

ENVIRONMENTAL
HUMANITIES

AVATAR

AND NATURE SPIRITUALITY

BRON TAYLOR *editor*

WILFRID LAURIER
UNIVERSITY PRESS

Wilfrid Laurier University Press acknowledges the financial support of the Government of Canada through the Canada Book Fund for our publishing activities.

Library and Archives Canada Cataloguing in Publication

Avatar and nature spirituality / Bron Taylor, editor.

(Environmental humanities series)
Includes bibliographical references and index.
Issued in print and electronic formats.
ISBN 978-1-55458-843-5 (pbk.).—ISBN 978-1-55458-881-7 (epub).—ISBN 978-1-55458-880-0 (pdf)

1. Avatar (Motion picture : 2009). I. Taylor, Bron Raymond, author, editor of compilation II. Series: Environmental humanities series

PN1997.2.A94A93 2013   791.43'72   C2013-903612-1   C2013-903613-X

Cover design by David Drummond. Front-cover image from iStockphoto. Text design by Daiva Villa, Chris Rowat Design.

© 2013 Wilfrid Laurier University Press
Waterloo, Ontario, Canada
www.wlupress.wlu.ca

This book is printed on FSC recycled paper and is certified Ecologo. It is made from 100% post-consumer fibre, processed chlorine free, and manufactured using biogas energy.

Printed in Canada

Every reasonable effort has been made to acquire permission for copyright material used in this text, and to acknowledge all such indebtedness accurately. Any errors and omissions called to the publisher's attention will be corrected in future printings.

Contents

PART I: BRINGING *AVATAR* INTO FOCUS

Prologue:
Avatar as Rorschach

BRON TAYLOR

I first saw *Avatar* shortly after its release in December 2009. Like most viewers, I found the bioluminescent landscape of Pandora stunningly beautiful. I was also moved by the storylines: the against-all-odds resistance by the native inhabitants of Pandora against violent, imperial invaders; the turncoats from the invading forces who join the resistance; and the love stories. Sure, there is the formulaic story—male and female find love, lose love, and find it again—but there is also the love of a people for their home and their wild flora and fauna, a contagious love that subverts the ecological and spiritual understandings of some invaders, leading them to take a stand with those they have come to exploit.

The film's producer, writer, and director, James Cameron, is adept at evoking emotional responses from his audiences and making huge sums of money along the way. Indeed, no one's films exemplify the blockbuster, money-making film genre better than Cameron's *Terminator, Aliens, Titanic,* and now *Avatar,* which banked $2.8 billion within the first two years after its release, 73 per cent of which came from outside the United States.[1] The figure would have been significantly higher had not the Chinese government cut short the film's run, reportedly out of fear that it might encourage resistance to development projects and the government's resettlement schemes (Stanton 2010). The film also gained wide recognition for its many technical innovations and won many awards, including best film drama and best director at the Golden Globe Awards (which is decided by

the Hollywood Foreign Press Association) and three of the nine Oscars for
which it was nominated (although not for best picture or director). The
attendance records and professional accolades provide one marker of the
film's appeal. But is there more to the film than tried-and-true narratives
of injustice being overcome and romantic dreams fulfilled? Is it significant
in some way other than for its technical achievements and profit making?

When I first saw the film, I certainly thought this might be the case. For
more than twenty years, I had been tracking the development and increasing global cultural traction of nature-based spiritualities, paying special
attention to how such spiritualities contribute to environmental activism.[2]
My book documenting these trends, *Dark Green Religion: Nature Spirituality and the Planetary Future* (2010), came out shortly before the release
of *Avatar*. In it, I argued that spiritualities that stress ecological interdependence and mutual dependence, involve deep feelings of belonging and
connection to nature, and express beliefs that the biosphere is a sacred,
Gaia-like superorganism, were taking new forms and exercising increasing
social and political influence. These sorts of nature-based spiritualities
generally cohere with and draw on an evolutionary and ecological worldview, and therefore stress continuity and even kinship among all organisms. They also often have animistic dimensions, in which communication
(if not also communion) with non-human organisms is thought possible.
Consequently, these "otherkind" are considered to have intrinsic value
(regardless of whether they are useful in some way to our own species)
and should be accorded respect, if not reverence. Uniting these Gaian and
animistic perceptions, I argued, is generally a deep sense of humility about
the human place in the universe in contrast to anthropocentric conceits,
wherein human beings consider themselves to be superior to other living
things and the only ones whose interests count morally.

In *Dark Green Religion*, I examined a wide range of social phenomena that expressed and promoted such spiritualities. Recognizing that
the evolutionary-ecological worldview that fuels dark green spirituality
has had only a century and a half to incubate and spread, and noting that
despite this, the trends I had identified were rapidly gathering adherents
and momentum, I speculated that we could be witnessing the nascent
stages of a new global nature religion. Such a religion would have affinities with some aspects of the world's long-standing and predominant religious and philosophical traditions, and it would, in some cases, fuse with
them, I suggested. Moreover, such dark green spiritualities could also *coex-
ist* (rather than fuse) with the environmentally progressive forms of the
world's long-standing religious traditions, uniting in common action to
protect the biosphere, even if profound differences remained about the

sources of existence. I also suggested that dark green religious forms might increasingly supplant older meaning and action systems, because the dark green forms more easily cohere with modern scientific understandings than religious worldviews involving one or more invisible divine beings. Consequently, the dark green forms could more easily adapt than most long-standing religions to new and deeper scientific understandings, especially when compared to religions that reify their "ultimate sacred postulates" by chiselling them, physically or metaphorically, into inviolable sacred texts.[3]

These were the possibilities running through my mind when I first saw *Avatar.* I had already spent considerable time looking at artistic productions, including documentaries and theatrical films that exemplified dark green spirituality; after seeing *Avatar,* I immediately thought it was another exemplar of such green religion. Moreover, as it broke box office records, I could not help but wonder if the film was evidence that global, cultural receptivity to the ideas prevalent in dark green religion was even more profound than I had previously thought. I also wondered if *Avatar* would prove to be the most effective "dark green" propaganda yet produced. In short, I thought, there might well be something exceptionally significant about the film, even if the ideas expressed in it were nothing new and even though some would conclude that the film was not great art. I suspected not only that *Avatar* was a *reflection* of the global emergence of dark green religion but that it might even effectively *advance* such spirituality and ethics.

In his public statements about the film, Cameron has expressed a clear intention to promote themes that are central to what I have called dark green religion. When accepting his Golden Globe Award for best picture, for example, he said: "*Avatar* asks us to see that everything is connected, all human beings to each other, and us to the Earth. And if you have to go four and a half light years to another, made-up planet to appreciate this miracle of the world that we have right here, well, you know what, that's the wonder of cinema right there, that's the magic" (Associated Press 2010). Soon after, in an Oprah Winfrey television special that was broadcast shortly before the Academy Awards ceremony, Cameron repeated this theme, adding, with delight, that at the climax of the film the audience had come to take the side of nature in its battle against the destructive forces of an expansionist human civilization. Here, without using the terminology of contemporary environmental ethics, Cameron expressed an affinity for deep ecological or biocentric theories, in which nature is considered to have intrinsic value. Indeed, according to an exchange during an *Entertainment Weekly* interview, it appears that Cameron was even on the radical side of biocentric ethics. When an interviewer asserted, "*Avatar* is the perfect eco-terrorism recruiting tool," Cameron answered in an equally provocative way, "Good, good, I like that one. I consider that a positive review. I believe in ecoterrorism" (Moorhead 2010).[4]

In the light of such statements, it seems clear that dark green themes and activist motivations underlay the film's production. Furthermore, the negative reaction to the film by most conservative commentators, whether political or religious, revealed significant concern that such views and imperatives might be gaining more adherents and cultural appeal. But while pundits and scholars speculated about the possible significance and influence of the film, they usually supplied little evidence to support their assertions. So I began to gather such evidence, establishing a website domain to track relevant information as it unfolded.[5] I knew that a more concerted inquiry was needed.

Avatar as Rorschach

Given my own response to the film and informed by the sociology of knowledge, I knew that generating a truly critical inquiry would be difficult.[6] I was keenly aware, for example, of my own tendency to view the film through pre-existing prisms. I therefore anticipated that many others would simply interpret the film through their own intellectual and cultural lenses, including scholarly perspectives grounded in postmodern philosophies, post-colonial critical theory, cultural anthropology, evolutionary biology, environmental ethics, and film studies, as well as perspectives rooted in ethnic and religious identities and other subcultures and enclaves, whether political, ideological, economic, tribal, or military.

The spiritual, moral, and political dimensions of the film have elicited wildly diverse reactions, nowhere more apparent than in the popular press and in cyberspace. The filmmaker and the film have been labelled pro-civilization and anti-civilization, pro-science and anti-science, un-American and too American, anti-Marine and pro-Marine, racist and anti-racist, anti-indigenous and pro-indigenous, woman-respecting and misogynistic, leftist and neo-conservative, progressive and reactionary, activist and self-absorbed. And, of course, there have been religious labels: pagan, atheistic, theistic, pantheistic, panentheistic, and animistic. More about all of these perspectives are provided in the following essays.

Observing the stunningly diverse and highly contested cognitive and emotional responses to *Avatar* reminded me of the famous Rorschach psychological test, in which individual reactions to ink blots shown on cards vary widely, presumably because of differences in the psychological constitution and cultural context of the test takers. While, as readers of this volume will find, there have been some surprising reactions to the film, it is also the case that if one were to know the cultural context and cognitive frames of the observers, it would usually be possible to anticipate their responses.

That different individuals and groups tend to perceive things differently is, on the one hand, a dynamic to be welcomed, because differently situated people may have insights that people placed elsewhere may not. On the other hand, it is a problematic tendency, for it is also possible for our cognitive frames to create a field of view in which other perspectives, as well as information that might disconfirm our expectations, remain out of focus. So it worried me when I thought about what insights might gleaned, or missed, when considering the film, given the strong human tendency to see what one expects, especially when we often remain insular, segregated in our own cultural enclaves, including supposedly enlightened, academic ones.

On a personal level, although the film *seemed* to exemplify what I had found in my previous research, I did not want to conclude too hastily that *Avatar* provided more evidence for my dark green theses. So, with regard to initial perceptions about the film's dark green themes and cultural significance, I thought I should suspend judgment, pay close attention to responses and interpretations of the film at variance with my own first impressions, and seek further information. I was concerned, however, about more than whether I might misperceive the meanings and significance of the film. In the initial months after its release, I noticed that in academic circles, there was little cross-disciplinary debate about it. Moreover, many of the scholarly views that were expressed struck me as "ivory towerish" in nature, disregarding the ways in which those not embedded in scholarly subcultures were responding to and often embracing the film—even seeing their own feelings and predicaments reflected in it. The tendency toward Rorschach-style, quick-reaction analyses seemed to me methodologically flawed. Last but not least, even though the film was replete with religious themes, in the first few months after the film was released, despite a great deal of public discussion and debate about the film, I could not find nuanced discussion of its religious dimensions.

For all these reasons, I thought a more judicious and interdisciplinary approach to the film and its reception was in order. Hoping to precipitate such an enquiry, in the spring of 2010, I issued a call for papers focusing on the spirituality and politics of *Avatar*. I eventually received more than thirty submissions. Several were published in the *Journal for the Study of Religion, Nature, and Culture*, which I edit; a wider array appear in this volume.[7]

The authors in the following pages express many points of view, sometimes, but not always, finding points of agreement. Each of them offers fascinating and important insights into the film and its putative significance. As I argue in my concluding reflections, despite my cautious approach, I think many of the essays provide further evidence of my argument in *Dark Green Religion* and my related initial impression about the film and its reception: *Avatar* reflects and dramatically presents dark green religious and ethical themes, and its commercial success is due in part to the profound, recently unfolding, and increasingly global changes in worldview that provide fertile cultural ground for dark green artistic productions. In short, the essays in this volume demonstrate that it is "good to think" about *Avatar*, as well as about the cultural trends that gave rise to it and the diverse and contested reaction to it.[8] These thoughts might even be of the kind that precipitate action, not on Pandora but right here on Earth.

★ ★ ★

Acknowledgements

I wish to acknowledge the support of the Rachel Carson Center for Environment and Society at Ludwig-Maximilians-Universität in Munich, Germany, which supported my writing and orchestration of this project while I was in residence there as a Carson Fellow in 2012. I am very grateful to the centre's directors, Christof Mauch and Helmut Trishler, for their invitation to study at this wonderful think tank, which provides scholarly habitat for scholars working at the intersection of the social sciences, environmental history, and the humanities. And I want to thank the fellows for many helpful conversations and recommendations about this and other, ongoing projects, as well as the staff and research assistants who provided such a warm welcome and were helpful in so many ways.

   This book has been a truly collaborative effort, not only by the contributors but also by reviewers and editors who labour on the *Journal for the Study of Religion, Nature, and Culture*, to which most of the writing in this book was originally submitted. The list of reviewers, many of whom offered helpful editorial suggestions as well, includes Paul Ray, Greg Johnson, Bart Welling, Pat Brereton, Terry Terhaar, Paula Willoquet-Maricondi, Rachelle Gould, Matthew Holtmeier, Randolf Haluza-Delay, Britt Istoft, and Stephen Rust. Those who did especially heavy lifting during the review process were David Barnhill, Adrian Ivakhiv, Lisa Sideris, Robin Wright, Robin Globus Veldman, Reyda Taylor, Joy Greenberg, and Joseph Witt. I received helpful leads to *Avatar*-related writing from Bernard Zaleha and Edward Noria, and especially helpful theoretical suggestions and recommendations from Carson Center Fellows Lisa Sideris, Anthony Carrigan, and Ursula Münster. I may have forgotten others who provided a good lead or insight along the way, and if so, I am grateful to them as well and regret their omission here.

Notes

1 *Avatar* Box Office Mojo, http://www.boxofficemojo.com/movies/?id=avatar.htm, updated 3 February 2013.

2 In 1991, I began publishing a series of articles about such phenomena (see Taylor 1991 to 2008) and orchestrated collaborative research leading to the book (Taylor 1995a).

3 The term "ultimate sacred postulates" is from anthropologist Roy Rappaport (1999), who argues that oral traditions are more likely to be environmentally adaptive than those based on writing because they are more flexible than those that put their religious guidelines down in inviolable, written, sacred texts.

4 For more on Cameron's long-standing environmental radicalism, see Renzetti (2009).

5 Shortly after seeing the film, for example, and hoping to track its reception and influence, I created an online venue to provide further information about the film; see "*Avatar* and Dark Green Religion" at http://www.brontaylor.com/environmental_books/dgr/avatar_nature_religion.html.

6 For the classic statements regarding the social construction of reality, the latter focusing on religion, see Berger and Luckmann (1966) and Berger (1969).

7 See the *Journal for the Study of Religion, Nature, and Culture* 5, no. 4 (2010) and 6, no. 2 (2012).

8 That species are not only "good to eat" but "good to think" was famously asserted by anthropologist Claude Lévi-Strauss ([1963] 1969, 89), who was expressing the idea that they are culturally and religiously significant in a number of ways. This is what I intend to suggest by borrowing the phrase here.

References

Associated Press. 2010. "James Cameron's 'Avatar' Wins Big at Golden Globes." *Access Hollywood*, 17 January. http://www.accesshollywood.com/james-camerons-avatar-wins-big-at-golden-globes_article_27831.

Berger, Peter. 1969. *The Sacred Canopy: Elements of a Sociological Theory of Religion*. New York: Anchor.

Berger, Peter, and Thomas Luckmann. 1966. *The Social Construction of Reality*. New York: Anchor.

Lévi-Strauss, Claude. (1963) 1969. *Totemism*. Reprint, Boston: Beacon Press.

Moorhead, John. 2010. "*Avatar*'s Success: Romantic Narratives and Dark Green Religion." *TheoFantastique*, 27 January. http://www.theofantastique.com/2010/01/27/avatars-success-romantic-narratives-and-dark-green-religion/.

Rappaport, Roy A. 1999. *Ritual and Religion in the Making of Humanity*. Cambridge, MA: Cambridge University Press.

Renzetti, Elizabeth. 2009. "James Cameron's *Avatar*: A Symphony in Blue and Green." *Globe and Mail*, 18 December. http://www.theglobeandmail.com/news/arts/james-camerons-avatar-a-symphony-in-blue-and-green/article1405271/.

Stanton, Pete. 2010. "China Pulls *Avatar* from Their Cinemas Fearing Civil Unrest." *Moviefone*, 19 January. http://blog.moviefone.com/2010/01/19/china-bans-avatar-from-their-cinemas-fearing-civil-unrest/.

Taylor, Bron. 1991. "The Religion and Politics of Earth First!" *The Ecologist* 21(6): 258–66.

―――. 1994. "Earth First!'s Religious Radicalism." In *Ecological Prospects: Scientific, Religious, and Aesthetic Perspectives*, edited by Christopher Key Chapple, 185–209. Albany: State University of New York Press.

―――. 1995a. *Ecological Resistance Movements: The Global Emergence of Radical and Popular Environmentalism.* Albany: State University of New York Press.

―――. 1995b. "Resacralizing Earth: Pagan Environmentalism and the Restoration of Turtle Island." In *American Sacred Space*, edited by David Chidester and Edward T. Linenthal, 97–151. Bloomington: Indiana University Press.

―――. 1996. "Earth First!: From Primal Spirituality to Ecological Resistance." In *This Sacred Earth*, edited by Roger Gottlieb, 545–57. New York: Routledge.

―――. 1997a. "Earthen Spirituality or Cultural Genocide: Radical Environmentalism's Appropriation of Native American Spirituality." *Religion* 17(2): 183–215.

―――. 1997b. "Earth First! Fights Back." *Terra Nova* 2(2): 29–43.

―――. 1998. "Religion, Violence, and Radical Environmentalism: From Earth First! to the Unabomber to the Earth Liberation Front." *Terrorism and Political Violence* 10(4): 10–42.

―――. 1999. "Green Apocalypticism: Understanding Disaster in the Radical Environmental Worldview." *Society and Natural Resources* 12(4): 377–86.

―――. 2000a. "Bioregionalism: An Ethics of Loyalty to Place." *Landscape Journal* 19(1–2): 50–72.

―――. 2000b. "Deep Ecology and Its Social Philosophy: A Critique." In *Beneath the Surface: Critical Essays on Deep Ecology*, edited by Eric Katz, Andrew Light, and David Rothenberg, 269–99. Cambridge: MIT Press.

―――. 2001a. "Earth and Nature-Based Spirituality (Part I): From Deep Ecology to Radical Environmentalism." *Religion* 31(2): 175–93.

―――. 2001b. "Earth and Nature-Based Spirituality (Part II): From Deep Ecology and Bioregionalism to Scientific Paganism and the New Age." *Religion* 31(3): 225–45.

―――. 2002. "Diggers, Wolves, Ents, Elves and Expanding Universes: Bricolage, Religion, and Violence from Earth First! and the Earth Liberation Front to the Antiglobalization Resistance." In *The Cultic Milieu: Oppositional Subcultures in an Age of Globalization*, edited by Jeffrey Kaplan and Heléne Lööw, 26–74. Lanham, MD: Altamira/Rowman and Littlefield.

―――. 2004a. "Revisiting Ecoterrorism." In *Religionen im Konflikt* [Religions in Conflict], edited by Vasilios N. Makrides and Jörg Rüpke, 237–48. Münster, Germany: Aschendorff.

―――. 2004b. "Threat Assessments and Radical Environmentalism." *Terrorism and Political Violence* 15(4): 172–83.

―――. 2005a. "Earth First! and the Earth Liberation Front." In *Encyclopedia of Religion and Nature*, edited by Bron Taylor, 518–24. London: Continuum International.

———. 2005b. "Radical Environmentalism." In *Encyclopedia of Religion and Nature*, edited by Bron Taylor, 1326–35. London: Continuum International.

———. 2008. "The Tributaries of Radical Environmentalism." *Journal of Radicalism* 2(1): 27–61.

———. 2010. *Dark Green Religion: Nature Spirituality and the Planetary Future.* Berkeley: University of California Press.

Introduction:
The Religion and Politics of *Avatar*

BRON TAYLOR

Readers who have not seen *Avatar* should do so before reading further, noting their own reactions and observations. For those unable to see the film and for those whose memory of the story and its pivotal moments would benefit from refreshing, the first section, below, provides a synopsis of the film. The second section surveys the approaches taken in the subsequent essays to guide those who may wish to pursue particular lines of inquiry. The introduction concludes by explaining both the "family resemblance" approach to social phenomena variously understood to be "religious" or "spiritual" and how this approach has shaped the terminology and framing of this volume.

Synopsis

Avatar is set on Pandora, a stunningly beautiful, often bioluminescent, and lushly vegetated moon circling a gaseous planet in the Alpha Centauri star system. There, in the year 2154, humans from the Resource Development Administration (RDA), a corporation with great political, economic, and military might that operates with the authority of Earth's Interplanetary Commerce Administration, has established a mining colony. The RDA seeks a rare mineral called "unobtanium," which is the most efficient superconductor known and is thus critically important to advanced energy systems and galactic economic enterprises. In a metaphorical allusion to the ways in which colonizers have often pursued the lands and resources of colonized peoples, *Avatar* quickly establishes that human beings have been waging a campaign to subjugate the Na'vi—tall, blue, humanoid (but tail-wagging) hunter-gatherer creatures who are the moon's indigenous inhabitants. The Na'vi stand in the way of the RDA's exploitive plans and ultimately mount a violent resistance against the invaders.

The RDA employs two entwined strategies in its campaign: one social, one military. The social strategy is scientific and is led by Dr. Grace Augustine, whose discipline is never clearly specified but resembles that of an anthropologist with a specialty in ethnobiology; when the film begins, she has already been studying Pandoran biology and Na'vi culture for some time. Although her primary passion is to learn about the moon's environment and the Na'vi's environmental and social systems, she is also there to provide information that may be useful to the RDA so that the corporation can gain the co-operation and pacification of the Na'vi, and thus access to the coveted energy conductor. If this strategy fails, the military strategy will take precedence: the RDA will then subjugate the Na'vi by force and take the unobtanium without their consent.

One of the soldiers brought to Pandora to help secure the unobtanium is a former Marine named Jake Sully. A paraplegic who lost the use of his legs in an earlier battlefield injury, he has been brought in to replace his deceased brother, who was participating in a genetic engineering program on Pandora that produces human-Na'vi hybrids (named "avatars")— beings with human consciousness in a Na'vi body. Augustine and her anthropologist assistant, Norm Spellman, also have Na'vi avatars, enabling them to breathe the Pandoran air, which is toxic to humans, and to interact with the indigenous inhabitants. Because Sully and his brother were identical twins with the same genetic structure, Sully can assume his brother's avatar body; combined with his military background, this accounts for his selection for the project. Working with Augustine's team, Sully is mandated to learn enough about the Na'vi to convince them to leave the regions that are targeted for commercial extraction. Failing that, he is to identify Na'vi vulnerabilities and thus ensure an easy military victory.

What the imperial forces do not anticipate is that Augustine, Spellman, Sully, and, later, a tough, no-nonsense Latina helicopter pilot and former Marine named Trudy Chacon will view what is happening to the Na'vi as fundamentally unjust and will join their resistance. Chacon, however, has no avatar body as she is a part of the military forces but not the avatar project. Augustine and Spellman, like many contemporary anthropologists, come to respect not only the environmental knowledge but also the nature spirituality of the Na'vi; so, too, does Sully, although he does not come to such respect scientifically.

There are two key aspects to Na'vi spirituality. On the one hand, they perceive the planet itself as a Gaia-like, organic, bio-neurological network, which they personify as the goddess Eywa. The Na'vi believe that Eywa does not take sides between different species on Pandora but rather promotes the balance and flourishing of the entire natural world. Augustine is obviously interested in but skeptical of the religious understandings that the Na'vi have about Eywa; early in the film, she seems to understand Eywa as akin to the laws of Pandoran nature.[1]

Na'vi spirituality also involves what could be called relational animism. With such animism, respect toward all other organisms, even dangerous prey animals, is obligatory. The Na'vi's animism is rooted in their belief that Eywa is "the author and origin of the vital interconnectedness of all its living things" (Wilhelm and Mathison 2009, xiv). But a special intimacy and bonding is also possible via a braid-resembling neural "whip" or "queue" that the Na'vi can entwine with other individuals and animals to deepen communion and communication with them. This sort of bonding enables Na'vi warriors to mind-meld with these animals and then hunt or engage in battle as though they were one being (8). They can establish this bond with creatures such as the direhorse and two flying creatures, the banshee and the Great Leonopteryx (in biological terms, an apex aerial predator), which the Na'vi call the *toruk* or flying king lion.

Based on what they learn from the Na'vi, Augustine and the others initially try to protect them by convincing RDA officials that Pandora's true wealth is in its natural systems and the living things that constitute them, not in the moon's minerals. Put simply, even though their motives for being there in the first place are clearly not altruistic, the scientists come to love the Na'vi, their knowledge and way of life, and even the habitats to which they belong. As Augustine puts it, "There are many dangers on Pandora, and one of the subtlest is that you may come to love it too much" (Wilhelm and Mathison 2009, epigraph). Although without a scientific background, Sully also falls in love with the people and the place, albeit in a different way than Augustine and Spellman. In his case, his love for Pandoran nature is due in no small measure to his expert guide into its beauties and mysteries, the lithe and beautiful Na'vi princess, Neytiri. The beginning of their relationship is rocky because of Sully's ignorance and disrespect of the forest and its creatures. But after the small luminescent woodsprites (the *atokirina'*), jellyfish-like "pure spirits" who are the seeds of the Tree of Souls (the *Vitraya Ramunong*) descend and alight on Sully, thus indicating their favour, Neytiri decides to take Sully to her parents.[2] Her father, Eytukan, is the chief of her Na'vi clan, the Omaticaya, and her mother, Mo'at, is their shaman-like spiritual leader. Mo'at, perceiving the will of Eywa, orders her daughter to teach Sully the Na'vi ways. Sully proves to be a courageous and astute student, and he is eventually initiated into the tribe, enters a romantic relationship with Neytiri, and mates with her.

In their own ways, especially as made possible viscerally through their avatar bodies, Augustine, Sully, and Spellman each come to love the Na'vi and to respect, if not embrace, their holistic ecological spirituality. This leads to a difficult situation, however, since they know of the RDA's plans and are complicit in pursuing its social strategy to pacify the Na'vi. Knowing that the RDA is on the brink of a military operation and having been initiated into the tribe, Sully desperately tries to convince the Omaticaya to leave their Hometree. (Each Na'vi clan has a Hometree, where they live and share their lives; the massive plant actually comprises a number of individuals of the same tree species that have grown together over time into a strong, interrelated organism.) While pleading with the Omaticaya, Sully reveals how he knows the RDA's military intention. In this way, he confesses the role that he and Augustine have played in the RDA's objectives. Having mated with Sully, Neytiri feels anguish and betrayal, and her entire clan rejects the human avatars. Shortly thereafter, the RDA forces—led by another former Marine, Colonel Miles Quaritch—attacks. Despite the efforts of Sully and his avatar comrades, and even though the helicopter pilot Trudy Chacon refuses orders to attack the Hometree, Quaritch's forces launch missiles that obliterate the Omaticaya's Hometree and kill many Na'vi, including Eytukan, scattering the survivors in agony and terror.

Soon after, back in their human bodies, Augustine, Sully, and Spellman are imprisoned after the RDA learn of their rebellion, but Chacon frees them, enabling Sully to return to his avatar body and prove his courage and good heart by bonding with the Leonopteryx, a rare feat in Na'vi history. Thus, Sully regains the trust of the Na'vi, who acknowledge him as the sixth Toruk Makto, conferring upon him the status of a warrior-leader, which he apparently shares with the Na'vi warrior and leader Tsu'tey. Clearly, however, as the Toruk Makto, Sully emerges as the greater of the two leaders.

Sully then asks Mo'at and the Omaticaya for help saving Augustine, who was shot by Quaritch during the battle over Hometree. Despite a ritual orchestrated by Mo'at at the Tree of Souls, Augustine dies. Before dying, however, as her own energies and memories pass into the Pandoran neuro-energetic field, she exclaims, "Eywa is real!" Sully then rallies the Omaticaya and other Na'vi clans to prepare for the next attack, which he knows is imminent. Indeed, Colonel Quaritch's next target is the Tree of Souls itself, since he thinks that destroying the spiritual heart of Na'vi culture will bring a quick end to the resistance. In another important spiritual moment, Sully—acting awkwardly, apparently because he is not used to praying, at least to Eywa—beseeches Eywa at the Tree of Souls for help defeating the RDA, even though Neytiri has told him that Eywa will not take sides in a battle.

Sully and Tsu'tey, a royal Na'vi warrior and Sully's former rival, lead the fight against the invaders. Despite the bravery of the resisting forces, the Na'vi are being overwhelmed by the superior technology of the RDA. Sully himself is saved by the valour of Chacon, who is killed by an RDA missile soon after. Spellman is shot and has to leave his avatar body, but he tries to rejoin the battle in his human body by using a breathing apparatus. Tsu'tey bravely attacks the *Valkyrie*, the airship laden with the bomb that is to destroy the Tree of Souls, but he suffers mortal wounds in the effort. Clearly, the RDA forces are superior, the Na'vi are losing, and it appears that soon Neytiri and Sully will join their fallen comrades. Then, just when all seems lost, hordes of the most dangerous Pandoran animals suddenly arrive—hammerheads, sturmbeests, viperwolves, and others—routing the imperial humans. As this occurs, an astonished Neytiri exclaims to Sully that Eywa has heard him.

Although Quaritch can see that the battle has turned against him, he fights on, now in a desperate and direct battle with Sully and Neytiri. Quaritch injures Neytiri and is about to kill her when Sully saves her, although in doing so, he is himself injured and his consciousness leaves his avatar and returns to his human body. Neytiri then saves Sully twice: first, by killing Quaritch with arrows just before he can deal a final blow to Sully and second, by providing him with a breathing apparatus after she finds Sully's human body and recognizes that he is suffocating in the Pandoran air, to which he has been exposed by Quaritch's attack. As Sully regains consciousness, he says to Neytiri, "I see you"—a Na'vi greeting that reflects a deep feeling of connection. Neytiri, relieved and crying, reciprocates, fully recognizing her mate even though he is then in his weak and fully human form. In another important event of the battle's denouement, Tsu'tey passes on his own leadership to Sully before dying from his wounds.

At the end of the film, the Na'vi allow Spellman and a few other humans who wish to remain on Pandora to do so. Sully, Neytiri, and the other Na'vi warriors, as well as Spellman, escort the RDA's survivors to their spacecraft, forcing them to leave the scarred but still beautiful moon. The implication is that Pandora will recover, but an obvious question remains unanswered: Will the invaders return? Sully's spirit and mind, through a ritual at the Tree of Souls, is permanently moved to his avatar body, eliminating the need for either the breathing apparatus or the avatar technology. Sully thus becomes a naturalized member of Na'vi society.[3]

Overview of Essays

The next chapter in this volume provides additional valuable background from film scholar Stephen Rust, who analyzes *Avatar*'s representations of social and ecological issues as they unfold within a form of cinema—the blockbuster melodrama—that is often criticized as socially and ecologically regressive. This is followed by historian of religion Thore Bjørnvig, whose careful analysis of Cameron's obsession with science and space exploration enhances our understanding of the passions that produced *Avatar*.

In part 2, the chapters focus on popular responses to the film. In its first two chapters, we travel to (cyber)space for two studies based on analyses of website forums, called "fandoms," that have been devoted to *Avatar*. Religion scholar Britt Istoft teases out various ways in which the spirituality of the film has been understood among its fans, most often as involving pantheistic and animistic perceptions, but also in ways more compatible with monotheistic traditions as well as with naturalistic metaphysics of interconnection. She shows that the fandom discourse generally includes calls for ecological lifestyles and environmental action, and argues that given these responses, and those of fan cultures inspired by the television and motion picture series *Star Trek*, it is reasonable to surmise that *Avatar* may kindle new communities with a complex mix of Pandoran and Earthly nature religion at their centre. In the next essay, cinema scholar Matthew Holtmeier, working with the views of the French critics Gilles Deleuze and Felix Guattari regarding the possibility of cinema and other art forms inspiring positive action in the world, focuses on two affective responses he sees in *Avatar* fandoms, which he labels "post-Pandoran depression" and "Na'vi sympathy." Only one of these, he contends, is likely to promote positive action in Earthly domains.

The next two chapters leave cyberspace for Earthly places. Rachelle Gould leads an interdisciplinary team of environmental studies scholars striving to understand "cultural ecosystem services" through a sophisticated qualitative and quantitative mixed-methods study. She and her colleagues integrate into this wider research reactions to the film *Avatar* among inhabitants of Hawai'i—both Native Hawaiians and those of other ethnicities. This fascinating study, set in a region with a relatively recent colonial history, shows how thoughtful and nuanced non-academicians can be about the sensitive historical, social, and ecological issues that *Avatar* raises. Many of these non-academics, Native and non-Native Hawaiians alike, appear to find resonance with and/or incorporate many of the film's ethical and spiritual themes; the apparent differences between different groups, however, are every bit as interesting as the similarities. Gould's essay is followed by a study led by sociologist Randolph Haluza-DeLay, which explores the way in which both Canadian environmentalists and the Canadian director of *Avatar* have appropriated the film to challenge tar sands mining in Alberta, Canada, as well as the ways (that some will find surprising) in which Christians from two different traditions in that region have responded to the film's spiritual and environmental themes.

Part 3 advances a number of critical perspectives on the film and its reception. Chris Klassen offers a feminist and post-colonial analysis, first noting that *Avatar* has affinity with ecofeminist spiritualities that emphasize the interconnectedness of all living things and acknowledging the environmentalist intention. But—contrary to enthusiastic readings of the film, including those that could come from an ecofeminist direction—Klassen renders a strong, negative judgment: *Avatar* presents "a thinly veiled misogynistic plot tied to a romanticization of indigeneity." Her analysis may give pause to *Avatar* enthusiasts.

Science and technology professor Pat Munday, in an interesting, contrasting way, takes up some of the issues examined by Klassen. Deploying what he calls "postmodern semiotics," Munday focuses on the affinities between the hunting practices of the indigenous Na'vi and those of non-indigenous American hunters. Like Klassen, he pays special attention to gender, noting that Na'vi hunters are both male and female, as are contemporary American hunters, both indigenous and non-indigenous. Munday finds in the practice of hunting a spiritual alternative to the dualisms of mainstream Western culture. He suggests, moreover, that such a spiritual hunting practice has affinities with the animistic spirituality expressed in *Avatar* and that this frame makes sense in the light of biophilia hypotheses. In contrast to Klassen, Munday sees in *Avatar*'s embrace of "woman the hunter" a progressive respect for both women and non-human organisms.

While all of the preceding articles engage the spiritual dimensions of the film, the next contributions make these their central focus. Engineering and computer science professor Bruce MacLennan, showing remarkable interdisciplinary range, advances an innovative perspective of the film with lenses rooted in Jungian archetypal psychology, evolutionary biology, and (like Munday) theories suggesting that *Homo sapiens* has an innate, albeit weak, tendency toward biophilia. For MacLennan, understanding biologically rooted archetypes and affective states can bring an appreciation of both culture and nature as important, entwined variables that are essential to understanding phenomena such as *Avatar* and its evocative power over its audiences.

Literature, religion, and environmental studies scholar David Barnhill demonstrates the continuities and discontinuities between *Avatar* and the work of American novelist Ursula Le Guin, who, in 1972, published *The Word for World Is Forest*. He examines the dystopian and utopian themes and the Gaian and animistic spiritualities in both works, building to an argument that, despite the problematics that inhere to both dystopian and utopian genres, both of these works provide a salutary focus on the ecological and social virtues needed to move *Homo sapiens* toward utopian visions while avoiding dystopian realities. Lisa Sideris concludes this section with a lucid exposition of the role of empathy in interspecies ethical concern and the way in which *Avatar* puts such affective states into play.

In wildly different ways, the next two chapters engage indigenous understandings related to the film. Musicologist Michael MacDonald examines indigenous music as a way of knowing through sound (acoustemology). He argues that had the composers been more directly engaged in relationship and solidarity with indigenous peoples, they could have made a more imaginative, evocative, and moving soundscape for the film while avoiding the ethical problem that often accompanies the colonial attitudes toward indigenous traditions—including sounds—as resources. Jacob von Heland and Sverker Sörlin take up epistemological questions in another way as they pursue the potential for cross-cultural understanding and for enhancing the resilience of environmental and social systems by integrating the traditional ecological knowledge of indigenous and local peoples with mainstream Western science. They do this by juxtaposing contemporary, supposedly post-colonial resilience science with *Avatar*'s depiction of the work and person of Dr. Grace Augustine. In Augustine, Von Heland and Sörlin see a powerful metaphor for both the peril and promise of engagement between indigenous peoples (and other local actors) and natural scientists and environmental conservationists as they struggle to understand, protect, and heal social-ecological systems.

In my concluding reflections, I survey the range of reactions to the film and wrestle, both as a scholar and personally, with what to make of the film and its contentious reception. Last but not least, in the afterword, Daniel Heath Justice, a Cherokee scholar of indigenous literatures, revisits *Avatar*, which he first discussed in a thoughtful review written soon after the film's release (Justice 2010), in the light of the reception to the film since then. In his reflections, Justice engages some of the perspectives expressed by the other contributors to this volume.

Of this I am confident: after reading *Avatar and Nature Spirituality*, open-minded readers will have a much more complicated, if not also conflicted, view of the film, its director, and its cultural, ecological, and ethical significance.

Family Resemblances, Religion, and Spirituality

Scholars have long debated the definition of religion and, more recently, have wrestled with the term *spirituality*. No consensus has emerged. Along with a growing number of scholars, I follow what we are calling the "family resemblance" approach to the study of what people have in mind when they use terms such as *religion* and *spirituality*. Such an approach leaves aside the fraught quest to demarcate where religion|spirituality ends, and where that which is not religion|spirituality begins. Those who take the family resemblance approach endeavour instead to explore, analyze, and compare the widest possible variety of beliefs, behaviours, and functions that are typically associated with these terms, without worrying about where the boundaries lie.

The family resemblance approach begins with recognition that there are many dimensions and characteristics to what people call religion|spirituality, and it rejects presumptions that any single trait or characteristic is essential to such phenomena. Instead, the focus is on whether an analysis of *religion-resembling beliefs and practices* has explanatory power.

In common parlance, of course, *religion* often refers to organized and institutional religious belief and practice, while *spirituality* is held to involve one's deepest moral values and most profound religious experiences. Certain other traits and characteristics are also often associated more with spirituality than religion. Spirituality, for example, is often thought to be more about personal growth and gaining a proper understanding of one's place in the cosmos than is religion, and it is often assumed to be entwined with a reverence for nature and environmentalist concern and action (Van Ness 1996; King 1996; Taylor 2001a, b). Careful observers will, therefore, be alert to the different ways in which people deploy these terms. Nevertheless, most of the traits and functions that scholars typically associate with religion are also associated with spiritual phenomena. From a family resemblance perspective, therefore, there is little *analytical* reason to assume that these are different kinds of social phenomena. The value of a family resemblance approach is that it provides analytic freedom to look widely at diverse social phenomena for their religious|spiritual dimensions. With such an approach, whether James Cameron believes in invisible divine beings (a trait some consider to be essential to religion) is worth analyzing, but we need not refrain from examining the religious dimensions of his films, or of their reception, based on whether Cameron's worldview includes that particular trait.[4]

Notes

1 In a mock *Confidential Report on the Biological and Social History of Pandora*, which purportedly draws on Augustine's research, Eywa is said to be "a kind of biointernet. She's a memory-keeper, a collective consciousness.... She logs the thoughts and feelings of everything that thinks and feels. Her function is to bring balance to

the systemic whole, one that is perfectly interdependent, biodiverse, self-regulating, and unified. But more than a network, she has a will. An ego. She guides, she shapes, she protects.... [But] Eywa does not take sides; Eywa will not necessarily save you. Her role is to protect all life, and the balance of life. She is, quite literally, Mother Nature" (Wilhelm and Mathison 2009, xv).

2 The Na'vi terminology was invented by Paul Frommer, a linguist from the University of Southern California hired to create the new language for the film.

3 In addition to the sources cited previously, in checking facts and details, I found this online source helpful: *Pandorapedia: The Official Field Guide* at http://www.pandorapedia.com/.

4 The family resemblance school began with Wittgenstein ([1953] 2001). For the most lucid exposition of the approach with regard to religion, see Saler (1993). For a short version of the approach, but longer than here, see Taylor (2007). For an even shorter version, see chapter 1 in Taylor (2010), also available online at http://www.brontaylor.com/pdf/Taylor--DGR_ch1.pdf. For a clear statement typical of those who object to the approach in religion studies, see Fitzgerald (1996).

References

Fitzgerald, Timothy. 1996. "Religion, Philosophy, and Family Resemblances." *Religion* 26(3): 215–36.

Justice, Daniel Heath. 2010. "James Cameron's *Avatar*: Missed Opportunities." *First Peoples: New Directions in Indigenous Studies*, 20 January. http://www.firstpeoplesnewdirections.org/blog/?p=169.

King, Anna S. 1996. "Spirituality: Transformation and Metamorphosis." *Religion* 26(4): 343–51.

Saler, Benson. 1993. *Conceptualizing Religion: Immanent Anthropologists, Transcendent Natives, and Unbounded Categories*. Leiden: Brill.

Taylor, Bron. 2001a. "Earth and Nature-Based Spirituality (Part I): From Deep Ecology to Radical Environmentalism." *Religion* 31(2): 175–93.

———. 2001b. "Earth and Nature-Based Spirituality (Part II): From Deep Ecology and Bioregionalism to Scientific Paganism and the New Age." *Religion* 31(3): 225–45.

———. 2007. "Exploring Religion, Nature, and Culture." *Journal for the Study of Religion, Nature, and Culture* 1(1): 5–24.

———. 2010. *Dark Green Religion: Nature Spirituality and the Planetary Future*. Berkeley: University of California Press.

Van Ness, Peter H. 1996. *Spirituality and the Secular Quest*. New York: Crossroad.

Wilhelm, Maria, and Dirk Mathison. 2009. *James Cameron's Avatar: An Activist Survival Guide*. New York: HarperCollins.

Wittgenstein, Ludwig. (1953) 2001. *Philosophical Investigations*. Reprint, Malden, MA: Blackwell.

Avatar: Ecorealism and the Blockbuster Melodrama

STEPHEN RUST

In March 2009, A. O. Scott, the chief film critic for the *New York Times*, asked the simple but provocative question "What kind of movies do we need today?" (Scott 2009). Faced with a global financial crisis, ongoing military conflict, and the increasing certainty of climate change, what were audiences to make of the steady diet of "fantasy, comedy, heroism" served up by corporate media's "blockbuster machinery"? "What we need from the movies, in the face of a dismaying and confusing real world," answered Scott, "is realism." Spotlighting the work of such independent filmmakers as Kelly Reichardt (*Wendy and Lucy*, 2008), Ramin Bahrani (*Goodbye Solo*, 2008), and So Yong Kim (*Treeless Mountain*, 2008), Scott argued that the techniques of Italian neo-realism—in which current social concerns are represented through on-location shooting, non-star actors, long takes, and deep focus cinematography—offer the best hope for revitalizing American filmmaking. *Wendy and Lucy*, for example, the story of a young homeless woman's search for her dog after she is arrested for shoplifting, bears a striking visual and thematic resemblance to Vittorio De Sica's *Bicycle Thieves* (1948) and *Umberto D* (1952). Wendy's final lines, "I'll come back. When I make some money I'll come back," are among the most relevant of any contemporary film, their message driven home as Wendy (played by Michelle Williams) quietly hops a freight train in the film's closing homage to the Depression-era classic *Wild Boys of the Road* (1933). Filmed in the suburbs of Portland, Oregon, *Wendy and Lucy* screened at such international film festivals as Cannes, was named the year's best film by the Dallas–Fort Worth and Toronto Film Critics Associations, and offered telling insights into life in a place where rates of unemployment, hunger, and homelessness are among the highest in the United States (see Oregon Department of Agriculture 2010; Law 2009; and Read 2010). Ask most Oregonians if they have seen *Wendy and Lucy*, however, and you will probably hear "no." But a great many of them have seen *Avatar* (2009).

A significant difference between blockbuster films like *Avatar* and independent films like *Wendy and Lucy*, of course, involves distribution and accessibility to broader movie-going audiences. By the year 2009, six media conglomerates had come to enjoy more than 90 per cent of North American box office revenues through their ownership of the major Hollywood studios and distribution deals with multiplex theatre chains. This situation forced independent films to compete for significantly smaller audiences at film festivals and arthouse theatres. For Scott, "neo-neorealist" filmmakers like Reichardt offer a vital counterweight to Hollywood.[1] Hollywood blockbusters, Scott argues, perform a disservice to society by rendering benign the "tyranny of fantasy entrenched on Wall Street and in Washington." Considering the line-up of studio blockbusters released in 2009—including *X-Men Origins: Wolverine*; *Watchmen*; *G.I. Joe: The Rise of Cobra*; and *Transformers: Revenge of the Fallen* (which collectively earned $1.7 billion globally)—it is tempting to agree completely with Scott.

The situation is more complex than Scott presents, though, because while Hollywood, Washington, and Wall Street clearly bolster one another, each subtly (but constantly) subverts the others to increase its own sphere of influence. *Avatar* itself likewise challenges Scott's argument because, in contrast to typical blockbusters, *Avatar* employs ecorealism—the representation of real world social and ecological concerns within the space of fictional narrative—to directly confront Western culture's addiction to fossil fuels. As Sean Cubitt (2005, 54) insightfully points out in a reading of David Attenborough's documentary series *The Blue Planet* (2001), "Scientific realism is often a matter of readjusting the unobservable so that it can be observed." In his own creative way, James Cameron, in *Avatar*, puts ecorealism into the service of melodrama, provoking viewers to see with their hearts and minds some of the most important social and ecological concerns of our time.

Avatar as Blockbuster
Despite its challenging message, *Avatar* remained situated within the film industry's typical capitalist funding and distribution models. Written and directed by James Cameron for Twentieth Century Fox (a subsidiary of

News Corporation), *Avatar* cost an estimated $500 million (Cieply 2009). Along with a massive production budget for state-of-the-art visual effects and star actors like Sigourney Weaver (who plays the scientist Dr. Grace Augustine), the film enjoyed an equally lavish marketing budget. To promote the film, Cameron partnered with several corporations known for their unsustainable business practices, such as McDonalds, Coca-Cola, and Mattel (Hampp 2010). Opening in December 2009 on more than ten thousand screens in more than one hundred countries, the film's $242 million opening weekend was virtually guaranteed by the blockbuster business model, which has bolstered Hollywood's bottom line since the mid-1970s.

This blockbuster production and distribution model was originally employed by Universal producer Lew Wasserman for Steven Spielberg's *Jaws* (1975). Wasserman built *Jaws* into a cultural event through a successful print and television advertising campaign (Gomery 2003). *Jaws* opened the same weekend in more than four hundred theatres and earned $100 million in less than six months to become the highest-grossing film to that date. Two years later, George Lucas's *Star Wars* surpassed the record set by *Jaws* and perfected the model by adding merchandizing to the mix.[2] Although films made to be blockbusters do flop, the model generally serves to minimize financial risk by combining (a) multi-million-dollar production budgets; (b) multi-million-dollar advertising budgets; (c) multi-million-dollar promotional deals for toys, video games, clothing, and other merchandise; and (d) targeted release dates in thousands of movie theatres around the world (Schatz 2008).

Recognizing the industry's shift in emphasis from playability (i.e., quality) to marketability, film historians often cringe at the word *blockbuster*. Yet *Avatar*'s cultural impact cannot be fully measured by economics. Today's blockbuster films typically earn 30 to 40 per cent of their theatrical profits during their opening weekend. *Avatar*'s opening weekend, however, accounted for less than 10 per cent of its total earnings. Dominating the box office for more than two months, *Avatar* earned more than $2.7 billion during its initial theatrical run to quickly become the highest-grossing film of all time.[3] *Avatar* achieved its phenomenal success with fans and critics by couching its progressive environmental message within what many still consider a regressive art form—the blockbuster melodrama. *Avatar* became a global cultural event because its groundbreaking 3-D visual effects blend with a musical score from composer James Horner (*Field of Dreams, Titanic*) to create a gripping narrative of love and war that invites viewers to reframe their perceptions of the world outside the theatre.

Avatar as Melodrama

Avatar's appeal transcends its blockbuster status, however, since it borrows from popular melodramatic forms. As democratic governments replaced monarchies in the wake of the American and French Revolutions, melodrama offered ordinary individuals the chance to imagine themselves as heroes. Over the past three centuries, melodrama has become the most popular method of storytelling in Western culture (Brooks 1976).

According to the *Oxford English Dictionary* (2010), in 1789 the English music historian Charles Burney coined the term *melo-drama* to describe the works of Italian composer Niccolò Jommelli (1714–74). Introducing dramatic action and ballet into his operas, Jommelli eschewed the period's typical consideration of story as an afterthought to highly decorative, technically challenging arias. In France, the term *mélodrame* (from the Greek *melos* "music" and the French *drame* "drama") came into use in 1802 to describe the century-old practice of blending song and dance into traditional forms of drama, as in Jean-Jacques Rousseau's *Pygmalion* (1762), a work created in partnership with composer Horace Coignet that is generally considered the first full melodrama (Branscombe 2001). Deriving from both the high opera and a popular oral tradition that began with medieval morality plays, folktales, and ballads, melodrama denotes a drama that is emotionally punctuated by music. Connotatively, however, the term is often used to describe stories that exhibit "strong emotionalism; moral polarization and schematization; extreme states of being, situations, actions; overt villainy, persecution of the good, and final reward of virtue; inflated and extravagant expression; dark plottings, suspense" (Brooks 1991, 58). Melodramas are set in symbolic worlds and typically conclude when the hero has vanquished evil and restored innocence. With highly visible recurring motifs—such as elements of *mise en scène* (props, costumes, sets, lighting)—melodramas operate through metaphor and moral confrontation to explore social conditions that are obscured by the hegemonic view of reality that is prevalent in the culture. As the literary critic Peter Brooks puts it, "Everything appears to bear the stamp of meaning, which can be expressed, pressed out from it" (Brooks 1991, 56). Burgeoning on the early-nineteenth-century stage, melodrama became the dominant narrative style in the most widely consumed forms of Western popular culture in each ensuing historical epoch, from the nineteenth-century novels of such writers as Victor Hugo, Charles Dickens, and Harriet Beecher-Stowe and the twentieth-century films of such directors as D. W. Griffith, Max Ophuls, and Douglas Sirk to the twenty-first-century multi-media extravaganzas of such writer/director/producers as Steven Spielberg, George Lucas, and James Cameron.

Following his success with such films as *The Terminator* (1984), *Aliens* (1986), and *Titanic* (1997), Cameron enjoyed complete creative control over the *Avatar* project. In one of the first major studies of ecological themes in American cinema, *Hollywood Utopia*, Pat Brereton (2005, 15) argues that in *Titanic*, "metaphorically, the humans become sacrificial victims for the sins of capitalism, which tries to ignore the innate potency of nature." Cameron brought a similar sensibility to *Avatar*. He even refused to back down when Fox Studio executives suggested he "leave some of the tree-hugging *FernGully* crap out of this movie" (Salamone 2010). Betting that viewers would feel moral outrage at The Company's treatment of the Na'vi, Cameron's film successfully tapped into audiences' increasing awareness of global warming and frustration over the wars in Iraq and Afghanistan. Paradoxically, however, the destruction of the Na'vi Hometree, like the sinking of the *Titanic*, required Cameron to fully exploit the blockbuster business model that is a hallmark of capitalist consumption.

Avatar's digital effects required state-of-the-art technology and took several years to complete (Duncan 2010). Audiences left theatres raving about the 3-D cinematography, however, because Cameron carefully interwove ecorealism with the film's music and sound effects to heighten viewers' emotional and ethical responses to characters and events. Sitting in a crowded theatre, viewers experience movies as individuals. But when so many individuals around the world share an experience like *Avatar*, its narrative can be understood as a powerful means of collective expression.

In her 1998 essay, "Melodrama Revised," Linda Williams (1998, 42) argues that as "the dominant mode of American cinema," melodrama adapts to changing social conditions by offering individual viewers a collective space to escape, displace, and yet at the same time, confront the overwhelming ethical and emotional paradoxes of life in a secular society. Williams, unlike Scott in the *New York Times*, recognizes the potential for viewers to make use of fantasy in Hollywood movies like *Avatar* as a means of negotiating and *seeing through* Washington and Wall Street's "tyranny of fantasy." Melodrama, according to Williams, "begins, and wants to end in a space of innocence.... The narrative proper usually begins when the villain intrudes upon the idyll" (65). These themes were expressed through *Avatar's* marketing campaign as well. For example, in September 2009, with *G.I. Joe: The Rise of Cobra* (based on Hasbro's popular Reagan-era action figures and television cartoon) still in theatres, the first *Avatar* action figures went on sale. Through the character of Colonel Quaritch, *Avatar* subverts the idyll of nationalism and militarism perpetrated by films like *G.I. Joe* and *Transformers*.

Invited by packaging and displays to pick up the boxes, buy the toys, and even use their webcams to create virtual avatars, fans knew that the angry-looking blue natives/aliens with the bows and arrows were the "good guys." Released in the run-up to the film, these toys also drew attention to the corporate military forces employed to secure fossil fuels in the real world. By 2010, according to ABC News, more than 110,000 private military contractors were operating in Afghanistan alone and an increasing number were being killed in combat (Wong 2010). "Back home these guys were Army dogs, Marines, fighting for freedom," Jake Sully says as he arrives on Pandora, "but out here they're just hired guns."

Seeing through the Eyes of the Melodramatic Victim-Hero

Jake Sully (played by Sam Worthington) is established as the melodramatic victim-hero in *Avatar*'s opening sequence. As a little-known actor before this blockbuster film, Worthington brings the quality of a blank slate to his protagonist. Because of his status as a blank slate, viewers are invited to share Sully's experiences of "cognitive estrangement," a term commonly used in science fiction studies to explain moments when a text suddenly jolts readers to "consider a question from a point of view that differs from their own" (Wald 2008, 1909). Speaking in voice-over while the camera delivers its first epic sweep across Pandora's stunning landscapes, Sully explains, "While I was lying there in the VA hospital [in the year 2154] with a big hole blown through the middle of my life, I started having these dreams of flying. I was free. Sooner or later though you always have to wake up." As Company officials explain Sully's new assignment, a cardboard coffin containing the dead body of his twin brother burns in a crematorium.

This is not an image viewers are used to seeing. In this moment, cognitive estrangement works by inviting the viewer to momentarily step outside of the narrative to consider the lives taken each day so that Western culture can carry on with business as usual. A similar moment occurs when the viewer learns that Sully is a former combat Marine who lost the use of his legs during a combat operation in Venezuela and is now confined to a wheelchair. That he was injured in Venezuela implies that Western forces back on Earth have invaded the country to secure its "unobtanium" (i.e., fossil fuels). Although his fellow Marines mock him for his disability when he arrives on Pandora, Sully's loyalties remain with the soldiers until his perceptions of nature are altered by his experiences with the indigenous Na'vi. Caught between his loyalties to his comrades in the military, the science team, and the Na'vi, Sully's outsider perspective provides audiences with a means of bridging vastly different worldviews.

Morphed into his avatar body, Sully invites audiences to experience cognitive estrangement by exploring Pandora from the perspective of a soldier. Analyzing the film's use of 3-D technology in relationship to ecological awareness, however, the science reporter Carol Kaesuk Yoon (2010) offers a different perspective: "Mr. Cameron somehow has the audience seeing organisms in the tropical-forest-gone-mad of the planet Pandora just the way a biologist sees them. With each glance, we are reminded of organisms we already know, while marveling over the new and trying quickly to put this novelty into some kind of sensible place in the mind." Yoon's description of how the film introduces viewers to Pandora nicely summarizes the process of cognitive estrangement. It is important to keep in mind, however, that while Augustine tries to teach Sully how to see "just the way a biologist sees," he initially pays little attention to her advice. While the scientists put their heads down to take samples, Sully impetuously rushes past the scientists and takes the audience with him into the forest. Rather than using a first-person perspective, the camera retains a third-person perspective, highlighting the hard Na'vi body that gives Sully the confidence to wander off from the group and into trouble. Armed with his machine gun and phallic swagger, Sully's status as protagonist invites viewers to enter the forest as conquering soldiers and not, as Colonel Quaritch crassly puts it, as "a bunch of limp-dick science majors." The forest feels "tropical-gone-mad" because Sully's gun becomes a motif critical to his adventures on the planet. The gun is also a means of engaging young male viewers, the target audience for most blockbuster films. Cognitive estrangement operates not only when the audience is introduced to the forest but also when Sully is confronted by the large jungle cat known as the thanator and forced to abandon his weapon.

After he survives his encounter with the thanator, Sully's soldier-versus-scientist status becomes increasingly important to the narrative and thematic progression because the film implies that only a soldier can lead the Na'vi to victory. During Sully's first night in the forest, Neytiri decides not to shoot Sully with an arrow because she recognizes that, although he is ignorant "like a baby," he has "a strong heart." Sully is welcomed by the Na'vi (rather than killed) because he convinces them that he is not another scientist but "a warrior of the Jarhead clan." As a warrior, Sully becomes part of the indigenous community and thus enjoys an insider's perspective on the Na'vi that the avatar scientists were previously denied.

Through Sully's love affair with Neytiri (played by Zoe Saldana), viewers are introduced to the Na'vi's relationship with Eywa. Encouraged by Augustine to "see the forest" from Neytiri's perspective, Sully overcomes his cognitive dissonance and eventually lets go of his ego and accepts his embodied connection to the environment. The Na'vi do not worship Eywa metaphorically but phenomenologically, by uploading their memories at the Tree of Souls. After Quaritch destroys Hometree, Sully remains a soldier but shifts his allegiance from The Company to Eywa. Freed from having to directly align themselves with Augustine (and Sigourney Weaver's environmentalist star image),[4] viewers are invited to consider Quaritch, Neytiri, and Augustine's competing ideologies from Sully's point of view as protagonist. By asking viewers to experience Sully's moments of cognitive estrangement, the film enables viewers to navigate his experiences through multiple perspectives and ultimately to form their own conclusions about Eywa's ambiguous status as a deity.

When seen through Sully's point of view as a hired gun whose sympathies have shifted from The Company to the Na'vi, Quaritch's attempt to destroy the Na'vi's spiritual connection to Eywa prompts the viewer to reconsider historical events in the world outside the theatre. The destruction of Hometree and the attempted destruction of the Tree of Souls allude to the military means by which Western culture has historically masked environmental injustice. Seeking to exploit the tribe's spiritual attachment to nature, Quaritch tells his troops that destroying the Tree of Souls will "blast a hole in their racial memory so deep they won't come within a thousand klicks of this place ever again." For American audiences in particular, the attack on Eywa alludes to the treatment of the indigenous people in the United States whose ways of life were forever altered by westward expansion. In *The Way to Rainy Mountain* (1969), for example, N. Scott Momaday uses the word *deicide* to describe the effects of white settlement on the Kiowa, whose last Sun Dance was held on their reservation in 1890 after the great herds of wild buffalo had been wiped out by settlers. At the tribe's medicine tree in Oklahoma, Momaday's grandmother, Aho, watched as a cavalry brigade forcibly dispersed the tribe. Aho was forbidden without cause the central act of her faith; thereby, "for as long as she lived she bore a vision of deicide" (Momaday 1969, 10). Similarly, the attack on the Tree of Souls was an act of deicide.

In the headquarters of the unobtanium mining operation, such historical memories were mapped back onto present concerns about the socio-ecological price for Western entanglements in the Middle East. By the time he tells Augustine about Quaritch's plans to forcibly relocate the Na'vi, Sully has come to recognize that "when people are sitting on shit that you want you make them your enemy so you can justify taking it." In this moment, Sully demonstrates that cognitive estrangement has led him to fully shift his sympathies from The Company to the Na'vi. The audience is further led to connect the plight of the Na'vi with events in the real world through the exchanges that take place between the characters vying for influence over Sully. While imploring the head of mining operations, Parker Selfridge (played by Giovanni Ribisi), to make peace with the Na'vi as the narrative builds toward the climactic battle, Augustine articulates how she, as a biologist, sees Pandora:

AUGUSTINE: I'm not talking about some kind of pagan voodoo here; I'm talking about something real, something measurable in the biology of the forest.

SELFRIDGE: Which is what exactly?

AUGUSTINE: What we think we know is that there is some kind of electrochemical communication between the roots of the trees which the Na'vi can tap into.... The wealth of this world isn't in the ground. It's all around us. Get it?

SELFRIDGE: What have you people been smoking out there?

Concerned only with profits, Selfridge is unable to fit Augustine's discovery into his worldview. Like Selfridge, most people's responses to new information and evidence are shaped by their pre-existing moral and ethical frames (Nyhan and Reifler 2010). Unlike Sully, the blank slate, Selfridge responds to his own moment of cognitive dissonance with an *ad hominem* attack on Augustine: "What have you people been smoking out there?" Selfridge makes his worldview clear when he attempts to justify the attack by calling the Na'vi "blue monkeys" and explaining to Jake, "Look, killing the indigenous looks bad but there's one thing shareholders hate more than bad press and that's a bad quarterly statement." Through such exchanges, viewers are invited to understand the moral and emotional reasons behind Sully's decision to, as Quaritch puts it, "betray his own race."

As the tension in the film builds toward the final battle, Pandora and Eywa become increasingly conflated with Western culture's imperial conquest of native cultures and the socio-economic roots of global environmental change. As Sully tells Eywa, "Look into Grace's memories. She can show you the world we come from. There's no green there. They killed their mother." In this brief allusion to deforestation and climate change on Earth, Cameron's film serves notice that while twenty years of scientific consensus have not led to major changes in policy, change is happening below the surface in people like Sully in response to shifting cultural perceptions of the relationship between the individual and the planet. This shift in perception is made tangible in the film by Augustine's death at the Tree of Souls. After she is shot by Quaritch, Augustine dies among the Na'vi and is granted a sacred status that confirms the validity of her scientific observations. Augustine verifies Eywa's existence with her dying words,

"She's real." Her death also gives Sully the personal emotional motivation necessary to assume the stance of leader (Toruk Makto) and deliver his call-to-arms speech to the Na'vi (a motif reminiscent of *Henry V, Braveheart, Return of the King,* and so on). Metaphorically, then, audiences around the globe are prompted to understand the ensuing battle for Pandora as an allusion to the threat facing their own environment. By inviting viewers to see through the eyes of the melodramatic victim-hero, *Avatar* represents global environmental change as a scientific *and* moral catastrophe, just as former US vice-president Al Gore argues in his influential documentary *An Inconvenient Truth* (2006). Artists like Cameron recognize that melodrama can tap into the cultural zeitgeist and can thus become an effective means of promoting environmentalist worldviews and action.

While film historians initially used the term *melodrama* simply to describe films they considered "women's weepies," Thomas Elsaesser recognized melodrama's widespread use across a range of Hollywood film genres. In a 1972 essay, Elsaesser employs the term "the melodramatic imagination" to articulate the mode's ability to map the concerns of public/social space onto the private/domestic space of home and family in order to express "the anxiety, the moral confusion, the emotional demands, in short the metaphysics of social change" (1991, 73, 68).[5] This mapping enables *Avatar* to elicit a sweeping range of readings from its audiences. In China, for example, which in 2010 surpassed the United States in total carbon emissions and energy consumption, officials prevented distribution of *Avatar* to all but a few select 3-D theatres, reportedly over fears that its socio-ecological message might cause social unrest (Davies 2010, 19). Meanwhile, American conservatives and the Vatican criticized Cameron for promoting "anti-Americanism" and "nature worship" (Associated Press 2010). Environmentalists, for their part, have been divided over whether the film's ability to reach a wide audience justifies its ethnic stereotypes and simplification of complex socio-ecological concerns. There is no denying, however, that Cameron's blend of melodrama and ecorealism provoked diverse responses.

Conclusion: Melodrama and Ecorealism

In the vast majority of Hollywood films, as Linda Williams (1998, 42) puts it, "supposedly realist cinematic *effects*—whether of setting, action or narrative motivation [through such formal devices as continuity editing and musical punctuation]—most often operate in the service of melodramatic *affects*" (emphasis in original). Historically, this realism/melodrama relationship traces to what Raymond Williams (1977) describes in "A Lecture on Realism" as three defining characteristics of realism that developed in eighteenth-century bourgeois drama: social extension (i.e., the qualities of tragic heroism were extended to characters of lower social ranks), an emphasis on the contemporary world, and an emphasis on secular action (i.e., narrative causes and effects were no longer of a metaphysical or religious order). As noted above, this shift in realism soon found its way into melodrama, a form that was developed during this period by composers like Jommelli and Rousseau. "Realism," as Jackie Byers (1991, 12–13) puts it, traditionally "depends on the assumption that the social world can be adequately explained, through social science methods, and that adequate representation is possible. Melodrama has no such confidence; irrational forces exist in the world." In order to understand the development of ecorealism in films like *Avatar*, it is thus important to bear in mind that realism and melodrama are not mutually exclusive but operate in historical and formal tension with one another.

As a result of the dialectic relationship between realism and melodrama, new forms of realism have emerged over time in response to melodrama's tendency to mask social problems with excess pathos and easy answers. Naturalism, neo-realism, and direct cinema, for example, were each developed by filmmakers who recognized that complex issues rarely fit into clearly defined metaphors of good versus evil. As a reactive mode, however, melodrama's power lies in its ability to "give material existence to the repressed": in other words, to interrogate realism and inspire new shifts in perception (Byers 1991, 19). The emergence of ecorealism in the blockbuster melodrama can therefore be understood as a response to contemporary social and ecological conditions and a sense among filmmakers like James Cameron that traditional forms of realism have proven unable to fully articulate the postmodern social condition. After *Avatar*'s release, Cameron commented that the film "doesn't try to accurately represent the earth's environmental issues," but he hoped it would elicit "emotions in viewers that can push them to take action" (Salamone 2010). Whereas other forms of realism have historically sprung up in opposition to Hollywood, ecorealism was developed by artists within the mainstream film industry who were willing to exploit the blockbuster melodrama in an effort to support environmental protection and indigenous rights.

Avatar's combination of sound and images asks viewers to imagine the true social and environmental costs of humanity's reliance on fossil fuels. As The Company's spaceship enters into orbit over Pandora, the sublime image of a moon that looks much like the viewers' own planet comes into view. As the craft descends, Sully turns to look through the windshield of the ship. The next shot cuts to a flyover view of the landscape that reminds viewers of the film's first shot. Here, however, the unbroken forest canopy of Sully's dream is interrupted by the reality of a massive earthmover and dump trucks (dubbed "Hell trucks" to suggest how they desecrate paradise) working in the unobtanium mine. From this deep-focus establishing shot of the mine, the film cuts to a soft-focus perspective with the earthmover in the background. Individual men come into focus as they walk alongside the Hell trucks in the foreground. As the men and trucks move toward the viewer, the cinematography heightens the effect of cognitive estrangement. Especially in 3-D, the relative sizes of the men and trucks momentarily invite viewers beyond the screen to their mental images of contemporary mining operations. The images of the unobtanium mine bear a remarkable resemblance to the Alberta oil sands, Chile's open-pit copper mines, and West Virginia's mountaintop coal mines. Viewers are similarly prompted throughout the film to experience cognitive estrangement and thus to reconsider their perceptions of the relationships between mechanized life-ways and organic ones.

As a blockbuster, *Avatar* reached audiences around the world by means of a capitalist business model that has become firmly established in Hollywood. As a melodrama, however, *Avatar* connects with audiences by employing a narrative style that has become deeply rooted in the cultural imagination. Inviting viewers from across the political spectrum into the safe space of the cinema and deploying ecorealism to interrogate the relationship between militarism and environmental injustice, *Avatar*'s unprecedented success should fill us more with hope than with fear, although there is certainly reason for both.

Notes

1 Hollywood connotes not merely a place in California but the global space of corporate-controlled mass media production, distribution, and exhibition (Miller et al. 2005).

2 Television scholar Jonathan Gray (2010) recently coined the term *paratext* to describe the multiple proliferations of a given blockbuster text. *Avatar*'s paratexts include the original and extended 2-D and 3-D versions of the film, advertisements, promotional materials, studio and fan Internet sites, interviews with cast and crew, news stories, film reviews, billboards, toys, video games, DVDs, and so on.

3 Adjusted for inflation, *Avatar* ranked number fourteen on the all-time list of domestic earners within six months of its release; the film's adjusted global earnings, however, surpassed even *Gone with the Wind*, *Star Wars*, and *Titanic*, and the film has posted record Blu-Ray and DVD sales (Segers 2010).

4 On Earth Day 2010, for example, Sigourney Weaver and James Cameron testified on ocean acidification, climate change, and *Avatar* before a US Senate subcommittee (Weaver 2010).

5 Working independently of one another (and on either side of the Atlantic), German film historian Thomas Elsaesser and American literary critic Peter Brooks each coined the term *the melodramatic imagination* in drafts of their work in the late 1960s (a fact confirmed by both scholars in emails to the author).

References

Associated Press. 2010. "The Vatican Criticizes 'Avatar.'" *Hollywood Reporter*, 12 January. http://www.hollywoodreporter.com/news/vatican-criticizes-avatar-19420.

Branscombe, Peter. 2001. "Melodrama." In *The New Grove Dictionary of Music and Musicians*, edited by Stanley Sadie and John Tyrell, 360–63. New York: Grove.

Brereton, Pat. 2005. *Hollywood Utopia: Ecology in Contemporary American Cinema*. Bristol, UK: Intellect.

Brooks, Peter. 1991. "The Melodramatic Imagination." In *Imitations of Life: A Reader on Film and Television Melodrama*, edited by Marcia Landy, 50–67. Detroit: Wayne State University Press.

———. 1976. *The Melodramatic Imagination: Balzac, Henry James, Melodrama, and the Mode of Excess*. New Haven: Yale University Press.

Byers, Jackie. 1991. *All That Hollywood Allows: Re-reading Gender in 1950s Melodrama*. Chapel Hill: University of North Carolina Press.

Cieply, Michael. 2009. "A Movie's Budget Pops from the Screen." *New York Times*, 9 November.

Cubbit, Sean. 2005. *Eco-Media*. Amsterdam: Rodopi.

Davies, Caroline. 2010. "Avatar—Even in 2D—Reportedly Too Hot a Property for Chinese Censors." *The Guardian*, 19 January.

Duncan, Jody. 2010. "The Seduction of Reality." *Cinefex* 120: 68–146.

Elsaesser, Thomas. 1991. "Tales of Sound and Fury: Observations on the Family Melodrama." In *Imitations of Life: A Reader on Film and Television Melodrama*, edited by Marcia Landy, 68–88. Detroit: Wayne State University Press.

Gomery, Douglas. 2003. "The Hollywood Blockbuster: Industrial Analysis and Practice." In *Movie Blockbusters*, edited by Julian Stringer, 72–83. London: Routledge.

Gray, Jonathan. 2010. *Show Sold Separately: Promos, Spoilers, and Other Media Paratexts*. New York: New York University Press.

Hampp, Andrew. 2010. "Marketers Hop on Augmented Reality Bandwagon to Promote 'Avatar.'" *Advertising Age*, 19 November. http://adage.com/article/madisonvine-news/advertising-marketers-augmented-reality-push-avatar/140661/.

Miller, Toby, Nitin Govil, John McMurria, Richard Maxwell, and Ting Wang. 2005. *Global Hollywood 2*. London: British Film Institute.

Momaday, N. Scott. 1969. *The Way to Rainy Mountain*. Albuquerque: University of New Mexico Press.

Nyhan, Brendan, and Jason Reifler. 2010. "When Corrections Fail: The Persistence of Political Misperceptions." *Political Behavior* 32(2): 303–30.

Oregon Department of Agriculture. 2010. "Household Food Security Drops in Oregon and US." 27 January. http://www.oregon.gov/ODA/news/100127food_security.shtml (site discontinued).

Oxford English Dictionary. 2010. "Melodrama." http://www.oed.com.

Read, Richard. 2010. "Oregon Unemployment One of Worst in Nation." *The Oregonian*, 2 January. http://www.oregonlive.com/business/index.ssf/2010/01/oregon_unemployment_one_of_wor.html.

Salamone, Gina. 2010. "James Cameron on 'Avatar': Fox Wanted Me to Take Out 'Tree-Hugging,' 'Ferngully' Crap." *New York Daily News*, 18 February. http://www.nydailynews.com.

Schatz, Tom. 2008. "The Studio System and Conglomerate Hollywood." In *The Contemporary Hollywood Film Industry*, edited by Paul McDonald and Janet Wasko, 13–42. London: Blackwell.

Scott, A. O. 2009. "Neo-Neo Realism." *New York Times*, 19 March.

Segers, Frank. 2010. "'Avatar' Breaks 'Titanic' Worldwide Record." *Hollywood Reporter*, 25 January. http://www.hollywoodreporter.com/news/avatar-breaks-titanic-worldwide-record-19914.

Wald, Pricilla. 2008. "Cognitive Estrangement, Science Fiction, and Medical Ethics." *The Lancet* 371(9628): 1908–9.

Weaver, Sigourney. 2010. "Protecting Our Oceans for Earth Day." *Huffington Post*, 22 April. http://www.huffingtonpost.com/sigourney-weaver/protecting-our-oceans-for_b_547198.html.

Williams, Linda. 1998. "Melodrama Revised." In *Refiguring American Film Genres*, edited by Nick Browne, 42–88. Berkeley: University of California Press.

Williams, Raymond. 1977. "A Lecture on Realism." *Screen* 19(1): 61–74.

Wong, Katie. 2010. "US Contractor Deaths Soaring in Afghanistan." *ABC News*, 16 July. http://abcnews.go.com/blogs/politics/2010/07/us-contractor-deaths-soaring-in-afghanistan/.

Yoon, Carol Kaesuk. 2010. "Luminous 3-D Jungle is Biologist's Dream." *New York Times*, 18 January.

Outer Space Religion and the Ambiguous Nature of *Avatar*'s Pandora

The conflict in *Avatar* revolves around the dichotomy Earth-Pandora, in which Earth and its representatives, in the form of the RDA corporation and its mercenaries, symbolize most obviously an instrumental, imperialistic, and exploitive stance toward nature and indigenous peoples. The very first scenes from Pandora, which depict gigantic mining machines digging into the forest, succinctly illustrate the exploitive way of perceiving nature, which Cameron criticizes by means of *Avatar*. At first, it is mainly the ferocious cruelty of Pandoran nature that is shown, thus implicitly justifying the imperialistic attitude of the Earthlings. When a small expedition led by Grace Augustine lands in the jungle, Jake Sully, in his Na'vi-human avatar body, is attacked by a predator. Fleeing, Sully becomes separated from the expedition and has to survive on his own at night. He fashions a torch and tries to defend himself against a pack of viperwolves. However, the moment he is saved by Neytiri, the jungle changes from a dark, aggressive place full of terrors to a peaceful, magical forest alive with bioluminescent trees and plants. Soon Sully, pursuing an indignant Neytiri, is contacted by Eywa, the goddess of Pandora, through Eywa's messengers, seeds of the Tree of Souls, prefiguring his destiny as the one to save the Na'vi, and Pandoran nature, from destruction at the hands of Earthlings.

Thus, not only is Sully initiated by Neytiri into a "mystical" aspect of Pandoran nature, so different from the supposed "hell" that the representatives from Earth are fighting, but he is also contacted by the vast, living bionet of Pandora in the form of the messengers of Eywa. At this moment, the ambiguous, technology-like character of Pandoran nature becomes evident. First, as we know from Earth, bioluminescent flora and fauna can develop spontaneously through natural evolution. Yet the movie conveys to the viewer a sense that there is something artificial about the Pandoran instances of bioluminescence, if for no reason other than its resemblance to neon LED lighting. Second, and more important, the bioluminescence corresponds visually to the movie's representation of avatar equipment brought to Pandora from Earth: the equipment's bluish hues mimic the blue of the Na'vi bodies and the many blue and violet colours of the Pandoran night forest. This equipment is, of course, quintessentially technological, yet without it, the mystical ambiguity of Pandora's nature would have entirely escaped the perception of the invaders from Earth. Thus, on a symbolic level, the audience is nudged toward an understanding of both a deeper connection between the avatar technology and Pandoran nature and the fundamental difference between this technology and the exploitive and warlike technology of RDA.[1]

The avatar technology is more refined and sophisticated than the crude, abusive technology of mining and warfare and shares many affinities with Pandoran nature and the way the Na'vi interact with it. These affinities become apparent when considering (1) that Pandoran nature is a kind of biological Internet;[2] (2) that this bionet has a conscious superstructure called Eywa; (3) that the Na'vi can connect physically through the optic fiber-like tendrils at the ends of their braids to similar "cables" of various animals and trees on Pandora; (4) that the Na'vi can upload their minds to Eywa; (5) that the Na'vi, by means of the Tree of Souls, are basically able to perform the same feat as that of the avatar technology—namely, transfer the mind from a human body to a Na'vi avatar body; and (6) that Sully is able to communicate with Eywa through the Tree of Souls.[3] These affinities between Pandoran nature and the avatar technology expose the ambiguous nature of both. That this is so, however, has been contested.

Elizabeth Rosen (2011) argues that Cameron's movies before *Avatar* expound a highly ambivalent portrayal of technology. Although on the surface they appear to be technophobic, they in fact portray technology in a more complex, ambivalent way as "a potential source of both horror *and* wonder" (109). This ambivalence, Rosen argues, "vascillates between the possibility that technology holds out to help humankind form either the ultimate dystopian world, or the ultimate utopian one" (113). According to Rosen, the ambivalence even runs as deep as to question the distinction between the organic and the technological. As she puts it, in Cameron's movies the "line between human and technology has already been crossed:

we *are* our technology" (115). Rosen does not see this in *Avatar*, in which technology is portrayed as only evil and nature is portrayed in a naive, nostalgic fashion. I do not agree with this point of view; rather, I propose that Rosen's analysis of Cameron's movies before *Avatar* also applies to *Avatar*. Perhaps the strong presence of dark green religious character traits in the movie has led her to conclude that Pandora is simply an allegorical portrayal of original and pristine (Earth) nature and the need to protect it. But *Avatar* also subtly promotes another kind of religion: outer space religion.

Throughout *Avatar*, nature is portrayed as sacred and as having intrinsic value; thus, the movie's religious aspects can be meaningfully interpreted by means of the concept of "dark green religion" (Taylor 2010). The ambiguity of Pandoran nature, however, calls for additional analytical measures. Here, the concept of "outer space religion" is useful. I define outer space religion as a system of thoughts, behaviours, and sentiments that centre on the conviction that salvation is to be found in outer space, or in activities and ideas connected to outer space. Activities may encompass both ritual behaviour and the production of scripture centred on space exploration, steps toward the colonization of space, or the search for and communication with extraterrestrial intelligences. In many cases outer space religion is devoid of divine (i.e., supernatural) beings. Often, however, extraterrestrial beings function like divine beings typically do in religious phenomena. Salvation may come in many forms, but it is usually defined by a moment or process of transcendence of an Earthbound mode of existence. Technology often plays a crucial role in the salvational scheme, and sometimes, but not always, it leads to a blurring or eradication of the nature-technology dichotomy. Space-related transcendence may also yield privileged knowledge, immortality, cosmic consciousness, an experience of the sublime, and so on. As it will sometimes be an implicit and unrecognized (and perhaps even denied) form of religion, it may be fruitful to concretize its contents by comparing it to well-known types of religion (Bailey 1997). Apocalypticism is a particularly useful analytic category. Outer space religion encompasses a dualistic worldview in which dreams of a transcendent new realm and the attainment of purified new bodies play a crucial role, and it combines elements of eschatology, revelation, and ascension (Collins 1979; Geraci 2010).[4]

The Historical Roots of *Avatar*'s Ambiguous Portrayal of Nature and Technology

As the fan site avatar-forums.com makes clear (and as many of the contributions in this book bear witness to), *Avatar* is typically understood as advocating a return to living in harmony with nature and as an incitement to environmentalist action. Cameron endorsed this understanding by releasing the DVD version of the movie on Earth Day, 22 April 2010, and in various statements (see, for example, Taylor's epilogue in this volume). He is openly involved in environmental activism, as exemplified by his participation in the battle against the Belo Monte Dam on the Xingu River in Brazil (Brooks 2010). He also started the Home Tree Initiative, the goal of which was to plant one million trees before 2011.[5] As his biographer Rebecca Keegan (2009, 255) puts it, "*Avatar* is Cameron's spiritual and ecological call to arms disguised as an adventure about a planet with ten-foot-tall blue aliens." Because all of this points to *Avatar*'s preoccupation with Earth environmentalism, it is easy to overlook the outer space setting of the movie, but taking it seriously helps to explain the ambiguity that pervades *Avatar*'s portrayal of nature.

As the astronauts of the Apollo missions looked back from space and saw the whole Earth from their elevated position, some of them reported strong feelings of responsibility for the well-being of Earth's ecosystems. Stewart Brand, the originator of the *Whole Earth Catalog*, lobbied NASA for a picture of the whole Earth seen from space because he thought that the global distribution of such an image would change the world into a better place. Although it perhaps did not have such far-reaching ramifications, the image did become an emblem for the environmental movement. In the long run, NASA was prompted to incorporate a more Earth-centred eco-awareness into the grand visions of space exploration and colonization (Poole 2008). As Robert Poole argues, the unexpected outcome of the Apollo program was, in a sense, a return to Earth. The tension between the movement away from Earth and the movement toward it has persisted in space exploration and in imaginative depictions of outer space (ibid).

Participants in the two movements have been categorized by William Bryant (1995) as "progressives," with an outward perspective away from Earth, and "environmentalists," with an inward perspective toward Earth. Each side responded differently to the image of the whole Earth, and each used it for their own cause. The environmental movement found support for a worldview "in which humanity was destined to destroy the Earth and itself unless it mended its ecologically unsustainable ways and found common ground for working and living together on a frail and finite planet" (44–45). In contrast, for the Enlightenment-inspired believers in progress, the images were "further compelling evidence that man was destined forever to explore and conquer nature in an evolutionary journey toward an ever more exalted state of humanness," and in this scheme, space exploration was of paramount importance (45). As a consequence, the images of the whole Earth can be "read as a site of contest between the environmentalist and progressive ideologies" (45). This conflict is also found in *Avatar*.[6]

There were also similarities between progressives and environmentalists (Bryant 1995, 47). Among these were "a discourse of 'survival' requiring a universalization (or, perhaps more appropriately, globalization) of all human beings into a single type" (54). The survival theme centred on things like the population explosion, nuclear war, and ecological catastrophes. But the two factions' responses to these dangers differed. Whereas the environmentalists wanted to stay on Earth and fight the consequences of technological overdevelopment, the progressives wanted to leave Earth in order to establish colonies elsewhere, thus ensuring the survival of the human race despite the potential catastrophes threatening life on Earth (55–56). Notwithstanding their different solutions, both believed in progress, harboured apocalyptic worldviews, and were looking for salvation (57). Furthermore, through the image of Earth seen from space, the two conceptual domains influenced each other. In Bryant's words, "the image of the Earth and the image of the spaceship that brought the image of the Earth were conflated," as is reflected in the expression "Spaceship Earth," probably coined by Buckminster Fuller in 1951 (51). By the very power of the Spaceship Earth metaphor, the two conceptual domains cross-fertilized each other.

Thus, while spaceships came to be viewed as more Earth-like, "more naturalized and less artificial," Earth came to be viewed as a spaceship: that is, as "a product of human technology, to be operated and even fixed by humans armed with the proper manual" (53). In somewhat extreme terms, "To see Earth as a spaceship is to see it as a machine, and to treat it as such" (54). Indeed, according to Peder Anker (2005, 239), the space exploration of the Apollo era spawned an "ecological colonization of space." Through trying to create ecologies for manned space exploration vehicles, the concept of Earth's ecosystems was, in turn, "colonized" by a managerial conception of Earth's ecology based on the analogy with the space cabin. The idea of "Spaceship Earth" was taken up by Stewart Brand, and the idea that Earth's threatened environments could be saved through technology was presented in the *Whole Earth Catalog* (Anker 2005). Analogously, Andrew Kirk has singled out the intimate connection between technology and environmentalism in Stewart Brand's variety of ecological awareness, and the "unbridled technological optimism" of the *Whole Earth Catalog*. According to Kirk (2001, 375), "Counterculture environmental politics embraced the seemingly contradictory notion that the antimodernist desire to return to a simpler time when humans were more closely tied to nature could be achieved through technological progress." Perhaps no one has put the connection between space exploration and ecology, and the concomitant evaporation of the distinction between nature and technology, so succinctly as Marshall McLuhan. In a 1973 essay, he contended that the first satellite to orbit Earth, the Soviet *Sputnik 1*, might "be an extension of the planet itself," and thus, "by putting the planet inside a man-made environment, nature ended. Everything that was called nature in preceding centuries ended at that moment, and instead the planet became an art form, an ecologically programmable environment" (McLuhan 2003, 208).[7] In this light, and given Cameron's predilection for space exploration, it is no wonder that nature has an ambiguous character in *Avatar*.

James Cameron's Pro-Space Activities

Cameron has expressed his excitement about space exploration not only in movies but also in pro-space activism. He is a member of both the Mars Society, an organization that lobbies for the human exploration and colonization of Mars, and the Planetary Society, which promotes the exploration and colonization of the solar system. He is an avid spokesman for space exploration and colonization, and he often airs his views of these matters. In 1999, Cameron was planning a TV miniseries and an IMAX feature film about the exploration and colonization of Mars (Clark 1999). (This plan was never realized.) From 2003 to 2005, he was a member of the NASA Advisory Council (Cameron 2010b). He plans to shoot a 3-D movie in the International Space Station (Rosenberg 2009), and in 2007, he began lobbying NASA to mount a 3-D camera of his design on the Mars rover "Curiosity." The latter project was scrapped by NASA in 2011 ("Transcript" 2005; Chow 2010; David 2011).

Cameron recognizes the importance of public support for space exploration and sees his own role as filmmaker as an important asset in this regard; in his view, the creation of science fiction visions may influence future space programs (Mone 2005; Cameron 2010b). In a keynote presentation at the first conference on the exploration of space held by the American Institute of Aeronautics and Astronautics (AIAA) in 2005, Cameron stated: "I've been asked lots of times by folks at all levels of NASA, what can we do better to reach out to the public? Well, two things. One, tell the story better. Two, have a better story to tell" ("Transcript" 2005; see also Kelly 2005). He continued, "What do rockets burn for fuel? Money. Where does the money come from? Comes from people.... Why do they give the money? Because they share the dream. So if you want to look at it that way, rockets really run on dreams."[8]

Space exploration may inspire the public in several ways. According to Cameron, space exploration could play a decisive role in keeping the

United States on track as the leading country in the world. It would yield an "inspirational dividend" that would boost everything from self-image to geopolitical stature. In order for this to come true, heroism is needed— though of a special kind: "Young kids need something to dream about, something to measure their value system against. Going to Mars is not a luxury we can't afford, it's a necessity we can't afford to be without" ("Transcript" 2005). US President Barack Obama's cancellation of his predecessor George W. Bush's Constellation program in 2010 did not throw Cameron off course (Bush 2004; Obama 2010; "NASA's Project" 2011). Instead, he endorsed Obama's new strategy for NASA and reiterated the importance of creating dreams in order to mobilize public support for space exploration (Cameron 2010a). Cameron has, though, been forced to think along slightly different lines when considering what stories are worth telling; since near-term plans for manned flights to Mars have been cancelled, the Mars exploration angle may no longer be worth pursuing (Boyle 2011).

Avatar's potential to build support for space exploration has been recognized by the pro-space movement: for example, some questioned why NASA did not quickly seize the opportunity presented by Avatar to arouse public interest in space and support for NASA activities (Cowing 2009, 2010). But NASA has begun doing so. In connection with the discovery of exoplanets, Charles Bolden, NASA's chief administrator, mentioned Pandora of Avatar in a speech to the Americian Astronomical Society. NASA subsequently produced a small series of public announcements on NASA TV concerning "the many contributions of the agency's Earth science program to environmental awareness and exploration of our home planet" (Bolden 2010; "Cameron Shares" 2010).[9] This series featured imagery from Avatar and excerpts from speeches by Cameron.[10]

James Cameron and Outer Space Religion

Although Cameron is certainly very dedicated to the space cause, the discussion above is not enough to ascertain the presence of outer space religion in Avatar; some retrospection is needed. At age fifteen, Cameron had tears in his eyes as he watched Neil Armstrong and Buzz Aldrin set foot on the moon, and the first time he saw a shuttle launch, he cried ("Transcript" 2005; Kelly 2005). Since his youth, he has been an avid reader of science fiction, favouring authors such as Arthur C. Clarke and Robert Heinlein (Keegan 2009, 7). Stanley Kubrick's 2001: A Space Odyssey (1968)—co-written with Arthur C. Clarke—made an unforgettable impression on Cameron and was a major reason why he became a filmmaker. He was fascinated by both the mystical content of the movie and its revolutionizing special effects (Keegan 2009, 10–11). The mystical content that drew in the young Cameron was an integral part of Arthur C. Clarke's science fiction, which displayed a strong preoccupation with religious themes and often cast technology as a catalyst for transcendence. In both fictional and popular scientific works, Clarke projected apocalyptic narrative structure and images onto the science and technology of the future, which fits well with the definition of outer space religion (Bjørnvig 2012). As is often the case with outer space religion, Clarke's work does not contain a notion of supernatural beings or powers. Instead, alien creatures or artifacts often display abilities that are indistinguishable from those of divine beings.[11]

Cameron does not believe in God, but he does believe in the power of religion: "We are all wired with the need to feel that there is some greater sense of purpose and order, that it all somehow makes sense, and that some great force is watching over us" (quoted in Keegan 2009, 8). Keegan summarizes Cameron's view: "Some of us choose heaven, some of us outer space, but most of us need to feel there's something out there smarter and more benevolent than we are" (86). Cameron was influenced by Clarke's outer space religion, which, like the religion of technology generally, constructs technology as the means to transfiguration, whether salvific, apocalyptic, or both. Examining previous movies by Cameron confirms this.

In *The Abyss* (1989), Cameron portrays extraterrestrial beings living at the bottom of the sea on Earth, reflecting his fascination with "inner space": that is, the sea as an alternative to outer space. The aliens inhabit what should probably be understood as a giant spaceship resting on the sea bottom. The spaceship, however, has an organic-looking shape, and the technology used by the alien creatures looks similar to biological organisms. The video montage of Earthly evils shown to the human protagonist at the end of the movie, for example, appears on a screen made of a material that seems to be indistinguishable from the material from which the extraterrestrial beings are formed. The plot revolves around the confrontation between the aliens and the technology of the representatives of Earthly military. Thus, we see the same antagonism between two kinds of technology as in *Avatar*: crude, abusive, aggressive Earth technology and a more sophisticated, peaceful technology of a seemingly semi-organic type. Moreover, the alien wielders of this technology are portrayed as angelic beings. Indeed, at the end of the movie they act in the role of divine judges of humanity's evil, Earthly ways, thus confirming the presence of apocalypticism and the outer space religious notion that salvific potential arises from the obliteration of the nature-technology dichotomy.[12] The aliens themselves are clearly inspired by underwater, bioluminescent sea creatures and, like Pandoran nature in its "mystical" aspect, there is something paradoxically artificial in their appearance. Visually, the difference between natural and artificial, nature and technology, is questioned in *The Abyss*, which brings to mind the concept of "cyborg."

The term *cyborg* was coined by Clynes and Kline (1966) in an article about the future prospects of humanity in outer space. Instead of dealing with the problems of transporting a biosphere into space, they suggest, it may be a better idea to turn humans into cyborgs, hybrids of technology and biology, thus transforming them into something more compatible with existence in outer space and rendering the need for a biosphere obsolete (Davis 2004, 152–53). Subsequently, the term *cyborg* was appropriated by Donna Haraway (1991) to signify the postmodern eradication of various culturally entrenched dichotomies, such as the dichotomy between the natural and the technological—in the context of this discussion, a highly significant dichotomy. Haraway's more expansive use of the term no longer signifies hybrids between nature and technology but rather the evaporation of the semantics of the opposition itself. In the cyborg-postmodern mode of existence, the very distinction between the natural and the artificial, the biological and the technological, has ceased making sense. It is, in my view, this postmodern way of perceiving nature that parts of Cameron's oeuvre reflect. Indeed, as McVeigh and Kapell (2011, 1) note, "the visions presented in his [Cameron's] films have been consistent and resonant visions of the contemporary zeitgeist." Recalling *Avatar*'s outer space setting, it is not without relevance that musings on the indistinguishability between technology and nature in relation to extraterrestrial civilizations abound in writings on the search for extraterrestrial intelligence (see, for example, Davies 1995; Armstrong 2012; and Hughes 2004).[13]

In his documentary about deep-sea exploration, *Aliens of the Deep* (2005), Cameron's predilection for casting the sea as parallel to outer space is repeated. Arthur C. Clarke often drew the same parallel: he saw underwater exploration as a surrogate for space exploration and thus, inevitably, conferred many outer space religious character traits on the sea (Keegan 2009, 83; Bjørnvig 2012). Notably, in *Aliens of the Deep*, part of the deep-sea exploration team consists of SETI (search for extraterrestrial intelligence) scientists and astrobiologists. In one scene, Cameron is involved in animated discussions with some of these scientists about the prospects of discovering alien life. Thus, the connections between sea, space exploration, and alien life stand out (see also Matsos 2003). At the end of *Aliens of the Deep*, Cameron envisions the first encounter between humans and aliens living under the ice of Europa, one of Jupiter's moons. Again, the form of the aliens is inspired by underwater, bioluminescent organisms. Thus, the connection between sophisticated, cyborg-like "organic technology," bioluminescent alien life, and outer space is strikingly prominent in Cameron's productions.[14]

There may be more to Cameron's choice of bioluminescence as a central visual marker, however, than his fondness for deep-sea diving. The phenomenon lends itself easily to a symbolic understanding that draws meaning from metaphors that cluster around the concept of "light" as truth, awakening, spiritual illumination, the divine, and so on (Werblowsky and Iwersen 2005). Thus, a major reason why Cameron repeatedly returns to this visual theme may be that it stirs culturally entrenched metaphorical connections between light and the supernatural, between the *non*-natural and the divine. Furthermore, given the Na'vi's visually prominent facial feature of luminous spark-like spots, it is tempting to see the light symbolism of *Avatar* more narrowly connected to Western esoteric, mystical ideas present in Neoplatonism, Hermeticism and Gnosticism. In these traditions, light signifies a higher, spiritual level of being as opposed to a lower, material one (Werblowsky and Iwersen 2005). It is, moreover, tempting to see parallels between the luminous spots of the Na'vi—and bioluminescence on Pandora in general—and the Manichaean idea that sparks of the divine are trapped in the material world (Davis 2004, 110–13). As the glimpses of Eywa obtained through Grace Augustine's connection to the Tree of Souls seem to suggest, the essence of Pandoran nature is, in some sense, pure light. Furthermore, the many connections between Gnosticism and the modern religious fascination with technology noted by Erik Davis (2004) makes it easier to understand how a technologized nature, a cyborg hybrid of the natural and the artificial, may accumulate religious significance of a special kind.[15]

Apocalypticism, Dualism, and Cognitive Dissonance in *Avatar*

There is great power in creating an alienating dualism in people's lives, a state of cognitive dissonance, and then pointing the way to its dissolution.[16] This pattern is typical of utopianism and apocalypticism. Both concepts are relevant in relation to the religious aspects of *Avatar* and both can precipitate political activism.[17] Here, however, I will focus on apocalypticism. As Robert M. Geraci (2010, 9) points out in a study of apocalyptic artificial intelligence, "Apocalypticism refers to (1) a dualistic view of the world, which is (2) aggravated by a sense of alienation that can be resolved only through (3) the establishment of a radically transcendent new world that abolishes the dualism and requires (4) radically purified bodies for its inhabitants." According to Geraci, the apocalyptic dualism centres on a battle between good and evil, and this battle surfaces in *Avatar* as the dichotomy of Earth versus Heaven (Pandora).[18] In *James Cameron's Avatar: An Activist Survival Guide*, Maria Wilhelm and Dirk Mathison (2009, ix) portray life on Earth as a hell and Pandora as a distant paradise in the heavens: "I look around at the garbage-strewn, high-tech squalor here and see in the murky distance that much better place—pristine Pandora, opalescent in the velvet darkness." Pandora is cast as the source of salvation for Earth: "I see our scarred Earth, renewed and revived. The oceans returned to blue, a world washed clean and begun again. Like it once was. I can't help but wonder if Eywa called out to us, at risk to herself, so that she might save Earth" (xvii).[19]

This way of portraying the gulf dividing Earthly and Pandoran existence speaks to religiously inclined, eco-oriented people, who seem to be numerous among *Avatar* fans, as is evident from the thread on avatar-forums.com titled "Ways to Cope with the Depression of the Dream of Pandora Being Intangible."[20] Here, people have joined in a mutual feeling of disappointment in face of the fact that Pandora and what it represents is out of reach—intangible. This feeling, and the effect it has on those who have it, was dubbed the "Pandora Effect" by one fan.[21] The depression that comes from being on the wrong side of the dualistic gulf between Earth and Pandora typically conforms to the following pattern: The movie is like a dream of a higher reality that at first energizes. Then comes the realization that it was only a dream and subsequent feelings of depression. Joining the *Avatar* forums gives some comfort, but the movie has created a rift in normal, Earthly reality that seems to forever render that reality colourless and depressing. And at all times, the movie is on one's mind.[22]

Although people react in different ways, nearly all attempt to overcome the dualism and the ensuing cognitive dissonance created or intensified in their lives by *Avatar*.[23] Some suggest the possibility of creating a virtual Pandora on the Internet, a kind of matrix in which fans can immerse themselves.[24] Some try lucid dreaming, a way of consciously controlling one's dreams, as a method to revisit Pandora.[25] Some change their lifestyles and take action in their own lives by living in a more "natural," ecologically sound way.[26] Some try to get out into nature and experience it up close and find a beauty on Earth that might compare to the beauty of Pandora.[27] Others hope that progress in spaceflight technology will enable humanity to go to other worlds. It is worthwhile to examine this last response in some detail since doing so reveals that not only can *Avatar* incite environmentalist passions, but it can also appeal to outer space religiosity by igniting dreams of leaving Earth, thus bearing witness to *Avatar*'s potential for promoting science, space exploration, and even the search for extraterrestrial intelligence and for extrasolar planets.[28]

On avatar-forums.com, for example, "futureman" admits: "I am starting to get mad at NASA for not making space ships that could take me to such a magical place."[29] "Woodsprite" relates: "I had a strong disbelief in life on other planets, and believed we were the only ones created in the universe... but this movie made me want to believe it, and it eventually convinced me that it's possible."[30] "Kxanì Kato" has been wanting to leave Earth since the age of six, and *Avatar* somehow makes it all fall into place: "Even if we wait until 2029, only the absolute luckiest of us will ever have the chance of reaching a planet like pandora. I finally realize why I have been so obsessed with space and astronomy my entire life. It's that hidden desire. I've wanted to be an astronaut since I was 6 years old. I've finally found out why.... Again Avatar has opened my eyes. I believe the only way to cure my case of the Pandora Effect is to leave this earth, if only for a day."[31] Thus, the responses of some *Avatar* viewers suggest that Cameron has created the kind of heroism and purpose that is needed to fuel the rockets that will take humanity out among the planets. The mechanism used to create this aspiration is an apocalyptic dualism, the dissolution of which—so *Avatar* suggests—can only be found beyond Earth.[32]

The apocalypticism of *Avatar* becomes even more evident in light of the final point of Geraci's fourfold definition of apocalypticism. The "radical purified bodies" necessary to inhabit the new, transcendent realm where the apocalyptic dualism is overcome are vividly present in *Avatar* in the form of the Na'vi avatar body donned by Sully as he merges with Pandoran nature. One of the most powerfully moving scenes of *Avatar* is when the paraplegic Sully stands upright for the first time in his new avatar body, his toes digging into the Pandoran soil and his sensory apparatus overflowing with Pandoran sensations of smell, sound, vision, and taste. Here, Sully is resurrected in a new purified body, enabling him to leave behind the Earthly trappings of both the greedy, corporate army and his own diminished body. The urge to leave the fallen human body in favour of resurrection in an avatar body on Pandora has been felt strongly by some *Avatar* fans: "AlphaNavi" writes, "I believe I am a Na'vi trapped in this human shell."[33] Indeed, some commentators have noticed that the very act of watching the 3-D spectacle of *Avatar* may produce a virtual experience of having been in a Na'vi body. For some, leaving the movie theatre is experienced as a fall from an elevated existence (Lertzman 2010; Croken 2010).

The Artificial Nature of Pandoran Paradise

Holmes Rolston III (2007) argues that a distinction between nature and culture, and culture's subset technology, must be upheld even though Earth's nature is gradually being synthesized. Rolston draws the distinction between "spontaneous nature and deliberated culture" and states, "Artifacts are the products of culture; they are nature cultured, and culture is something else from wild nature." Yet, as the sphere of human influence is spreading over the surface of Earth and into almost all conceivable ecological niches, nature is gradually becoming more and more cultured. There will always be areas where biological entities will grow and live spontaneously with little or no human influence. But as Earth becomes increasingly managed, it also becomes, in a sense, synthetic: "Nature as it once was, nature as an end in itself, is no longer the whole story. Nature as contrasted with culture is not the whole story either. One can dwell on the extremes in either direction. Much of life does take place in the symbiotic zone" (Rolston 2007).

Perhaps Cameron's ambivalent portrayal of Pandoran nature is a kind of mythical reflection of Rolston's (and Haraway's) basic point: that much of nature has already become synthetic. On one level, Cameron constructed Pandoran nature so that it could function as a symbol of Earth's nature as it, to some dedicated environmentalists, ought to be: pristine, unspoiled, wild. As I suggest, however, Pandoran nature is ambiguous both on a visual level and through its correspondence with the avatar technology. Again, this paradox may be explained if we take heed of *Avatar*'s science fiction setting and outer space religious character traits. According to Sharona Ben-Tov (1995, 46), science fiction is an American genre with an ambivalent stance toward nature. While it embodies the Cartesian dualism of modern science with its instrumentalist view of nature, it also longs for the paradisaical, limitless nature of the "American frontier." This impels the genre to re-create nature by artificial means, and the genre itself may function as a "paradise machine" that constitutes a simulacrum of the lost paradise. Ben-Tov's analysis of the "artificial paradise" proposes that science fiction constitutes a break with nature: "The moment of suspended disbelief when a reader accepts the images of interstellar travel is also a moment of implicit, conspiratorial belief in the ideology of progress" (5). Ben-Tov concludes, "As soon as we picture a spaceship, we mentally unroll the map of objectified space; we enter the mass dream of collective technological power; we participate in a drama about remaking the universe in our image" (130; see also 34). What Ben-Tov describes is outer space religion's propensity for transcending nature while at the same time longing for it—although in an artificial, re-created form.

Following Ben-Tov, Cameron's *Avatar* reiterates the religious drama of the "captivity tale," in which the soldier hero suffers a fall and must resist the temptation to "accept being absorbed into the native tribe"—but it does so with a twist, radicalizing the pro-native stance of the obvious model of the film *A Man Called Horse* (1970). Even though Sully follows the mythic pattern by becoming a "soul-dier" and rejuvenates himself through the hunter's killing, which gives "him the same bond with the land's spirits that Native

Americans were believed to possess," his going native is not momentary (Ben-Tov 1995, 104, 107). Indeed, by being resurrected in a native body, Sully could not go more native. However, Sully's Na'vi body is *not* a natural product of spontaneous evolution but the outcome of the splicing of Na'vi and human genes. Although organic through and through, Sully's avatar body is the artificial result of technological manipulation and is therefore a cyborg. It is in this body that Sully experiences ultimate freedom; thus, Sully, even as Ben-Tov's "soul-dier," subtly conforms to the science fiction ideology since "limitlessness is the very basis for his personal integration of technology and nature" (108).

Consequently, the avatar theme reverberates with complex layers of symbolic meaning. One of these relates to apocalypticism and the relation between the audience and the medium of cinema itself. As the audience in the darkened theatre is sucked into the magic 3-D world of Pandora, so Jake Sully is sucked from his wheelchair into the glowing fairyland of the "real" Pandora. And as Sully is resurrected in his avatar body, so is the audience, by force of identifying with Sully. By participating in the hyper-reality of *Avatar*, the audience inhabits the paradise machine identified by Ben-Tov. Some of the most gripping scenes in *Avatar* are played out in relation to the avatars, as exemplified when Sully stands in his new avatar body, revelling in Pandoran sensations. Another example is near the end of the movie, when Neytiri compassionately embraces Sully's suffocated, naked human body. For a moment, the illusion is broken and the prelapsarian mirage of the movie evaporates. But in the end, it is not the avatar body that Sully abandons but his human shell. For Sully, as for the audience in the grip of the movie, resurrection in a perfect cyborg body awaits and the promise is given that the painful dualism between polluted, fallen Earth and pristine, paradisaical Pandora may be transcended.

Conclusion

Given the Earth-centred evironmental message of *Avatar*, it may seem paradoxical that the movie also implies that the solution to the dualism that it creates may be found in space. This paradox, however, becomes easier to understand when the historical convergence of progressive and environmentalist ideologies—and their religious expressions in outer space religion and dark green religion, respectively—are taken into consideration. Likewise, it comes as less of a surprise that we find apocalypticism and technoscience entwined in *Avatar*. The apocalyptic genre's close affiliation to science fiction—and thus, by implication, to outer space religion—has been noted, and not the least in relation to the works of Arthur C. Clarke (Kreuziger 1982, 1986; Bjørnvig 2012). Indeed, apocalypticism developed in a dialectical relationship with science and astronomy in medieval and Enlightenment Europe (Fried 2000), and millenarian ideas have long suffused technology (Noble 1999). As Geraci demonstrates in *Apocalyptic AI* (2010, esp. 56–71), in relation to scientific research in artificial intelligence, apocalyptic narratives can function as a means of obtaining funding for scientific endeavours.[34] While the goal of Cameron's outer space religious apocalyptic as expressed in *Avatar* is surely to mobilize the public to take environmentalist action, it simultaneously encourages space research and exploration.

As noted, the stance toward nature and technology in *Avatar* is ambivalent. Although Cameron sides with nature against the negative effects of technology-driven exploitation, he does not criticize technology per se but only the crude, abusive, destructive technology deployed to promote social and ecological imperialism. In contrast, the movie's sophisticated avatar technology mirrors Pandoran nature and, following the film's internal logic, is the bridge to understanding it and becoming part of it, thus constituting a pathway to redemption. The cyborg avatar bodies mirror the cyborg-resembling Pandoran nature, and in the process of the continual reflection between the two, the semantic dichotomy between nature and culture/technology is blurred. As such, *Avatar* tries to bridge the fundamentally different worldviews of progressive outer space religion and environmentalist dark green religion. It does so by returning the spectator, through a highly complex symbolic journey, to the historical point of convergence between the two different worldviews. One might say that *Avatar* is a powerful dark green religious myth that shares some of its historical roots with outer space religion, roots that float free of Earth's gravity field just as the roots of the plants growing on the Hallelujah Mountains of Pandora float free of the tangled jungle below.

Notes

1 At first, the avatar technology is harnessed by RDA in order to make the Na'vi move away from the coveted sources of unobtanium; it is, however, inherently subversive, precisely because it is the pathway into the mystical nature of Pandora.

2 Grace Augustine's announcement that there are more neural connections in Pandoran nature than in the human brain is reminiscent of statements about the Internet; see, for example, White (1987, 85–87) and "Futuretalk" (2008).

3 On Pandoran nature having something technological about it, see Autino (2010), "petersattler" (2010), Crain (2010), Linnitt (2010), and Istoft (2010 and this volume).

4 The idea that religion and modern space activities may be connected is not new; see, for example, Noble (1999, 115–42), Horrigan (1986), and Michaud (1986). Regarding connections between religion and technology in general, see Noble

(1999), Stahl (2001), and Davis (2004). Speaking in history-of-religions terms, we are dealing with such comparative types as "millenarianism," "apocalypticism," and "gnosticism" as they connect to technology; see Bjørnvig (2005, 2012). The science fiction genre's apocalyptic dimension has been analyzed in Kreuziger (1982, 1986).

5 The Home Tree Initiative was begun by Twentieth Century Fox Home Entertainment in collaboration with Earth Day Network; see http://www.earthday.org/avatar. For additional examples of Cameron's eco-activism, see Taylor and Ivakhiv (2010, 389). The Home Tree Initiative succeeded and surpassed its goal of planting a million trees; see Johnston (2011).

6 For the connection between space exploration and environmentalism, see Noel (2005), and on science fiction movies and the view from space of the whole earth, see Brereton (2005, 140, 151–53).

7 See also Brereton (2005, 152) and, in general, Turner (2006), which traces in considerable depth Brand's synthesis of the natural and the artificial.

8 Cameron's presentation was given at the AIAA's "First Space Exploration Conference: Continuing the Voyage of Discovery," 31 January–1 February 2005; see program at https://www.aiaa.org/ProceedingsDetail.aspx?id=5771.

9 *Avatar* has begun to seep into discourse about SETI and the search for exoplanets (Hsu 2010).

10 On the connection between imagination and space policy, see McCurdy (1997).

11 Regarding "religion" without transcendent, or supernatural, entities, see arguments in favour of a (more) "flexible" definition of religion that does not rest on the notion of transcendent beings in Taylor (2010, 40, 158–60, 177–78); see also Taylor's introduction to this volume. For functional versus substantial definitions of religion, see Istoft (2010 and this volume) and Arnal (2000).

12 Here again I disagree with Rosen, who contends that the apocalyptic elements in Cameron's movies are strictly secular and thus can only point the way to a utopian solution devoid of any divine interference; this fails to take into consideration the role of the aliens in, for example, *The Abyss*. Although they can be considered natural, not supernatural, beings, they nevertheless occupy the very same roles that otherwise would have been occupied by God, angels, or gods. On religious aspects of *The Abyss*, see Keegan (2009, 83–86).

13 The emerging paradigm of "Next Nature" also embraces the notion that nature and technology are becoming indistinguishable; see Sterling (2010).

14 SETI enthusiasts have had both positive (Autino 2010) and skeptical (Shostak 2010) reactions to *Avatar*.

15 Davis's comment on *Avatar* only partly reflects my own (Davis 2010).

16 For the concept of "cognitive dissonance," see Festinger, Riecken, and Schacter ([1956] 2008). The utility of the concept in connection with millenarian and apocalyptic movements has been disputed (O'Leary 2000; Geraci 2010, 16, 171n23), but it is an illuminating term in the present context. Renee A. Lertzman (2010) has also pointed out *Avatar*'s radical splitting up of the world into good and bad and has likened the longings inspired by *Avatar* with longings for a lost paradise, as has Ryan Croken (2010), who vividly describes the duality created by *Avatar*: "Epiphany and counter-epiphany collide in your mind."

17 For the "progressive, even pro-active, agency" of utopia in Hollywood movies, see Brereton (2005, 23).

18 On the apocalyptic aspects of *Avatar*, see also Barnhill (2010 and this volume).

19 In addition, in the fictive universe of the book, artifacts, plants, and animals have already been imported to Earth. Some of these may, it turns out, be dangerous to the environment on Earth but many have the potential to purify various habitats on Earth (see, e.g., Wilhelm and Mathison 2009, xiii, 115, 134, 137).

20 See http://www.avatar-forums.com/showthread.php?43-Ways-to-cope-with-the -depression-of-the-dream-of-Pandora-being-intangible.

21 "Keeper of Na'vi," 31 December 2009, 08:30 p.m., at http://www.avatar-forums.com/ showthread.php?43-Ways-to-cope-with-the-depression-of-the-dream-of-Pandora -being-intangible/page24.

22 See, for example, "Ryan," 2 January 2010, 09:48 a.m., at http://www.avatar-forums .com/showthread.php?43-Ways-to-cope-with-the-depression-of-the-dream-of -Pandora-being-intangible/page51. See also Croken (2010) and Holtmeier (2010 and this volume); but some *Avatar* fans deny that they are "isolated, anti-social, psychologically mixed-up dreamers" (Istoft 2010 and this volume).

23 As O'Leary (2000) points out, proselytizing is not the only way to overcome cognitive dissonance surfacing in apocalyptic movements; the thread dealt with here indicates that sharing the results of the Pandora Effect in itself reduces cognitive dissonance.

24 See "Grif," 5 January 2010, 04:47 p.m., at http://www.avatar-forums.com/showthread .php?43-Ways-to-cope-with-the-depression-of-the-dream-of-Pandora-being-intang ible/page66.

25 See "It's Possible to Visit Pandora" at http://www.avatar-forums.com/showthread .php?434-It-s-Possible-to-Visit-Pandora&highlight=LUCID+DREAMERS.

26 See, for example, the posting by "Neytiri," 26 December 2009, 11:21 p.m., at http:// www.avatar-forums.com/showthread.php?43-Ways-to-cope-with-the-depression -of-the-dream-of-Pandora-being-intangible.

27 See, for example, the posting by "The_Duke," 29 December 2009, 12:45 p.m., at http://www.avatar-forums.com/showthread.php?43-Ways-to-cope-with-the -depression-of-the-dream-of-Pandora-being-intangible/page8.

28 See, for example, the posting by "Shomvu," 5 January 2010, 01:22 a.m., at http://www.avatar-forums.com/showthread.php?43-Ways-to-cope-with-the -depression-of-the-dream-of-Pandora-being-intangible/page64.

29 "futureman," 30 December 2009, 10:16 p.m., at http://www.avatar-forums.com/ showthread.php?43-Ways-to-cope-with-the-depression-of-the-dream-of-Pandora -being-intangible/page18..

30 "Woodsprite," 3 January 2010, 04:13 p.m., at http://www.avatar-forums.com/ showthread.php?43-Ways-to-cope-with-the-depression-of-the-dream-of-Pandora -being-intangible/page61.

31 "Kxanì Kato," 5 January 2010, 10:45 a.m. This post has been removed from avatar -forums.com.

32 Cameron's manipulation of his audience has been noticed by some fans; as "neyt-irifanboy" says: "I believe Cameron intended to get us addicted by making us fall in love, not only with the characters, but the whole world where it [*Avatar*] takes place" (28 December 2009, 04:38 a.m).

33 "AlphaNavi," 29 December 2009, 02:30 p.m., at at http://www.avatar-forums.com/
    showthread.php?43-Ways-to-cope-with-the-depression-of-the-dream-of-Pandora
    -being-intangible/page9.
34 A similar point has been made by Bryant (1995) in relation to the progressive myth
    and outer space.

References

Anker, Peder. 2005. "The Ecological Colonization of Space." *Environmental History*
    10(2): 239–68.
Armstrong, Rachel. 2012. "Any Sufficiently Advanced Civilization Is Indistin-
    guishable from Nature." *Next Nature*, 18 February. http://www.nextnature.net/
    2012/02/any-sufficiently-advanced-civilization-is-indistinguishable-from
    -nature/.
Arnal, William E. 2000. "Definition." In *Guide to the Study of Religion*, edited by
    Willi Braun and Russell T. McCutcheon, 21–33. London: Cassell.
Autino, Adriano V. 2010. "Avatar, a Movie of This Time." *SETI League.* http://
    www.setileague.org/reviews/avatar.htm.
Bailey, Edward I. 1997. *Implicit Religion in Contemporary Society.* Leuven, Belgium:
    Peeters.
Barnhill, David Landis. 2010. "Spirituality and Resistance: Ursula Le Guin's *The
    Word for World Is Fores*t and the Film *Avatar.*" *Journal for the Study of Religion,
    Nature, and Culture* 4(4): 478–98.
Ben-Tov, Sharona. 1995. *The Artificial Paradise: Science Fiction and American
    Reality.* Ann Arbor: University of Michigan Press.
Bjørnvig, Thore. 2005. "Science, Apocalyptic, and the Quest for Meaning in the
    SETI Movement: An Examination of the Interfaces between Science Fiction,
    Religion, Science and the Search for Extraterrestrial Intelligence (SETI)."
    Master's thesis, University of Copenhagen.
————. 2012. "Transcendence of Gravity: Arthur C. Clarke and the Apocalypse
    of Weightlessness." In *Imagining Outer Space: European Astroculture in the
    Twentieth Century*, edited by Alexander C. T. Geppert, 127–46. Basingstoke:
    Palgrave Macmillan.
Bolden, Charles F. Jr. 2010. "Keynote Address by NASA Administrator Charles F.
    Bolden Jr., American Astronomical Society Winter Meeting, January 5, 2010."
    NASA. http://www.nasa.gov/pdf/415511main_Bolden_AAS_Remarks_010510
    .pdf.
Boyle, Alan. 2011. "'Avatar' Director Targets Spaceflight." *Cosmic Log*, 6 June.
    http://cosmiclog.nbcnews.com/_news/2011/06/06/6797375-avatar-director
    -targets-spaceflight?lite.
Brereton, Pat. 2005. *Hollywood Utopia: Ecology in Contemporary American Cin-
    ema.* Bristol, UK: Intellect Books.
Brooks, Bradley. 2010. "James Cameron: 'Victory' in Brazil Halting Dam." *3 News*,
    15 April. http://www.3news.co.nz/James-Cameron-Victory-in-Brazil-halting
    -dam/tabid/1160/articleID/151237/Default.aspx.

Bryant, William. 1995. "The Re-Vision of Planet Earth: Space Flight and Environmentalism in Postmodern America." *Over Here: A European Journal of American Culture* 36(2): 43–63.

Bush, George W. 2004. "President Bush Announces New Vision for Space Exploration Program." Press notice, The White House, 14 January. http://history .nasa.gov/Bush%20SEP.htm.

Cameron, James. 2010a. "The Right Way Forward on Space Exploration." *Washington Post*, 5 February. http://www.washingtonpost.com/wp-dyn/content/ article/2010/02/04/AR2010020402439.html?hpid=opinionsbox1.

———. 2010b. "Rockets Run on Dreams." 14 February. *Mars Artists Community*. http://marsartists.blogspot.com/2010/02/james-cameronlone-voice-in -wilderness.html

"Cameron Shares NASA's Exploration of Earth in 'Avatar' Videos." 2010. *NASA*, 24 August. http://www.nasa.gov/topics/earth/features/avatar.html.

Chow, Denise. 2010. "James Cameron Wants to Film Mars in 3-D." *Space.com*, 30 April. http://www.space.com/8321-james-cameron-film-mars-3.html.

Clark, Greg. 1999. "Cameron Sending Two Missions to Mars." 25 August. *Space .com*. http://www.space.com/sciencefiction/cameron_mars_speech_825. html (site discontinued).

Clynes, Manfred E., and Nathan S. Kline. 1966. "Cyborgs and Space." *Astronautics*, September.

Collins, John J. 1979. "Introduction: Towards the Morphology of a Genre." *Semeia* 14: 1–19.

Cowing, Keith. 2009. "Avatar: A Stunning New World That NASA Is Ignoring." *NASA Watch*, 17 November. http://www.nasawatch.com/archives/2009/11/ avatar-a-stunni.html.

———. 2010. "Avatar: A Stunning New World That NASA Continues to Ignore." *The Astrobiology Web*. 18 January. http://www.astrobiology.com/news/ viewnews.html?id=1364.

Crain, Caleb. 2010. "Don't Play with That, or You'll Go Blind: On James Cameron's *Avatar*." *n+1*, 1 January. http://nplusonemag.com/dont-play-or-youll-go-blind.

Croken, Ryan. 2010. "No Garden to Get Back To: Understanding Post-*Avatar* Ecological Depressive Disorder." *Religion Dispatches*, 28 January. http://www .religiondispatches.org/archive/culture/2226/no_garden_to_get_back.

David, Leonard. 2011. "Sorry, James Cameron: NASA Nixes 3-D Camera for Next Mars Rover." *Space.com*, 28 March. http://www.space.com/11241-nasa -mars-rover-3d-camera-james-cameron.html.

Davies, Paul. 1995. *Are We Alone? Philosophical Implications of the Discovery of Extraterrestrial Life*. London: Penguin Books.

Davis, Erik. 2004. *TechGnosis: Myth, Magic, and Mysticism in the Age of Information*. New York: Three Rivers Press.

———. 2010. "Aya Avatar: Drink the Jungle Juice." *TechGnosis.com*, 7 January. http://www.techgnosis.com/chunkshow-single.php?chunk=chunkfrom -2010-01-06-2204-0.txt&printable=1.

Festinger, Leon, Henry W. Riecken, and Stanley Schacter. (1956) 2008. *When Prophecy Fails*. Reprint, London: Pinter and Martin. Kindle edition.

Fried, Johannes. 2000. "Awaiting the Last Days.... Myth and Disenchantment." In *Apocalyptic Time*, edited by Albert I. Baumgarten, 283–303. Leiden: Brill.

"Futuretalk." 2008. "Global Brain: The Internet Could Become Conscious by Mid-2030s." *FutureBlogger*, 15 March. http://memebox.com/futureblogger/show/158.

Geraci, Robert M. 2010. *Apocalyptic AI: Visions of Heaven in Robotics, Artificial Intelligence, and Virtual Reality*. New York: Oxford University Press.

Haraway, Donna J. 1991. "A Cyborg Manifesto: Science, Technology, and Socialist-Feminism in the Late Twentieth Century." In *Simians, Cyborgs, and Woman: The Reinvention of Nature*, 149–81. New York: Routledge.

Holtmeier, Matthew. 2010. "Post-Pandoran Depression or Na'vi Sympathy: *Avatar*, Affect, and Audience Reception." *Journal for the Study of Religion, Nature, and Culture* 4(4): 414–24.

Horrigan, Brian. 1986. "Popular Culture and Visions of the Future in Space, 1901–2001." In *New Perspectives on Technology and American Culture*, edited by Bruce Sinclair, 49–67. American Philosophical Society Library Publication No. 12. Philadelphia: American Philosophical Society.

Hsu, Jeremy. 2010. "A Million Questions about Habitable Planet Gliese 581g (Okay, 12)." *Space.com*, 1 October. http://www.space.com/scienceastronomy/habitable-alien-planet-gliese-581g-facts-101001.html.

Hughes, Paul. 2004. "Exotic Civilizations: A Possible Answer to Fermi's Paradox." *Enthea*. http://enthea.org/writing/exotic-civilizations-a-possible-answer-to-fermis-paradox/

Istoft, Britt. 2010. "*Avatar* Fandom as Nature-Religious Expression?" *Journal for the Study of Religion, Nature, and Culture* 4(4): 394–413.

Johnston, Marsha. 2011. "Avatar Home Tree Initiative Plants over 1 Million!" *Earth Day Network*, 20 January. http://www.earthday.org/blog/billion-acts-green/2011/01/20/avatar-home-tree-initiative-plants-over-1-million.

Kapell, Matthew Wilhelm, and Stephen McVeigh, eds. 2011. *The Films of James Cameron: Critical Essays*. Jefferson, NC: McFarland.

Keegan, Rebecca. 2009. *The Futurist: The Life and Films of James Cameron*. New York: Crown.

Kelly, John. 2005. "Director James Cameron Works with NASA on Future Mars Mission." *Space.com*, 9 February. http://www.space.com/entertainment/ft_cameron_mars_050209.html.

Kirk, Andrew. 2001. "Appropriating Technology: The *Whole Earth Catalog* and Counterculture Environmental Politics." *Environmental History* 6(3): 374–94.

Kreuziger, Frederick A. 1982. *Apocalypse and Science Fiction: A Dialectic of Religious and Secular Soteriologies*. American Academy of Religion Academy Series. Chico, CA: Scholars Press.

———. 1986. *The Religion of Science Fiction*. Bowling Green, OH: Bowling Green State University Popular Press.

Lertzman, Renee. 2010. "Desire, Longing and the Return to the Garden: Reflections on *Avatar*." *Ecopsychology* 2(1): 41–43.

Linnitt, Carol. 2010. "The Sacred in James Cameron's *Avatar*." *Journal of Religion and Film* 14(1). http://www.unomaha.edu/jrf/Vol14no1/Reviews/Linnitt_Avatar.html.

Matsos, Helen. 2003. "James Cameron IV: The ET Challenge." *Astrobiology Magazine*, 6 November. http://www.astrobio.net/interview/661/james-cameron-iv-the-et-challenge.

McCurdy, Howard E. 1997. *Space and the American Imagination*. Washington, DC: Smithsonian Institution Press.

McLuhan, Marshall. 2003. "Art as Survival in the Electric Age." In *Understanding Me: Lectures and Interviews*, edited by Stephanie McLuhan and David Staines, 206–24. Cambridge, MA: MIT Press.

McVeigh, Stephen, and Matthew Wilhelm Kapell. 2011. "Introduction: Persistence of Visions—Approaching the Films of James Cameron." In Kapell and McVeigh, *The Films of James Cameron*, 1–13.

Michaud, Michael A. G. 1986. *Reaching for the High Frontier: The American Pro-Space Movement, 1972–84*. New York: Praeger.

Mone, Gregory. 2005. "Director of PR." *Popular Science*, February.

"NASA's Project Constellation and the Future of Human Spaceflight (Historical Information)." 2011. SpacePolicyOnline.com Fact Sheet, 24 May. http://www.spacepolicyonline.com/pages/images/stories/Constellation_Fact_Sheet_May_2011.pdf.

Noble, David. 1999. *The Religion of Technology: The Divinity of Man and the Spirit of Invention*. New York: Penguin.

Noel, Daniel C. 2005. "Space Exploration." In *Encyclopedia of Religion and Nature*, edited by Bron Taylor, 1585–88. London: Continuum International.

Obama, Barack. 2010. "Remarks by the President on Space Exploration in the Twenty-First Century." *NASA*, 15 April, John F. Kennedy Space Center. http://www.nasa.gov/news/media/trans/obama_ksc_trans.html.

O'Leary, Stephen. 2000. "When Prophecy Fails and When It Succeeds: Apocalyptic Prediction and the Re-Entry into Ordinary Time." In *Apocalyptic Time*, edited by Albert I. Baumgarten, 341–62. Leiden: Brill.

"petersattler." 2010. "AVATAR Is Not about Nature." 7 January. http://www.slate.com/discuss/forums/post/3567052.aspx.

Poole, Robert. 2008. *Earthrise: How Man First Saw the Earth*. New Haven: Yale University Press.

Rolston, Holmes III. 2007. "Technology Versus Nature: What Is Natural?" *University of Aberdeen*. http://www.abdn.ac.uk/philosophy/endsandmeans/vol2no2/rolston.shtml.

Rosen, Elizabeth. 2011. "'You Have to Look with Better Eyes Than That': A Filmmaker's Ambivalence to Technology." In Kapell and McVeigh, *The Films of James Cameron*, 109–23.

Rosenberg, Adam. 2009. "James Cameron on Past and Future Plans to Shoot in Outer Space." *MTV Movies Blog*, 14 December. http://moviesblog.mtv.com/2009/12/14/james-cameron-on-past-a-future-plans-to-shoot-in-outer-space/.

Shostak, Seth. 2010. "Life at the SETI Institute: Strip-Mining 'Avatar.'" *Huffington Post*, 18 January. http://www.huffingtonpost.com/seti-institute/life-at-the-seti-institut_b_427337.html.

Stahl, William A. 2001. *God and the Chip: Religion and the Culture of Technology.* Canadian Corporation for Studies in Religion. Waterloo, ON: Wilfrid Laurier University Press.

Sterling, Bruce. 2010. "Essay: Next Nature Intro." *Next Nature*, 9 August http://www.nextnature.net/2010/09/next-nature-intro-by-bruce-sterling/.

Taylor, Bron. 2010. *Dark Green Religion: Nature Spirituality and the Planetary Future.* Berkeley: University of California Press.

Taylor, Bron, and Adrian Ivakhiv. 2010. "Opening Pandora's Film." *Journal for the Study of Religion, Nature, and Culture* 4(4): 384–93.

"Transcript of Closing Keynote Address by James Cameron at the AIAA's First Space Exploration Conference." 2005. *SpaceRef*, 9 February. http://www.spaceref.com/news/viewsr.html?pid=15381.

Turner, Fred. 2006. *From Counterculture to Cyberculture: Stewart Brand, the Whole Earth Network, and the Rise of Digital Utopianism.* Chicago: University of Chicago Press.

Werblowsky, R. J. Zwi, and Julia Iwersen. 2005. "Light and Darkness." In *The Encyclopedia of Religion.* 2nd ed., vol. 8, edited by Lindsay Jones, 5450–55. Detroit: Thomson Gale.

White, Frank. 1987. *The Overview Effect: Space Exploration and Human Evolution.* Boston: Houghton Mifflin.

Wilhelm, Maria, and Dirk Mathison. 2009. *James Cameron's* Avatar: *An Activist Survival Guide* (London: HarperCollins).

PART II: POPULAR RESPONSES

Avatar Fandom, Environmentalism, and Nature Religion

BRITT ISTOFT

The science fiction movie *Avatar* has generated a large and diverse fan culture, mainly on the Internet. By investigating religious or spiritual trends found in the most popular international fan forums on the Internet, avatar-forums.com and naviblue.com, and, to a lesser extent, associated sites such as Tree of Souls Forum, I shall illuminate the extent to which nature is often seen as sacred by fans. My central question is this: Are *Avatar* fandoms developing some kind of nature-related spirituality of either a conventionally religious or a more secular, religion-resembling variant? To explore this question, I will focus on fans' interpretations of Eywa; their views on religion, spirituality and science; and the ways in which fans practise the insights they claim to have gained from viewing the movie. I will also consider how *Avatar* fandom might develop in the future: specifically, whether it will, like the fandom associated with *Star Trek*, be inspired to pursue some envisioned future utopia while developing its own distinctive mythology.

Popular Culture and Religion

Although popular culture often reflects traditional religious themes and imagery, it often also creates its own stories and myths, providing people with identity and meaning (Forbes and Mahan 2000, 1–20). When fans organize their lives around a film or television series, this activity could be regarded as religious, or at least as analogous to religion. *Star Trek* and

Star Wars exemplify how fantasy and science fiction movies and television series can draw very devoted and even religiously creative fans.

Religion may, of course, be defined in many ways. Substantive defini-tions of religion focus on the essence of religion. They tend to emphasize a relationship with one or more higher beings or a transcendental realm. Functional definitions of religion stress the systems of meaning making that religion provides. My own approach to the concept of religion is that of the broader functionalist variant, because narrow definitions can obscure how new forms of religiosity arise, as well as the way in which the very concept of religion may be under transformation among non-academics. A similar approach has shaped the inquiry in this volume and in *Dark Green Religion* (Taylor 2010, 1–4). Today, people increasingly speak of spiritual-ity instead of religiosity, for in popular parlance, at least, the two concepts are not completely interchangeable: the term *spirituality* is seen as more personal than the word *religion*, which tends to be more associated with institutions and dogma. Interestingly, "spirituality" is also a concept that tends to consecrate otherwise secular fields, such as psychotherapy and political activism (Taylor 2001a, 176).

Fan Cultures

The study of fan cultures is relatively new. The pioneering work in the field, *Textual Poachers*, was written by Henry Jenkins in 1992. Jenkins sees media fans as literary nomads, always on the lookout for a new text, or rather a new understanding of the known text, whether it be a literary work, a movie, or a television series. According to Jenkins, fans use mass media texts in innovative and meaningful ways. Specifically, they extend the ori-ginal universe to a "meta-text" that contains much more information on persons, lifestyles, and values than did the original text. Fans are therefore not passive recipients but active consumers, and they construct meaning in texts collectively, often creating communities that are more democratic than the surrounding society (Jenkins 1992). If Jenkins is right, there is basis for a comparison with religion, as the created meta-text can be said to con-stitute a meaningful mythology for the community. Besides, members of the community perform rituals, relating to the meta-text by way of role playing, pilgrimages to the places where the original myth took place (for instance, films studios), or integration of the values of the various myths—such as tolerance, gender equality, or environmental concerns—into daily practice.

Star Trek

One of the best-studied of these fan cultures is the one inspired by the television and motion picture series *Star Trek*. From its start in the late

1960s, *Star Trek* dramatized ideas of personal identity, gender relations, interspecies relationships, and alternative political forms. Dedicated fans have continued to fill out this utopian and mythological universe.

Not that religion plays a positive part in the *Star Trek* universe. On the contrary, in the utopian world of *Star Trek*, religion has faded away in the human world, and more enlightened secular humanist principles have taken over. This is clearly a reflection of the humanism and atheism of *Star Trek*'s creator, Gene Roddenberry (Alexander 1991). The United Federation of Planets, the joint governmental institution of nations and planets in the twenty-fourth century, seeks to bring peace to the galaxy, although it follows the principle of non-interference in "primitive" cultures, which are often characterized by having religious institutions.[1]

Star Trek fans argue that by watching *Star Trek* and applying its lessons, one can make the world a better place. They emphasize the Prime Directive (forbidding interference in another culture), the co-operative governing structure of the United Federation of Planets, and, in particular, the Vulcan philosophy of IDIC (Infinite Diversity in Infinite Combinations) as values that are needed if we are to survive into the twenty-fourth century. IDIC is only discussed explicitly in one episode of the original series but has been turned into an entire worldview by fans, because they see the IDIC philosophy as summarizing key messages of *Star Trek* (Jindra 1999, 221).[2] IDIC is thus the most central concept in *Star Trek* fandom. The principle of diversity is, to fans, first and foremost symbolized by the ethnic, racial, and gender diversity of crew members on the various starships in the series. But fans attribute to IDIC many values and practices—for example, tolerance, vegetarianism, and the fight against AIDS—and many fans trace their commitment to feminism, gay rights, pacifism, or multiculturalism to *Star Trek*'s IDIC philosophy (McLaren 1999, 234).

The future utopia of *Star Trek* is, however, not seen by fans as an inevitable state. The vision must be achieved. Fans encourage each other to make "real life" more like *Star Trek* (Jindra 2000, 168). They are often successful in this regard, supporting funding of space programs and community service projects and raising funds for charities (Istoft 2008, 150–69). *Star Trek* fans organize in local communities, but they also meet at conventions, where bonds between fans can be strengthened. Something approximating an orthodox canon has developed, consisting of the five television series, the eleven films, and a library of authorized commentary, including novels, audio materials, and survey volumes. In summary, *Star Trek* has affinities with a religious outlook, providing an ideology and a myth that orient its fans in the world and promoting action toward its envisioned utopia.[3]

Star Wars

Another long-standing fandom phenomenon is related to the six *Star Wars* films, the original trilogy (1977–83) and the prequel trilogy (1999–2005). Part of this fandom easily meets most conventional definitions of religion. In contrast to *Star Trek*, the main characters in the first trilogy of *Star Wars* are not explorers or diplomats but rebels fighting againt the evil Galactic Empire personified by Darth Vader. The second trilogy travels back in time to a period before the empire, telling the story of Darth Vader's transformation from Jedi knight to servant of the dark side of the Force. The tendency among *Star Wars* fans to create religious (or at least religion-resembling) societies based on the films is as obvious as it is among *Star Trek* fans.

George Lucas has stated that his intention with *Star Wars* was to stimulate interest in already established religions, not to found a new religion (Moyers 1999). Many fans, however, found in *Star Wars* a persuasive ethical system. Many refer to the Jedi knights and form a code of behaviour and belief from the evidence of Yoda, Obi-Wan Kenobi, Qui Gong Jinn, and Luke Skywalker (Brooker 2002, 6). Some fans consider the film scripts to be sacred.[4] The central tenet of the Jedi Creed is that expressed by Obi-Wan Kenobi in *Star Wars: A New Hope* (1977), the first of these motion pictures: the Force is "an energy field created by all living things. It surrounds us and penetrates us. It binds the galaxy together." For many other fans, the *Star Wars* saga has been a defining influence in their lives, informing their beliefs and ethics.

Avatar: A Green Message

Although it is possible to find many messages in *Avatar*, the movie speaks most obviously against the destruction of nature and indigenous peoples on Earth. When the human "Sky People" descend on Pandora, Earthly nature has already been decimated. Cameron's green agenda is also outlined in the book published simultaneously with the movie's release, Maria Wilhelm and Dirk Mathison's (2009) *James Cameron's* Avatar: *An Activist Survival Guide*, with the additional subtitle *A Confidential Report on the Biological and Social History of Pandora*. This volume provides a detailed field guide to Pandora with an introduction urging the supposed future reader to rebel against those destroying the Earth.

The movie does not only depict the destruction of primeval rainforests and indigenous cultures; on a more positive note, it shows a planet-orbiting moon working well as a collectively connected entity. This resembles the view of the biosphere articulated in the Gaia hypothesis by the British atmospheric scientist James Lovelock, who likens the biosphere to a self-regulating organism (Lovelock [1979] 1995). Furthermore, *Avatar* has a happy ending: nature and the oppressed win over commercial interests and greed. Like Gene Roddenberry and George Lucas before him, Cameron has articulated his environmentalist motivation for making the movie, even, on several occasions, endorsing radical environmentalism.

Avatar: The Fandom

Like *Star Trek*'s fictional languages—Klingon, Vulcan, and Romulan, among others—a native tongue of Pandora had to be invented. Paul Frommer, a linguist from the University of Southern California, was hired for this purpose. In addition to creating the rules and structure of the language, he invented about one thousand words. Today, however, the language has gained a much larger vocabulary thanks to its fans, who use the Internet site learnnavi.org to learn and further develop the language. On the many Internet fan sites, some of the communication takes place in Na'vi, and most of the users have adopted a Na'vi name, such as Neytiri or Toruk Makto, or a name descriptive of their practice or general identity as "avatarians," like eywa_devotee, DreamWalks, GaiaWarrior, or Human No More. Other traditional fan activities—for instance, the creation of fan fiction expanding on the original universe—can also be seen on the sites.[5] Role playing has been undertaken by some groups, especially in the United States.[6] The most distinguishing mark of *Avatar* fandom seems, however, to be attachment to nature, empathy toward animals, and an awareness of the need to take care of the environment. Strong humanitarian convictions are also discernible, as are mystical leanings and a general tolerance toward a wide range of religious, spiritual, and philosophical beliefs and practices.

Of the two main fan sites studied for this project, avatar-forums.com had, on 13 September 2010, a total of 7,845 members, 34 categories, 11,887 subjects, and 319,165 posts. (By 11 March 2012, those numbers had grown to 12,517 members, 37 categories, 14,685 subjects, and 397,317 posts.) Naviblue.com on the same 2010 date had 5,450 members, 16 categories, 2,836 subjects, and 239,548 posts. (On 11 March 2012, the forum had a total of 8,110 members, 16 categories, 3,387 subjects, and 514,231 posts.) New members join the two forums every day, although it must also be said that many of the original members have become less active. Several of these latter fans, at least on avatar-forums.com, still read the discussions, as seen when an old member now and then starts a new subject, seeking out old friends.[7]

Proportionately more subject categories deal with games, role play, and entertainment on naviblue.com than on avatar-forums.com. Although it is possible to find discussions that touch on religion and green issues under many categories, on naviblue.com, I focused on the category "Hometree"

(129 subjects and 4,009 posts on 13 September 2010, and 202 subjects and 5,259 posts on 11 March 2012), and on avatar-forums.com, I focused on the categories "Na'vi Culture and Language" (382 subjects and 8,127 posts on 13 September 2010, and 439 subjects and 9,435 posts on 11 March 2012), "Pandora" (329 subjects and 8,642 posts on 13 September 2010; 354 subjects and 9,494 posts on 11 March 2012), "Human and Environmental Rights Forum" (330 subject and 4,373 posts on 13 September 2010; 423 subjects and 5,368 posts on 11 March 2012), and "The Na'vi Movement" (81 subjects and 1,943 posts on 13 September 2010; 186 subjects and 2,772 posts on 11 March 2012). I read the content of these categories meticulously and also sought to get an overall impression of the other categories on the two forums. My research involved analyzing selected posts that shed light on nature religion among *Avatar* fans.

The first and greater part of my research drew on discussions on the two forums dating from January 2010 until June 2010. The second part focused on discussions on the two forums from October 2010 until 11 March 2012. For the latter part of the research, I also—to a limited extent—drew on the increasingly active Learn Na'vi site (learnnavi.org) as well as on three partner sites of avatar-forums.com: the Tree of Souls Forum (tree-of-souls.com), the Avatar Prime site (avatarprime.net) and Avatar Wiki (avatar.wikia.com). New developments in the online fandom since the original investigation in 2010 are Avatar Nation, a podcast created in spring 2011 and dedicated to the movie and its fans, and Avatar Meet, an information site for *Avatar* fan meetings, of which there were two in 2011 at the EMP museum in Seattle in connection with an *Avatar* exhibition there.[8] A further fan meeting took place in June 2012, also in Seattle, and a meeting is planned for 2013 in Washington, DC.

Factors such as the gender, age, and location of the individual fans on the two main forums were difficult to establish. On avatar-forums.com, fans mostly stated their location in the form of their native country but also often as Pandora. Age was sometimes stated during discussions, but I had to surmise the gender of participants from their chosen avatarian name or icon. On naviblue.com, this information is likewise difficult to obtain. From the information available, it seemed that the majority of fans were American, but English-speaking countries like Canada, New Zealand, and England were also well represented. Several Germans, Swedes, Poles, Turks, and even Chinese were active on avatar-forums.com. When it comes to age, many fans seem to be in their early twenties, but a large proportion are probably younger. Some very active fans, however, have stated that they are in their thirties or older. Male and female fans were, according to my interpretation of their names and icons, represented equally.

Interestingly, one finds representatives from other fandoms on the two forums: for instance, the username of one of the active participants on avatar-forums.com is Spock, referring to the most important alien character from the original *Star Trek* series.

Eywa: Goddess, Computer, or Nature?

One of the frequently discussed topics on avatar-forums.com and naviblue.com, especially in the first months after the release of the movie (although the subject has often been taken up again when new members join the forums) has been how to understand Eywa. A central question in this regard has been whether Eywa is a sentient entity or a scientific concept.

In many respects, *Avatar* coheres with ideas developed in twentieth-century paganism (Hutton 2001). The villains are the anti-ecological humans, or "Sky People," coming to exploit Pandora because of their greed for unobtanium. The inhabitants of Pandora, the Na'vi, are tribal warriors and shamans living in close harmony with their environment. The human hero, Jake, is saved and brought to the tree village of the Omaticaya clan when Neytiri, the Na'vi heroine, sees seeds of the Tree of Souls, so-called woodsprites, land on Jake and interprets this as a message from Eywa.

A personification of nature reminiscent of some forms of both pagan and New Age spirituality can also be seen in the scenes in which the Na'vi try to save the human scientist Grace Augustine, who is fatally wounded by a gunshot, by appealing to Eywa to transfer her soul permanently to her avatar. They do not succeed, but Grace's last words describe her soul melting into the consciousness of Eywa herself. Furthermore, before the final battle, Jake *prays* to Eywa for help, imploring her to search Grace's mind and memory to understand the danger from the Sky People. However, to Neytiri, Eywa appears to be a more impersonal force, indicated by Neytiri's statement to Jake that Eywa takes no sides since she is only committed to maintaining the balance of life. Later, however, when the battle seems to be lost for the Na'vi, the animals of Pandora come to their rescue and take part in the battle. This convinces Neytiri that Jake's prayer must have been answered, suggesting the possibility of a more immanent and involved divine consciousness infusing life on Pandora.

On the one hand, these events indicate that Eywa is actually a super-ordinate divine intelligence with a will of her own. On the other hand, it is repeatedly stated, both during the film and in the published *Activist Survival Guide*, that she is more like a bio-Internet and a collective consciousness that "logs the thoughts and feelings of everything that thinks and feels" (Wilhelm and Mathison 2009, xv). Jake's prayer may also be seen in this perspective, since he contacts Eywa by linking his queue to the illuminated tentacles of the Tree of Souls, thus connecting neurally as to a computer network. Cameron himself has described the Tree of Souls as the central input-output station of the moon Pandora (Maher 2009). This raises the possibility of a panentheistic worldview in which everything participates in the divine universe but the sum is greater than the parts: there is an overarching divine intelligence at work.

The ambiguity in the movie on the subject of Eywa is reflected in discussions among fans. As a rule, Eywa is seen in light of Lovelock's Gaia theory. Many, however, interpret the (secular) Gaia theory in a religious way, seeing Gaia as a goddess, as, for instance, this female fan, who identifies Eywa with her Wiccan-inspired triple goddess: "I feel the Na'vi and my own spiritual beliefs are very similar.... I have a maiden Artemis the goddess of the hunt and forests a mother Selene the goddess of the moon and a crone Hecate the queen of witches and dark places. But this triple goddess is a form of her full glory her whole and united one goddess which is where my heart lays."[9] In other words, the many goddesses are aspects of the same entity, a universal goddess, which this fan can identify with Eywa. Others see Eywa more like a metaphor, arguing that she "is more just Pandora itself. A living earth, that works kind of like a computer of sorts, or perhaps more a living organism."[10] Understandings about Eywa seem as diverse as the views regarding the Force in Star Wars fandom. The Force is often interpreted as a purely impersonal energy, in accordance with the first Star Wars trilogy, but it is also seen as a personal deity with a will of its own, in accordance with the second trilogy; this leaves room for fans to find affinities with diverse religious convictions, from Zen Buddhism to Christianity.[11]

Most Avatar fans seem, however, to view the Na'vi religion and way of life as pantheistic or animistic because it is "all about the unity of life and communication with nature."[12] A comparison to pagan shamanistic traditions is also common.[13] That paganism seems to play an important role among many fans is not surprising considering its significant role in Avatar, where the Na'vi live as hunter-gatherers in a forest full of spirits and embraced by Eywa, to whom all living creatures are connected. Some fans have objected to the Na'vi universe being pagan, emphasizing that Eywa is a monotheistic goddess, the spirits of the forest being only her envoys. Others find such a perspective to be intolerant, reminding them of monotheistic religions that have suppressed pagans and indigenous people, whose religious beliefs have been considered primitive and spiritually dangerous. For some fans, this problem is overcome by reference to known indigenous people in the past who have had "monotheistic" beliefs in an overall Great Spirit: for instance, the Iroquois, who are seen by some as a model of the Omaticaya clan.[14] This provides a glimpse of what fans may view as acceptable religion and non-acceptable religion—or rather spirituality, for the word *religion* is often seen as negative in contrast to the term *spirituality*.

The Concept of Religion among Fans

Contempt for the term *religion* is expressed by many fans who object to viewing the Na'vi culture as religious. The argument is often that Eywa is not a god because she is "real": in the sense that one can "plug in" to her, she is touchable, not a fabrication. One fan wrote, "She [Eywa] was created by the life of the planet, itself. She exists as an electro-chemical phenomenon generated by that life. Her existence is not based on faith. She exists whether anyone believes in her or not. . . . So I wouldn't say that the Na'vi are religious. They deeply revere Eywa and their planet's eco-system, but their reverence is based on fact, not faith."[15] Another fan, like several others, expressed hope for "a culture with NO religion. not anti religion just 'no religion.'"[16]

Some fans accept the term *religion* as being, at least to some extent, an apt one in describing the culture of the Na'vi, as articulated in this contribution from Toruk Makto: "The 'religion' of the na'vi is far more appealing and just all around better than any religion offered here on earth because it is actually based on something tangible."[17] Generally, fans exhibit a widespread tolerance toward many different beliefs and practices, although Christianity is often severely criticized for its anthropocentrism and for its intolerance toward other traditions.[18] Many subscribe to the idea of all religions having the same essence, as expressed by a Swedish fan with the username Svansfall, who characterized himself as "worshipper of Eywa": "I tend to believe that most of the different versions of deities and spiritualities are all really the same thing, only seen and interpreted differently by different people."[19] Another fan, Tslolam, had for a long time "believed in a creator (God)" but also in an energy, which he identified as the Daoist concept of "chi." However, it was not until he saw *Avatar* that he was able to combine the two, since "the idea of Eywa seems to encompass a great many religions we have here on Earth. She is both the creator and spirit of Pandora, as well as the energy that flows through all living things."[20] But how do fans put their newfound insights into practice, and does their view of religion have any impact on these practices?

Fan Practices: Depression and Healing through Reconnecting to Nature

After the release of the movie, there was a prolonged media discussion about fans being depressed by not living on Pandora, even resulting in suicidal thoughts. The representation of fans as isolated, anti-social, psychologically mixed-up dreamers has a long and, it seems, enduring history, despite the academic rehabilitation of fan-cultures since the publication of Jenkins's *Textual Poachers* in 1992. Understandably, fans have reacted to such a portrait of *Avatar* enthusiasts. On avatar-forums.com, for example, several individuals have commented on depression among fans, including one named Deep Ecology, who wrote:

> I saw the really horribly misrepresentative CNN story about people experiencing post-avatar type feelings. The psychologist that they interviewed offered, in my opinion, a really simplistic and inaccurate analysis of the phenomenon: people who get caught up in "fantasy" are lacking something in their "real" experience and need to make general adjustments in their lives with regards to work, family, friends, etc.... I don't think this is true, or, at least, it's not the whole story. I think the strong response to Avatar has a much more specific origin, having to do with a profound and perhaps spiritual questioning (or rejection) of the structure of human society and how that influences our relationship to nature and to one another. [21]

Another fan, eywa_devotee, wrote: "My gut feeling is Avatar causes depression in people who can see what is going on with the world, not necessarily that they cannot go to Pandora. It is sobering that our HUMAN species has caused devastation that makes the worst scenes in Avatar look like a practical joke in comparison."[22]

According to some fans, an effective way to heal the depression is to reconnect with nature by way of meditation. Ethereal Blue Being, for example, wrote that such an approach does not involve worship but, instead, is simply "to experience many different levels of existence, realities, dimensions. universes."[23] Many fans achieve feelings of oneness with nature through meditation, as this fan wrote, "I've only begun to meditate after watching Avatar. I find it to be an amazing stress reducing experience. I have no way to explain it but it's almost like I feel 'one' with everything. When I meditate its always a must for me to do it when I'm surrounded by pure nature. If you haven't tried it already nature truly enhances your meditation experience."[24] Oneness with nature is also the focus of a contribution from a fan, Regenweald, who lives in the Hebrides: "Sometimes, when I sit on a rock, soaking in the environment and creatures about me, I transcend the mundane and my 'Soul' soars within me. So...I am not in prayer, nor meditation, but just sitting empty. Why should I experience such moments of exhilaration?...Am I being reached out to?"[25] Regenweald received the following answer from a fellow fan: "The transcendent is found in silence like you are experiencing...when you look for the goddess you can see her everywhere but she is to be found inside of you."[26]

Some fans advocate controlling the world by positive thinking. Interestingly, these same fans are also those who tend to personify Earth or Eywa as a sentient divine being. For instance, one female fan, Neytiri, modelling herself after the movie's heroine, wrote: "What you focus on is what you reap. Think positive. Reap positive."[27] The previously mentioned eywa_devotee wrote in emphatic capitals: "DO NOT BE AFRAID, YOU HAVE IT IN YOUR POWER TO CHANGE IT," explaining that hope lies in letting go of the past and realizing that "we are one being."[28] This is in line with Bron Taylor's observation that those who personify Earth or Gaia—in this case Eywa—as a goddess are more likely to be optimistic about humans' ability to change their destructive uses of technology and to believe that positive changes can be created by "magic" or positive thinking than those who see Earth or Gaia more as a purely ecological process (Taylor 2001b, 238–42).

Inward practice and belief in Eywa should, according to many fans, lead to practical responsibility for nature: "The Goddess is alive and well... and she is not happy about her creatures being destroyed and her gardens being paved over" and "believing in Eywa is believing that all of us are connected, and that we have a responsibility on this Earth to make it a better place, and not fight among each other for no reason. You defend life, you protect each other, and you defend the environment."[29] Making Earth into Pandora is not a call to "start living on the Amazon Rainforest," as one fan put it. Although a long and heated discussion on the benefits of primitivism and living "in the wild" occurred on avatar-forums.com between 25 January 2010 and 8 October 2011, the consensus appeared to be that the ideal is rather to learn from the Na'vi's general view of Eywa and nature—for instance, by using self-replenishing energy resources.[30] Advice from fans on practical ways of honouring Eywa cover recycling, rejection of the traditional economy, planting community farms, buying organic products, and driving fuel-efficient vehicles, as well as reconnecting with nature and one's "own true self."[31] As in *Star Trek* fandom, the underlying ideology of the movie inspires fans to make positive changes in the Earthly world. Avatar-forums.com is by far the most radical of the two forums, debating human and environmental rights, urging boycotts of certain corporations, and considering whether mating on Pandora might be homosexual (most users are not inclined to think so).[32] Most discussions debate practices that can be incorporated into the everyday life of fans, although there is evidence of broader political initiatives, which I discuss below.

Fan Practices: Vegetarianism, Manifestos, and Activism

Food was often discussed by fans: for example, whether "avatarian" interconnectedness enjoins vegetarianism, even though the movie itself does not support this perspective.[33] In this respect, *Avatar* fans resemble those of *Star Trek*, who attribute values of their own to the rather ill-defined Vulcan concept of IDIC. Some *Avatar* fans defend their meat-eating practices using the movie in support. While one fan wrote, "I read that some of you wish to become vegetarians. I had that thought too," he ended up arguing that meat eating remains acceptable if you follow Na'vi practice and "just show some respect to the animal that got killed," thanking its spirit.[34] In contrast to some other (mostly male) deer-hunting fans on avatar-forums. com, this fan said nothing about whether he hunted animals himself. Others expressed strong objections to meat eating in a society in which industrial farming is the norm.[35] Such sentiments have affinity with those vegetarian or vegan fans who have strong feelings of friendship toward non-human animals.

Svansfall, quoted above, wrote of his own experience in connection with his interpretation of the message of the film. To him, the sanctity of life is extended to non-human animals: "I for one do not believe that human life is any more, nor less valuable than the life of any other living being on this planet. This belief of mine is nothing I will impose on anyone else, and I am with my own actions a hypocrite, as I still eat fish, even though I do not eat meat from mammals."[36] Svansfall's reluctance to eat meat from mammals has to do with his life on an ecological farm, where he has developed a friendship with the animals, in particular "cows and bulls."[37]

Although one online commentator considers one of the characters in the movie, Trudy Chacon, as an eco-martyr and role model for radical environmentalists, I have found no references in fandom either to this character or to violent environmental action.[38] Actually, on the two Internet forums, I have found only a few fans encouraging others to more radical forms of activism on behalf of the environment, such as animal rights or similar causes. However, some fans support strong action against whalers, as practised by the Sea Shepherd Conservation Society. This *Avatar* fan from New Zealand is one of them: "Take action against Japanese whalers in Antarctica, they are putting severe strain on the eco-system there. And 60% of Japanese harpooners incorrectly harpoon the whale they are catching causing severe pain to the whale. A big boat with a bulbous bow made out of titanium is what we need. Then we can use that to ram the Japanese whaling fleets ships."[39] This fan specifically alludes to the Sea Shepherd Conservation Society and its anti-whaling operations—perhaps in particular to the collision between the Sea Shepherd vessel *Ady Gil* and a Japanese whaling support vessel in January 2010, actions shown on the Animal Planet cable television channel.[40] But such incitement to activism is rare on the fan forums.

Worth mentioning, however, is a more moderate political initiative in which several users of avatar-forums.com established the Na'vi Movement, which—at the time of this writing—had its own independent site at navimovement.com (the site has since been discontinued). Only the name of the Na'vi Movement betrays its origin in the fan culture, which was quite deliberate, according to the founders.[41] One of these, unil_mi_tokx, wrote after the first draft of the new movement's manifesto had been made: "Something new is happening. At first I thought I was crazy for being so drawn to a movie. Then we all became connected and soon we wanted to change what we are doing to Our Mother.... Together, we can really make a difference to our own Pandora."[42] The draft generated much disagreement, however, in particular with regard to statements in the original draft promoting monogamy (in imitation of the Na'vi's lifelong bonding) and opposing abortion (as an expression of respect for all life). Because of intense critique, these views were deleted from the manifesto. Another controversy erupted over an emphasis on the extraordinary worth of human life. The original wording, "The sanctity *of human life* shall not be abused under any circumstances" was later changed to "The sanctity *of life* shall not be abused" (my emphasis).[43] Through this debate, anthropocentrism was gradually rejected, although the final wording of the manifesto sought to harmonize humanism and environmentalism, stating, "The Na'vi Movement is both an environmental and human rights movement."[44]

The manifesto referred positively to environmentalists, including Rachel Carson and Bill McKibben, and stated that "pollution and destruction of the environment is a violation of human rights." The manifesto was meant to be a reminder to fans and the general public about environmental and human rights questions, but first and foremost, it was designed as a forum for signing petitions requesting politicians to act on environmental issues. Although this particular form of activism has ceased, the discussions and the incitement to act politically on behalf of the environment have continued at the "Human and Environmental Rights" thread on avatar -forums.com, and in particular at the avatar-forums.com–derived Tree of Souls Forum.[45] Some long-term fans, like unil_mi_tokx, who had hoped that the Na'vi Movement would make a big difference, have been disappointed, but new fans have adopted more modest environmental goals.[46] An interesting new development is a Russian equivalent of the Na'vi Movement, "The Public Ecological Movement of the Na'vi," with its own site at pandoraworld.su, announced on avatar-forms.com.[47]

Most of the fans who are active on the two fan forums that I studied cannot be characterized as radical, but they are, by their own accounts, trying to act on their convictions. Although some fans, such as Svansfall, have a background in eco-paganism, others—like Tslolam, who had been torn between Christianity and Daoism—seem to have found a new nature religious insight when confronted with the portrait of Eywa in *Avatar*. The same could be said of unil_mi_tokx, one of the founders of the Na'vi Movement, to whom a new world opened after he saw the movie. This does not mean, however, that these fans adopted unconditionally the worldview of the movie. Rather, as is the case in other fandoms, they focused on certain elements of the story—in particular, Eywa and the connection between all living beings—and ignored others, such as the violent resistance toward opponents. Although a few members of *Avatar* fandom are interested in military technology and express sympathy toward the Sky People, the technological violence in the movie has evoked little response among fans. Neither has the escapist idea of leaving one's Earthly body behind to inhabit some imagined avatar. On the contrary, fans have objected to the media view of them as unrealistic dreamers and have asserted that the way to make the Pandoran world come true is to work to protect the environment on Earth.

Fan Practices: Face-to-Face Activities

The first organized *Avatar* face-to-face gathering took place in June 2011. Fans, mostly from the United States, met on 4 June 2011 at the EMP (Experience Music Project) and Science Fiction Museum in Seattle for the opening of the museum's *Avatar* exhibit, *AVATAR: The Exhibition* (4 June 2011 to 3 September 2012). A subsequent meeting took place on 9 July 2011. The first meeting was attended mostly by fans from the Tree of Souls Forum, and the second mainly by fans from learnnavi.org, probably because the museum on this specific date had arranged a panel on the Na'vi language in which Paul Frommer, the linguist who developed the language, participated. Judging from the information and photos on avatarmeet.com, both meetings seem to have had a limited attendance by forum members, approximately twenty-one in June and thirty-five in July. However, another meeting took place at the EMP museum on 19–23 July 2012 and proved more successful in terms of number of participants: at least sixty-eight forum members from Europe, Canada, and the United States participated. The planning was more meticulous than in 2011, and early announcements made on a variety of fan forums included an advertising video containing highlights from the 2011 meeting.[48] Moreover, the planning committee included representatives from most of the major *Avatar* forums, and, signalling its intention, the meetup was titled "Uniting the Clans."[49] Besides the visit to Seattle and the museum, pre-meetup wilderness camping events and other activities took place.[50]

The EMP museum in Seattle was an excellent venue for a fan meeting, perhaps even comparable to the *Star Trek* set at the Universal Studios theme park in California, which has been a popular tourist site and fan meeting place for many years. With its sets, props, and costumes from the movie, interactive displays, and concept models, the exhibition in Seattle seemed to serve the same purpose for *Avatar* fans as the theme park in California does for *Star Trek* fans: for example, tourists and fans were filmed taking on characters' roles and acting out plots from the movie, which is the closest thing one can experience to being a part of the fictive universe. Playing Neytiri or Jake on the performance stage at the Seattle exhibition, directed by a virtual James Cameron, while watching one's avatar image on a screen may be compared to being filmed while sitting on the bridge of the starship *Enterprise* in the *Star Trek* theme park.[51] At the annual *Star Trek* conventions, one can find *Star Trek* literature, artwork, costume contests, rock music, and appearances by *Star Trek* actors (Istoft 2008, 158). The same was the case at the opening day of the Seattle *Avatar* exhibit on 4 June 2011. At this event, James Cameron himself made a speech, and a panel with cast members Giovanni Ribisi (Parker Selfridge), CCH Pounder (Mo'at), and Laz Alonso (Tsu'tey) was arranged, as were drum circles and a jewellery workshop.[52]

Participation in *Star Trek* conventions has been described—at least in the *Star Trek* universe—in almost mystical terms as a time warp (in which time travels faster than the speed of light; Van Hise 1990, 90). One might argue that for some devoted fans, convention attendance represents a secular pilgrimage, where fans, like pilgrims in conventional pilgrimages, are, in a sense, "out of time," liberated from everyday roles and hierarchies (Porter 1999). The *Avatar* fan meetings in Seattle provide fans with an opportunity to step outside their everyday social roles into a world where a love of *Avatar* unites participants into a community that transcends racial, ethnic, gender, or class lines. Experiencing the fan community as a family is expressed by many fans, not least by those attending the meetups in Seattle. In a later discussion of the 2011 fan meeting on the Tree of Souls Forum, one participant in the event expressed his feelings this way: "Reading all of these replies really does make me realize that even though we have only met briefly, we really are a kind of family, but connected not by relation or same geographical region, but by an idea/concept that I really couldn't explain."[53]

Like the convention setting in *Star Trek* fandom, the Seattle meeting for this fan can be seen as representing *communitas* and spiritual liminality, notions developed by anthropologist Victor Turner in connection with religious pilgrimages (Turner 1969; Turner and Turner 1978); it is a moment out of time in which the fan experiences a sense of egalitarian community with the other participants. Like *Star Trek* convention attendance, the Seattle meeting can be seen as a secular pilgrimage. The *Avatar* online communities seem on the brink of establishing a tradition of an annual meeting. Since the Seattle exhibition was not permanent, the community is looking for new locations in Washington, DC for the next meeting, called "AvatarMeet 2013: Journey to the Eastern Sea." If the Seattle meeting in June 2013 proves successful, the time may have come to establish an independent convention—something perhaps presaged by the name a fan gave to the 2012 Seattle meeting, "Avatarcon II."[54]

Conclusion

The fans on the two fan forums avatar-forums.com and naviblue.com, as well as on the other major fan forums studied, have taken the universe found in *Avatar* and begun adding their own creative dimensions to it. While a mythological or metaphysical consensus may not yet have emerged, it may unfold along with further Pandoran movies: the plan is for *Avatar 2* to premiere in 2014. Clearly, the construction of a meaningful new world is already in progress, as seen by fans learning the language of the Na'vi, taking on Na'vi names and identities, and developing the *Avatar* universe with new stories about the characters in the movie.

The potential of *Avatar* fandom for the production of nature religion is clear, as is its ability to provide fans with meaning and an ethical orientation to the world. Although the studied fan forums express, primarily, pantheistic or animistic spiritualities of nature, many fans also regard Eywa as a living goddess and identify her with the biosphere. The sacredness of Eywa/Earth has influenced fans' environmental practices because they have come to believe that one way to venerate Eywa is by living ecologically. In a way that resembles the responses of *Star Trek* fans, *Avatar* devotees encourage each other to make life on Earth a better place, modelled on their understandings of the virtues of Na'vi culture. As in other fandoms, *Avatar* fans show considerable creativity. Yet—at the time of this writing, at least—those in *Avatar*'s fandom seem to ritualize less than do those in fandoms associated with *Star Trek* and *Star Wars*. This may be because *Avatar* fans meet mainly on the Internet, in contrast to *Star Trek* fans, who also meet locally and during international conventions. As discussed, however, this is slowly changing as face-to-face contacts have begun and may become more extensive. Indeed, there seems to be a will for collective action and for community among those moved by the film. In any case, the *Avatar* fandom has raised consciousness among many fans, promoting environmental concern and action, and is contributing to the recent tendency in the Western world to see nature as "sacred, imbued with intrinsic value, and worthy of reverent care" (Taylor 2010, ix).

Notes

This research was carried out in two periods: results from the initial period, from January to June 2010, were published in Istoft (2010); some but not all of that material is replicated here. Subsequent research, conducted in the winter of 2011/2012, enabled analysis of whether more communal and face-to-face activities were unfolding, as they had with other science fiction and fantasy fandoms.

1 Although the portrayal of religion in the *Star Trek* series is generally negative, in some episodes from the *Deep Space Nine* and *Voyager* series, a more positive approach may be seen, especially through the spiritual experiences of the Native American commander Chakotay. The approach to religion in *Voyager* is akin to New Age spirituality, which is closer to the overall *Star Trek* worldview than are most institutional and doctrinal forms of religion. See McLaren and Porter (1999, 101–15). See also Kraemer, Cassidy, and Schwartz (2001).

2 The philosophy of IDIC is discussed in the episode "Is There in Truth No Beauty?" *Star Trek: The Original Series*, season 3, episode 5 (1968–69).

3 For *Star Trek* as an origin myth, see McLaren (1999).

4 See "The Jedi Creed" at http://www.jedicreed.org. See also http://www.temple ofthejediorder.org. Jedism has not yet gained official recognition as a religion in England and Australia, but according to the 2001 UK census, 390,127 respondents listed their religion as Jedi, while in Australia, 70,509 people declared that they were followers of the Jedi faith and that they believed in "the Force." See "Jedi 'Religion' Grows in Australia," *BBC News*, 27 August 2002, http://news.bbc.co.uk/2/ hi/entertainment/film/2218456.stm, and "Jedi Makes the Census List," *BBC News*, 9 October 2001, http://news.bbc.co.uk/1/hi/uk/1589133.stm.

5 See, for instance, http://www.naviblue.com/hometree/component/kunena/35 -Avatar-Related-Writing-Poetry, or http://www.avatar-forums.com/forumdisplay .php?50-Fan-Fiction.

6 See, for instance, "L.A.R.P.: Live Avatar Role Playing" at http://www.youtube.com/ watch?v=yk2vR8w2sjc.

7 See, for instance, "Wameyn," 30 November 2011, 10:35 p.m., "Going through My Avatar Friends List...," at http://www.avatar-forums.com/showthread.php ?17082-Going-through-my-Avatar-friends-list.

8 Here are the websites mentioned in this paragraph, with some information about their memberships as of 11 March 2012: http://www.learnnavi.org—5,424 members, 80 categories, 15,022 subjects, and 532,196 posts; http://www.tree-of-souls .com—1,071 members, 33 categories, 4,692 subjects, and 168,353 posts; http:// avatarprime.net—886 members, 17 categories, 803 subjects, and 7,601 posts; http://james-camerons-avatar.wikia.com/wiki/Avatar_Wiki—primarily occupied with editing articles on the *Avatar*-universe, but also has a small forum with 78 members, 5 categories, 177 topics, and 1,315 posts; http://avatar-nation.net; and http://avatarmeet.com.

9 Ean Menari Kimberly, "Na'vi Religon?" http://www.naviblue.com/hometree/ component/kunena/15-The-Hometree/725-Navi-Religon?limit=25&start=25.

10 Elequin, 4 January 2010, 10:54 a.m., "The 'Eywa' Theory," http://www.avatar -forums.com/showthread.php?773-The-quot-Eywa-quot-Theory.

11 Information on Jedism as a syncretistic religion—where one can be a Wiccan Jedi,

a Christian Jedi, a Buddhist Jedi, or an agnostic Jedi, for example, but where Jedi-ism is also a religion or way of life in its own right—is available under "Home" and "Temple Doctrine" on http://www.templeofthejediorder.org.

12 fluffyinside, "Na'vi Religon?" http://www.naviblue.com/hometree/component/ kunena/15-The-Hometree/725-Navi-Religon?limit=25&start=25.

13 fella, "Na'vi Religon?" http://www.naviblue.com/hometree/component/kunena/ 15-The-Hometree/725-Navi-Religon?limit=25&start=25.

14 Dan AKA, "Na'vi Religon?" http://www.naviblue.com/hometree/component/ kunena/15-The-Hometree/725-Navi-Religon?limit=25&start=25. The term *Iroquois* is no longer used by scholars of the association of clans in the Haudonesaunee confederacy. They tend rather to refer to the specific clans involved. However, in popular parlance the term *Iroquois* is still in use.

15 ScottWashburn, 16 June 2011, 03:10 p.m., "The Navi, Eywa, and Religion," http:// www.avatar-forums.com/showthread.php?16212-The-Na-vi-Eywa-and-Religion.

16 nerys, "Na'vi Religion?," http://www.naviblue.com/hometree/component/ kunena/15-The-Hometree/725-Navi-Religon?limit=15&start=30.

17 Toruk Makto, 4 January 2010, 05:15 a.m., "The 'Eywa' Theory," http://www.avatar -forums.com/showthread.php?773-The-quot-Eywa-quot-Theory.

18 See, for instance, Nightweaver20xx's annoyed answer to a proselytizing Chris-tian on the fan forum: Nightweaver20xx, 13 June 2010, 11:23 p.m., "How Do You Meditate to Eywa," http://www.avatar-forums.com/showthread.php? 8602-How-do-you-meditate-to-Eywa/page10.

19 Svansfall, 9 February 2010, 01:31 p.m., "The Way of Eywa," http://www.avatar-forums .com/showthread.php?5215-Way-of-Eywa/page2.

20 Tslolam, 2 February 2010, 08:26 a.m., "The Way of Eywa," http://www.avatar-forums .com/showthread.php?5215-Way-of-Eywa.

21 Deep Ecology, 28 January 2010, 07:56 p.m., "Article on Na'vi Movment/ Pandora on Earth," http://www.avatar-forums.com/showthread.php?4549-article -navi-movement-pandora-earth/page2.

22 eywa_devotee, 22 January 2010, 04:45 a.m., "Sick of the NIGHTMARE! Time to WAKE UP!" http://www.avatar-forums.com/showthread.php?3520-Sick -of-the-NIGHTMARE-Time-to-WAKE-UP!.

23 Ethereal Blue Being, 7 June 2010, 07:07 p.m., "How Do You Meditate to Eywa," http:// www.avatar-forums.com/showthread.php?8602-How-do-you-meditate-to-Eywa/ page10.

24 Ateyo 'uniltiranyu, 9 June 2010, 10:43 p.m., "How Do You Meditate to Eywa," http:// www.avatar-forums.com/showthread.php?8602-How-do-you-meditate-to-Eywa/ page10.

25 Regenweald, 3 August 2011, 01:46 a.m., "The Na'vi, Eywa, and Religion," http:// www.avatar-forums.com/showthread.php?16212-The-Na-vi-Eywa-and-Religion/ page6.

26 Transcend, 3 August 2011, 09:26 a.m., "The Na'vi, Eywa, and Religion," http://www .avatar-forums.com/showthread.php?16212-The-Na-vi-Eywa-and-Religion/page6.

27 Neytiri, 24 January 2010, 02:47 a.m., "Sick of the NIGHTMARE! Time to WAKE UP!" http://www.avatar-forums.com/showthread.php?3520-Sick-of-the -NIGHTMARE-Time-to-WAKE-UP!/page2.

28 eywa_devotee, 24 January 2010, 02:19 a.m., "Sick of the NIGHTMARE! Time
    to WAKE UP!" http://www.avatar-forums.com/showthread.php?3520-Sick
    -of-the-NIGHTMARE-Time-to-WAKE-UP!/page2.

29 Transcend, 2 August 2011, 10:56 a.m., "The Na'vi, Eywa, and Religion," http://www
    .avatar-forums.com/showthread.php?16212-The-Na-vi-Eywa-and-Religion/page5;
    Nightweaver20xx, 9 June 2010, 01:07 p.m., "How Do You Meditate to Eywa," http://
    www.avatar-forums.com/showthread.php?8602-How-do-you-meditate-to-Eywa/
    page10.

30 For the discussion on primitivism, see "Living Na'vi Style... in the Wild," http://www
    .avatar-forums.com/showthread.php?4015-Living-Na-vi-Style-in-the-Wild!-!. On
    learning from the Na'vi, see Arthur, 27 January 2010, 08:13 a.m., "A Movement
    Begins," http://www.avatar-forums.com/showthread.php?1745 -A-Movement
    -Begins/page8.

31 See, for instance, Neytiri, 28 January 2010, 05:16 p.m., and Elyannia, 28 Janu-
    ary 2010, 07:44 p.m., "Challenging People to Change," http://www.avatar-forums
    .com/showthread.php?4613-Challenging-People-to-Change, and eywa-devotee,
    28 February 2010, 10:33 p.m., "Toruk Makto Calls to You Time to Wake Up," http://
    www.avatar-forums.com/showthread.php?8327-Toruk-Makto-Calls-to-you-Time
    -to-Wake-Up!

32 See debates at "Human and Environmental Rights," http://www.avatar-forums.
    com/forumdisplay.php?26-Human-amp-Environmental-Rights; "Ecocommu-
    nalism," http://www.avatar-forums.com/showthread.php?9828-Ecocommunal
    ism; and "Na'vi Homosexuality," http://www.avatar-forums.com/showthread
    .php?7296-Na-vi-homosexuality.

33 See, for instance, Theorist, 8 April 2010, 04:22 a.m., and Sempu, 8 April 2010, 07:12 a.m.,
    "What Do You Guys Think about This? About Food:]," http://www.avatar-forums
    .com/showthread.php?10750-What-do-you-guys-think-about-this-about-food.

34 Walas00, 19 January 2010, 11:21 a.m., "Eating Meat," http://www.avatar-forums
    .com/showthread.php?3030-Eating-meat.

35 See, for instance, Taw tìran, 21 January 2010, 03:18 a.m., "Vegetarian?" http://www
    .avatar-forums.com/showthread.php?3154-Vegetarian. See also the discussions on
    "What Do You Guys Think about This? About Food:]," http://www.avatar-forums
    .com/showthread.php?10750-What-do-you-guys-think-about-this-about-food.

36 Svansfall, 12 January 2010, 05:03 a.m., "A Movement Begins," http://www.avatar
    -forums.com/showthread.php?1745-A-Movement-Begins/page3.

37 Svansfall, 29 January 2010, 02:09 p.m., "Article on Na'vi Movement/Pandora
    on Earth," http://www.avatar-forums.com/showthread.php?4549-Article-on
    -Na-vi-Movement-Pandora-on-Earth/page3.

38 See Karl Burkart, "Is Avatar Radical Environmental Propaganda?" *Mother Nature
    Network*, 4 January 2010, http://www.mnn.com/technology/research-innovations/
    blogs/is-avatar-radical-environmental-propaganda.

39 Spock, 26 January 2010, 05:05 p.m., "Suggestions for Actions for the Environmental
    Movement," http://www.avatar-forums.com/showthread.php?4313-Suggestions
    -for-Actions-for-the-Environmental-Movement.

40 See Sea Shepherd, http://www.seashepherd.org/, and the video "Whale Wars,"
    Animal Planet, http://animal.discovery.com/tv/whale-wars/.

41 See unil_mi_tokx, 20 January 2010, 11.15 p.m., "A Movement Begins," http://www
.avatar-forums.com/showthread.php?1745-A-Movement-Begins/page8.

42 Unil_mi_tokx, 11 January 2010, 10:45 p.m., "A Movement Begins," http://www.avatar
-forums.com/showthread.php?1745-A-Movement-Begins.

43 On these discussions, see "Navi Movement Project—You Can Help," http://www
.avatar-forums.com/showthread.php?4041-Na-vi-Movement-Project-You-can
-help!, and "My Problems with the Na'vi Movement," http://www.avatar-forums
.com/showthread.php?2036-My-problems-with-the-Na-vi-Movement.

44 The manifesto was part of the navimovement.com site, which has been discontinued. Part of the manifesto can be seen in Svansfall's contribution, 12 January 2010, 05:03 a.m., on "A Movement Begins," http://www.avatar-forums.com/
showthread.php?1745-A-Movement-Begins/page3.

45 See "Human and Environmental Rights," http://www.avatar-forums.com/forum
display.php?26-Human-amp-Environmental-Rights, and "Environmentalism,"
http://www.tree-of-souls.com/environmentalism.

46 Unil_mi_tokx, 5 September 2010, 10:49 p.m., and DarkPontiac, 4 September
2010, 10:16 a.m., "Sick of the NIGHTMARE! Time to WAKE UP!" http://www
.avatar-forums.com/showthread.php?3520-Sick-of-the-NIGHTMARE-Time-to
-WAKE-UP!/page3; and Txim-Asawl, 11 September 2010, 04:50 a.m., "Sick
of the NIGHTMARE! Time to WAKE UP!" http://www.avatar-forums.com/
showthread.php?3520-Sick-of-the-NIGHTMARE-Time-to-WAKE-UP!/page4.

47 See http://pandoraworld.su; Bolo, 25 December, 02:31 a.m., and 26 December 2011,
12:28 p.m., "A Movement Begins," http://www.avatar-forums.com/showthread
.php?1745-A-Movement-Begins/page12.

48 See, for instance, "AvatarMeet 2012," http://forum.learnnavi.org/2012-meetup;
"Seattle Meetup 2012," http://www.tree-of-souls.com/seattle_meetup_2012; and
http://www.naviblue.com/hometree/component/kunena/18-Member-Meetup/
501639-Avatar-Meet-up-2012.

49 The following forums are represented on the planning committee: *Learn Na'vi*,
http://www.learnnavi.org; *Tree of Souls Forum*, http://www.tree-of-souls.com;
Avatar Forums, http://www.avatar-forums.com; *NaviBlue.com*, http://naviblue
.com/hometree; and *Avatar Wiki*, http://james-camerons-avatar.wikia.com/wiki/
Avatar_Wiki.

50 See "2012 Event Calendar: Pre-Meetup Events," http://avatarmeet.com/?m=3&s=7.

51 The Avatar exhibition program is no longer available on the EMP Museum's
homepage, but on YouTube, one can see videos of the performance stage at the
exhibition. See, for instance, http://youtube.com/watch?v=JxclxM7PVFk.

52 An *Evening Magazine* video about the Avatar exhibition at the EMP Museum can
be seen at http://www.youtube.com/watch?NR=1&v=5WwoPhnE7kA&feature=
endscreen.

53 Aketuan, 12 June 2011, "Anything about June 4th Meetup," http://www.tree-of
-souls.com/meetups/4213-anything_about_june_4th_meetup-2.html.

54 Drewan, 8 June 2011, "Anything about June 4th Meetup," http://www.tree-of
-souls.com/meetups/4213-anything_about_june_4th_meetup.html.

References

Alexander, David. 1991. "Interview with Gene Roddenberry: Writer, Producer, Philosopher, Humanist." *The Humanist*, March/April. http://www.stjohns -chs.org/english/STAR_TREK/humanistinterview/humanist.html.

Brooker, Will. 2002. *Using the Force: Creativity, Community and Star Wars Fans*. London: Continuum International.

Forbes, Bruce David, and Jeffrey H. Mahan, eds. 2000. *Religion and Popular Culture in America*. Berkeley: University of California Press.

Hutton, Ronald. (1999) 2001. *The Triumph of the Moon: A History of Modern Pagan Witchcraft*. Oxford: Oxford University Press.

Istoft, Britt. 2008. "Trekkies, Jedi-Knights and Pop Witches: Fantasy and Science Fiction as Religion." In *Recent Releases: The Bible in Contemporary Cinema*, edited by G. Hallbäck and A. Hvithamar, 150–69. Sheffield, UK: Sheffield Phoenix Press.

———. 2010. "Avatar Fandom as Religious Expression?" *Journal for the Study of Religion, Nature, and Culture* 4(4): 394–414. doi:10.1558/jsrnc.v4;4.394.

Jenkins, Henry. 1992. *Textual Poachers: Television Fans and Participatory Culture*. New York: Routledge.

Jindra, Michael. 1999. "'Star Trek to Me Is a Way of Life': Fan Expressions of Star Trek Philosophy." In Porter and McLaren, *Star Trek and Sacred Ground*, 217–30.

———. 2000. "It's about Faith in Our Future: Star Trek Fandom as Cultural Religion." In Forbes and Mahan, *Religion and Popular Culture in America*, 165–79.

Kraemer, Ross S., William Cassidy, and Susan L. Schwartz. 2001. *Religions of Star Trek*. Boulder, CO: Westview Press.

Lovelock, James. (1979) 1995. *Gaia: A New Look at Life on Earth*. Reprint, Oxford: Oxford University Press.

Maher, Kevin. 2009. "Avatar: Pictures of James's Cameron's Fantastic New World." *Sunday Times*, 8 December.

McLaren, Darcee L. 1999. "On the Edge of Forever: Understanding the Star Trek Phenomenon as Myth." In Porter and McLaren, *Star Trek and Sacred Ground*, 231–43.

McLaren, Darcee L., and Jennifer E. Porter. 1999. "(Re)Covering Sacred Ground: New Age Spirituality in *Star Trek: Voyager*." In Porter and McLaren, *Star Trek and Sacred Ground*, 101–15.

Moyers, Bill. 1999. "Cinema: Of Myth and Men". *Time* magazine, 26 April. http://www.time.com/time/magazine/article/0,9171,990820,00.html.

Porter, Jennifer E. 1999. "To Boldly Go: *Star Trek* Convention Attendance as Pilgrimage." In Porter and McLaren, *Star Trek and Sacred Ground*, 245–70.

Porter, Jennifer E., and Darcee L. McLaren, eds. 1999. *Star Trek and Sacred Ground: Explorations of Star Trek, Religion and American Culture*. New York: State University of New York Press.

Taylor, Bron. 2001a. "Earth and Nature-Based Spirituality (Part 1): From Deep Ecology to Radical Environmentalism." *Religion* 31(2): 175–93.

———. 2001b. "Earth and Nature-Based Spirituality (Part 2): From Earth First! and Bioregionalism to Scientific Paganism and the New Age." *Religion* 31(3): 225–45.

———. 2010. *Dark Green Religion: Nature Spirituality and the Planetary Future.* Berkeley: University of California Press.

Turner, Victor. 1969. *The Ritual Process: Structure and Anti-Structure.* Ithaca, NY: Cornell University Press.

Turner, Victor, and Edith Turner. 1978. *Image and Pilgrimage in Christian Culture.* New York: Columbia University Press.

Van Hise, James. 1990. *Trek Fan's Handbook.* N.p.: Movie Publisher Service.

Wilhelm, Maria, and Dirk Mathison. 2009. *James Cameron's* Avatar: *An Activist Survival Guide.* New York: HarperCollins.

Post-Pandoran Depression or Na'vi Sympathy: *Avatar*, Affect, and Audience Reception

MATTHEW HOLTMEIER

A new ecosophy, at once applied and theoretical, ethico-political and aesthetic, would have to move away from the old forms of political, religious and associative commitment.

—Félix Guattari

On 20 August 2010, eight months after the motion picture *Avatar* was released, *Entertainment Weekly* interviewed director James Cameron regarding the film's re-release, which was about to take place in approximately a thousand theatres in the United States alone. In this interview, Cameron was asked a question about *Avatar*-inspired depression: interviewer Benjamin Svetkey (2010) noted that "there were reports that some of those fans were so upset Pandora didn't really exist outside your movie, they fell into serious depressions after leaving the theater." Cameron chalked this up to "hyperbole," observing, "Everybody writes in purple prose in the blogosphere." He suggested that if these feelings of depression do exist, "they should just go on a damn walk in the woods. Or go snorkeling." Unfortunately, such action does not seem to be an adequate solution for these individuals experiencing *Avatar*-inspired depression, nor do these feelings seem as easy to brush off as Cameron made it out to be. It appears that individuals have instead looked back to the film as a way of coping, a strategy that has simply exacerbated their own depression. This depression suggests a particular relationship with our world and environment that needs to be examined more carefully because it establishes a worldview contrary to what Cameron describes in his interview with *Entertainment Weekly*—a recursive relationship with the film that leads fans to return to the fictional world of Pandora rather than seeking change in their lived realities. Although *Avatar* may have an environmentally proactive side, in order to create a clearer view of *Avatar's* effects on fan communities, the film needs to be examined in relation to the depression it engenders in some of its fans.

Post-Pandoran Depression: The Return of the Same Fiction

The phenomenon that I am calling "post-Pandoran depression" was first reported by CNN in an online article titled "Audiences Experience 'Avatar' Blues" (Piazza 2010), which traces the activity of a thread on a website forum dedicated to *Avatar* (www.avatar-forums.com). CNN reported that as of 11 January 2010, over a thousand posts had been added to the forum on the topic of *Avatar*-induced depression. The original thread—at 772 posts alone—was closed on 6 January 2010, and a series of new threads with a similar name was soon created. "Ways to Cope with the Depression of the Dream of Pandora Being Intangible (Part 2)" started the new series, clocking in at 385 posts. Part 3 followed with 504 posts, and Part 4 was still running at 1,576 posts as of 2 August 2010. These posts have since been consolidated as the website underwent improvements, and the new count stands at 3,573 as of 28 February 2013. While the thread has effectively died, this points to another 500 posts between 2010 and the last post in 2011. This total, 3573 posts, attests to the longevity and impact well beyond the number that CNN originally reported. My research is based on reading threads on *Avatar* forums dedicated to the topic of post-Pandoran depression to determine whether fans return to the fictional world of Pandora to cope with their depression or seek change in their immediate environments. First, I provide a sample of responses that illustrate the ways in which fans talk about the film in these forums and what their discussion suggests about their personal experience with post-Pandoran depression. Second, I categorize each response according to whether the individual freely admits to feelings of post-Pandoran depression or offers a method of coping that involves immediately returning to the film or the fictional world of Pandora. Finally, I look at media-based responses to *Avatar* uploaded to social networking sites such as YouTube that are indicative of a different response to the film, which I describe as "Na'vi sympathy."

Although no data is available documenting what proportion of the audience has experienced post-Pandoran depression, the first-hand accounts from people describing this phenomenon provide evidence of its potency, if not its prevalence. The basic response of those who have identified themselves as suffering from post-Pandoran depression has been that after viewing *Avatar*, their own world seemed lacklustre. As one writer described it, leaving the theatre is like waking up from a dream.[1] Unfortunately for the individuals feeling depressed after the movie, the dream does not fade. The typical reaction reported by those feeling post-*Avatar* depression is that of seeking ways to reimmerse themselves in the Pandoran world: in other words, to prolong the dream. Writers recommend remedies such as listening to the film's soundtrack, painting Pandoran landscapes, and going back to the theatre to see the film repeatedly. While these activities might allay the feeling of post-Pandoran depression, they also create an endless cycle of reimmersion into *Avatar*'s fictional world. Whether or not such reimmersion alleviates the reported depressed feelings, those feelings are at least indicative of a particular relationship between these *Avatar* viewers and the world. More importantly, the relationship between audiences and the world that post-Pandoran depression typically creates runs counter to what Gilles Deleuze describes as the task of an ethical cinema.

Deleuze (1925–95) was a French philosopher well known for his critique of modern capitalism and for his collaboration with the psychoanalyst Félix Guattari. Much of Deleuze's philosophy is Spinozist and Nietzschean in orientation; he turned his attention to film analysis later in his career. While Deleuze's work with film is well known for the examination of time and movement in the cinematic image, I want to address the potential for his cinematic ethics to be used for an ecological or ecosophical critique. An ecosophical approach to Deleuze's work would examine the viewer's relationship with a film and the resulting impact on her or his immediate environment. In his works on film, *Cinema 1* and *Cinema 2* (1986, 2000), Deleuze contends that a film's ethical efficacy depends on its ability to construct a viewer's relationship with the world. An analysis of audience responses to *Avatar* points to several potential types of relationships engendered by the film. Deleuze, aware of the potential for the construction through film of both positive and negative relationships, outlines four relationships with film through a set of archetypal characters: "The formidable man of good or the devout person (he for whom there is no question of choosing), the uncertain or indifferent (he who does not know how to, or is unable to choose), the terrible man of evil (he who chooses a first time, but can then no longer choose...), finally the man of choice or belief (he who chooses choice or reiterates it)" (1989, 177). Although such characters are recognizable as formal pieces of a story, Deleuze's ethical consideration of these characters stems from how they treat choice. More specifically, each "character" describes a particular relationship *with* or belief *in* the world and one's ability to affect the world. Despite being defined as characters, Deleuze qualifies these descriptions, specifying that "it is not simply a question of a film-content: it is cinema-form...which is capable of revealing to us this higher determination of thought, choice, this point deeper than any link with the world" (178). While it would be difficult to make a direct connection between a single one of these ethical relationships and *Avatar*, post-Pandoran depression has much in common with the first three archetypes, which all limit choice or one's connection with the world in the same the way post-Pandoran depression limits choice by leading fans to continually choose Pandora over our world. As a result, *Avatar*'s ability to function as Deleuze's ethical cinema, in which the viewer "chooses choice" and belief in one's ability to change the world, is shown to be stunted by the depression that viewers of *Avatar* describe online.

The most prominent thread on avatar-forums.com that describes post-Pandoran depression is the ever-growing "Ways to Cope with the Depression of the Dream of Pandora Being Intangible." As the title of the thread suggests, forum participants have offered a number of ways to cope with post-Pandoran depression. These methods of coping, however, rely on re-establishing or reinforcing a link between the viewer and the fictional world of Pandora. Most of the posted suggestions come from individuals who are already engaged in their described remedy, suggesting that a number of people are actively pursuing these activities. One user suggested, for example, that the afflicted "listen to the soundtrack" and offered, "i'm writing an avatar sequel. The writing gets my mind distracted."[2] For this commentator, listening to the soundtrack leads back to aural experiences of *Avatar*, while writing an *Avatar* sequel reinvokes Pandora's fictional realities. Others posted more complicated suggestions; for example, one wrote, "Spend your time on this forum, or volunteering in your free time, instead of getting high or drinking, twiddling your thumbs, being apathetic and complaining about how bad the world is."[3] While this post urges going out into the world and volunteering instead of being apathetic, it also suggests spending time on *Avatar* forums as a way to cope. Furthermore, the same writer concluded, "The only way you can fill the emptiness you feel after this movie, is to jump on the leonopteryx," referring to the fictional birds that the natives of Pandora ride in the film. Suggestive of the cliché "jump on the bandwagon," this post recommends replacing something in our world with something from the fictional world of Pandora and thus seems to perpetuate a desire to live in the film's "reality."

While the previous examples provide creative methods of coping, a common suggestion from forum participants is to view the film repeatedly. One such user recounted: "The first time after I woke up the next day after watching it I 'had' to see it again. I have seen it four times now, and soon to be a fifth. I think watching it takes away that depression."[4] Clearly, this is lucrative for those who profit from the film, but following Deleuze, it makes sense to ask: What do these responses mean for the ethical value of *Avatar*? Focusing on post-Pandoran depression, one could argue that *Avatar* leads to the opposite of the reaction that Deleuze envisions for an ethical cinema. Whereas Deleuze's cinematic ethics include, as described by Ronald Bogue (2010, 129), "choosing to choose…belief in the possibilities of the world," the individuals affected by post-Pandoran depression choose *Avatar* instead. In other words, rather than a belief in the possibilities of the world, they choose the endless repetition of Pandora's fictional components. And rather than being enabled to take ethical action in the world, the viewers who are affected by post-Pandoran depression are unable to act because they desire participation with a fictional universe. A short survey of the first one hundred posts of the thread "Ways to Cope with the Depression of the Dream of Pandora Being Intangible" shows that far more responses are illustrative of a relationship that leads to a repetition of Pandora's fictional components rather than to action in the world. Specifically, twenty-three offered solutions that involved returning to Pandora's fictional world. The remainder of the one hundred posts were either off-topic or short comments affirming what another respondent had written. Although this is a small sampling considering the popularity of the movie, it provides a sense of the relationship between post-Pandoran depression and fan culture—or more specifically, fan culture's popularity as a solution to *Avatar*-inspired feelings of sadness. Just as significantly, only a few of the responses in this sample suggested real-world community-based solutions.

Post-Pandoran depression, however, is only one of the symptoms associated with *Avatar*'s remarkably widespread popularity. Another reaction, which I call "Na'vi sympathy," does seem to produce in audiences what Deleuze envisions for ethical cinema. By Na'vi sympathy, I mean sympathy for the indigenous peoples of *Avatar*'s Pandora and their habitats. While the Na'vi and Pandoran nature are fictional, many viewers recognize that they symbolize nature and indigenous people on Earth. Some of these viewers espouse Na'vi sympathy and use the film to reflect on and spur action in their own Earthly world.

Na'vi Sympathy and the Three Ecologies: Subjectivity, Social Organization, and the Environment

Rather than encouraging fans to recreate the world of Pandora, as post-Pandoran depression does, Na'vi sympathy prompts fans to take action in the social and material environments of our world. I follow Félix Guattari's ecosophical approach to the issue of Na'vi sympathy because it helps to illustrate the interrelated nature of audience subjectivity, resulting social formations, and positively shifting relations with the environment. Guattari (1930–92) was a French psychoanalyst who is known for his collaboration with Deleuze and his work at the La Borde clinic in France, where he practised innovative methods of psychoanalysis. Guattari has also been associated with ecological philosophy, or what he called "ecosophy." Although Arne Naess coined the term *ecosophy* almost two decades earlier, Guattari uses the term without reference to Naess. This lack of reference on Guattari's part reflects the difference between these writers while obscuring their similarities, such as their shared Spinozist insistence on connections between different communities and ecologies. Despite Guattari's seeming unawareness of ecosophy's origins, his approach to the concept is useful in analyzing *Avatar* because he foregrounds the possibility for popular forms of entertainment to rearrange approaches to the environment on a large scale. As Gary Genosko (2009, 157) notes, for Guattari, "'popular' works...held promise because of the potential publics they catalyzed." If it is the case that empathetic responses to *Avatar* found online are catalyzing individuals to take action in our world and toward our environments, Na'vi sympathy functions antithetically to a disempowering post-Pandoran depression, thus seeming to realize the hope in Deleuze's ethics that film can function positively in the world, fostering both social and environmental mobilization.

While Guattari's ecosophical method does explicitly promote concern for the environment, it also treats ecosystems as a model for critical interpretation: in other words, the interrelated nature of life and physical environments in an ecosystem operates similarly to the interrelation Guattari sees between subjectivity and physical environments. This model is particularly apt for looking at the effects of *Avatar* and Na'vi sympathy, because Na'vi sympathy first appears to promote an affective response in some viewers, who then attest to this in Internet forum posts that express themes like "I once was lost, but now am found." Na'vi sympathy appears again in the more social calls-to-arms and the formation of online communities, as can be found at avatar-forums.com and other online fan sites. These sites have evolved as "discourse communities," groups of people sharing language, ideas, and values. Finally, forum users suggest and sometimes personally describe actions impacting the material and social environments. This development seems to fit what Guattari (2000, 67–68) hoped for in ecosophy, "a multi-faceted movement, deploying agencies and dispositives that will simultaneously analyse and produce subjectivity," which will be different from "old forms of political, religious and associative commitment." In other words, Guattari defines a political potential that operates as a complex and interrelated set of factors rather than as a cohesive or identifiable group of people. By looking at the individuals displaying Na'vi sympathy, one finds a set of individuals or a multitude both "analyzing" *Avatar* and "producing" subjectivities informed by the film. Guattari's basic ecosophical premise is that once people's minds change toward an issue, they will affect the social configurations around this issue and the issue's state of being in reality. Likewise, he believed, the resulting social configurations will in turn change more people's minds and prompt them to take collective action, with the possible building of social networks and movements toward environmental and social mobilization.

This seems to be precisely what director James Cameron had in mind when he said during a fundraiser for the Natural Resources Defense Council, "*Avatar* asks us all to be warriors for the earth." Although this may not be a new perspective to the green community, what is unique about the film is that its emotional impact has enlisted "warriors for the earth" from individuals not previously engaged in green causes, while also, apparently, bolstering the resolve of those who are already committed to the environment. A form of conversion narrative can be found in forum posts online that details some posters' new-found commitment to the environment, which is evidenced by statements to the effect that "*Before* I didn't care about the environment, but after *Avatar* I actively notice the environment around me." One user on avatar-forums.com, for example, dedicated a thread to this phenomenon, leading the comments that followed with "okay so before the movie avatar i was one of those jerks who always littered and after avatar i became like an eco-warrior or something."[5] Other posters echoed this statement. One, referring to his own attitudes, wrote, "after avatar everything changed."[6] Others reaffirmed their own commitment to environmentalism: "well, i've been very eco-friendly all the time anyway, it just opened my eyes a little wider."[7] Another writer admonished the original poster with Platonic militancy, "No I have always picked up trash left by others. It's good that you have woken up to the truth. Please for all of us don't forget the lessons you have learned."[8] These comments reveal the forum participants' subjective view of the environment while also illustrating how *Avatar* has affected the environmental facet of their subjectivity. Perhaps sensing this potential of *Avatar* and its online communities, one fan created a thread dedicated to planting trees across the world titled "How Avatar Has Empowered You and This Community—Community Tree Planting Tracker."[9] Although the first-hand accounts of changed habits may be more indicative of the film's positive effect and its affective nature, threads like "Community Tree Planting Tracker" show that the community itself has become an environmental motivator. In these ecosophical communities, what Henry Jenkins (2010) has called "*Avatar* activism" emerges. While such online responses are limited to how these users *feel* and do not reveal what they actually *do*, they do show the writers' affinities with the mental component of Guattari's three ecologies, which, as he argues, is important in shaping the social and environmental components. The fourth comment above ("Please for all of us don't forget the lessons you have learned"), for example, is illustrative of this interrelation between subjectivity and social spheres in that it contributes to shaping the social formation by invoking group values. Finally, if indeed these words are followed by actions, the effect of these subjectivities on the environment will be the result of individual and political action to clean up and protect environmental systems.

In terms of how *Avatar* has mobilized social formations, one can examine Internet media productions that called for action instead of describing a personal experience. Guattari's social ecology can be understood as a set of collective values upon which individuals in a social formation take action. In a way, the examples of the individual posters above already describe a social ecology in that they highlight a collective value regarding the treatment of litter. Already, it seems that the ecologies are intermingling. *Avatar*'s influence, however, has spawned other media creations that incorporate direct calls for personal and collective action. Adam Hintz (2010), for example, posted a YouTube video that is far more socially oriented than the previous examples of conversion narratives because it offers a set of values for its audience instead of describing a personal change. In his video, he proclaims, "If you really want to be as free as the blue people in the movie *Avatar*, you need to walk away from civilization. You need to go tribal. You need to start living with the planet, instead of against it." Hintz thus provides an example of an empathetic response to the natives of Pandora and, perhaps, of a desire to become one, by suggesting a tribal lifestyle as opposed to the lifestyle of "the farmer" or "the industrialist." Although the extent to which this affects the environment is debatable, the comments appended to this video show that others share his desire for a tribal way of living in harmony with nature, even if this concept is varied and vague.

Several communities around the world have also taken the experience of the indigenous peoples of Pandora as parables of their own lives. A notable example is the Achuar people of Ecuador who gained attention after Cameron bussed them to Quito for a 3-D screening of *Avatar* (Spitzer 2010). I am unsure whether the Achuar exemplify Na'vi sympathy, however, because they did not come to the film on their own, nor did they change their lifestyle as a result; one tribeswoman even critiqued *Avatar* for its violent nature. The residents of Bil'in in the West Bank, however, organized a protest against the West Bank barrier by dressing up as Na'vi, having made a connection between the displacement of the Na'vi in *Avatar* and the repression of Palestinians by Israel (Katib 2010). Connecting the real-world situation of Palestinians to the plight of the Na'vi reinvokes the empathetic and affective value of the film *Avatar*, while associating it with a context based in this world. This strategy was effective in reaching a wide audience as videos and images from the event quickly spread across the Internet. Adding to the potential emotional response from viewers familiar with *Avatar*, Israeli soldiers responded by firing tear gas at the protesters, just as the paramilitary troops attack the Na'vi in the film. The correlation between the nearly defenseless Na'vi and the Palestinian protesters, as well as between the paramilitary of the mining expedition and the Israeli Defense Forces, is unmistakable. An important goal of the ongoing Bil'in protests has been to generate media attention so that people across the world might understand the political situation in Israel; in this case, *Avatar* provided an opportunity to intensify media attention. The film also highlights the important interaction between mental and social ecologies: as uninformed or politically neutral individuals witness these images, they may well re-evaluate this political conflict. Although this issue does not concern the natural environment explicitly, treating the issue as inextricably linked to particular states of mind and relationships with the environment follows Guattari's logic that a healthy Earthly environment is inseparable from healthy social environments.

It is premature, and beyond the scope of the present analysis, to determine whether *Avatar* has had or will have a social, political, or environmental impact. The aforementioned examples, however, show that *Avatar* has changed the environmental and political opinions of some viewers, especially with regard to how to treat the planet and its peoples. To speculate on how *Avatar* might affect the environment, we may again consider Guattari's basic claim: subjectivity and social formations are so closely tethered that change to one means change to the other as well. If one agrees with this claim, the best place to look for material or social environmental change is in the personal experiences or stories of people who say, "After *Avatar*, I started cleaning up my environment and convinced others of the environment's importance" or "After *Avatar*, I better understand what the Palestinian people are going through." If this is indicative of an established or emergent ecosophy, a particular attitude toward the environment and interaction between subjective and social spheres, it is also an eco-philosophy based firmly in our world, even if it draws inspiration from a computer-generated universe.

Notes

1 Okoi, 26 December 2009, 11:12 p.m., "Ways to Cope with the Depression of the Dream of Pandora Being Intangible," http://www.avatar-forums.com/showthread .php?43-Ways-to-cope-with-the-depression-of-the-dream-of-Pandora-being -intangible.

2 Yunnydanis, 26 December 2009, 10:03 p.m., "Ways to Cope with the Depression of the Dream of Pandora Being Intangible," http://www.avatar-forums.com/showthread. php?43-Ways-to-cope-with-the-depression-of-the-dream-of-Pandora-being -intangible.

3 Neytiri, 26 December 2009, 10:21 p.m., "Ways to Cope with the Depression of the Dream of Pandora Being Intangible," http://www.avatar-forums.com/showthread .php?43-Ways-to-cope-with-the-depression-of-the-dream-of-Pandora-being -intangible.

4 Elequin, 27 December 2009, 5:06 a.m., "Ways to Cope with the Depression of the Dream of Pandora Being Intangible," http://www.avatar-forums.com/showthread.php?43 -Ways-to-cope-with-the-depression-of-the-dream-of-Pandora-being-intangible/ page2.

5 Stubydub, 2 March 2010, 6:56 p.m., "ive been thinking," http://www.avatar-forums .com/showthread.php?8501-ive-been-thinking.

6 Sullyjake1, 2 March 2010, 9:55 p.m., "ive been thinking," http://www.avatar-forums .com/showthread.php?8501-ive-been-thinking.

7 Abdisavatar, 2 March 2010, 10:21 p.m., "ive been thinking," http://www.avatar-forums .com/showthread.php?8501-ive-been-thinking.

8 Txen, 2 March 2010, 7:40 p.m., "ive been thinking," http://www.avatar-forums.com/ showthread.php?8501-ive-been-thinking.

9 Madman, 13 April 2010, 12:29 p.m., "How Avatar has Empowered you and this Community—Community Tree Planting Tracker," http://www.avatar-forums .com/showthread.php?10923-How-Avatar-has-empowered-you-and-this-community -amp-Community-Tree-Tracker.

References

Bogue, Ronald. 2010. "To Choose to Choose — To Believe in this World." In Afterimages *of Gilles Deleuze's Film Philosophy,* edited by D. N. Rodowick, 115–34. Minneapolis: University of Minnesota Press.

Deleuze, Gilles. 1986. *Cinema 1.* Minneapolis: University of Minnesota Press.

———. 1989. *Cinema 2.* New York: Athlone Press.

Guattari, Felix. 2000. *The Three Ecologies.* New York: Athlone Press.

Genosko, Gary. 2009. *Felix Guattari: A Critical Introduction.* New York: Pluto Press.

Hintz, Adam. 2009. "Avatar." *YouTube.* http://www.youtube.com/watch?v= kurdeuthw2i.

Jenkins, Henry. 2010. "*Avatar* Activism." *Le Monde diplomatique* (English edition), 15 September. http://mondediplo.com/2010/09/15avatar.

Katib, Haitham A. 2010. "Bilin Reenacts Avatar Film 12-02-2010 By Haitham Al Katib." *YouTube.* http://www.youtube.com/watch?v=chw32qg-m7e.

Piazza, Jo. 2010. "Audiences Experience 'Avatar' Blues." *CNN Entertainment*, 11 January. http://www.cnn.com/2010/SHOWBIZ/Movies/01/11/avatar.movie. blues/index.html.

Spitzer, Melaina. 2010. "Avatar in the Amazon." *The World*, 29 January. http:// www.theworld.org/2010/01/29/avatar-in-the-amazon/.

Svetkey, Benjamin. 2010. "James Cameron on Returning to *Avatar*." *Entertainment Weekly*, 20–27 August.

Transposing the Conversation into Popular Idiom: The Reaction to *Avatar* in Hawai'i

RACHELLE K. GOULD

NICOLE M. ARDOIN

JENNIFER KAMAKANIPAKOLONAHE'OKEKAI HASHIMOTO

Traditionally, Native Hawaiians have considered nature and culture inseparable (Maly 2001). For over a thousand years, Hawaiians have studied the movements, seasons, and structure of the land.[1] Many of today's Native Hawaiians profess a strong belief that Hawaiian culture would not exist without the land (Parion Noelani Neal, pers. comm.); however, historical events have often forcibly separated the Hawaiian people from their land (Herman 1999). In this article, we explore the perspectives of current residents of Hawai'i, both Native Hawaiians and those of other ethnicities, by analyzing their perceptions of *Avatar*.[2] We ask these questions: After a delayed period, what messages from *Avatar* do viewers retain? How do perceptions of the film relate to the present culture of Hawai'i?[3] Our analysis compares participants' responses along three axes: ethnicity (Native Hawaiian versus residents of other ethnicities), engagement with forests (those with relatively high and low levels of engagement with Hawaii's forests), and level of education. Although many people consider Hollywood's portrayal of these issues oversimplified and trite, our data suggest that discussion of the film can provide insight into sensitive topics that may otherwise be difficult to broach.

Historically, Hawaiian culture has exemplified a close relationship with the land, largely developed and solidified through the people's dependence on farming and fishing for their livelihoods (Kamakau 1991, 23). Historians and Native Hawaiian storytellers describe how Hawaiians' hands became stained from the brown dirt, hardened by the lava rock, and calloused by the tools they made (Kalani Flores, pers. comm.). There was "fluidity between culture and environment" (Herman 1999, 80); in this culture, the human/ecosystem relationship was an integral component of a productive lifestyle (McGregor 1996). Working with nature equalled life; nature was life (Christiano Hashimoto, pers. comm.). In traditional Hawaiian culture, there is a saying: If the land is taken care of, the land will take care of us (Kalani Flores, pers. comm.).

Today, many Native Hawaiians retain this close connection to the land and ocean (Trask 1991). The arrangement of the land has changed dramatically—for instance, a Western system of land ownership has replaced the traditional land management system, which did not conceptualize individual ownership of land (Herman 1999). But Native Hawaiians often describe their ancestors' knowledge of their natural surroundings as powerful (Andrade 2008). Connections such as these are described among indigenous cultures throughout the world (e.g., Burgess et al. 2005; Takano, Higgins, and McLaughlin 2009); for contemporary Native Hawaiians, that historical connection is equally intense and motivating. This link gives Native Hawaiians a sense of spiritual connectedness and cultural belonging, which may contribute to a contemporary Native Hawaiian sense of identity (Kehaulani E. Crawford, pers. comm.). This study is informed not only by our data but also by informal observations based on the authors' experience in the community (see the Methods section). Formal and informal observations suggest that many Native Hawaiians feel a strong connection to the land and that this connection cannot be adequately expressed with words, particularly English words.

Yet for reasons we hope to elucidate, Native Hawaiians indicated that their reflection on the film *Avatar* was at times helpful in explicating their feelings of connection to the land and how historical events have affected that connection. This research was spurred by pilot work conducted in January 2010, during which we explored the values associated with Hawaii's forests. At that time, we were struck by respondents' repeated and unprovoked references to *Avatar*; these often profound references encouraged us to explore further the feelings evoked by the film. *Avatar*'s story addresses intense political, societal, and cultural issues. This research aimed to use the film as a vehicle for understanding more about a geography that, as many of our respondents brought to our attention in our pilot work, resonates with some of the film's principal messages.

For several reasons, the geographical, cultural, and historical aspects of Hawai'i offer a rich setting in which to explore reactions to the film. First, the archipelago's history provides a poignant parallel to the film. Hawaii's vibrant, highly functioning society was taken over by colonizing powers in recent historical memory (Liliuokalani 1990; McCubbin and Marsella 2009), and that takeover was associated with the control and commercialization of land and natural resources (Levy 1975; Ralston 1984). A complex spiritual and ancestral connection with the land has been an integral part of Hawaiian culture since before the time of the takeover (Trask 1991); this intertwined political and spiritual history has formed a society sensitive to the tensions dramatized in *Avatar*. Second, many of the state's residents are of Native Hawaiian ancestry—360,000 individuals (approximately 30 per cent of the state population) identified themselves as at least part Native Hawaiian in the 2000 census (US Census Bureau 2010); their ancestors have lived in the Hawaiian islands for generations. Third, a recent renaissance of traditional Hawaiian culture has brought traditional beliefs, philosophies, and worldviews to the forefront (Linnekin 1983; Harden 1999; Meyer 2003). Many of these philosophies, such as that of the spirits of ancestors and deities being embodied in the non-human world (Trask 1991), have parallels in *Avatar*.[4] Fourth, Hawaii's society is highly modernized and diverse; people commonly attend films and otherwise participate in popular culture events, and thus, many people in Hawai'i have been exposed to *Avatar*.

The relatively recent history of Hawai'i also includes a number of examples of a growing body of Native Hawaiian activists referring to tradition and cultural practices in protests of land-based action. The discourse of *mālama'āina*, or "care for the land," has become a common component of efforts focused on land, culture, and the intersection of the two (Linnekin 1983). For instance, there has been active and, at times, vitriolic debate on Hawai'i Island over the spiritual and cultural implications of geothermal energy extraction (largely because Pele, a powerful Hawaiian deity, is the goddess of the volcano's energy) and of the construction of large telescope complexes on the summit of Mauna Kea, which is considered by many to be a sacred mountain (Zimmerman 2005). The story of Kaho'olawe, a small island that was used intensively by the US Navy for bombing practice in the late 1960s and early 1970s, provides another example of both the abuse of land and a culturally imbued protest against military control and action (Blackford 2004). These and other issues illuminate the history in Hawai'i of relating infringements on indigenous land rights to cultural practices and traditions, as was arguably done in the film *Avatar*.

Certain films denoting historical events have had notable impacts on societal awareness of those events. *Schindler's List* (1993), for example, evoked a flurry of response and reaction to the Holocaust in both popular and academic forums. Although some critiqued it as bending historical detail, many people emphasized how moving and metaphorically eye-opening the film's representation of the Holocaust was (Classen 2003). Similarly, *Dances with Wolves* (1990) has been discussed in scholarly work (e.g., Appleford 1995; Bovey 1993) with a mixture of appreciation for addressing issues in need of societal attention and criticism of its romanticization and simplification of native cultures. These examples suggest that the cinematic fictionalization of real-world issues can be problematic but can also generate constructive public discourse. Film and popular media scholars note that such portrayals may be particularly effective in sparking emotional responses and spurring discussion as they "open a space of possibility that achieves its impact especially by the fact that it is not identical with reality" (Classen 2003, 82). Cultural researchers such as Appleford (1995) suggest that people of indigenous heritage may appreciate cinematic representations of their culture, even if the details are inaccurate: that is, the value of presenting the idea of their worldview outweighs the damage that some contend, or fear, may be caused by inaccuracies. Building from this body of work, we investigated whether *Avatar* presents an opportunity to explore elusive human/nature relationships and particularly challenging post-colonial narratives even though its messages and storyline may be considered oversimplifed.

Methods

This study was conducted as a component of a larger study aimed at understanding the cultural ecosystem services, or intangible benefits provided by ecosystems (Chan et al. 2012), associated with forests in Kona (Gould, forthcoming). We conducted a mixed-methods study, using a combination of techniques to produce qualitative and quantitative data. Mixed-methods studies, which are based on the premise of triangulation (Babbie 2001), employ a variety of methods with the intention of offsetting weaknesses of individual methods with the strengths of others (Singleton, Straits, and Straits 1993). In this way, the study design can decrease the likelihood that the data reflect biases of particular data-collection strategies (Maxwell and Loomis 2002).

The study collected data through surveys, interviews, and informal observation. The majority of the surveys and interviews focused on cultural ecosystem services; questions about *Avatar* were asked near the end of both survey and interview protocols. The lead author lived in the South Kona community for six months during 2009–10, and the third author is Native Hawaiian, is from the study area, and has lived in Hawai'i her entire life. The research team conducted surveys and interviews in Kona, Hawai'i Island, in summer 2010. The delay between the release of *Avatar* in December 2009 and our data collection allowed us to address how the film impacted respondents in the medium term. Although the delay may have hindered the ability of some participants to fully remember details of the film, we believe that the time lag strengthened our ability to explore bigger-picture issues by shifting the research focus toward sustained conceptual impact of the film. We summarize our methods below; see Gould, Ardoin, and Hashimoto (2010) for more detailed descriptions of techniques and analyses summarized here.

In-Person Survey

We conducted the surveys with a convenience sample of residents of the South Kona area. We worked in public places (parks and grocery stores) and solicited the participation of passersby. Given that much of the survey's content referenced upland forests, we recruited people to complete the survey by asking, "Would you be willing to share your thoughts about *mauka* [upland] Kona?" Therefore, although the survey sample was not random, the recruitment verbiage was neutral to perceptions of the film *Avatar*. The average respondent required twenty-three minutes to complete the survey. A total of 205 individuals completed the survey (124 male, 80 female, one unidentified). Ages ranged from eighteen to eighty-one, with an average of forty-six. The *Avatar* section of the survey comprised thirteen questions. Eleven questions used to produce quantitative data (see table 1) assessed opinions of the film and its messages and the degree to which the film inspired specific emotions in people. All but the last two questions produced quantitative data. The two final questions requested more general thoughts on the film and its message, producing qualitative data (see table 1).

Interviews

In addition to the highly structured surveys, the research team conducted twenty-one semi-structured interviews. The interview sample was purposefully selected to represent a diversity of relationships with Hawaii's forests. The interview sample included fourteen males and seven females with ages ranging from thirty-four to seventy-four years. Like the surveys, interviews covered topics related to uses of and values pertaining to Hawaii's upland forests, and respondents were recruited without mention of *Avatar*. Interviews lasted from one and a half to four hours. *Avatar* was discussed at the end of each interview. The interview guide included four topics regarding the film: (1) what the respondent thought of the film, (2) the film's main messages, (3) whether the film related to the previous discussion about cultural ecosystem services, and (4) whether the respondent was glad that the film addressed the topics it did.

Data Analysis

We analyzed the qualitative and quantitative data concurrently, using themes emerging from each technique to guide our exploration of the other (Maxwell 2005). In both the quantitative and qualitative analyses, we catalogued and summarized various perceptions of the film and then asked whether those perceptions differed among people with a range of ethnic backgrounds, levels of education, and degree of involvement with the forest. Throughout this paper, to increase clarity, we describe respondents using the ethnicity with which they indicated that they "most identified," even though this simplifies ethnic heritage.

We digitally recorded and transcribed interviews. We analyzed qualitative data—from interviews as well as from the two open-ended questions on the survey—using a thematic coding scheme.

Our quantitative analyses explored respondent *opinions* of the film on three levels. (See table 1; hereafter, we label these "opinion" questions.) Quantitative analyses also explored six *emotions* that respondents may have felt in response to the film. (See table 1; hereafter, we label these "emotion" questions.) We analyzed how these responses related to the three primary demographic axes: ethnicity, level of education, and level of involvement with forest (a constructed scale). Because the data from our five-point scale are ordinal, and the distances between the points are arbitrary, we used the Wilcoxon-Mann-Whitney test (Mann and Whitney 1947; Wilcoxon 1945) to examine possible relationships between responses and demographic characteristics.

Results and Discussion

Of the 205 respondents who completed the survey, 125 (61 per cent) had seen the film *Avatar*. Of the 70 individuals who had not seen it, 24 (12 per cent of the total sample) had heard enough discussion of it that they felt qualified to answer questions related to it. Therefore, 149 survey respondents answered the questions about *Avatar*. Of the 21 in-depth interviewees, 15 had seen the film; all "interview" responses below are from these 15 individuals.

Emotions and Opinions Related to the Film

Preliminary statistical analyses of the quantitative data revealed four significant differences. However, when the Bonferroni correction was applied to account for the high number of relationships tested, none of these results

TABLE 1: SURVEY ITEMS

Question category	Question	N	Response mean[a]	Response standard deviation
Opinion	Overall, how much did you like the movie?[b]	147	4.3	0.9
Opinion	How much did you like the special effects?	147	4.5	0.8
Opinion	How much did you like the story?	144	4.0	1.1
Message agreement	How much do you agree with the first message you gave?	130	4.6	0.9
Message agreement	How much do you agree with the second message you gave?	106	4.5	1.0

Please rate on the 1–5 scale how *Avatar* created (or didn't create) the following emotions for you:

Question category	Question	N	Response mean[a]	Response standard deviation
Emotions	Angry	132	2.9	1.5
Emotions	Disgusted	133	2.8	1.6
Emotions	Frustrated	134	2.9	1.5
Emotions	Hopeful	134	3.6	1.4
Emotions	Proud	128	2.8	1.6
Emotions	Spiritual	132	3.6	1.5
Messages	What do you think were the main messages of the movie – what was the movie trying to say to us?		n/a	n/a
Other thoughts	Is there anything else you would like to say about the movie and/or your reaction to it, or to what others have said about it?		n/a	n/a

a Quantitative responses were scored using a five-point Likert scale where "1" indicates the negative response (negative or "not at all") and "5" indicates the positive response (positive or "most definitely").
b For respondents who had not seen the film but felt qualified to answer questions about it, the survey administrator replaced the word "you" with "people you've talked to" for all questions.

remained significant.[5] Thus, we report these results as suggestive rather than as statistically significant.

In the "emotion" questions, we asked respondents to rank the degree to which the film inspired in them the feeling of six emotions: angry, disgusted, frustrated, hopeful, proud, and spiritual. We found four patterns in these answers. (See table 2 for the complete results.) First, respondents who identified as Native Hawaiian were more likely than those who

TABLE 2: TEST STATISTICS FOR MANN-WHITNEY TESTS COMPARING RESPONDENT GROUPS

Emotions elicited as reported by Native Hawaiian and white respondents

	Angry	Disgusted	Frustrated	Hopeful
Mean (std dev) Native Hawaiian	3.1 (1.7)	2.9 (1.6)	2.9 (1.6)	3.6 (1.5)
Mean (std dev) white	3.0 (1.4)	2.7 (1.6)	2.8 (1.5)	3.5 (1.3)
Mann-Whitney U	1039	1007	1033	1035
Z[a]	−.32	−.79	−.63	−.61
Significance (2-tailed)	.751	.428	.530	.539

Emotions elicited as reported by respondents with higher and lower levels of engagement with forest

	Angry	Disgusted	**Frustrated**	Hopeful
Mean (std dev) higher engagement	**3.3 (1.6)**	3.0 (1.7)	**3.3 (1.5)**	3.6 (1.4)
Mean (std dev) lower engagement	**2.6 (1.4)**	2.6 (1.5)	**2.5 (1.5)**	3.6 (1.4)
Mann-Whitney U	**1757**	2056	**1677**	2360
Z[a]	**−2.57**	−1.42	**−3.17**	−.21
Significance (2-tailed)	**.010**	.157	**.002**	.831

Emotions elicited as reported by respondents with higher and lower education levels

	Angry	Disgusted	**Frustrated**	Hopeful
Mean (std dev) lower education	3.0 (1.5)	2.9 (1.7)	**3.3 (1.5)**	3.5 (1.4)
Mean (std dev) higher education	2.8 (1.6)	2.7 (1.6)	**2.6 (1.5)**	3.6 (1.3)
Mann-Whitney U	2174	2170	**1768**	2289
Z[a]	−.52	−.67	**−2.59**	−.31
Significance (2-tailed)	.602	.503	**.009**	.754

a   The Z-statistic can be interpreted similarly to the t-statistic; Z-values greater than 1.96 indicate significance at the 0.05 level and Z-values greater than 2.58 indicate significance at the 0.01 level. The significance level is an estimation of confidence that a difference like the one in our data would occur by chance alone; for example, a significance value of 0.002 indicates a 0.2 per cent chance that the difference in ratings between two groups would have occurred by chance. Results significant at the 0.05 level (before Bonferroni correction) are bolded.

Proud	Spiritual	Liked overall	Liked plot	Liked special effects
3.3 (1.7)	3.6 (1.5)	4.2 (0.9)	4.0 (1.1)	4.5 (0.7)
2.5 (1.5)	3.5 (1.4)	4.3 (0.8)	3.9 (1.0)	4.5 (0.7)
715	981	1329	1205	1271
−2.18	−.55	−.08	−.66	−.52
.029	.582	.939	.507	.605

Proud	Spiritual	Liked overall	Liked plot	Liked special effects
3.1 (1.7)	3.8 (1.6)	4.2 (1.0)	4.0 (1.1)	4.4 (0.8)
2.6 (1.6)	3.6 (1.4)	4.3 (0.9)	4.0 (1.0)	4.5 (0.7)
1948	2198	2795	2698	2770
−1.33	−.79	−.34	−.30	−.47
.183	.428	.732	.765	.639

Proud	Spiritual	Liked overall	Liked plot	Liked special effects
2.8 (1.6)	3.5 (1.4)	4.3 (0.9)	3.9 (1.0)	4.4 (0.8)
2.9 (1.7)	3.8 (1.5)	4.2 (0.9)	4.1 (1.1)	4.5 (0.7)
2126	2030	2773	2299	2671
−.32	−1.31	−.22	−1.71	−.67
.748	.191	.823	.088	.501

identified as Caucasian/white to report that the film made them feel proud ($p < 0.05$ before Bonferroni correction; Mann-Wilcoxon-Whitney test, U=715, Z=2.18). This finding is consistent with past work on societal perceptions of films (e.g., Appleford 1995) as well as with findings from our qualitative data; our qualitative work suggested that people of indigenous descent more frequently expressed a sense of pride related to the film's story than those without a genealogical connection to the pro-indigenous messages in the film.

Past interaction with Hawaii's forest also may have affected people's reactions to the film. Respondents with a higher degree of engagement with the forest reported higher levels of frustration ($p < 0.05$ before Bonferroni correction; Mann-Wilcoxon-Whitney test, U=1768, Z=2.60) and higher levels of anger ($p < 0.05$ before Bonferroni correction; Mann-Wilcoxon-Whitney test, U=1757, Z=2.57) than those with less engagement with the forest. This result may suggest that respondents with higher levels of interaction with the forest may have higher levels of emotional connection with that ecosystem; therefore, the forest-exploitation aspect of the film may have spurred more anger and frustration among those respondents than among those who rarely interact with the forest.

In addition, respondents with lower levels of education (no formal education, grade school, middle school, or high school) reported stronger feelings of frustration than those with higher levels of education (community college, four-year degree, or graduate degree) ($p < 0.05$ before Bonferroni correction; Mann-Wilcoxon-Whitney test, U=1587, Z=2.378).[6] A straightforward rationale for this result is not obvious, but it may stem from those with higher education levels having more exposure to critical analysis, which is often emphasized in higher education. Perhaps those respondents would be less frustrated by the short-sightedness portrayed by the film's characters than would those who are less familiar with the rhetorical devices commonly used in artistic works. Additional qualitative data probing why individuals rated each emotion as they did, which we did not collect, would be helpful in further illuminating the reasoning behind their responses.

We found no significant differences in the three "opinion" responses (see table 1) when respondents were compared along the three demographic axes.

Messages of the Film

Collectively, survey respondents provided 242 messages from the film.[7] The messages were diverse and nuanced. (Table 3 provides a selection of responses representative of the more common subcategories.) In presenting our results, we often highlight ethnicity of respondents (see table 3) because this is often an important distinction in the Hawaiian context and since this axis provided interesting comparisons in a number of cases.

Table 3 presents an overview of selected responses to the questions about the film's main messages. In the "#" column, we indicate the number of survey respondents who identified the message, and the next four columns report percentages describing the division of that small pool of respondents by ethnicity. However, because this question was free-response, these quantitative results cannot be seen as representative of the population and thus are only included as description.

Joint analyses of the survey and interview data sets revealed four overarching themes. These themes emerged from combined qualitative data from surveys and interviews.

1. Respecting the land and the people who live on the land

When asked about the messages of the film, the majority of respondents discussed some variant of a theme that we categorized as "Take care of nature." Of the 242 messages provided in surveys, 103 (43%) were coded in the main category of "Take care of nature." Although this may in part be due to the previous content of the survey, which was related to Hawaii's forests, it nevertheless indicates that many respondents considered the film to have an "environmental" message.

Thirty-nine of the "Take care of nature" responses (16% of all messages provided) were coded as "Preserve nature and save environment" or "Take care of the life of the forest"; people of diverse ethnic backgrounds gave these responses. Examples of "Preserve nature and save environment" include "conserve the forest" and "have to save the environment." An example of the "Take care of the life of the forest" subcategory is one respondent's statement that "we tend to use forests as a resource just for our needs, but we tend to forget that other creatures...have their own needs. We have a responsibility to restore their environment if we damage it."

In addition to these responses related to "nature" overall, eight respondents (5% of the 149 survey respondents who answered questions about *Avatar*) specifically mentioned nature and people jointly. For instance, one Native Hawaiian respondent gave as a message of the film "respect each culture: land, resources, environment, people." Another Native Hawaiian respondent represented the concept of conserving both nature and culture by combining two negatively phrased messages: "subjugation of another culture" and "destruction of another rainforest." Similarly, ten respondents (7%) provided messages that were coded as "humans lose if take down forest." These messages—such as one Native Hawaiian respondent's

TABLE 3. SELECTION OF MAIN MESSAGES AS REPORTED BY SURVEY RESPONDENTS.

Categories and Number of Responses			Ethnicity				
Main category	Subcategory	#	Native Hawaiian	White	Other indigenous	All other[a]	Example
Composition of *Avatar* survey sample (for reference)			27%	45%	9%	19%	
Take care of nature[b]	Preserve nature and save environment	33	36%	39%	9%	15%	"not destroy nature"
Culture	Connection to land	11	30%	60%	0%	0%	"importance of connection with our plant brothers"
Indigenous rights	Anti-subjugation of natives	10	20%	30%	40%	10%	"Indigenous people don't need saving by white people."
Preserve nature	Humans lose if take down forest	10	50%	30%	0%	20%	"Care for the earth, you are caring for yourself."
Take care of nature	Mother Nature	9	22%	22%	33%	22%	"The land is living. Mother Nature is a human being too."
Human nature	People are evil, destructive, greedy	9	11%	67%	11%	11%	"people's greediness, selfishness, stupidity"
Culture	Respect culture	8	50%	25%	13%	13%	"appreciate culture and why certain thing are done that way"
Human nature	Exploitation for personal gain or profit	7	29%	43%	14%	14%	"how we can destroy our earth all for profit, and it's easy to lose a whole culture in the process"

TABLE 3, *continued*

Categories and Number of Responses			Ethnicity				
Main category	Subcategory	#	Native Hawaiian	White	Other indigenous	All other[a]	Example
Composition of *Avatar* survey sample (for reference)			27%	45%	9%	19%	
Lessons	Understanding others	7	14%	71%	14%	0%	"importance of communication between cultures"
Real world	Could and does happen anywhere	6	50%	17%	17%	17%	"The movie speaks the truth a little bit – but just in alien form; they didn't want to use humans because of media and stuff."
Spiritual	Animism	6	67%	0%	0%	17%	"All natural things have a soul."
Human nature	Transcending Race	5	40%	40%	0%	20%	"Tolerate people who look different."
Preserve nature	Balance	4	25%	75%	0%	0%	"Preserve our forest because it plays important part in the balance of life."
Preserve nature	All connected	4	25%	50%	0%	25%	"Earth and people are connected."
Real world	Military is bad	4	0%	75%	0%	25%	"The military is bad."
Corporations	Corporations hurting environment	3	33%	67%	0%	0%	"Evil corporations can take over and rape the land."

TABLE 3, *continued*

Categories and Number of Responses			Ethnicity				
Main category	Subcategory	#	Native Hawaiian	White	Other indigenous	All other[a]	Example
Composition of *Avatar* survey sample (for reference)			27%	45%	9%	19%	
Corporations	Corporations defiling natives	3	0%	33%	33%	33%	"If the indigenous people have something that the industrial complex wants, it will take it."
Lessons	Cannot take what's not yours	2	0%	50%	0%	50%	"not to take advantage of other planets, situations, or things we are not entitled to"
No message or don't Remember	Liked special effects	2	50%	50%	0%	0%	"I don't think I was looking for a message; it was fun and had good special effects."
Spiritual	Connection between land and spirit	2	0%	0%	100%	0%	"Humanity needs to reconnect with the natural world because the unnatural world does not support us spiritually; and people who are conscious of that tend to be more socially responsible."

a Rows are ordered based upon the number of responses in each sub-category (the "#" column). Percentages do not always add up to 100 per cent because of rounding errors and some respondents' refusal to provide ethnicity. Readers interested in the complete list of responses may contact the lead author.
b Of the ethnicity category described as "All other," 53 per cent comprised people of three ethnicities common in Hawai'i: Filipino, Chinese, and Japanese.

statement that "we cannot survive without resources, nature; we cannot duplicate nature, no matter the technology"—reflected the basic idea of ecosystem services: that ecosystems provide humans with essential benefits. Half of the responses in this category came from Native Hawaiians, perhaps partly because of the cultural orientation described above, which suggests a reciprocal relationship between land and people.

The two main film themes described by a white male in his fifties, who is a long-time island resident active in Hawaiian affairs, summarized the idea of the intertwined responsibility for people and nature: "*Mālama* [take care of] the *ʻāina* [the land, literally "that which feeds"]. *Mālama* the people on the *ʻāina*. That's probably it."

2. Link between people and land

One of the frequently mentioned concepts most salient to this exploration was the intensity of the Native Hawaiian connection to the land. Many respondents noted its similarity to the relationship between the Na'vi and the land of Pandora.

In the surveys, eleven respondents (7%) provided messages that were coded as "Culture: Connection to land," a category exemplified by one Native Hawaiian respondent's message that "they [the Na'vi] were trying to protect their culture and the 'tree of life.'" Respondents providing these "Connection to land" messages were ethnically diverse; one white respondent mentioned "people's emotional ties to the forest," while another white respondent said that the film taught us about "what you're able to draw from the land and forest, if you're close to it, spiritually."

In contrast to the diversity of the "Connection to land" category, it is interesting to note that of the six messages that were coded as "Spiritual: Animism," four came from Native Hawaiian respondents, one from a Chinese/Japanese individual whose family has lived in Hawai'i for "generations," and one from a respondent who refused to provide ethnicity. As examples of this category, three Native Hawaiian respondents described messages from the film as "plants have feelings, and everything revolves around the forest," "all natural things have a soul," and "the forest is a living thing—you must respect it."

Two respondents provided messages addressing the spiritual nature of the human-land connection (categorized as "Spiritual: Connection between land and spirit"); again notably, both of the responses in this coding category came from people of indigenous descent, although not, in this case, Native Hawaiian heritage. A Native American respondent said that one of the film's messages was a "connection between land and spirit." One respondent of Māori heritage (the indigenous people of New Zealand) gave this as a message: "Humanity needs to reconnect with the natural world because the unnatural world does not support us spiritually, and people who are conscious of that tend to be more socially responsible. We need the forest."

Interviewees detailed some of the ideas expressed in the surveys. One Native Hawaiian in his fifties said, "I could relate to the blue guys [the Na'vi]." When asked why, he responded with a statement about the poorly understood meaning of natural features: "Ah, about people just coming in, and just building things, and knocking things down. And not understanding what that shoreline, or that hill, means. And just, 'I'm gonna do my subdivision.'"

One Native Hawaiian respondent in his thirties expressed similar ideas related to the depth of meaning that can be associated with land and the features on it. He explicitly made a connection between that depth of meaning and indigeneity, or perhaps longevity of tenure in a place: "All aboriginal people, people who have identified themselves with a place, or have evolved with a place, probably felt the same, or have similar feelings... that land, that tree was their mother. I mean, that was part of their existence.... Their symbiosis between the forest and that culture, or that people, was so close that they'd die. They just, [pause] they would have died if that forest was gone."

Two white male respondents, both in their early sixties, suggested that the connection that the Na'vi have with their ecosystem is an appealing but unrealistic idea. The words of these two individuals in the two quotations that follow reveal the striking similarity of their comments:

> I'm sympathetic with the views that the story portrayed.... I certainly am attracted to the idea that there is a more perfect relationship between humans, or some kind of human-like things, and the forest. You know, that there's a way that they live together in wonderful [pause] and I think it's sort of a fantasy, but it's a nice fantasy.

> You have a people that seem to be very plugged into their environment and physically plugged into other species, I mean you can tell me how that can possibly evolve [laughing]. But, so some of it is unrealistic, but they are obviously a people that are very guided and that idea has a lot of appeal. I'm not sure it's quite so realistic.

However, respondents with Native Hawaiian ancestry did not see the Na'vi connection as far-fetched. Two interviewees powerfully expressed their thoughts using noticeably similar language. One respondent suggested that people with backgrounds different from his might not understand the connection.

And I think maybe that's why I connected with…that movie, 'cause when I saw them communicating with the plants, I knew *exactly* what they were doing. And it's, for me, it's *not* an animated thing for me. When I saw them understanding their plants, I said, "I know what they're talking about."…Which kinda surprised me—that some guy in Hollywood would understand that. I thought that was kinda cool. (Native Hawaiian male, late fifties)

I guess one thing for me is the connection to the forest, and learning from the forest, and quote "talking to the trees," that's not something that's at all strange to me, in that movie. I have no idea what other people think…they'd think, "Oh, that's far-fetched," or "that's fantastic," or that's, you know, "living in a fantasy world." That wasn't a stretch for me. (Native Hawaiian male, mid-thirties).

3. People hold diverse perspectives, but underlying human tendencies exist. Another common theme, which builds upon the preceding theme of the link between people and land, was the need to recognize and respect diversity in cultures and perspectives. Conceptually intertwined with comments on this diversity of perspectives, however, was a message that human beings share certain innate qualities: on the one hand, an affinity for "nature," and on the other, greediness, destructiveness, and pursuit of profit.

Many survey respondents provided variants on the idea of respecting different cultures and backgrounds. Eight responses (representing 5% of respondents) were related to the need to "respect culture" (these were categorized as "Culture: Respect culture"). We coded comments regarding understanding and respecting a diversity of perspectives as "Lessons: Understanding others" (7 respondents, 5%) and "Human nature: Transcending race" (5 respondents, 3%). One Native Hawaiian respondent listed two messages that succinctly encompass many of the messages in two of these categories. His first message, which reflected the eight messages coded as "Respect culture," was "the importance of keeping a culture alive." He represented the "Understanding others" subcategory with his second message: "the importance of communication between cultures."

For seven of the fifteen interviewees who had seen *Avatar*, the film evoked comments about different perceptions of the world. These comments often suggested that differences in perception correspond with differences in ethnic background and that awareness and effort are needed to increase understanding of those differences. For example, a white respondent in her sixties said: "It's true that Native Hawaiians are very spiritual, very linked to the land…. The mining people [in the movie] had a sense of entitlement. It's the same problem with people [who come to Hawai'i] from the mainland. They think: our way is right, and your way is superstitious. While on the mainland, there's a big separation between religion and culture, the Hawaiian can't separate religion and culture. There is a total lack of respect with the Western coming in; they don't get that the 'āina [land] is a living, breathing thing." Although this woman could also be considered a "Westerner" from the mainland, her comments throughout the interview suggested that her many years on the island, combined with her study of Native Hawaiian perspectives and active involvement in community affairs, may have added to a perspective atypical of newcomers.

Another respondent, a Native Hawaiian woman in her late fifties, provided nuanced reflection on the different relationships to the environment portrayed in the film. In her view, "the two main [messages] were that if you're disconnected you're going to behave badly, and if you're connected you won't." However, in concordance with the implication of the white woman's quote directly above, she doesn't view "connectedness" as a static, pre-determined state. Previously in the interview, she had discussed the need to recognize that everyone and everything is a part of the "whole" and that dividing ourselves along so many lines is ultimately unhelpful. In reference to *Avatar*, she said: "I think that people from the disconnected group were able to join the connected group is an important message, but there again, it misses the mark that we've talked about, that even the disconnected guys are part of the whole.... The us- and them-ness was perpetuated. So, that would be my concern, is that it perpetuates the notion that we cannot become whole."

Likewise, Appleford (1995, 100) suggests that films such as *Dances with Wolves* perpetuate an "otherness" that leaves intact "the ideological division between Self and Other, white and Indian." Our results are consistent with Appleford's critique: many of our respondents, such as the woman quoted above, did not feel that the connection to the natural world—or the lack thereof—was limited to people of any particular ethnic background. Instead, a number of survey and interview respondents implied the existence of innate human propensities. Many respondents spoke of the underlying human affinity for the "natural" world in ways that resemble E. O. Wilson's notion of "biophilia" (Wilson 1984). For instance, one white interviewee in his fifties commented about the reason for the film's success: "The popularity of the movie had to indicate that people weren't there looking at the special effects; they're interested in the message.... A lot of people have seen that movie one, two, three, four times.... All the greenery that shows there, and [writer/director James Cameron's] depiction of how a human can integrate, or a being can integrate themselves into a natural environment...that's soothing to the viewer's soul to see that, and it wasn't any, you know, grand story."

Similarly, some respondents discussed the negative aspects of human behaviour without reference to ethnic differences. Nine survey respondents (6%) made statements about what they considered to be innate human greediness: for instance, "people's greediness, selfishness, stupidity," "humans are evil," and "humans in general are pretty destructive." Seven respondents (5%) made statements that we coded as "Human nature: Exploitation for personal gain or profit," stressing the human propensity to pursue profit. None of these respondents connected these characteristics to ethnicity; rather, respondents mentioned them more as general statements about the human condition. To emphasize this point, some interviewees explicitly stated that greedy and destructive behaviour is not connected with ethnicity. For instance, a white respondent in his early thirties said: "I don't wanna say it's white man, because I think that even the Hawaiian, Inuit, or whoever else around the world can still have those drives to do those bad things, you know, and destroy things."

4. Portraying the plight of native peoples worldwide, and particularly the history of Hawai'i

The final emergent theme was the mistreatment of native peoples around the world and, specifically, in Hawai'i. In the survey, ten respondents (7%) provided messages that we coded as "Indigenous rights: Anti-subjugation of natives." These messages were expressed in diverse ways and by people of many ethnic backgrounds (see table 3). A Native American respondent, for example, described one of the film's messages as being that "indigenous wisdom and tradition should be honoured at all costs," and a Hispanic respondent stated a similar idea: "leave indigenous people alone." A white respondent expressed the same idea with ironic sarcasm: "the people [Na'vi] shouldn't worry about it, because eventually they'll get casinos like the Indians."

When describing the film's messages, six respondents (4%) expressed statements along the line that this abuse "could and does happen anywhere." Three of these six comments were made by Native Hawaiians and one by a Native American respondent who stated that the film "delved into tribal tradition as a whole—not just in Hawai'i—and a lot of the crises they've dealt with."

Four survey respondents referenced the universality of the phenomenon of domination of native people but specifically mentioned that the situation portrayed in the film mirrored the story of Hawai'i. One of these four said, "You can see how the *haoles* [common parlance in Hawai'i for white people] do it to everyone—the Hawaiians, Indians. Egyptians did it to South Africans, the British did it to Hawaiians, etc."

Of the fifteen interviewees who had seen *Avatar*, nine discussed the similarity of the film's story and Hawaii's story, and many referenced the global nature of the problem. Although two interviewees (one Native Hawaiian and one white) commented that the film portrayed a highly·clichéd indigenous society, both nevertheless contended that the film addressed deep and important topics. One interviewee—a Native Hawaiian man in his thirties—described the impact of the modern world on traditional cultures in general and in Hawaiian culture in particular, in this way:

> I think the movie was really trying to say that in certain areas of this world, if this world keeps going down the track that it's going, people will [pause], will die. And maybe not physically [pause], but Hawaiians will not be called Hawaiians anymore. They'd be a thing of the past. Um, we'd evolve into something else. Our names would be lost. That whole culture would be gone. And, and I think if it hasn't happened, it's probably happening already—um, to other cultures. They've just completely lost their cultural practices.

In a similar way, a white woman in her sixties described the congruence between the film's plot and the situation in Hawai'i, along with the global nature of the scenario:

> It was about special interests wanting resources, wanting to take down that tree that was in the way of the resources. We have that same situation here.... It was very obvious in the movie: it didn't matter what they [the Na'vi] did or felt.... They [*Avatar*'s creators] came to Hawai'i and they took our story. But it's not a unique story; it's what the Western world did to the Native Americans on the mainland, too. It happened all over.

Discussing the film led a Native Hawaiian in his fifties, as well, to explain Hawaii's statehood in grim terms:

> Well, that's why Hawai'i is part of the United States—because "the natives didn't deserve this place. They just don't know how to maximize the return on it. They're just squandering it away. So let's take it from 'em, turn it into this prosperous place. And if they die, so what?"

In another sweeping comment, a Native Hawaiian respondent in his mid-thirties encompassed many of the messages discussed above—the message of differing views of land, that of the Native Hawaiian link to the land, and that of the symbolic relevance of the film to the situation in Kona, Hawai'i:

> I think there are a lot of the newcomers here...want to come here and "we want to learn to dance hula, and want to *mālama 'āina*"...but I don't know if they truly get it.... The movie might be sort of symbolic of some

of the challenges facing Kona, and especially Kona because the population is shifting to a very Caucasian population.... That is a challenge of just a different perspective and outlook of what the forest is—some place to be accessed, and some place to be able to go hiking and to do whatever you want, and to take pictures of birds, or to do this thing. Then it's a whole different outlook on it; it's not a genealogical connection. They don't come from that place. It's sort of: this is America, and we can access wherever we want.... There's no idea or thought that this is where I come from...this is who I am, this is where I'm born from. It's a completely different outlook.

This response touches on profound issues related to perception of land and the gravity involved in combining differing perceptions, with specific reference to the situation in contemporary Hawai'i. The respondent raises issues central to study of values related to forest, and the context of *Avatar's* storyline seems to have encouraged formulation of this potentially controversial message.

Connection of Themes to Other Scholarly Work

This study's four emergent themes, which are detailed above, are consistent with scholarly works addressing similar issues. The theme of respecting the land and the people associated with it is being explored in a number of academic realms (Chan et al. 2007; Khan and Bhagwat 2010; Adams et al. 2004). A large and diverse body of literature addresses a second theme: the spiritual and cultural dimensions of the link between people and land (e.g., Herman 1999; Maly 2001). A third theme—the diversity of perspectives of different peoples with respect to land—is similarly addressed both explicitly and implicitly in a variety of fields (Berghoefer, Rozzi, and Jax 2010; White 1967). The tragic but common subjugation of native peoples, which emerged as a fourth theme, is discussed by scholars with respect to native peoples worldwide (Pulver and Fitzpatrick 2008) and specifically in Hawai'i (Trask 1991; McCubbin and Marsella 2009).

Connection to Cultural Ecosystem Services

As was described above, this study was part of a larger project investigating the cultural ecosystem services (CES) associated with Hawaii's forests. When interview respondents were asked if the discussion of *Avatar* related to the preceding discussion of CES (which constituted the bulk of their interviews), all but one of the respondents saw a connection.

The CES concept deals with the intangible benefits that ecosystems provide to people, although it is important to note that CES analysts do not necessarily attempt to monetize those benefits, as do many other ecosystem services analysts (e.g., Fisher et al. 2008). A CES analysis attempts to characterize connections between ecosystems and humans that are difficult to define, and often even more difficult to quantify or encapsulate—connections related to, for instance, spirituality, aesthetics, sense of identity, and cultural heritage.

For many scholars, intuition and experience demonstrate the depth and interdependence of connections between nature ("ecosystems"), spirituality, and culture. It is often unclear, however, how to approach and characterize these connections such that they are appropriately included in a decision-making sphere. The development of methods to adequately study and portray this connection is the subject of much research and thought (e.g., Chan et al. 2012). Given that CES research addresses the connections between ecosystems and topics such as spirituality and cultural heritage, the story of the Na'vi, with their tree-based deity who protects and nurtures the ancestors, provides a fictional setting for discussions related to CES. For instance, the Native Hawaiian in his mid-thirties mentioned above said: "[Avatar's story] relates to identity...it relates to the ecosystem. Well, they're kinda one and the same. For me, anyway, the ecosystem is what has made my identity, is what has made me who I am." This statement, precipitated by reflecting on the film, is closely aligned with theoretical concepts related to CES (such as the notion that ecosystems can contribute to the formation and maintenance of people's sense of identity). Our study, exemplified by reflections such as this respondent's, suggests that representing issues through artistic and cultural mechanisms such as film may provide a conceptual platform that facilitates discussion of these interconnections.

Popular Media and Societal Beliefs and Practices

Many survey and interview responses expressed doubt that viewers of Avatar would retain the "deeper messages" of the film. However, our survey data indicate that the vast majority of people (n = 143, 96% of the 149 survey respondents who answered questions about Avatar) were able to identify moral messages from the film months after viewing it. A middle-aged male interview respondent, who called himself "Japanese on paper but Hawaiian at heart," said, "I think a lot of people...from Hawai'i got that message," by which he meant the message of how it's wrong to change "a whole society...because of what you need or want." The implication of his comment is that in a place like Hawai'i, where some of the film's messages closely reflect historical and contemporary events, those messages are especially salient. The data reported here support his statement.

Many of our respondents indicated that they were deeply passionate about the basic issues that they felt the film addressed—issues such as indigenous rights and the spiritual connection between people and land. To explore further the respondents' opinions about the film's treatment of such topics during the interviews, we explicitly asked respondents: "Are you glad that the movie addressed the issues it did?" A few interviewees expressed disappointment about how the film addressed certain social issues: for instance, respondents suggested that the film's treatment of indigenous rights was a cliché, its treatment of spirituality superficial, and its portrayal of anti-colonialism violent. However, all interviewees suggested that they were glad the film had addressed the issues that it did. One white male in his fifties called it "a statement in a movie form." A Native Hawaiian in her fifties described her appreciation by saying: "I think it translates, or transposes, the conversation into popular idiom. So it can be a good springboard for discussion with a variety of age ranges and economic backgrounds, and geographic backgrounds." Again, our data support this respondent's claim.

Interviewees noted the significance of the opportunity of using a block-buster film as a springboard for discussion of issues such as indigenous rights and post-colonialism. Two Native Hawaiian interviewees remarked that the presence of *Avatar*'s plotline in a blockbuster film may be a marker of societal change. One said that the film and its success "signal a different time we're in." The other stated, "When I was growing up, I just don't think [this kind of movie] would have been made." Both of these respondents indicated that the anti-imperialist, pro-indigenous sentiment in the movie would not have been socially acceptable even twenty years ago. Survey respondents also expressed appreciation for the film's messages: when asked for additional thoughts on *Avatar*, 15 of 149 respondents (10%) indicated that the film had an important or appealing message. As one respondent said, "I am heartened that it seems that many people did hear what the theme was, even though times are dark."

Three interviewees were skeptical, however, regarding the possibility that the film would precipitate positive changes in the world. One referred to *Avatar* as "just a movie." But another respondent who doubted that the film would spur massive change thoughtfully noted, "Very seldom in human history does one thing make a difference. It's a series of events over a period of time that has attitudes evolve. This is just one."

Conclusion

This study was limited in a number of ways. First, our respondent pool was a non-random survey sample. Second, our sample size was not large enough to demonstrate statistically significant quantitative results. We also had an underrepresentation of women in the interview sample.

Despite these limitations, our findings provide insight into the reception of *Avatar* in Hawai'i and ideas for further research. First, our quantitative data suggest that people of different backgrounds had different emotional responses to the film; these data thus lay groundwork for future research into the variegated societal response to powerful films and the implications of those varied responses. For instance, our finding that those with more interaction with the forest reported more feelings of anger and frustration than those with less interaction with forest ecosystems suggests that such exposure might cultivate emotional attachment to those ecosystems, which can even be evoked through symbolic representations of them—in this case, through cinematic art. The idea that art can evoke and affect humans' emotional and spiritual connection to the natural world is discussed in a number of forums (e.g., Taylor 1993; Kellert 2005), and our findings reinforce that possibility. Similarly, our finding that the film seemed to evoke in respondents of Native Hawaiian heritage greater feelings of pride than in those of white European heritage suggests that even simplified and archetypal artistic portrayals of indigenous societies may be appreciated by native peoples (as discussed in Appleford 1995).

Our qualitative findings suggest that the majority of respondents in our sample derived powerful messages from *Avatar*. With respect to many of the messages, ethnic background did not appear to dictate respondents' interpretation of the film, but for some of the messages, respondents of different ethnicities seemed to relate to the film differently. Specifically, our qualitative data suggest that people of varying backgrounds retained pro-environment messages from the film, including of the importance of humans connecting to the land, and readily identified the connection between Hawaii's history and *Avatar*'s plotline. The data also suggest that respondents of Native Hawaiian background more frequently identified and related to messages regarding animism and the need to respect culture than did white respondents. However, the use of questions on the survey precludes the use of statistical analyses to explore relationships between messages and demographic data, including ethnicity, education, and age.

Overall, the messages that respondents garnered represented contemporary issues, including the nature of cultural and spiritual connections to land, post-colonial political power relations, subjugation and displacement related to natural resource extraction and use, and questions of property and domain. These issues are relevant not only to Hawaii's history but also in Hawai'i today. As many respondents indicated, the film is not likely to create a tidal wave of change; however, the depth and diversity of responses suggest that the film may help increase awareness of and dialogue about important environmental, cultural, and natural-resource issues in ways that are relevant to residents of Hawai'i and many other areas of the world.

Using *Avatar* to promote discussion allowed unconventional explora-tion of these issues. Our interaction with survey respondents was brief; a fictional story facilitated a depth of discussion that would have otherwise been difficult to achieve given the relatively short relationship between researchers and interlocutors. It is also worth noting that our principal interviewer and three of the five survey administrators were white; the focus on *Avatar* may have increased respondents' comfort with expressing anti-colonial views, because they were superficially discussing the agreed-upon antagonists in a fictional story.

The idea of investigating perceptions of the forest in Hawai'i through the lens of a recent blockbuster film may seem outlandish. Many of our respondents, however, all of whom were selected without any mention of *Avatar*, had strong reactions to the film. Moreover, those reactions precipi-tated discussion about profound spiritual, cultural, and historical concepts related to the connection between people and the land. These relationships represent a core of the human experience, but are often difficult to articu-late. Using the platform of a film to explore such ideas, issues, and experi-ences may help provide insight when that insight is particularly important.

Notes

We are grateful to many people: survey respondents, interviewees, colleagues in Hawai'i, survey administrators (Anna Doty, Theodora Gibbs, and Iberia Zafra), and anonymous reviewers. We also thank our funders: the Heinz Family Foundation, Stanford Graduate Fellowship, Stanford Interdisciplinary Graduate Fellowship, Stan-ford School of Earth Sciences, and Stanford Center for Conservation Biology.

1 Archaeologists estimate that human settlement in Hawai'i began sometime between 300 and 800 CE (Graves and Addison 1995).

2 Contemporary transliteration of the Hawaiian language includes two diacritical marks: a macron lengthens vowels, and an 'okina marks a glottal stop. We have included diacritical marks in Hawaiian words; however, for Hawaiian words that have been modified to fit English grammar (e.g., *Hawaiian* and *Hawaii's*), we omit diacritical marks.

3 See Scott (1998) for discussions of post-colonial theory.

4 In Hawaiian language and culture, for example, 'aumakua refers to ancestral guardian spirits, or "deified ancestors who might assume the shape of" of animals, plants, rocks, or clouds (Pukui and Elbert 1986, 32). Akua is translated as "god, goddess, spirit" (ibid., 15); however, akua can be more like a force, a formless spirit that is not necessarily supernatural (as discussed in Taylor 2010) or humanoid, but which can inhabit, embody, and be embodied by places.

5 The Bonferroni correction is a statistical method applied when many relation-ships are tested, increasing the likelihood that a given result will fall within the range of statistical significance by chance (Samuels and Witmer 2003). The Bon-ferroni method indicates that, for our study, the level of certainty needed to claim

95 per cent confidence is 0.05 (the desired p-value) divided by nine (the number of response categories tested); none of the results described below fall within this corrected confidence level. Nakagawa (2004) offers a criticism of the Bonferroni procedure.
6 There was no significant correlation between level of education and level of involvement with the forest (Spearman's rho: r=0.055, p=0.420.)
7 Some survey respondents described only one main message.

References

Adams, W. M., R. Aveling, D. Brockington, B. Dickson, J. Elliott, J. Hutton, D. Roe, B. Vira, and W. Wolmer. 2004. "Biodiversity Conservation and the Eradication of Poverty." *Science* 306(5699): 1146–49.

Andrade, Carlos. 2008. *Hā'ena: Through the Eyes of the Ancestors*. Honolulu: University of Hawai'i Press.

Appleford, R. 1995. "Coming out from behind the Rocks: Constructs of the Indian in Recent United States and Canadian Cinema." *American Indian Culture and Research Journal* 19(1): 97–118.

Babbie, Earl R. 2001. *The Practice of Social Research*. 9th ed. Belmont, CA: Wadsworth Thomson Learning.

Berghoefer, Uta, Ricardo Rozzi, and Kurt Jax. 2010. "Many Eyes on Nature: Diverse Perspectives in the Cape Horn Biosphere Reserve and Their Relevance for Conservation." *Ecology and Society* 15(1): Article No. 18.

Blackford, M. G. 2004. "Environmental Justice, Native Rights, Tourism, and Opposition to Military Control: The Case of Kaho'olawe." *Journal of American History* 91(2): 544–71.

Bovey, S. 1993. "Dances with Stereotypes: Western Films and the Myth of the Noble Red Man." *South Dakota Review* 31(1): 115–22.

Burgess, C. P., F. H. Johnston, D. Bowman, and P. J. Whitehead. 2005. "Healthy Country: Healthy People? Exploring the Health Benefits of Indigenous Natural Resource Management." *Australian and New Zealand Journal of Public Health* 29(2): 117–22.

Chan, K.M.A., R. M. Pringle, J. Ranganathan, C. L. Boggs, Y. L. Chan, P. R. Ehrlich, P. K. Haff, N. E. Heller, K. Al-Krafaji, and D. P. Macmynowski. 2007. "When Agendas Collide: Human Welfare and Biological Conservation." *Conservation Biology* 21(1): 59–68.

Chan, K.M.A., Anne Guerry, Patricia Balvanera, Ratana Chuenpagdee, Mary Ruckelshaus, Xavier Basurto, Jordan Levine, Sarah Klain, Ann Bostrom, Rachelle Gould, Ben Halpern, Neil Hannahs, Bryan Norton, Roly Russell, Terre Satterfield, Debra Satz, and Ulalia Woodside. 2012. "Where Are 'Cultural' and 'Social' in Ecosystem Services? A Framework for Constructive Engagement." *BioScience* 62(8): 744–56.

Classen, C. 2009. "Balanced Truth: Steven Spielberg's *Schindler's List* among History, Memory, and Popular Culture." *History and Theory* 48(2): 77–102.

Fisher, B., K. Turner, M. Zylstra, R. Brouwer, R. de Groot, S. Farber, P. Ferraro, R. Green, D. Hadley, J. Harlow, P. Jefferiss, C. Kirkby, P. Morling, S. Mowatt,

R. Naidoo, J. Paavola, B. Strassburg, D. Yu, and A. Balmford. 2008. "Eco-system Services and Economic Theory: Integration for Policy-Relevant Research." *Ecological Applications* 18(8): 2050–67.

Gould, Rachelle. 2013. "Cultural Ecosystem Services and Reforestation in Hawai'i." Ph.D. dissertation, Emmett Interdisciplinary Program in Environment and Resources, Stanford University, Palo Alto, CA.

Gould, Rachelle K., Nicole M Ardoin, and Jennifer Kamakanipakolonahe'okekai Hashimoto. 2010. "'Mālama the 'āina, Mālama the People on the 'āina': The Reaction to *Avatar* in Hawai'i." *Journal for the Study of Religion, Nature, and Culture* 4(4): 425–56.

Graves, M. W., and D. J. Addison. 1995. "The Polynesian Settlement of the Hawaiian Archipelago: Integrating Models and Methods in Archaeological Interpretation." *World Archaeology* 26(3): 380–99.

Harden, M. J. 1999. *Voices of Wisdom: Hawaiian Elders Speak.* Honolulu: Booklines Hawai'i.

Herman, R.D.K. 1999. "The Aloha State: Place Names and the Anti-Conquest of Hawai'i." *Annals of the Association of American Geographers* 89(1): 76–102.

Kamakau, Samuel Manaiākalani. 1991. *The People of Old.* Honolulu: Bishop Museum Press.

Kellert, Stephen R. 2005. *Building for Life: Designing and Understanding the Human-Nature Connection.* Washington, DC: Island Press.

Khan, M. S., and S. A. Bhagwat. 2010. "Protected Areas: A Resource or Constraint for Local People? A Study at Chitral Gol National Park, North-West Frontier Province, Pakistan." *Mountain Research and Development* 30(1): 14–24.

Levy, Neil. 1975. "Native Hawaiian Land Rights." *California Law Review* 63(4): 848–85.

Liliuokalani. 1990. *Hawaii's Story by Hawaii's Queen.* Honolulu: Mutual.

Linnekin, Jocelyn S. 1983. "Defining Tradition: Variations on the Hawaiian Identity." *American Ethnologist* 10(2): 241–52.

Maly, Kepā. 2001. *Mālama pono i ka 'āina: An Overview of the Hawaiian Cultural Landscape.* Hilo, HI: Kumu Pono Associates LLC.

Mann, H. B., and D. R. Whitney. 1947. "On a Test of Whether One of 2 Random Variables Is Stochastically Larger Than the Other." *Annals of Mathematical Statistics* 18(1): 50–60.

Maxwell, Joseph. 2005. *Qualitative Research Design: An Interactive Approach.* 2nd ed. Applied Social Research Methods No. 41. Thousand Oaks, CA: Sage.

Maxwell, Joseph A., and Diane M. Loomis. 2002. "Mixed Methods Design: An Alternative Approach." In *Handbook of Mixed Methods in Social and Behavioral Research,* edited by A. Tashakkori and C. Teddlie, 241–72. Thousand Oaks, CA: Sage.

McCubbin, L. D., and A. Marsella. 2009. "Native Hawaiians and Psychology: The Cultural and Historical Context of Indigenous Ways of Knowing." *Cultural Diversity and Ethnic Minority Psychology* 15(4): 374–87.

McGregor, D. P. 1996. "An Introduction to the Hoa'āina and Their Rights." *Hawaiian Journal of History* 30: 1–27.

Meyer, Manu. 2003. *Ho'oulu: Our Time of Becoming. Hawaiian Epistemology and Early Writings.* Honolulu: Ai Pohaku Press.

Nakagawa, S. 2004. "A Farewell to Bonferroni: The Problems of Low Statistical Power and Publication Bias." *Behavioral Ecology* 15(6): 1044–45.

Pukui, Mary Kawena, and Samuel H. Elbert. 1986. *Hawaiian Dictionary.* Honolulu, HI: University of Hawai'i Press.

Pulver, L.R.J., and S. A. Fitzpatrick. 2008. "Beyond Sorry: The First Steps in Laying Claim to a Future That Embraces All Australians." *Medical Journal of Australia* 188(10): 556–58.

Ralston, C. 1984. "Hawai'i 1778–1854: Some Aspects of Maka'ainana Response to Rapid Cultural Change." *Journal of Pacific History* 19(1): 21–40.

Samuels, Myra L., and Jeffrey A. Witmer. 2003. *Statistics for the Life Sciences.* 3rd ed. Upper Saddle River, NJ: Pearson Education.

Scott, James C. 1998. *Seeing Like a State: How Certain Schemes to Improve the Human Condition Have Failed.* New Haven, CT: Yale University Press.

Singleton, Royce A., Bruce C. Straits, and Margaret Miller Straits. 1993. *Approaches to Social Research.* 2nd ed. New York: Oxford University Press.

Takano, T., P. Higgins, and P. McLaughlin. 2009. "Connecting with Place: Implications of Integrating Cultural Values into the School Curriculum in Alaska." *Environmental Education Research* 15(3): 343–70.

Taylor, Bron. 1993. "Evoking the Ecological Self: Art as Resistance to the War on Nature." *Peace Review* 5(2): 225–30.

———. 2010. *Dark Green Religion: Nature Spirituality and the Planetary Future.* Berkeley: University of California Press.

Trask, Haunani-Kay. 1991. "Coalition-Building between Natives and Non-Natives." *Stanford Law Review* 43(6): 1197–213.

US Census Bureau. 2010. State of Hawai'i Census 2000 Summary File 1.

White, L. 1967. "Historical Roots of Our Ecologic Crisis." *Science* 155(3767): 1203–7.

Wilcoxon, F. 1945. "Individual Comparisons by Ranking Methods." *Biometrics Bulletin* 1(6): 80–83.

Wilson, E. O. 1984. *Biophilia.* Cambridge, MA: Harvard University Press.

Zimmerman, Naupaka. 2005. "The Nature of Identity and the Identity of Nature: Hawaiian Perspectives on Persons and Place." Bachelor's thesis, Committee on Degrees in Environmental Science and Public Policy and the Department of Anthropology, Harvard University, Cambridge, MA.

Watching *Avatar* from "AvaTar Sands" Land

RANDOLPH HALUZA-DELAY

MICHAEL P. FERBER

TIM WIEBE-NEUFELD

As in the fictional world of Pandora, humans in Alberta function within a resource-based economic system with weighty environmental, social, and cultural consequences. Oil extraction has long been a major part of Alberta's economy. As conventional oil reserves have declined, it has become profitable to exploit alternative sources such as the bitumen-soaked sand and shale that make up the Alberta oil sands. Developing these reserves requires considerably more energy and water and produces more carbon emissions than developing conventional oil.[1] Also called "tar sands," Alberta's oil sands are promoted as third in size to the petroleum reserves of Saudi Arabia and Venezuela, and essential to North American energy security. Balanced against energy, ecosystem degradation, employment, and economic benefits are costs such as pollution and water depletion, cultural and health impacts on Aboriginal communities, and transfer of natural capital from the public to the coffers of corporations (Adkin et al. 2008; Nikiforuk 2008). Oil is Earth's parallel to Pandora's unobtanium.

Industry and the provincial and federal governments have aggressively defended the oil sands. Industry public relations campaigns have explicitly framed Alberta's identity in the context of energy production, with an extensive marketing campaign using the slogan "Alberta IS Energy."[2] Similarly, the Alberta Enterprise Group, a collection of industry insiders, has repeatedly made the identity-constructing declaration "Energy is what makes us Albertans." But the rapid expansion of oil sands "development" is highly contentious in Alberta. Aboriginal, environmental, and religious organizations have launched local and transnational campaigns targeting corporations, investors, and governments (Haluza-DeLay and Carter, forthcoming). One strategy by international environmental groups characterized the oil sands as a contemporary version of the *Avatar* storyline. Launched in March 2010, the "AvaTar Sands" campaign targeted Americans and included ads in major media outlets like *Variety*, news releases, and a website.[3] Ads compared northern Alberta's Aboriginal peoples to the Na'vi. Website videos depicted the horror of Na'vi characters responding to the devastated Alberta landscape. The campaign requested Americans contact their government and reject Alberta's "dirty oil." Albertans noticed the campaign. The day after the *Variety* ad, the Canadian Association of Petroleum Producers (CAPP) responded with news releases and a special page on its website (http://www.capp.ca/avatar) in order to counter claims of environmentalists that "Pandora's unobtanium mining is Alberta's tar sands" (Mittelstaedt 2010; CAPP 2010). Even James Cameron, the producer-director of *Avatar,* became involved, calling the oil sands a "black eye" for Canada. Invitations for him to visit the region came from indigenous and environmental groups, and eventually from Alberta Premier Ed Stelmach (Bennett 2010). Intense media scrutiny met his subsequent trip and meetings in Alberta in late September 2010.[4]

It is upon this contested landscape, with purported parallels between the oil sands and the movie narrative, that Albertans watched *Avatar.* Because some of the public discourse has focused on the nature spirituality of the movie, our investigation queried how religious Albertans might respond to *Avatar*.[5]

Studying *Avatar* in Alberta

Our approach resembles what Gellert and Shefner (2009, 193) call "structural fieldwork," wherein "the deep familiarity with people and locales" offers analytic traction on the political-economic world-system. Haluza-DeLay has been conducting long-term participant observation with the environmental and religious justice organizations of Alberta (Haluza-DeLay 2012; Haluza-DeLay and Carter, forthcoming; Kowalsky and Haluza-DeLay 2013). This ethnographic work illuminates the technocratic closure of debate over the ecological and social effects of extensive oil sands development and the general reliance of the provincial government on oil and gas revenues. It corresponds to the analysis of the discursive representations of the oil sands/tar sands in the media and in the official record of the provincial legislature (Davidson and Gismondi 2011).[6] We build on this foundation by adding evidence gathered in focus groups in specific churches, which serves as the basis of this chapter.

Focus groups were conducted in May and June 2010 with Albertans in three churches in the city of Edmonton. As the provincial capital and largest city in the northern half of the province, Edmonton serves as the supply and transportation hub for the oil sands, which lie a five-hour drive further north. Focus groups were held in two Mennonite churches and one Pentecostal church, with eleven, nine, and nine adults respectively, for a total of twenty-nine participants. Participants responded to announcements in the various churches inviting them to discuss the movie and their perceptions of it. Our contact with various churches had already shown there was ferment about the movie and the spiritual and environmental themes it seems to express. Participation was roughly equal in terms of gender. All participants were white. They included a wide range of occupations, length of residence in Alberta, and income status. Specific demographic and biographical information was not collected because it was most likely that personal experiences coupled with the social influences of participant relationships were more salient. The sample was not expected to be formally representative of Albertans. Instead, it provides insight into ways in which Albertans negotiate meanings of a cinematic powerhouse, particularly amidst the cultural politics of the oil sands and the CAPP and AvaTar Sands campaigns. The extensive media attention to the movie and the debate about its purported parallels with the oil sands meant that participants had generally thought through the issues they were asked about during the focus group discussions.

Each focus group took the form of a wide-ranging group conversation with moderate guidance by the research team.[7] Responses were solicited through group conversation and participants were encouraged to respond to each other. Because each group was composed of individuals in pre-existing relationships, the focus groups also encoded organizational context. The main advantage of focus groups is the interaction among participants; the main disadvantage is that individual responses may be submerged by more dominant perspectives in the group. Focus groups are particularly beneficial in understanding the connections that participants make among the components of a topic as they engage in interaction with each other.

The focus group in one of the Mennonite churches was held during the adult Sunday school hour with participants who had already seen the movie. At the Pentecostal church's request, the movie was shown one evening at a private home to an existing fellowship group and the focus group discussion followed the viewing. At the third church, the movie was shown one evening at the church and the focus group discussion was held the following week.

Focus groups were videotaped and a notetaker recorded discussion and observations of non-verbal behaviour. Rough transcripts were prepared. Analysis of the transcripts followed a top-down, open coding system with the categories "nature," "culture," "religion," and "environmental problem-solving" imposed but with subthemes developed in a way that follows tenets of grounded theory as detailed by Creswell (1998) and Charmaz (2005). Videotaping and observation of the focus groups enabled analysis that could include non-verbal behaviours as well as the spoken word.

Alberta Christians Watching *Avatar*

We describe these Christians' responses to *Avatar* in the theoretically imposed categories of "religion," "nature," "culture" (here referring to how cultural products incorporate underlying social values and collective narratives), and "environmental problem-solving."[8] Each of the first three themes points in significant ways toward the final theme: environmental problem-solving in personal and/or collective ways. Since space is limited, the analysis herein focuses on material that contributes to understanding environmental problem-solving by these Albertans.

In each section, commonalities between focus groups and individuals are emphasized, although differences are also noted. Most of these participants located themselves outside the polarized positions prevalent in the Albertan oil sands discourse. They demonstrated the capacity to autobiographically reflect upon their positionality, drawing on themes of interconnectivity (or ecological holism) in *Avatar* but also identifying its insufficiency for addressing the problems of the oil sands in Alberta.

Religion

Critics have sometimes asserted that *Avatar* presents a nature-based spirituality. If so, the apparent pantheism could be problematic for Christians. However, most participants of all three groups had little problem with this aspect of the movie. The primary ways in which participants perceived religion and spirituality in *Avatar* involved recognizing an integrally religious dimension to the movie and comparing it to their own faith, sometimes by reinterpreting the movie's worldview in light of their own theologies. These responses were seen in each focus group in roughly equal proportions.

The inherent religiosity of the movie was repeatedly identified by participants in all three focus groups. For example, Sully's reference to his "birthday"—the day he transmigrated his human being into a Na'vi body at the end of the movie—was discussed in two of the focus groups as having deep religious overtones. At another time, a Mennonite participant referred to Sully "orchestrating their [the Na'vi's] salvation." The Pentecostal group and members of one of the Mennonite focus groups referred to Sully "praying" when he tried to communicate on his own with Eywa, the Na'vi name for the planet's interconnected life force or divinity. Sully's effort engendered discussion in each group. The interconnectivity of Pandora was what Christian participants in all three focus groups most frequently said resonated with their own faith perspectives; this will be discussed in the "nature" section below.

Participants in all three focus groups repeatedly observed that *Avatar* was not presenting a Christian spirituality and indicated that they did not expect theological accuracy. A Mennonite participant, one of the most enthusiastic fans of the movie, repeatedly stated his faith in Jesus Christ, apparently stressing that he could enjoy the film without feeling as though his Christian faith was threatened. When a similar comment was made in the other two groups, participants nodded and verbally concurred. At no time did anyone indicate rejection of the movie or its theme of ecological interconnectivity. One participant in one Mennonite group referred to the Gaia hypothesis, Matthew Fox, and Teilhard de Chardin. Fox and de Chardin are twentieth-century theologians associated with the "creation-spirituality" tradition. The Gaia hypothesis, which has both scientific and religious implications, was discussed in the other Mennonite focus group as well.

More than the Mennonite groups, the Pentecostal group discussed the movie in terms of it being "New Age" or "Eastern" influenced. Said one Pentecostal participant, "Definitely a bit of an Eastern philosophy or a Buddhist philosophy—all interconnected and energy flowing through everyone.... Seems more Eastern than our individualistic North American philosophy." However, this comment was embedded in the flow of conversation that showed theological reinterpretation of the content of the spirituality presented in the movie. Prior to this point, a participant had reframed the immanent Eywa as a personal deity:

> One thing that struck me was the phrase "Eywa heard you." They were reaching out to God and God heard them. We sometimes forget from a Christian perspective that God is there. We don't experience it. They reached out and God answered in the midst of the evil and the chaos.

Slightly later, another exchange occurred among different participants in the same focus group:

> There was a line when the main character became an avatar and he noticed how sensitive she [Neytiri, the female Na'vi protagonist] was to sights and sounds of her land—he had to heighten his sense of awareness in order to

fit in. We often hear suggestions of how to be deliberate in our pursuit of Christ, like, disciplining our minds and listening to the Holy Spirit—it is important for strong daily day-to-day Christian life.

The next participant responded,

> Thinking of it in Christian terms, the energy is totally not what I feel as a Christian—I don't believe in that…but if you look at the whole thing and try to change it into Christianity, it is similar—he was reborn out of humanity and into Na'vi—there are similarities to their energy and the Holy Spirit—it could be like Christianity…fighting evil; together fighting the humans, who in this case represent evil.

Hearing this discussion of the interconnectivity of Pandora as a form of the immanent presence of God in creation, a third participant concluded, "I was uncomfortable with the New Age Mother Earth stuff—but now that I see it in the Holy Spirit perspective…" The participant left unsaid but implied more acceptance of the ecological orientation of the movie in Christian terms. The exchange demonstrates a process of reinterpreting the nature spirituality of the movie to be congruent with participants' existing beliefs.

Some focus group participants felt that the Christian narrative would be more effective than the spirituality presented in *Avatar*. One Mennonite woman said, "When I saw them [the Na'vi] crying out to the tree, I thought, 'How sad, there's not anyone there.'" Others agreed with her. In the film, there is a moment when Sully tries to talk directly to Eywa and is told by Neytiri that it isn't going to work. Two of the focus groups referred to this as "prayer" and discussed how the movie showed that one cannot pray to Earth because it cannot "hear." They felt that the movie simplified the divine by removing the complexity of divine personhood and relationality; this became the most often described divergence between *Avatar* and Christian forms of religiosity and was one reason why several participants asserted that Christianity is more complicated than the "simpler" spirituality of the movie. Participants expressed other reasons for seeing the Christian narrative as more effective and preferred. One Mennonite participant commented, for example, "There are lots of options to see biblical principles, but it doesn't go the whole way…. But I didn't expect it to, so no big deal." Another Mennonite participant pointed out that Christianity is more than ethics. Others agreed and each focus group explicitly stressed that Christianity is about Jesus Christ. Furthermore, each focus group referred to the ease of "plugging in" in the movie, with the tenor of each focus group's discussion represented well by one person's observation that "this is a perfect spirituality for our computer age."

Ultimately, the spirituality in *Avatar* was appealing to the focus group participants, but each group decided that connection to nature or the divine in our world is a more intricate process than is depicted in the film. In each group, the complexity of the religious perspective was also connected to the complications involved in solving real-life problems. Several women in one of the Mennonite groups kept probing other focus group participants—with some frustration—about both the legitimacy of the violence of the movie's ending and how Christians in Alberta can address injustices related to Aboriginal peoples. Both Mennonite groups discussed whether peaceful alternatives to Pandora's exploitation were possible, a concern that is consistent with the characteristic focus of Mennonites as a peace church.[9]

This problem-solving dimension will be discussed more fully below but is important to mention here because it is central to the participants' perceptions that the Christian faith is more complex than the spirituality presented in the movie. Nevertheless, because they appreciated the ecologically oriented spirituality dramatized in the film, these Christians viewed *Avatar* in ways that allowed them to take lessons from the main themes of the movie and apply them within their Christian belief structure.

Nature

The participants' religious interpretation of *Avatar* was closely connected to an environmental dimension. Two themes characterize participant perspectives on nature and *Avatar*—the movie highlighted their appreciation of the natural world, and it reinforced that care for creation is part of Christian faithfulness. Numerous participants said that they found aesthetic, experiential, and spiritual richness in nature. Participants often associated the ecological interconnectivity of Pandora with their religious beliefs and perceptions of God. The exchange presented earlier in the Pentecostal group about this interconnectivity or Eywa being like the Holy Spirit is one example. A similar position was expressed in one of the Mennonite groups: "I loved the pure spirits as they floated around. And Jake didn't even recognize them.... [Their purpose] was the replenishing of souls...like places of oasis.... [In our Christian perspective] this is the Creator and you can't separate Creator and Creation."

The movie reinforced a sense of nature's divine beauty. Said one participant in a Mennonite focus group, "I'd love to be in that world—its beauty, how everything is. I mean, I love our forests, and our forests aren't [even] quite as cool as with the fibre-optic plug-in." The next speaker continued the thought, "[The movie] made me appreciate the world we have because a lot of things are similar [on Pandora] but enhanced." Each focus group and nearly every participant made a complementary comment or non-verbally signalled agreement. One Mennonite participant's observation that the "oneness and connectedness impressed me most" was repeated by well over half the participants in the three groups. Pandora's interconnectedness was compared to that of Earth. It is easy to see interconnectivity on Pandora, but participants pervasively referred to Earth's ecology as being similar, if not so visually spectacular. They positioned humans as part of this inter-connectedness, with consequences, as represented by the comment of a Mennonite man: "To me it's sort of sad that people don't realize that… we have an effect with every breath we take or even every step.… And when Neytiri was telling Sully he was like an ignorant child and I can look back and see that in myself how ignorant I've been." He explained this intercon-nectiveness of all creation as one of the key resonances of the movie with his Christian faith. Such a close association of Creator and created hints at a strong form of immanence that contrasts with the more traditional streams of Christian transcendence; it may even represent a deepening of reverence for nature among Christians. In retrospect, it would have been productive to pursue the question of how this understanding of nature was operationalized in their everyday lives. Primarily, participants like this man linked it to what they saw as a duty to care for creation.

Participants repeatedly acknowledged that humans have degraded Earth. Members of each focus group felt the environmental message of *Avatar* was consistent with a Christian stance. The following exchange in the Pentecostal group paralleled exchanges in the other two groups. One person observed, "It [an environmental message] is underpinning the entire movie. Like what [another participant] said—it makes you aware how much of the earth has been destroyed in greedy gain. In a Christian perspective, God has given us the earth to take care of it, but we have not done a good job of it." This observation was followed by another person in the group: "We are stewards and we are not meant to waste what we have. God must look at us and be disappointed just as we are sometimes disap-pointed with our churches." After hearing the numerous expressions of the need for stewardship of Earth in her focus group, another of the Pen-tecostals responded with astonishment, "How can you *not* be an environ-mentalist and a Christian?" From this comment, it seems like a reasonable supposition that some form of environmental concern has become com-monplace in these Canadian Christian churches.

Culture
Participants observed that *Avatar* presents a critique of their society. They also recognized that *Avatar* presents particular cultural narratives and identifies some of these, including tropes about the moral superiority of

indigenous lifestyles (e.g., the noble savage or "Ecological Indian"), colonialism and the Great White Hero, and the beneficial use of violence. In the interests of brevity, we focus primarily on the latter.

The Mennonite focus groups criticized the movie for concluding with the colonial outsider who saves the day, but no one in the Pentecostal group mentioned this. In the context of extended discussions, various Mennonite participants made such comments as "[Sully] was kind of annoying—that he can be the great white guy that can do all" and "He's the traditional male who is going to come in from the outside and save the day." Both Mennonite groups included people who had participated with campaigns for justice for the Lubicon Cree native band in northern Alberta, and they drew parallels between *Avatar* and the historic colonization of Canada's indigenous peoples and its contemporary manifestations.[10] Aboriginal peoples were briefly mentioned in the Pentecostal group, but there was no further discussion of issues related to them.

Another cultural narrative referred to by participants of some of the groups was the myth of the superhero and its association with the use of violence to eradicate injustice—that is, the "myth of redemptive violence" (Lawrence and Jewett 2002; Wink, 1999). The interplay among participants in one of the Mennonite groups portrays the way this theme was perceived:

DP: I've heard parallels with the Gulf [British Petroleum's Deep Horizon oil spill in the Gulf of Mexico, April 2010]. All it's lacking is a big battle.
[DH then described theologian Walter Wink's perspective that "faith in the Western world is in the efficacy of violence.... We are 'saved' by violence."]
N: But the female protagonist was appalled by violence.
[Several participants then pointed out that Neytiri shot the military commander, and that Sully and the Na'vi people were saved by violence. This discussion continued back and forth among three members.]
DI: [The movie] perpetuates violence.
N: I had to turn away.
DI: I mean, there's the GI Joe effect and I resent that. It [the movie] perpetuates a thought process.

This "thought process" is part of a culture of violence. The other Mennonite group also had an extended discussion about how the movie's violence represented a dominant thought process in North American society. One participant was particularly vocal, arguing,

It's the typical myth of redemptive violence [other participants nodding here]. Jesus' message is so opposite, so this [movie, Sully] was like the Anti-Christ. I hear what you are all saying [about the creativity, magic, interconnectivity and other positive aspects of the film that other participants had described] but I just can't see that. That [violence] theme is so dominant in our culture. Hollywood depicts the problem as using power to get what you want and then using greater power to win the day. I was reminded of Clint Eastwood's—what's that movie?... *Unforgiven* [1993].... [In both movies] 95 per cent of it presented the use of power as a problem, then in the end they had to use power.

During the discussion that followed, another participant, who had been very positive about the movie, thoughtfully observed that the success of the movie showed that its narrative was deliberately constructed to connect with moviegoers. In the same group, another participant drew together the spiritual, ecological, and military themes, ending with, "the storyline is a direct result of the ways we live, even if it's sort of chastising." Similarly, in the other Mennonite focus group, a participant (DI) summarized, "The oneness and connectedness impressed me most. The GI Joe part probably sells [the movie] to others." According to him, the message of ecological interconnectedness would get heard by the general public only if it was embedded in the more culturally resonant narrative of heroic violence.

In contrast, there was little discussion of this theme in the Pentecostal group, although participants pointed out that the movie was a direct critique of American militarism, consumerism, and even imperialism. References were made to Afghanistan, Iraq, and the movie's use of the language of "shock and awe" and "fight terror with terror" as similar to that deployed by the Bush administration in the United States. Several times in this focus group, people referred to the movie as portraying the battle between good and evil, and they gave this battle Christian resonance: "When they came together to fight, from a biblical perspective it was like Gideon [a figure from Hebrew biblical history] and a few men who looked like so much more than they were but could not win against all of the power [their enemies] had. The final battle [in the movie] reminded me of this—it was impossible but they did it. When we trust in God things can happen beyond the natural." The closest that the Pentecostal group came to discussing the potential problem of redemptive violence was near the end, when another participant observed, "It is amazing—the whole deal of how you [we, the viewers] are betraying your own people—the movie got us to cheer for the non-humans. They [the moviemakers] created the empathy for killing the humans!" The main significance of this comment is that it was not responded to by others in the Pentecostal group, although the lateness of the night may have contributed to the lack of response. While the problematic of violence was recognized by individuals in each group, the Mennonite groups discussed the topic much more extensively. One particularly vehement Mennonite participant excoriated the creativity of the filmmakers that had been so thoroughly appreciated by others, asking, "You want to talk about creativity? How about some creativity in solutions?"

Environmental Problem-Solving
Moving from a general pro-environmental position to specific forms of action was difficult for members of all three groups. Although they had no trouble acknowledging the film's critique of cultural and environmental exploitation and chastising both the oil sands and the oil-driven and consumerist society in which they live, discerning what to do with such a critique was difficult for participants.

A Pentecostal participant commented, "I don't think anyone stands up and says 'Yeah for tar sands.' But, at the end of the day we like to buy our cars. We like our SUVs. I love my SUV and it never even goes off-road." Another in the same group insisted, "To some degree we're stuck. If you want to get out of it you are living a counter-culture life. In all respects, you can't drive to Calgary. You can't fly to Ontario to see your family.... We're stuck in the system, and we like the system, even though we hate what it does to the earth." Similar comments were voiced by people who had found the movie's ecological holism so appealing. However, in all three focus group, criticisms of the oil sands or general environmental destruction were met with rejoinders indicating that the critic was being inconsistent for maintaining both a critique and an automobile.

The question of the oil sands, despite their obvious destructiveness, was even more difficult to resolve, although participants compared the film to this issue. The Pentecostal group had a particularly thorough discussion of the oil sands. One of these participants had recently participated in an aerial tour of the oil sands and described the visible destruction there. "Most of those on the flight were environmental folks and their perspective was great, great horror. When you fly over the things, it is incredible." He later described the larger tailings ponds as "the absolute rape of the Earth." The group recounted what they knew of problems in the environment and social fabric of local communities, although without mentioning Aboriginal peoples. When one participant ended by saying, "I think we are so accustomed to getting things cheap that we just want cheap gas and that is our expectation—so of course we keep driving these industries," the group moved to a discussion of their own lifestyles as built on convenience, comfort, ready goods, and automobiles for easy travel.

While the Pentecostal group positioned the conflict in *Avatar* as one of good versus evil, this dichotomous framing did not fit the oil sands and their lives, nor did the *Avatar* solution. As one summarized: "We do care about the environment. But we can only do what we can do. We can't stop it [oil sands degradation]. What difference could we make? Could we form our army to fight that? Like the movie—there is that helplessness feeling. We don't want our earth to crumble, but with the big item issues can we really do something? It is hard to say 'Yes, you can.'" Similarly, other participants made a connection between the movie and Alberta but expressed the ambiguity of "real life." "The film is stacked against resource extraction. But our ethical issues are harder. Our ambulances run on oil, and our homes are heated," said one Mennonite participant.

When asked for alternatives to the climactic battle with which the movie culminates, the focus groups struggled. "The entire movie is set up to come to this conclusion," complained one participant in a Mennonite group. The other Mennonite group did discuss possible alternatives, such as Eywa sending out an electromagnetic pulse that would disable machinery (a possibility consistent with the laws of Pandoran nature and the film's plot). The group also brought up the classic H. G. Wells novel *War of the Worlds*, in which the bacterium from the common cold infected and eliminated the alien invaders. "This is a different way for the ecology to 'fight,'" said one participant, contrasting it to the aggressive and self-aware response of Pandora's creatures. In a variety of ways, the film left focus group participants with few resources to engage in environmental problem-solving.

So, if participants rejected the idea that the violent solutions arrived at in *Avatar* could be applied to the social and environmental damage associated with the oil sands, what is left? Many of the participants in the study were captivated by the autobiographical journey of the main character, as represented in this comment during a Mennonite focus group discussion: "I was interested in how the main character, Jake Sully, changes through the course of the movie. I would like to find out more about how that could happen." In fact, this participant was so captivated by the drama around this character that he did not notice societal complexities that the other participants elaborated: "I was so focused on what Jake's experience was out of it, that of the one person's transformational experience, that I was not able to take away some of these other takes such as the environmental, business, and military themes. Then I heard all these environmental messages and questions—how you make broad change—that's daunting. I felt it was more about how we change as an individual and not how we change society." For other participants as well, this personal transformation was the important message of the movie. Carrying it into their personal lives, some noted that they recycled or tried to engage in various pro-environmental behaviours. Others pointed out, however, that Sully starts out as part of the military culture, and they questioned the extent of his transformation. Participants saw the movie as Sully's personal journey but disagreed on the extent to which individual change is the movie's core application for environmental problems: perhaps it is merely a hook for some of the larger themes of environment and exploitation.

Avatar as Resource in the Alberta Context

These focus groups demonstrated how some Canadian Christians in the oil-producing province of Alberta are drawing on themes in *Avatar* and making connections with their local context. These Albertan Christians have an affinity with notions of ecological interconnectivity but feel ambivalence because of the difficulties of sustaining congruence with corresponding environmental values. Yet it seems clear that, at least for these self-selected group participants, nature is important morally and experientially and entwines with their religious beliefs. They had little difficulty drawing their own faith-oriented interpretations from *Avatar* about ecological holism and a responsibility to care for creation. In general, they saw parallels between the environmental degradation on Pandora and oil sands extraction in northern Alberta. Yet they recognized their immersion in a petroleum-fuelled economic boom and had difficulty imagining alternatives. While appreciative of the movie, participants saw *Avatar* as simplistic—its storyline, spirituality, and political-economic solutions too simple for the complexities of contemporary society.

The common cultural understanding of Alberta is that of a province with an economy dependent upon the oil and gas sector; the "common sense" aspect of Albertan identity is one intimately connected with energy production (Takach 2010). This is reinforced by a provincial government heavily invested in the oil sands, devoting extensive money and bureaucratic power to attracting corporate investment and staunchly defending and promoting the industry (Davidson and Gismondi 2011; Gailus 2012; Nikiforuk 2008).

Institutional religious actors have recently begun to weigh in on the oil sands issue. In 2009, Roman Catholic Bishop Luc Bouchard (2009), whose northeastern Alberta diocese includes the oil sands, wrote a public pastoral letter describing the oil sands projects. In his summation, he wrote, "Any one of the above destructive effects provokes moral concern, but it is when the damaging effects are all added together that the moral legitimacy of oil sands production is challenged." At a Catholic social justice conference in February 2010, Bishop Bouchard recounted the predominant response to his letter as "Tell Bishop Bouchard I will stay out of his God business if he will stay out of the oil sands business" (Warnica 2010). This sort of response reflects the strong cultural conviction that religious beliefs should be separate from such issues.

Some Alberta trucks carry bumper stickers that read "I Am Alberta Oil"—with the first two words highlighted in red, subtly identifying with the divine "I Am" of Judeo-Christian scriptures. Bob McKeon (2010) rejoindered, however, that from his own Christian perspective, this is an idolatrous statement. To such Christian activists, human identity and purpose should be grounded in a theology rooted outside the prevailing socio-political culture (Hiemstra 2009). Religious communities have sometimes provided such "autonomous spaces" to raise moral concerns and duties within a framework that does not simply accept cultural narratives authorizing the exploitation of resources or supporting the idea of redemptive violence (Billings 1990). Some questioning of the cultural hegemony of oil in Alberta was evident in the focus group participants.[11] The oil sands are increasingly developing into a more contentious issue as Albertans such as these focus group participants begin to struggle with the ethical issues it raises. At the same time, since the socio-structural issues of a petroleum-based society seem so large, these Alberta citizens remained uncertain about how to live in a way that is consistent with their felt desires within the conditions of this society.

Sully's journey of transformation—a "crossing" (Tweed 2006) from human disconnection and exploitation to Na'vi holism—is presented by Avatar as one narrative for environmental change. These Christian viewers welcomed that narrative, while questioning other themes they perceived in Avatar, including its apparent embrace of violence. In this way, the movie required of its protagonist, and of these viewers, a sort of reflexivity—the ability to think back upon themselves relative to the social circumstances in which they are embedded (Adams 2006; Archer 2007; Ferber 2006). They cannot literally cross, as did Sully, so viewers have to become reflexive about their own socio-cultural and environmental predicaments. Reflexivity could be a counterforce to habituated participation in the treadmill of environmental destruction, but both self-reflexivity (personal lifestyle analysis) and cultural reflexivity (political-economic and socio-cultural analysis) are required.

Our experience with the focus groups indicates that Avatar is part of a growing "culture of enchantment" (Gibson 2009). Although this culture does not appear to have the characteristics of what Taylor (2010) calls "dark green religion," which holds nature itself as sacred and worthy of reverential care, participants' valuation of the ecological interconnectivity of *Avatar* went beyond a sense of religious obligation. Movies like *Avatar* may provoke reflection by viewers, but they are ultimately products of their culture, too. As Christians in Alberta navigate the complex terrain between faith commitments and social, political, economic and cultural milieux, *Avatar* becomes one more tool in the process. Their reflections on the movie highlight the difficulty of discerning effective solutions for the environmental problems of our world while still embedded in the contrary sensibilities of an exploitive cultural milieu.

Notes

1 Nikiforuk (2008) provides the most accessible account of the oil sands history, production processes, relation to provincial political and economic systems, and environmental and social impacts.

2 From 2010 to 2012, an industry-sponsored website, http://www.albertaisenergy.ca, was active and linked to by numerous government and corporation actors in the province. Television and radio ads were prominent and posted on YouTube. The website has been discontinued and the URL now reverts to the Canadian Association of Petroleum Producers (CAPP) website. As of February 2013, some campaign materials can be found on the corresponding Facebook site.

3 The original website (http://www.avatarsands.org) was active until late summer 2010. The ad can be found by searching Google images for "AvaTar Sands," and at http://www.capp.ca/avatar and http://dirtyoilsands.org/files/AVATARSANDS_ Variety_Final_PRINT.pdf. Several versions of the videos can be found on YouTube with the same search term.

4 For news clippings and videos, see http://dirtyoilsands.org/dirtyspots/category/ avatarsands.

5 See Bron Taylor's extensive discussion on *Avatar*, including this spiritual dimension, at http://www.brontaylor.com/environmental_books/dgr/avatar_nature_ religion.html.

6 Both terms are used but by different actors, resulting in a discursive war of positioning. "Oil sands" has become more widely used. Although governments used "tar sands" in the past, that label has now been cast as a pejorative only used by "radical environmentalists."

7 Each focus group began with an explanation of the research as required by the university's Research Ethics Committee. The preamble assured participants that what we sought was an open discussion and that we were interested in their own thoughts and were not looking for any particular results. Interaction among participants, such as disagreeing or asking probing questions of other participants, provide some confidence in the validity of the process and their discussions. The following questions were used to guide the discussions if necessary, although in most cases, the focus groups had already broached the topic before we specifically asked about it:

   1. What was significant about *Avatar* for you? What did you like or think about the movie?

   2. What parts of the movie resonated with your Christian faith?

3. What parts of the movie do you find a problem in terms of your Christian faith?
4. How do you feel about the changes in Jake Sully's perspectives and allegiances in the movie?
5. To what extent do you think there's an environmental message in the movie? Do you agree or disagree with this message?
6. How do you perceive the movie as an environmental story for Alberta?

8 As Ivakhiv (2007) points out, these three categories are "folk constructs," and what is meant by "culture" is particularly unclear.

9 The largest Pentecostal denomination, the Assembly of God, was once a "peace church" with conscientious objection and non-violence as official church positions until 1967 (Alexander 2009).

10 See Ominayak and Thomas (2009) for a full discussion of the historic and present injustices faced by the Lubicon Cree. An ecumenical coalition of Canadian churches known as the Aboriginal Rights Coalition eventually folded into a multidimensional ecumenical justice coalition of ten church denominations known as Kairos (http://www.kairoscanada.org), and Friends of the Lubicon was among the most active non-governmental solidarity organizations.

11 The word *hegemony* is used here in a Gramscian manner, as structures of thought and practice wherein the populace consents to the status quo (ergo, loose regulation and increasingly destructive extraction). Manufacture of hegemony is a cultural process (Crehan 2002); in Alberta, it is intimately linked to the production of Albertans' identity as energy producers, the government's defence of oil sands production, and elites espousing that there are no alternatives for economic prosperity in the province (Adkin et al. 2008; Davidson & Gismondi 2011).

References

Adams, Matthew. 2006. "Hybridizing Habitus and Reflexivity: Towards an Understanding of Contemporary Identity?" *Sociology* 40(3): 511–28.

Adkin, Laurie, Byron Miller, Naomi Krogman, and Randolph Haluza-DeLay. 2008. *Political Ecology and Governance in Alberta.* Workshop funded by the Social Science and Humanities Research Council of Canada, University of Alberta, Edmonton, Alberta.

Alexander, Paul. 2009. *Peace to War: Shifting Allegiances in the Assemblies of God.* Telford, PA: Cascadia.

Archer, Margaret S. 2007. *Making Our Way through the World: Human Reflexivity and Social Mobility.* New York: Cambridge University Press.

Bennett, Dean. 2010. "Alberta Hopes James Cameron's Oil Sands Comments Won't Open a Pandora's Box." Canadian Press/*MSN Entertainment*, 21 April. http://entertainment.ca.msn.com/movies/canadian-press/article.aspx?cp-documentid=23971008.

Billings, Dwight B. 1990. "Religion as Opposition: A Gramscian Analysis." *American Journal of Sociology* 96(1): 1–31.

Bouchard, Bishop Luc. January 2009. "A Pastoral Letter on the Integrity of Creation and the Athabasca Oil Sands." http://www.dioceseofstpaul.ca/index.php?option=com_docman&task=doc_download&gid=14&Itemid=5&lang=en.

CAPP. 2010. "Canadian Oil Is Responsible Energy." *Canadian Association of Petroleum Producers.* http://www.capp.ca/aboutUs/mediaCentre/NewsReleases/Pages/Avatar.aspx.

Charmaz, Kathy. 2005. "Grounded Theory in the Twenty-First Century: Applications for Advancing Social Justice Studies." In *Handbook of Qualitative Research*, 3rd ed., edited by Norman K. Denzin and Yvonne S. Lincoln, 507–35. Thousand Oaks, CA: Sage.

Crehan, Kate A. F. 2002. *Gramsci, Culture and Anthropology.* Berkeley: University of California Press.

Creswell, John W. 1998. *Qualitative Inquiry and Research Design: Choosing among Five Traditions.* Thousand Oaks, CA: Sage.

Davidson, Debra J., and Mike Gismondi. 2011. *Challenging Legitimacy at the Precipice of Energy Calamity.* Berlin: Springer.

Ferber, Michael P. 2006. "Critical Realism and Religion: Objectivity and the Insider/Outsider Problem." *Annals of the Association of American Geographers* 96(1): 176–81.

Gailus, Jeff. 2012. *Little Black Lies: Corporate and Political Spin in the Global War for Oil.* Calgary: Rocky Mountain Books.

Gellert, Paul K., and Jon Shefner. 2009. "People, Place, and Time: How Structural Fieldwork Helps World-Systems Analysis." *Journal of World-Systems Research* 15(2): 193–218.

Gibson, James William. 2009. *A Reenchanted World: The Quest for a New Kinship with Nature.* New York: Metropolitan Books.

Haluza-DeLay, Randolph. 2012. "Giving Consent in the Petrostate: Hegemony and Alberta Oil Sands." *Journal for Activist Science and Technology Education* 4(1): 1–6. http://www.wepaste.org/jaste4.1.html.

Haluza-DeLay, Randolph, and Angela Carter. Forthcoming. "Scaling Up: Strategies and Opportunities in Opposing the Oil Sands Status Quo." In *Political Ecology and Governance in Alberta*, vol. 1, edited by Laurie Adkin, Byron Miller, and Naomi Krogman. Toronto: University of Toronto Press.

Hiemstra, John L. 2009. "Canada's Oil Sands Developments as Icon of Globalization." In *Globalization and the Gospel: Probing the Religious Foundations of Globalization*, edited by Michael W. Goheen and Erin Glanville, 179–98. Vancouver: Regent Press.

Ivakhiv, Adrian. 2007. "Religion, Nature and Culture: Theorizing the Field." *Journal for the Study of Religion, Nature, and Culture* 1(1): 47–57.

Kowalsky, Nathan, and Randolph Haluza-DeLay. 2013. "Homo Energeticus: An Ellulian Analysis of the Alberta Tar Sands." In *Jacques Ellul and the Technological Society in the Twenty-First Century*, edited by Helena Mateus Jeronimo, Jose Luis Garcia, and Carl Mitcham. Berlin: Springer.

Lawrence, John Shelton, and Robert Jewett. 2002. *The Myth of the American Superhero.* Grand Rapids, MI: William B. Eerdmans.

Mittelstaedt, Martin. 2010. "Environmentalists Back Avatar for Oscar." *The Globe and Mail*, 4 March. http://www.theglobeandmail.com/arts/awards-and-festivals/environmentalists-back-avatar-for-oscar/article1209178.

McKeon, Bob. 2010. "Base Energy Policy on Christian Values." *Western Catholic Reporter*, 24 May.

Nikiforuk, Andrew. 2008. *Tar Sands: Dirty Oil and the Future of a Continent.* Vancouver: Greystone Books.

Ominayak, Bernard, and Kevin Thomas. 2009. "These Are Lubicon Lands: A First Nation Forced to Step into the Regulatory Gap." In *Speaking for Ourselves: Environmental Justice in Canada*, edited by Julian Agyeman, Peter Cole, Randolph Haluza-DeLay, and Pat O'Riley, 111–22. Vancouver: University of British Columbia Press.

Takach, Geo. 2010. *Will the Real Alberta Please Stand Up?* Edmonton: University of Alberta Press.

Taylor, Bron. 2010. *Dark Green Religion: Nature Spirituality and the Planetary Future.* Berkeley: University of California Press.

Tweed, Thomas. *Crossings and Dwellings: A Theory of Religion.* Cambridge, MA: Harvard University Press.

Warnica, Richard. 2010. "Bishop Assesses Fallout from Letter," *Edmonton Journal*, 28 February.

Wink, Walter. 1999. *The Powers That Be.* New York: Doubleday.

PART III: CRITICAL, EMOTIONAL
& SPIRITUAL REFLECTIONS

Becoming the "Noble Savage":
Nature Religion and the "Other" in *Avatar*

CHRIS KLASSEN

James Cameron's *Avatar* is a visual playground with awe-inspiring special effects that foreground a wondrous expanse of constructed "nature." As a film dealing with the increasingly popular theme of the preservation and romanticization of nature, Cameron and his team appear to have drawn heavily on an ecofeminist vision of what Bron Taylor (2010) calls "dark green religion." Many viewers have been inspired by Cameron's offering. The multiple responses that viewers have had to this blockbuster film points to the multiple readings available (see Istoft 2010). Drawing on Stuart Hall (1993), I perceive the meaning of *any* cultural product as unfixed, even if a given producer encodes a preferred meaning into the production. In the case of *Avatar*, the preferred meaning seems to point to environmental awareness. I am not interested, however, in that preferred meaning. I am struck, instead, by a reading of *Avatar* that highlights a thinly veiled misogynistic plot tied to a romanticization of indigeneity underlying the seemingly feminist ambience. This is not the only possible reading of *Avatar*, but it is one that suggests scholars and fans should consider some of the less appealing implications of this film.

Avatar is the story of a disabled Marine, Jake Sully, who serves as a go-between for the human paramilitary force to negotiate colonization with the indigenous people of Pandora, the Na'vi. As he engages with them, in an avatar body designed to look Na'vi, he becomes enamoured of their holistic worldview. Eventually, he leads the Na'vi in fighting off the human colonists, and he rejects his crippled body for permanent embodiment in his Na'vi avatar form. Although we are presented with a number of strong female characters who are champions for the divinely feminine natural world—specifically Dr. Grace Augustine, the scientist trying to learn about the Na'vi and Pandora; Trudy Chacon, the military pilot who defects with Sully; and Neytiri, the daughter of the Na'vi chief and shaman—the only one allowed to survive is the alien "Other," Neytiri, the constructed female who represents the dynamics of a nature-goddess–worshipping, tribal people who are themselves represented as ecologically noble savages embodying primitive ecological wisdom and who live on a moon named for the bringer of all evil in the form of a woman: Pandora.[1] I argue that *Avatar*, while possibly providing a vision of ecologically and spiritual survival against the machine of capitalism, reinforces the dominant ideologies of patriarchal and capitalist hegemony, not the least of which is the dominant ideology of the (white) masculine hero who supersedes his indigenous teachers to become the saviour of nature and a threatened way of life. I begin by showing the ways in which the film seems to play into a cultural ecofeminist vision of nature religion, tying together the interconnections of all living entities in the body of the goddess with an appeal to what Kay Milton calls "the myth of primitive ecological wisdom" (1996). I then address such questions as, Who is the ecological noble savage, and how is this image constructed and co-opted? *Avatar* allows viewers to simultaneously identify with this Other while recasting it in hegemonic forms of (white) masculinity. I end with some suggestions for an oppositional and cautionary reading of the gendered and (post-)colonial dynamics found within the story: namely, the sacrifices of an indigenous worldview of harmony and, more critically, the sacrifices of the human women and Na'vi male leaders, which are needed to allow Sully to become the heroic Other.

"Who's This Eywa?": Ecofeminist Nature Religion

Bron Taylor introduced the concept of "dark green religion" in his 2010 book by that name. Dark green religion is characterized by "a deep sense of belonging to and connectedness in nature, while perceiving the earth and its living systems to be sacred and interconnected" (13). While dark green religion is manifested in many varieties, including both naturalist and supernaturalist renditions, contemporary Paganism (or Neopaganism) could be seen to represent its general worldview (see Taylor 2010, 224). Contemporary Paganism itself is multifaceted and polyvocal. Even so, the dominant forms of Paganism in North America today (including Wicca, feminist Witchcraft and Druidry) are heavily influenced by a particular form of ecofeminist ideology.[2]

Ecofeminism involves the integration of environmentalism and feminist theory. Its primary premise is that the way dominant society sees and treats the natural world is similar and related to the way it sees and treats women and any other marginalized group (racial, ethnic, economic, etc.). That said, it is important to remember that ecofeminism involves myriad approaches. Some ecofeminists see the relationship between nature and women as discursive, constituted by social practices and patriarchal attempts to control the material world represented as feminine. Others see a more inherent connection between women and nature, a connection that is largely due to the reproductive role women play, bearing the physical body of new human life. This latter approach fits within the purview of cultural feminism, which typically maintains a strict distinction between male/masculine and female/feminine. *Avatar* transmits echoes of specifically cultural feminist approaches to ecofeminism, approaches that appeal to many contemporary Pagans. "Ecofeminist theory," writes Heather Eaton (2005, 29) of these cultural approaches, "envisions alternative philosophical and social conceptual frameworks based on benign human and human–earth relations, rather than on mutually supporting systems of domination." In other words, cultural ecofeminists see the connection between women, or the feminine, and nature as naturally formed rather than, as other ecofeminists would argue, as a result of patriarchal hierarchic systems of power associating nature (or matter), the body, and the feminine as weak and inferior to spirit, the mind and the masculine.

Some proponents of cultural ecofeminist envisioning are particularly concerned with spirituality and a resacralizing of nature and the feminine. As Val Plumwood (1992, 10) suggests, "Cultural ecofeminism aims to remedy ecological and other problems mainly through the creation of an alternative 'women's culture' (the 'authentic female mind' in the words of Charlene Spretnak) based on revaluing, celebrating and defending what patriarchy has devalued, including the feminine, non-human nature, the body and the emotions." These cultural ecofeminists tend to present imagery of Earth as the body of the goddess and the relationship between all living beings as a spiritual as well as a physical relationship. They are often involved in the reconstruction of ancient Pagan worldviews for the modern era (although not all contemporary Pagans can be classified as cultural ecofeminists). Echoes of this position are found in *Avatar* in the presentation of the mother goddess, Eywa, and of the relationship between all living creatures on Pandora.

Susan Griffin, as a poetic voice of this cultural ecofeminism, speaks of Earth as "my sister." This relationship is one of connection and familiarity. Griffin (1989, 103) writes: "She is as delicate as I am; I know her sentience;

I feel her pain and my own pain comes into me, and my own pain grows large and I grasp this pain with my hands, and I open my mouth to this pain, I taste, I know, and I know why she goes on, under great weight, with this great thirst, in drought, in starvation, with intelligence in every act does she survive disaster." This affective placement of the natural world in relation with the self is one of the resounding themes echoing through *Avatar*. The main protagonist, Sully, comes to understand the indigenous Na'vi's, and ultimately his own, relationship with Pandora in similar ways. Pandora is alive and the Na'vi are a part of that livingness, not separated in either imagination or biology, as the humans believe themselves to be. *Avatar* could be viewed, then, as a visionary solution to the ecological problems on "real-life" Earth, as articulated by cultural ecofeminists. Carol P. Christ (1989, 314), for example, argues that "the preservation of the earth requires a profound shift in consciousness: a recovery of more ancient and traditional views that revere the connection of all beings in the web of life and a rethinking of the relation of humanity and divinity to nature." The process of envisioning alternatives is central to ecofeminism, particularly in cultural approaches to ecofeminism. As Rosemary Radford Ruether declared in 1991, "[Ecofeminism] needs visionaries to image how to construct a new socioeconomic system and a new cultural conscious-ness that would support relations of mutuality rather than competitive power. For this one needs poets, artists and liturgists, as well as revolution-ary organizers, to incarnate more life-giving relationships in our cultural consciousness and social system" (quoted in Eaton 2005, 35). Could *Avatar* be an answer to this call?

Cameron envisions a spiritual world in which the highest, most sacred force is the Mother Goddess, Eywa, who is the integration of all energies on Pandora. This vision is tied to a representation of a pre-colonized and pristine Pandora, which is characterized by a mutual relationship between Na'vi, animals, vegetation, and the energies shared between them all. Cameron infuses these relationships with scientifically "provable" char-acteristics, as measured by the scientist, Augustine, allowing the viewer to take up the vision as plausible. He also positions these relationships in opposition to a capitalist, militarized world, a scenario that, once again, follows an ecofeminist pathway. Noël Sturgeon suggests that one of the places in which ecofeminism originally developed was in the anti-mili-tarist movement of the late 1970s and 1980s. Thus, for her, ecofeminism "develops its multivalent politics from that movement's analysis of the connections between militarism, racism, classism, sexism, speciesism, and environmental destruction" (Sturgeon 1997, 23–24). This connection can be seen clearly in the writing and political action of some ecofeminist

Pagans—such as Starhawk—who work against a worldview in which militarism backs corporate capitalism to limit access to natural resources to those with political and social power over the majority of people. Starhawk (1990, 74) draws an explicit connection between "earth-based spirituality," or what might be called "nature religion," and ecofeminism: "When we start to understand that the Earth is alive, she calls us to act to preserve her life. When we understand that everything is interconnected, we are called to a politics and set of actions that come from compassion, from the ability to literally feel *with* all living beings on the Earth. That feeling is the ground upon which we can build community and come together and take action and find direction." Starhawk calls that living Earth "Goddess" and, by doing so, contributes to the construction of an immanentist theology, which Cameron's mythology in *Avatar* seems to replicate.

Avatar gives us a world in which nature is sacred, "where a tribal clan, the Na'vi, worships the connections among all living things" (Denby 2010). It would seem, on the surface, that Cameron, in his construction of the world of Pandora, is one of the visionary artists whom Ruether (1991) lauds. However, a closer look at the characterizations and narrative shows another cultural and political trajectory under the surface. We hear echoes of ecofeminist and Pagan concerns, but in forms that would concern many critics of cultural ecofeminism.

One of the concerns commonly articulated about cultural ecofeminism is that it reinforces naturalized gendered dualisms. As Carolyn Merchant (1990, 102) writes, "In emphasizing the female, body, and nature components of the dualities male/female, mind/body, and culture/nature, radical [cultural] ecofeminism runs the risk of perpetuating the very hierarchies it seeks to overthrow." The construction of a nature-based, goddess-worshipping society that honours women can be perceived as a reification, in reverse, of the dualisms. Catriona Sandilands (1999, 16) suggests that "the emergence of nature as female (seen in terms such as Mother Earth, virgin forests, the rape of the wild) is understood [by cultural ecofeminists] to originate in the repudiation of woman; the construction of male separation from nature is justified in terms of nature's apparently feminine attributes." In reclaiming value for the feminine/female, many cultural ecofeminists continue the association of the feminine/female with nature in a way that reverses the prior devaluation of the two. Nature is still conflated into the feminine or femaleness. In cultural ecofeminist discourse, nature includes the body and women are still associated with bodily functions. Nature, in the human body and beyond, is feminine and good. Culture—particularly mechanistic, technological, and militaristic culture heavily influenced by reason—is masculine and morally suspect.

In *Avatar*, the reification of nature disallows most usages of "culture," represented as overwhelmingly oppressive, as a means for addressing the problems at hand. Even the use of modern military skills by the transformed Sully in defence of the Na'vi has only limited value, although the film incorporates little direct critique of these limitations. (This is a thread I will pick up again later.) As a society living in connection with the natural world envisioned as a goddess, the Na'vi are associated with the female and the body by virtue of their placement and embrace of nature. It is significant that they use minimal clothing to cover their bodies; clothing is a product of culture and, in moderate climates, a way to hide the body. However, the hero of the story does not originate in this "natural" setting. He is a high-tech military man who is defined by his mind rather than his disabled body, which he eventually discards. Not only is this a problematic representation of the disabled body as being without value, but in discarding this "flawed" male human body, Sully chooses to become the Other: the more natural and, by association, feminine/feminized Na'vi body. This could be construed as an ecofeminist move. He does not, however, consciously blur the boundaries between the dualisms of nature/culture or masculine/feminine, showing them to be constructions. Rather, he recasts the Other into a stronger, physically able version of himself. He transforms this new Na'vi body into a masculine hero by drawing on human military skills that are anathema to cultural ecofeminism, appropriating the desirable elements of the feminine, such as connection with nature, into his reinforced maleness. Sully becomes the Other, but it is an Other constructed in his own image.

"This Is Our Land": Becoming the Other

As I have argued elsewhere (Klassen 2008), the feminizing of nature, particularly in a form of holism based on an immanent (Earth-based) goddess, tends to be heavily invested in "the myth of primitive ecological wisdom" (Milton 1996). This perspective is tied closely to tropes of the noble savage and what Shepard Krech III (1999) has termed the "ecological Indian." *Avatar* continues the narrative of becoming the Other, the "noble ecological savage," in a way that prioritizes white, or colonial, agency over that of indigenous peoples.

In becoming the Other, Sully goes through a process of self-othering not unlike that described by Nicholas A. Germana in reference to eighteenth- and nineteenth-century German Orientalism. As Germana (2010, 81) describes it, "Self-Othering...was a curious rhetorical strategy which involved *two* distinct forms or acts of Othering—imaginative constructions of the oriental Other with whom one could identify and the western imperial Other, against whom one was seeking to construct an identity." German Romantic thinkers identified themselves with the victims of British and French imperialism—particularly in India—and, in doing so, showed themselves to be superior to these European Others. However, Germana is clear that the German construction of the Oriental was nonetheless imaginary, as all Orientalist constructions of the time were. In much the same way, we can see the construction of the indigenous Other in *Avatar* as a foil against which the "imperialism" of capitalist America can be contrasted. In becoming Na'vi, the characterization of Sully says less about what it might mean to be indigenous than about what it could mean to be the "right kind" of Euro-American and, as I will show shortly, the "right kind" of white male in an ecologically sensitive era.

The idea of becoming the Other, and particularly of the white American/Westerner becoming the indigenous Other, is not a new phenomenon in dominant Western cultural discourse. There are myriad examples of whites "playing" Indians that reinforce the cultural acceptance of the choices that Sully makes in this most recent version. A notable parallel story can be found in the 1990 MGM film *Dances with Wolves*, wherein the protagonist, played by Kevin Costner, is a US military man who comes to know and defend an Indian tribe threatened by the expansion of white colonial society after the Civil War. Another good example of this trope is the historical figure of Grey Owl (the British Archibald Belaney) who "played" Indian at a legendary level in early-twentieth-century Canada (eventually, himself, being appropriated for the Hollywood spectator and immortalized in the visage of Pierce Brosnan in the 1999 film *Grey Owl*, directed by Richard Attenborough). Grey Owl can be connected with *Avatar* beyond the simple taking on of the indigenous role. For Grey Owl, it seems, playing Indian was a necessary part of loving nature. So, too, with Sully. He *must* take on the persona and, eventually, the permanent body of a Na'vi to show a true connection with the natural world. Alaster Bonnett (2006, 323) points out that "Grey Owl was probably right to imagine that he would not get far as an authentic 'Indian,' and *that his ecological message would not be taken seriously*, if he did not 'look the part'" (my emphasis). The ecological message is one that is increasingly part of the American common tongue. As Americans see themselves as more and more ecologically aware and part of the solution to environmental problems, there is a strong impetus to connect to an American image of ecological sustainability: the American Indian.

Rayna Green (1988, 48) persuasively argues that the figure of the noble savage—and, tied to that figure, the act of "playing" Indian—is an essential part of American identity and culture: "In playing Indian, certainly

Anglo-American players are connecting to the America that existed before European invasion; they are connecting to the very beginnings of the mythological structure called America." However, this playing requires the death of real Indians. Americans who idealize their version of the "authentic" Indian are "disappointed in the truth of what happens and continues to happen to Indians in America," so "they reconstruct the Indian presence in an acceptable version," with themselves in the role of Indian. "Indians are in effect loved to death through playing Indian, while despised when they want to act out their real traditional roles on the American landscape," writes Green, referencing the massacre at Wounded Knee as one example (50). In *Avatar*, the story of conquest and colonialism is recast as one of triumph over the heartless grasp for commodities: what could have been, or should have been, if indigenous peoples only had the right kind of leader and the right kind of motivation. Their actual leaders, however, cannot supply this leadership and motivation. The Na'vi chief, Eytukan, is killed in the attack on the Hometree. His successor, Tsu'tey, is also subsequently killed by the human military force. Neither can take on the necessary role of leading the Na'vi people into victory. The one who can supply this leadership is, in fact, a product of that very heartless economy, and the triumph comes in the form of military might of a more "natural" kind—the animals themselves become soldiers at the request of this white man to Pandora's goddess. Eywa hears Sully's prayer and provides the animal reinforcement troops to vouchsafe the Na'vi victory. As Green (1988, 49) points out about earlier versions of this play acting, "What could not be converted to a sterilized and non-specific American iconography from a very distinctly Indian one...had to be converted, by non-Indians, to one in which non-Indians played the Indian role, and thus could control the meaning." *Avatar* takes this play acting to a new level by allowing a white male to actually inhabit an indigenous body.

The indigenous body that Sully inhabits is, as an *indigenous* body, also an ecological body. The indigenous Other is an ecological Other. In 1991, Kent Redford brought the concept of the ecologically noble savage into environmental conservation discourse. This notion, itself an echo of the earlier romantic vision of the noble savage, places indigenous peoples in a relationship with nature that is marked by simplicity and a static positioning outside of history. Redford writes, "Despite evidence to the contrary, indigenous people continue to be credited with natural respect for ecology and a commitment to sustainable methods of resource use under all conditions." An even more extensive explanation and examination of the ecologically noble savage trope, or what Shepard Krech III (1999) calls the "Ecological Indian," was later developed by Douglas Buege (1996), Sandy Marie Anglás

Grande (1999), and Krech himself (1999). The characterization of the Na'vi in *Avatar* can be seen as another example of this Ecological Indian.

The myth of the ecologically noble savage, argues Buege (1996, 72), is invoked in a variety of popular and academic sources "by Euro-Americans who desire something from native peoples." What is it that is desired? Since this myth represents indigenous peoples as "ecologically responsible role models" (73), they presumably provide a source of wisdom and inspiration for those concerned with the ecological destruction to which modern Western society has contributed. Buege states, "Ecologically noble people have either rejected Western society or they have yet to experience the fruits of global capitalism, retaining their traditional culture. They have a deep concern for their environment and will do *anything* to protect it from harm. In short, these people live in harmony with the natural cycles and the animals and plants in their surroundings" (75). Buege provides an example of this trope within literature: Tolkien's Woses from *The Lord of the Rings*, who are "archaic, yet noble 'creatures' who live isolated from the more 'modern' peoples of Middle-earth" (74). The Na'vi are another example. The conflict around which *Avatar* centres is the very conflict of modern, global capitalism cast as culture against a more simple life lived "in harmony with the natural cycles." However, not only are the Na'vi living in harmony with nature, but they, like Tolkien's Woses, represent a "lost way of life" (75). When Sully petitions the goddess Eywa for help, he recounts the troubles of Earth, couched in the metaphors of cultural ecofeminism. "They killed their Mother," he says. Once Earth was green and now it is lost. The existence of the Na'vi on Pandora provides a hope, as Buege said of the Woses, "that such lifestyles may continue to exist" (75). Furthermore, this scene reinforces what Krech (1999, 22) sees as essential to the Ecological Indian trope: "Habitually coupled with its opposite, the Nonecological White Man, the Ecological Indian proclaims both that the American Indian is a nonpolluting ecologist, conservationist, and environmentalist, and that the white man is not." This trope is played out in the contrast between the militarized colonial humans and the Na'vi, and it can be seen in Sully's assessment of the Na'vi as not being willing to give up their Hometree for "light beer and jeans."

The popularity of *Avatar* suggests that the message of "primitive ecological wisdom" is one that many viewers are eager to hear. However, Buege takes this image and parses out some consequences. The distinction we see in the myth of the ecologically noble savage between indigenous peoples and modern capitalism—in our case, between the Na'vi and the humans—creates "an ideological distance between ourselves and native peoples" (1997, 76).[3] This distance serves to limit the acceptance of indigenous peoples into contemporary modern life, and "assists us in disregarding current political issues involving distanced 'Others'" (ibid.). While the Na'vi do not represent any actual indigenous human people, the trope fits within common assumptions of indigeneity. In fact, Cameron himself identified a connection in his own imagination between the Na'vi and a tribe of indigenous peoples of Brazil, the Xikrin-Kayapo, who have been trying to block construction of a hydroelectric plant on the Xingu River that could destroy their traditional hunting grounds (Adams 2010). Slavoj Žižek (2010) cautions us to be wary of Cameron's "superficial Hollywood Marxism," which, Žižek says, "concerns a young rich person in crisis who gets his (or her) vitality restored through brief intimate contact with the full-blooded life of the poor." Although I am discussing a fictional construction, the multiple implications for real indigenous communities and individuals remain.

Grande (1999, 309) emphasizes these implications when she suggests that the myth of the ecologically noble savage presents "Indian-ness" as "the elixir" to fix white civilization. This concept oversimplifies a complex set of identities. And, as Grande points out, oversimplification equals dehumanization. "Even though the current typification of American Indians can be viewed more positively," she writes, "insofar as any stereotype serves to objectify otherwise dynamic entities, and conscript otherwise complicated voices, it remains a pernicious phenomena [*sic*]" (313). Krech (1999, 26) agrees: "While this image may occasionally serve or have served useful polemical or political ends, images of noble and ignoble indigenousness, including the Ecological Indian, are ultimately dehumanizing. They deny both variation within human groups and commonalities between them." At question here is the idea of authenticity. As both Buege and Grande point out, the myth of the ecologically noble savage is a construct of Euro-Americans, who then expect all indigenous peoples to fit the mould. If they do not, they are no longer considered authentically "Indian." While some American Indians have embraced this image (Krech 1999), Buege (1997, 83) suggests that "the 'ecological nobility' accredited to certain primal peoples is a state of perfection in which human beings live in harmony with the natural world. It is something to strive for, a pinnacle for Euro-Americans to aspire to. It is not a condition that most First Peoples, faced with direct threats to their cultural integrity, can afford to pursue." The myth of the ecologically noble savage perpetuates the ways in which Euro-Americans, who still hold much of the power of legal and social identity construction, see indigenous peoples. It can also limit the ways in which indigenous peoples are given space to represent themselves, or at least to have their representations taken seriously by non-indigenous people.

Avatar not only promotes the myth of the ecologically noble savage, but it also provides a vicarious opportunity for viewers to strive for this pinnacle. For we see both a continuance of the myth of the ecologically noble savage and the desire and eventual culmination of the striving toward this state of perfection. Sully, a representative of the modern capitalist domain, transverses the distance between "civilization" and "nature" to become a Na'vi. He becomes the Other. He is the one who can inspire us to transform our ecologically damaged world back into a pristine paradise. The emphasis is always on the past; the indigenous Other never takes us into the future, into innovation, but only backward. I use the masculine pronoun in this description consciously. As in the myth of the noble savage, which identifies the simplistic nobility of the indigenous people as "natural," so too is this noble savage naturally "masculine." As Bonnett (2006, 330) points out in analyzing the "masculine" facial expressions and postures that made Grey Owl appear "authentically Indian," "the dignity of the warrior, of the brave and fearless man of honor is etched too deep in the noble savage's visage for this look... to be available to women." Yet this is a masculinity that is informed by concepts associated with femininity and a feminized nature. Just as the myth of the ecologically noble savage requires the death of real Indians, so too Sully's becoming the Other in Avatar requires the death of the Na'vi male leaders. The white male is thus in control of the image of the noble savage. The association with femininity works similarly. Sully's becoming the ecologically noble savage, for whom nature is feminized in the Mother Goddess, requires the death of "real"—that is, human—women. The male must be able to control the image of femininity.

If the plot we find in Avatar had been narrated through the eyes of Neytiri or Augustine, we would have a very different story. From the perspective we are given, however, we are drawn into Sully's life and encouraged to identify with him as hero. With Sully the hero embodying the noble savage persona, we have not only an identification with a racial and cultural Other but also an appropriation of a gendered Other. I say "appropriation" instead of "identification" because we do not see an active feminization, or even a conscious questioning of gender in this film. We see a usurpation of an aspect often associated with the feminine—an ethic of care—for the reinforcement of a dominant masculine ideal of the warrior.[4] It is imperative in examining how Sully becomes the Other that we explore his relationships with the women in the film.

In the relationships between Sully and the human women, we see an interesting dynamic. We have two main women characters: Augustine, the scientist, and Chacon, the soldier. Both of these women have taken on arguably male roles, at least in a traditional sense. Thus, one could conclude that the filmmaker was either consciously trying to shift gendered assumptions or that by the year 2154, society has changed sufficiently that these women are no longer seen as exceptional. These are optimistic positions that would be more convincing if we were later able to see how either of these women triumphed in her struggle against the "evils" of the corporate capitalistic RDA Corporation. These characterizations could be seen, instead, as "a gesture to feminist interventions of the past 30 years," as Joanne Clarke Dillman (2007) classifies the strong female characters in another futuristic film with a male hero, *Minority Report*. They are problematic masculine positions. The scientists are continually referred to, by the soldiers, in emasculating terms (such as "limp dick"). So, while Augustine takes on a traditional male role, she tarnishes it with her femininity. Her brashness and lack of interpersonal affection, however, seem to point to a deliberate attempt on her part to be "the man." Chacon seems more successful in the male role of soldier, even to the extent of using misogynistic slurs (such as "bitch") just like "the boys." Necessarily, though, both Augustine and Chacon die in combat. Their deaths are not meaningless. They die in service of justice; they are heroic, in that sense. But just as Eytukan and Tsu'tey need to die so that Sully can become the victorious leader, Augustine and Chacon must also die so that Sully can become the champion of feminized nature, the Mother Goddess, Eywa. Although aligned with Sully and the Na'vi, Augustine and Chacon represent progress, both technological and social. In terms of their social progress, they are human women with power, women who combine care with intelligence and reason. They clearly reject what Valerie Su-Lin Wee (1997) calls a "patriarchally approved brand of femininity which advocates the qualities of obedience, submission, weakness and inferiority for women." But even more significantly, they represent technological progress: they do *not* become the ecologically noble savage. Had they survived, we may have been left with a reading that ecological sensitivity need not be associated with indigeneity. This could contravene the message of the myth of primitive ecological wisdom. Sully cannot become the Other if these socially and technologically progressive women survive, and there is no place on a pristinely natural Pandora for these technologically progressive women. This reading sees Sully as integrating the feminized role of caregiver of nature with the masculinized role of leader. He cannot become the caring leader if equally, or even more authoritative, heroic women (who integrate the feminine and masculine in altogether different ways) are by his side. The hero—the naturally noble, masculine, stoic hero—stands alone even as he recognizes the connection of all life.

It is in these deaths that I see the not-so-inconsequential remnants of misogyny, which, as David Gilmore (2001, 9) reminds us, is nearly universal and is largely associated with an "affective ambivalence" that positions the hatred of women alongside a dysfunctional "gynophilia." In *Avatar*, this gynophilia is evident in the characterization of Neytiri and Eywa, who become constructions of ideal femininity—a femininity that embraces the heroic male figure. Neytiri, particularly, is modelled on one of the abiding images of female indigeneity in North America: the Indian Princess who rescues the white male (Valaskakis 1993). This image can also be seen in the popular 1995 Disney film, *Pocahontas*. Much like Pocahontas, Neytiri is the daughter of the chief and the shaman, destined one day to be shaman herself. She takes Sully under her wing and teaches him how to be Na'vi. Her role is complicated and she complicates Sully's role as leader and hero. She saves him while providing the guidance needed for him to save her people. It is her love, and his love for her, that is one of the motivating factors for Sully to switch his allegiances and become a "true" member of the tribe. Thus, Sully does not stand completely alone. He is given Na'vi companionship. The human women, however, although not actively denigrated, are simply not allowed to survive.

Rereading *Avatar*

I have argued here that *Avatar* may look in many ways like a visionary manifestation of an ecofeminist and even Pagan worldview, but alternate meanings with significantly different implications are available. Underlying the sense of spiritual interconnectedness between all living things and a sacralization of nature and the feminine, I also see a diminishing, even misogynistic, representation of human women and a construction of the Other that relies on common tropes of the noble savage tied to primitive ecological sensitivity. This constructed Other is not simply fictional but has multiple implications for real indigenous peoples.

With these arguments in mind, I propose a reading of *Avatar* as a cautionary tale. However, the caution is not the obvious—if we allow capitalist militarism to continue in its destructive path we will "kill our Mother"—although this reading may also be pertinent. Rather, in its appropriation of ecofeminism and indigeneity by Sully, the white human Marine, *Avatar* gives us a vision of what could happen if we respond to capitalist militarism with a version of militarism of our own, the "justified" warrior perspective. Violence seems to beget violence. In this reading, *Avatar* embodies the "shadow side" of dark green religion, as Bron Taylor (2010, ix) formulates it: "it might mislead and deceive; it could even precipitate or exacerbate violence."

Sully begins his narrative on Pandora with the statement, "There's no such thing as an ex-Marine." He proves this to be true in his use of military tactics to defend the Na'vi at the culmination of the film. Significantly, his attempts at peaceful and diplomatic solutions to the conflict between humans and Na'vi are unsuccessful. As he states, "I was a warrior who dreamed he could bring peace. Sooner or later, though, you always have to wake up." In fact, his military knowledge is the only element of "culture" that Sully brings with him into his transformation to the Other. This knowledge fits the Na'vi characterization of the noble savage because it identifies Sully as a warrior, a significant component of the stereotypically masculine Indian portrait. But he is no mere warrior; he is the greatest warrior, the Toruk Makto, the rider of the most fearsome beast. Sully brings his Marine skills with him as he becomes the Other. By using military force to defend the Na'vi and by calling on Eywa to join in that fight, Sully is ultimately successful in driving the humans of the Company off of Pandora. It is his "prayer" to Eywa that brings the needed reinforcement troops: the animals. We are eventually shown a solemn scene at the end in which the humans sulkily parade onto their transport with the "encouragement" of guns and spears in the hands of the Na'vi and a couple of their human supporters.

I see this as a cautionary tale for two reasons. The first is that as the humans are sent on their way, I can not help but hear in the back of my head, "We'll be back." *Avatar* ends with an obvious opening for further human-Na'vi conflict. Cameron's plan for sequels suggests that this opening is deliberate. What this suggests, however, is that Sully's military prowess and his transformation into the ultimate Other, as shaped by his own desires, did not solve the problem. At most, it created an impasse. What will happen when the humans return with even more force? *Avatar* provides us with a caution to remember that an immediate outcome is not actually a long-term solution.

Avatar is a cautionary tale in another way. Audre Lorde (1984) famously suggests that the master's tools cannot be used to dismantle the master's house. *Avatar* is one more example of evidence to support this statement. Even as Sully is attempting to fight against the military powers of the Company, he does so in a way that transforms the Other—those seen as living in harmony with all living beings—into himself, a Marine. Harmony is broken. The warrior is triumphant and as the humans are escorted off the moon, we see Na'vi soldiers, not hunters, lining the way. Again, this is a manifestation of, not an opposition to, a militaristic worldview. And the sacrifices necessary for this victory reinforce a dominant masculinity embodied within this worldview. The human women cannot survive to see this "victory." The male Na'vi leaders also must be sacrificed so that this "victory" can allow the white human Marine, Sully, to become the male and masculine triumphant noble savage, the leader of an indigenous people who have become what they originally were positioned against. Once again, as in so much produced by Hollywood, we are given a white masculine hero at the expense of indigenous and female identities. While this is not the only possible reading of this film, we, as scholars and fans, would be remiss to ignore the implications and the cautions that this reading suggests.

Notes

1 In Greek philosophy, Pandora was the first woman, designed by the gods to punish men for the theft of fire. She carried with her a jar holding all the evils of the world, as well as hope. Out of curiosity, she opened the jar and released the evils, but she closed it before hope could be released.

2 In *Storied Selves: Shaping Identity in Feminist Witchcraft* (2008), I explicate the uses of ecofeminism within the Pagan traditions of feminist Witchcraft. See that work for a detailed discussion of the development and implications of cultural ecofeminism in Pagan contexts.

3 "Ourselves" in this quotation refers to non-indigenous scholars. Buege identified himself as a Euro-American and directed his argument toward Euro-American scholars.

4 See Carol Gilligan (1982) on the ethic of care.

References

Adams, Guy. 2010. "The Real '*Avatar*': Cameron Shoots Amazon Tribe in 3D." *The Independent*, 8 September. http://www.independent.co.uk/arts -entertainment/films/news/the-real-avatar-cameron-shoots-amazon-tribe -in-3d -2073139.html.

Bonnett, Alastair. 2006. "Pale Face, Red Mask: Racial Ambiguity and the Imitation of 'American Indian' Facial Expressions." *Cultural Politics* 2(3): 319–38.

Buege, Douglas. 1996. "The Ecologically Noble Savage Revisited." *Environmental Ethics* 18: 71–88.

Christ, Carol P. 1989. "Rethinking Theology and Nature." In *Weaving the Visions: New Patterns in Feminist Spirituality*, edited by Judith Plaskow and Carol P. Christ, 314–25. New York: HarperCollins.

Denby, David. 2010. "Going Native: '*Avatar*' and 'Sherlock Holmes.'" *The New Yorker*, 4 January. http://www.newyorker.com/arts/critics/cinema/2010/ 01/04/100104crci_cinema_denby.

Dillman, Joanne Clarke. 2007. "*Minority Report*: Narrative, Images, and Dead Women." *Women's Studies* 36: 229–49.

Eaton, Heather. 2005. *Introducing Ecofeminist Theologies*. London: T&T Clark International.

Germana, Nicholas A. 2010. "Self-Othering in German Orientalism." *The Comparatist* 34: 80–94.

Gilligan, Carol. 1982. *In a Different Voice*. Cambridge, MA: Harvard University Press.

Gilmore, David D. 2001. *Misogyny: The Male Malady*. Philadelphia: University of Pennsylvania Press.

Grande, Sandy Marie Anglás. 1999. "Beyond the Ecologically Noble Savage: Deconstructing the White Man's Indian." *Environmental Ethics* 21: 307–20.

Griffin, Susan. 1989. "This Earth Is My Sister." In *Weaving the Visions: New Patterns in Feminist Spirituality*, edited by Judith Plaskow and Carol P. Christ, 105–10. New York: HarperCollins.

Green, Rayna. 1988. "The Tribe Called Wannabee: Playing Indian in America and Europe." *Folklore* 99(1): 30–55.

Hall, Stuart. 1993. "Encoding, Decoding." In *The Cultural Studies Reader*, edited by Simon During, 90–103. London: Routledge.

Istoft, Britt. 2010. "*Avatar* Fandom as Nature-Religious Expression?" *Journal for the Study of Religion, Nature, and Culture* 4(4): 394–413.

Klassen, Chris. 2008. *Storied Selves: Shaping Identity in Feminist Witchcraft*. Lanham, MD: Lexington Books.

Krech, Shepard III. 1999. *The Ecological Indian: Myth and History*. New York: W. W. Norton.

Lorde, Audre. 1984. *Sister Outsider: Essays and Speeches*. Berkeley: Crossing Press.

Merchant, Carolyn. 1990. "Ecofeminism and Feminist Theory." In *Reweaving the World: The Emergence of Ecofeminism*, edited by Irene Diamond and Gloria Feman Orenstein, 100–105. San Francisco: Sierra Club Books.

Milton, Kay. 1996. *Environmentalism and Cultural Theory*. London: Routledge.

Plumwood, Val. 1992. "Current Trends in Ecofeminism." *The Ecologist* 22(1): 8–13.

Redford, Kent. 1991. "The Ecologically Noble Savage." *Cultural Survival Quarterly* 15(1). www.culturalsurvival.org/ourpublications/csq/article/the-ecologically-noble-savage.

Ruether, Rosemary Radford. 1991. "Ecofeminism: Symbolic Connections between the Oppression of Women and the Domination of Nature." Loy H. Witherspoon Lecture in Religious Studies, University of North Carolina, 31 October.

Sandilands, Catriona. 1999. *The Good-Natured Feminist: Ecofeminism and the Quest for Democracy*. Minneapolis: University of Minnesota Press.

Starhawk. 1990. "Power, Authority, and Mystery: Ecofeminism and Earth-Based Spirituality." In *Weaving the Visions: New Patterns in Feminist Spirituality*, edited by Judith Plaskow and Carol P. Christ, 73–86. New York: HarperCollins.

Sturgeon, Noël. 1997. *Ecofeminist Natures: Race, Gender, Feminist Theory and Political Action*. New York: Routledge.

Taylor, Bron. 2010. *Dark Green Religion: Nature Spirituality and the Planetary Future*. Berkeley: University of California Press.

Valaskakis, Gail Guthrie. 1993. "Parallel Voices: Indians and Others—Narratives of Cultural Struggle." *Canadian Journal of Communications* 18(3). http://www.cjc-online.ca/index.php/journal/article/view/756/662.

Wee, Valerie Su-Lin. 1997. "The Most Poetic Subject in the World: Observations on Death, (Beautiful) Women and Representation in *Blade Runner*." *Kinema*, 57–71. http://www.kinema.uwaterloo.ca/article.php?id=284&feature.

Žižek, Slavoj. 2010. "*Avatar*: Return of the Natives." *New Statesman*. 4 March. http://www.newstatesman.com/film/2010/03/avatar-reality-love-couple-sex.

The Na'vi as Spiritual Hunters:
A Semiotic Exploration

PAT MUNDAY

As Gary Snyder (1969, 119) observes, "Something is always eating at the American heart like acid; it is the knowledge of what we have done to our continent, and to the American Indian." When confronted with this malaise, *Avatar* helps us "dramatize ideological contradictions and work out possible resolutions to them" (Ingram 2004, 5). In depicting an alien world where Na'vi people live in perfect ecological harmony, *Avatar* is a postmodern utopia epitomizing what Bron Taylor (2010, 14–22) calls "spiritual animism." Na'vi traditional ecological knowledge results in part from a global neural network—Eywa—that is the soul and mind of the moon Pandora.

From the perspective of modernist technoculture, Pandora appears to be an ideological contradiction. Modernism has largely severed spiritual connections—and communication—between humans and other animals on Earth.[1] Descartes and other architects of the early modern period facilitated this intellectual dichotomization of nature/culture, as is well documented by historian Carolyn Merchant (1980). In practical terms, developments such as industrialization, urbanization, and consumerism reshaped society in ways that reinforced this disconnection (Louv 2005; see also Shepard 1982). Some postmodern approaches seem to take this disconnect for granted, as with advocates of social construction who "rely on a humanist perspective about knowledge creation that privileges the cognitive sovereignty of human subject over nature" (Crist 2004, 5).[2] As environmental problems loom larger, healing the divide between humans and nature is an important aspect of addressing our spiritual alienation.

Avatar offers a spiritual alternative to the dominant Cartesian meta-narrative and presents a postmodern utopian ideology that deserves to be taken seriously. The film's popularity seemingly demonstrates longing for a lost world or, possibly, a newly imagined one. The lost world is the premodern—that is, pre-Cartesian—world of spiritual animism charac-terized in the Neoplatonic writings of Plotinus. As Ken Hillis (2009) puts it, *Avatar* is "indicative of a wider resurgence of such metaphysical beliefs." Some indigenous cultures, such as people of the North American Arctic and Subarctic, still experience this world of spiritual animism. Like *Avatar's* fictional anthropologist, Dr. Grace Augustine (played by Sigourney Weaver), real "advocacy anthropologists" such as Hugh Brody (2001) have articulated this sense of spiritual relationship and have defended it from the neolithic bias that saw agriculture as a step in social evolution.[3] Simi-larly, cultural anthropologist Richard K. Nelson (1983), after studying and living with the Koyukon people of central Alaska, became an eloquent spokesperson for their practical and spiritual intimacy with nature. Even ethologists, deeply impressed by the intelligence and co-evolved relation-ship of animals such as ravens and wolves, describe the spiritual ways in which indigenous peoples construct culture based on knowledge of and reverence for animal behaviour. Like the invasion of Pandora by Earth-lings, however, this reverence is in danger as the modernist disconnect with nature fosters disrespect for the natural world (Heinrich 1999; Marzluff and Angell 2005).

In Na'vi culture, both men and women participate in hunting, an activ-ity believed to be immoral by some contemporary scholars. When such scholars think about hunting, they often picture what Stephen Kellert calls "dominionistic/sport hunters" (1978, 416) who seek "mastery and control of nature" (2005, 34, 52). Such hunters are generally ignorant of nature, know little about the animals they hunt, tend to be detached from and fearful of wild animals, and are often obsessed about elaborate high-tech gear. In Cartesian terms, they are dualistic about the human/nature divide and their hunting tends to be a competitive activity where manufactured shortcuts are used to overcome the challenge (Petersen 2000). Trophy hunters with groups such as Safari Club International often fall into this category—the trophy may even belong to an endangered species (Williams 1991). One can imagine that if *Avatar's* Colonel Quaritch went hunting, he would be a dominionistic/sport hunter.

Critics who generally reject hunting in contemporary America might accept Na'vi hunting, given its deep cultural roots and apparent nutritional necessity. Na'vi hunting is, however, structurally similar to a particular form of hunting practised by many Americans. Petersen (2000) demonstrates that even in America—where dominionistic/sport hunters and utilitarian/meat hunters dominate hunting culture—many hunters epitomize another type called the "spiritual hunter" (see Swan 1995). Petersen builds on Kellert (1978), who found that about 18 per cent of hunters of the late 1970s were "naturalistic/nature hunters" who rejected excess technology and found in hunting a deep spiritual connection with the natural world. [4]

Among contemporary spiritual hunters, traditional archers appear to be especially attuned to the natural world. They eschew high-tech gear such as compound bows with pulleys and cams in favour of handcrafted bows and wooden arrows. Yana Robertson (pers. comm.), a member of the Robertson Stykbow family that builds these beautiful weapons in Forest Grove, Montana, explains:

> Every time I watch [Avatar] I love it more!... The framework behind Na'vi archery and traditional bowhunting are exactly the same. In this type of hunting a person must learn to examine and respect the forest. Just like the Na'vi, a traditional bow hunter must value and understand the animals and environment to make a good, clean kill. The traditional bowhunter goes into the woods to be in the woods, to listen to the birds and watch animal signs, just like the Na'vi do in Avatar. To hunt is to add an element of excitement while stalking or waiting for prey. To kill brings gratitude to the life you took and food you harvested. There is a very important correlation between Na'vi archery and traditional bowhunting: they both advocate the importance of learning from and respecting nature.

Ever since Saxton Pope learned about traditional hunting from Ishi, the last member of the Yana tribe, Americans have been rediscovering spiritual hunting values. Terry Tempest Williams, Gary Snyder, and Ted Kerasote have all written eloquently about this tradition. Richard K. Nelson (1996, 2) describes it in personal terms: "Hunting provides the most important staple foods in our home, deepens my sense of connection to the surrounding natural world, and sharpens my awareness that I am an animal, not separate from my fellow creatures but twisted together with them in one great braid-work of life. Hunting brings me into the wild and brings the wild into me."

Semiotics proves a useful tool in addressing the view of spiritual hunting portrayed in Avatar. In examining the meaning of signs and the ways in which they are structured to form a coherent narrative, the idea of hunting as a spiritual activity that connects people and nature stands in stark contrast to our culture's common understanding of hunting. Furthermore, semiotics helps explain spiritual hunting as an activity that transcends

Yana Robertson, of the Robertson Stykbow family, at full draw with her hunting bow. Self-portrait, September 2011.

modernist notions of "*man* the hunter" and addresses feminist critiques of hunting as a decidedly male-gendered activity. The latter is particularly important given *Avatar*'s portrayal of both men and women as hunters.

Avatar Semiotics

For postmodern theorists, semiotics is a key tool to investigate communication as a basis for connection between humans and other animals. The structuralist approach pioneered by Ferdinand de Saussure and developed by Claude Lévi-Strauss unfolds through the dialectical juxtaposition of opposing signs that give rise to new signs and meanings.[5] This method proves especially fruitful for understanding myth and other human narratives.

Semiotics also proves to be a good tool for analyzing film and understanding indigenous cultures. Many scenes in *Avatar* fit neatly into the simple model pioneered by Saussure, whereby a signifier such as Colonel Quaritch straps himself into an amplified mobility platform (AMP) suit and signifies (i.e., conveys an idea of) the modernist domination of nature with technology. As an overall dialectical narrative, the film portrays a binary, oppositional logic: the battle of the Resources Development Administration's (RDA) Security Operations (Sec-Ops, a private mercenary army) against the Na'vi clans of Pandora. At a more complex level beyond the simple oppositions of binary logic, the narrative of *Avatar* can be diagrammed nicely with a semiotic square, Greimas's (1987) tool of structural analysis for reading the narrative "grammar" of myth, novels, film, or other stories.[6] While the *Avatar* story can be told and interpreted from various standpoints, for a viewer sympathetic to the Na'vi perspective, it might begin with the privileged term H, the humans from RDA/Sec-Ops. The Na'vi (N) oppose these humans who want to displace them in order to mine Na'vi land for the mineral unobtanium:

Beyond this simple, binary opposition, we can consider additional terms generated by the diagonal, contradictory terms non-H and non-N. In the film, non-human avatars (~H), especially the one occupied by Jake Sully, are non-human hybrids that eventually become so sympathetic to the Na'vi cause that they join them in battle against Sec-Ops. On the other hand, humans wearing technologies such as the AMP suit are decidedly non-Na'vi (~N). The new opposition of ~N (men in AMP suits) and ~H (avatars) is especially interesting since they are both a sort of hybrid. Avatars are literally a genetic hybrid of human-Na'vi, whereas a man in an AMP suit is a hybrid like the man-machine cyborgs described by Haraway (1997). While both hybrids are technoscientific artifacts, the avatar is designed to be embedded in Na'vi culture whereas the AMP-man is disturbingly unlike anything native to Pandora. Thus, the *Avatar* narrative is not a simple dialectical opposition between humans and Na'vi but a more complex story that includes genetic hybrid avatars (~H) and man-machine cyborgs (~N):

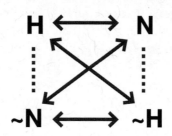

The defection of Jake Sully and other avatars from RDA/Sec-Ops to the Na'vi cause is a strong example of embodiment—what Haraway (2003) calls "material-semiotic natureculture." As a physically handicapped soldier who has lost the use of his legs and who might harbour some sense of bitterness and resentment over what he has sacrificed as a US Marine, Jake Sully is peculiarly situated to appreciate his new life as a human-Na'vi hybrid, an avatar in a Na'vi body. When Sully awakens for the first time in his Na'vi body, he exuberantly rips away the medical monitoring cables and IV drips, stumbles out of the lab, and runs through the outdoor exercise and garden area. Grace Augustine, an anthropologist and head of the avatar program, is also in her Na'vi body when she tosses Sully a native fruit. The sensuous scene of Sully eating it (19:03) is a reaffirmative depiction of the scene from the Garden of Eden when Eve gave Adam the forbidden fruit (Genesis 3:6–7). *Avatar* is, however, a postmodern interpretation that inverts "original sin" as "original knowledge." Instead of feeling shame at this strange fruit of knowledge that is forbidden to humans, Sully stands agape—a sign that he is wide open to everything Pandora has to offer. He is reborn and eventually embraces life as a Na'vi spiritual hunter, including requisite rites of passage. As he undergoes this transformation, "Sully's avatar makes him whole" (Hillis 2009).

Signs are everywhere in nature; they are not limited to human language or Pandora's neural network. Consider the hound scenting a fox or the bee homing in on a flower's infrared bull's eye.[7] As Deely (2004, 28) puts it, "The animal's survival depends upon getting right the manner in which the physical environment is incorporated into its world of objects, its Umwelt, when it comes to food, sex, and danger." The Umwelt constitutes the biological foundations for semiosis. In a larger sense, species evolve means for communicating through signs to other members of their species as well as to certain other species. This is what Jakob von Uexküll and Thomas Sebeok pioneered as the field of zoosemiotics (Radomska 2001; see also Sebeok 2001). Much of the emphasis in this field is on animal-human communication, beginning with Sebeok's research directive, as captured by Petrilli and Ponzio (2001, 20): "There is no doubt that the inner human world [Innenwelt], with great effort and serious study, may reach an understanding of non-human worlds and of its connection with them."[8] On Pandora, the Umwelt and Innenwelt merge in the great sign-system of Eywa.

Lévi-Strauss (1963, 89), in pondering the human side of communication between humans and other animals, writes, "Natural species are chosen not because they are 'good to eat' but because they are 'good to think.'" Lévi-Strauss theorizes that we "think with animals" as structural signs. In other words, in the human mind, animals serve as mental constructs in a larger mentalité or Innenwelt, especially in cultural myths. But I agree with eco-semiotician Andreas Roepstorff (2001) that Lévi-Strauss did not have it quite right. Using examples from Greenlanders' myths about and pragmatic interaction with animals, Roepstorff argues that for humans who live their lives enmeshed with wild animals, it can be a matter of thinking *along with* animals. We do not merely think using animals as signifiers for our ideas. Rather, non-human animals interact with us to produce meaning. In this way, animals are active agents in the co-construction of meaning, just as other people are. Greenlandic halibut fishermen, for example, watch seals to know when a glacier is becoming dangerously unstable and it is time to move from the area. Thus, Greenlanders construct meaning through interplay with the seals as active agents in the external world.

In the construction of meaning vis-à-vis non-human animals, Lévi-Strauss takes us the first step whereby animals serve as signs in our inner, mental world. Roepstorff, drawing from Sebeok's work, takes us a second step, with non-human animals as active, external agents in the construction of meaning. *Avatar* takes us a third step, into a world where the Na'vi can literally experience the world through the eyes and other senses of non-Na'vi animals, just as Sully experiences the Na'vi world through his avatar. When Sully or a Na'vi bonds with a direhorse, the two animals (human and non-human) see the world through another being's eyes. *Avatar*'s closing song (2:35:42) makes this point literally with the line, "I see me through your eyes." Ultimately, this engenders a world where humans (or the human-like Na'vi) are not limited to a sign-world based on what they think or on what they imagine animals to think. Instead, it is a world where signs have an intersubjective meaning that can be accessed by humans, non-human animals, and even plants such as the Tree of Souls (*Vitraya Ramunong*).

Sully does not easily gain an understanding of the signs that mark this strange new world. As an avatar seeking assimilation with the Na'vi, Sully first has to learn their ways. For more than a century, the greenhorn-to-hunter myth was a common trope in American literature, often with the greenhorn receiving spiritual and practical instruction from indigenous peoples. More recently, of course, this has also been a common theme in film. As direct sources for *Avatar*, critics often cite the films *Dances with Wolves* (1990), *FernGully: The Last Rainforest* (1992), and *Pocahontas* (1995). There are strong parallels in these films in terms of the depiction of the relationship between indigenous peoples and modernist culture, and the depiction of the defector/hero from modernist culture trying to save the indigenous peoples. Compared with *Avatar*, however, there is one major difference: none of these films depict spiritual hunting. The opening scene of *Dances with Wolves* does depict a buffalo hunt with the transitional character Lt. John J. Dunbar (played by Kevin Costner) on his way from modernism to understanding indigenous ways. Dunbar blazes away with a modern Winchester repeating rifle, seemingly killing as many buffalo as possible. After the buffalo are killed, neither Dunbar nor his Sioux hosts express a sense of reverence for the animal's life or spirit.

As a precedent for the spiritual hunting depicted in *Avatar*, the *Leatherstocking Tales* of James Fenimore Cooper serve as a better model.[9] Although most readers probably assume that the protagonist, Natty Bumppo ("Natural Bumpkin"), was a white orphan adopted by Mohicans, there are numerous signs in Cooper's novels that point to Bumppo as a hybrid or "half-breed" figure—a mixed-race child born of Native American and white European parents. Barbara Mann (1998) persuasively makes this point with an argument based on historical notions of race, Cooper's sources, and explicit clues in Cooper's novels. While not a genetically modified product of technoscience like Sully's avatar, Bumppo is a white man who is embedded in an exotic culture and environment. Like Sully's avatar, this immersion allows him to embody the qualities of the indigenous people and to deeply appreciate their relationship to the environment. Raised by his Mohican family, Bumppo learns to respect nature, to find God and moral goodness in nature, and, when hunting, to kill only what he needs (Nash 1967).

To become a hunter and warrior, Bumppo undergoes key rites of passage. He acquires the name Deerslayer after his would-be lover, Judith Hutter, gives him the rifle Killdeer, and he becomes a proficient hunter. So proficient, in fact, that he can kill an elk without really seeing it—merely by intuiting its shape upon seeing the tips of its antlers among the branches. When he puts this extraordinary skill to work in instinctually whirling around to shoot an Indian who is taking a bead on him, the dying Indian renames Bumppo/Deerslayer "Hawkeye." These key events cast the hunter as a killer of animals and the warrior as a killer of men. They are rites of passage in a durable American trope widely used in American frontier narratives (Callahan 2005; Leverenz 1991; Slotkin 2000).

Director Michael Mann based his film *The Last of the Mohicans* (1992) on Cooper's novel of the same name and opened the film with a spiritual hunting scene. Although the film is largely about events that took place in 1757 during the French and Indian War, the opening scene draws solidly, if not literally, from Cooper's portrayal of Bumppo as Deerslayer in the pre-war era. In the scene, Hawkeye (formerly Deerslayer) and his Mohican brother Chingachgook are hunting and come upon an elk. The animal runs through the thick forest, and just as all but the antlers disappear from view, Hawkeye kills it with a single shot. Chingachgook and Hawkeye stand over the dead elk and together chant a ritual prayer of thanks. The English subtitles read, "We're sorry to kill you, Brother. We do honor to your courage and speed, your strength." The simple ritual is a small but representative glimpse of deeply complex ways in which indigenous peoples spiritually connect with non-human animals and the environment. The well-studied hunter-gatherers of the Ju|'hoansi minority group (sometimes called !Kung San) of the Kalahari, for example, believe themselves to be in constant, intimate contact with their environment and the animals they hunt. Complex rituals and rites of passage define spiritual connection with non-human animals, especially highly valued prey such as the eland (Lewis-Williams and Beisle 1978). The Ju|'hoansi listen to the hunting cries—"tssik!" and "tsá!"—of stars in the clear night sky. Mothers hold up their infants, sing a special song, and ask the stars to give their child a hunter's heart (Van der Post 1961).[10] For the traditional Ju|'hoansi, stars are like the Na'vi's Tree of Souls (*Vitraya Ramunong*)—the place where Sully asks Eywa to look into Dr. Augustine's mind in order to know why and how to help the Na'vi people.

Like Natty Bumppo, Sully has to undergo key rites of passage. These include bonding with a direhorse (*pa'li*), mastering archery, learning to track and observe wildlife, killing a hexapede (*yerik*), and bonding with a mountain banshee (*ikran*). Reminiscent of the opening scene of *Last of the Mohicans*, the *Avatar* scene in which Neytiri guides Sully to the hexapede (the *yerik* hunt beginning at 1:04:19) is central to the film as a moment of truth when Sully makes the transition from child to adult. Neytiri and Sully stalk carefully within range. Sully takes a shooter's stance and draws his bow. The hexapede looks at him and flares the large fan structure on its head. Sully releases his arrow, which strikes low behind the shoulder—about where the heart would be on an Earthly deer or elk. The hexapede drops instantly. Sully approaches with knife drawn to administer the *coup de grâce*, uttering a ritual Na'vi phrase. The English subtitles read, "I see you Brother and thank you. [He ends its life with his knife.] Your spirit goes with Eywa. Your body stays behind to become part of The People." Neytiri approves, saying, "A clean kill. You are ready." By this, she means that Sully is ready for his final rite of passage into Na'vi adulthood: becoming an *Ikran Makto* by bonding and learning to fly with a mountain banshee (*ikran*). The ritual hunting prayers from *Last of the Mohicans* and *Avatar* express the deep sense of reverence that spiritual hunters feel for their prey. As Kellert (quoted in Petersen 2000, 56) writes, "The nature hunter...felt the need to confront and rationalize the death of the animal. Motivated by a genuine...respect for wildlife, the nature hunter faced the paradox of inflicting violence on a world that was the object of great affection." For a spiritual hunter, killing is not a final act. It is a spiritual transition; it acknowledges the unity of life and death, and accepts that pain and suffering are inherent in life. In analyzing Snyder's poem "The Genji Story," Ling Chung (2005, 52) writes, "Killing, the physical blow, is part of a ritual, it is meant to help the bird pass over the threshold of death so that it can transform into human form and act as the novice's guardian spirit."

Complex stories may consist of numerous semiotic systems that carry the story's meaning and bring about closure. Although the opposition between human and Na'vi is the main governing semiotic system in *Avatar*, the diegesis (and its visual portrayal) also hinges on the hunter's spiritual transformation. In semiotic terms, the narrative for spiritual hunting looks like this:

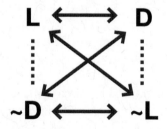

The story of hunter and prey is a meeting between Life (L) and Death (D). In killing the prey, hunters face their own mortality and vulnerability, bringing about an apparent state of Death (D). But the prey's death is not

final—it is a state of non-Life (~L) marked by the ritual prayer of gratitude. Consuming the prey's flesh—non-Death (~D)—feeds The People
and honours the prey's spirit.[11]

There are some major differences regarding spiritual hunting between
Cameron's film and either Cooper's novels or Mann's *Last of the Mohicans* film. Although Bumppo (Hawkeye) is a human raised by Mohicans
from infancy, Sully's avatar is a technologically engineered human–Na'vi
hybrid who, by the movie's end, has been with the Na'vi just a few months.
Bumppo hunts with an exotic weapon, a flintlock rifle, whereas Sully
hunts with the traditional Na'vi longbow. Although female Na'vi, with the
exception of Neytiri, seemed conspicuously absent from the hunter/war-
rior rite-of-passage scenes, they are totally absent from Bumppo's world.
Furthermore, Bumppo is intensely homosocial and awkward with women,
whereas Sully and Neytiri form an intimate bond.[12]

From a structuralist semiotic point of view, *Avatar's* Neytiri substitutes
for Chingachgook in *Mohicans*. But this change is a profound paradigmatic
substitution. In conventional tropes, paradigmatic substitution proceeds
based on alignment. In the code for Western films, for example, Bumppo's
Chingachgook, the Lone Ranger's Tonto, and the Cisco Kid's Pancho are all
more or less equivalent as inferior non-whites. The postmodern Western
Dead Man (1995, directed by Jim Jarmusch) inverts this trope. Whereas
William Blake (played by Johnny Depp) has a Native American sidekick
named Nobody (played by Gary Farmer), the wounded Blake utterly
depends on Nobody as his guide to the spirit world and the threshold from
life to death. The narrative of *Dead Man* deconstructs the irreconcilable and
contradictory meanings of classic Western films and their myth of the frontier. Once again, *Avatar* takes this paradigmatic substitution a step further.
Neytiri, as a female, poses a major challenge to the modernist Western trope
of "man the hunter," let alone white man as the *master* hunter.

In this way, *Avatar* is a reconstruction project. As Sully's spiritual guide,
Neytiri cures him of modernist insanity. The elder daughter of the Omaticaya clan leader, Eytukan, and the spiritual leader (*tsahìk*), Mo'at, Neytiri
is destined to become the next spiritual leader. She is an expert bowhunter,
direhorse (*pa'li*) rider, and mountain banshee (*ikran*) aviator (*Ikran
Makto*). She meets Sully after he gets separated from a scientific exploration party (33:32). When darkness sets in, Sully makes a spear, dips it into
a tarry plant substance to make a torch, and, with childlike clumsiness,
attracts a pack of dangerous viperwolves (*nantang*). Because a woodsprite
(*atokirina'*)—a very pure and sacred spirit from the Tree of Souls (*Vitraya Ramunong*)—gives Neytiri a sign that Sully is special, she saves him
from the viperwolves, shooting two of the fierce creatures with her only

arrows, stabbing another one with her knife, and driving off the rest with blows from her bow. In delivering the *coup de grâce* to a wounded viper-wolf, she offers an apology. This scene contrasts sharply with the hunting scene described earlier, where giving thanks is central to the act of killing. When Sully tries to thank her for saving his life, Neytiri responds angrily (she learned English at Augustine's school), "Don't thank, you don't thank for this. This is sad. Very sad only.... This is your fault. They did not need to die." When he protests, she replies even more emphatically, "Your fault! Your fault! You're like a baby, making noise, don't know what to do." But Neytiri does save him. Returning to Hometree (*Kelutral*), woodsprites swarm over Sully and confirm her instincts.

Through such scenes, the role of Neytiri as "woman the hunter" integrates hunting competence with a deeply spiritual sense of connection with nature. By casting a woman in this role, *Avatar* challenges us to imagine a possible world in which women can be hunters and warriors as well as spiritual leaders. Signifying a woman in this way may be as important a contribution to our understanding of dark green religion as the notion of a world in which all things are connected.

Woman as Spiritual Hunter

Although seldom depicted in Western literature or studied by Western anthropologists, women hunters are found in ethnographic accounts. Ju|'hoansi women scout the bush for game and some are expert trackers who contribute significantly to their husbands' hunting success (Biesele and Barclay 2001). Iñupiat women commonly call animals into close range so their husbands can kill them (Bodenhorn 1990). In some areas of the Philippines, Agta women are almost universally expert with bow and arrow. They hunt frequently with men, with other women, and alone (Estioko-Griffin and Griffin 1981). In *Avatar*, Neytiri excels at all hunting-related activities: she stalks Sully silently through the treetops and saves him from the viperwolves; she silently guides him to observe a viperwolf with pups and to kill a hexapede, and, as a warrior, ultimately saves Sully by shooting two arrows through Colonel Quaritch's chest at the end of the "Battle for Pandora."

Avatar stubbornly refuses to yield to simple, modernist "good versus bad," "man versus nature," or "man versus woman" dialectical semiotics. Even postmodern feminists fall into this modernist trap of objectification and reductivism when contemplating nature, animals, and hunting. In considering spiritual hunters, which she called "holy hunters," Marti Kheel (1995, 87, 105) seeks to "examine how the textual discourse on hunting ethics has functioned both to camouflage and to legitimate violence and biocide," concluding that men hunt and kill out of a psychological need to "deny all that is female within themselves." In semiotic terms, this would make it impossible to explain "woman the hunter." No wonder, then, that the role of women as hunters—whether in ethnology, contemporary culture, or fiction—makes some ecofeminists uneasy. Although most were initially silent on the issue, others have argued that women who hunt buy into patriarchal ideology and perpetuate their own subordination (Fitzgerald 2005). After the publication of Mary Zeiss Stange's *Woman the Hunter* (1997), the argument that women can hunt as a matter of moral responsibility for their own sustenance and as a form of connection/reciprocity with nature could not be ignored. One could argue, in fact, that ecofeminists opposed to spiritual hunting essentialize women, reinforce modernist nature/culture and female/male dichotomies, and erect a new dualism between traditional cultures and postmodern holistic approaches to engagement with nature. In semiotic terms, ascribing fixed, gendered meanings of "woman the gatherer" (W) and "man the hunter" (M) sets up a binary opposition as a myth or narrative of conflict.

As we expand the narrative with the subordinate terms in a semiotic square, contemporary ecofeminism (~M) and contemporary patriarchy (~W) occupy the contradictory signs in the ongoing conflict:

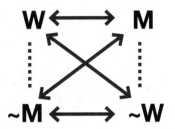

As a template for understanding and perhaps moving beyond the conflict, however, this narrative structure has several problems. The aforementioned problem of essentializing women as gatherers or non-hunters makes it difficult to understand the role of Neytiri in *Avatar*, let alone the role of real-life women such as Mary Zeiss Stange or Agta women. Furthermore, it neglects the damage done to nature by all human activities. The footprint of a home disrupts ecosystem functions in the area in which it is erected, a plot of land for a cultivated crop displaces native plants and animals, and the materials for our computers must be mined from the earth. All of these activities are potentially more damaging to the environment than hunting, which can be a sustainable activity that does not, over time, reduce a non-human animal's population or damage its habitat.

As a scholar who has made significant contributions to ecofeminism and material semiotics, Donna Haraway (2008, 295–96)—always one to demolish easy generalizations and ideological positions—discusses a birth celebration at which participants ate the new mother's placenta (cooked with onions) and then explains why she (Haraway) also ate, with gratitude, a feral pig hunted, killed, cooked, and served by a colleague at a departmental gathering:

> There is no way to eat and not to kill, no way to eat and not to become with other mortal beings to whom we are accountable, no way to pretend innocence and transcendence or a final peace....
>   ... To repeat myself, outside Eden, eating means also killing, directly or indirectly, and killing well is an obligation akin to eating well. This applies to a vegan as much as to a human carnivore.

Beyond the basic problem whereby some ecofeminists deny the possibility of woman-the-hunter, some feminists push the argument to another level by considering nature to be a term aligned with female. Thus, taming or domesticating a wild, non-human animal is a paradigmatic substitution for conquering—or even raping—a woman. In applying ecofeminist theory to *Avatar*, Randy Malamud (2010) finds a paradox. Although the Na'vi demonstrate a deep sense of environmental connection, they also dominate direhorses and banshees in seemingly brutal and aggressive ways. He cites bloggers as evidence that *Avatar*'s director and audience are "merely reiterating the same old anthropocentric prejudices under the cover of a flashy new veneer." One blogger found the Na'vi neural link with direhorses to be a one-way sort of mind control, a form of human domination and animal abuse. Another was upset that the film suggests that "humans have the right and the duty to dominate, 'tame,' and make use of animals—that nonhuman animals are resources and tools." The blogger was particularly outraged over the scene where Sully chooses a banshee, seeing it as a brutal "no means yes" sort of rape: "It is Jake's duty, while the animal fights him off, to "bond" with the animal by overpowering him, tying him up, climbing on top of him, and inserting a part of his body into the body of the animal while his victim desperately fights him off.... This was not a scenario in which each party sought out the other, for mutual benefit. The being in power dominated/raped the "lesser" being" (Malumud 2010, 16–17). Malamud and the bloggers offer an incisive critique. Given the anthropological examples of women who hunt and Stange's argument regarding "woman as hunter," however, I do not find either Malamud's or Kheel's analyses convincing. In a semiotic sense, it is wrong-headed to inscribe nature as female and thus to conclude that activities such as hunting or the domestication of animals necessarily entail a *sexist* form of subjugation.[13] Although Western narrative forms are often structured as stories of men conquering nature (Kolodny 1975), this is not always the case in anthropology, fiction, or film. Essentializing wild, non-human animals as females (let alone as women) to be conquered simply does not fit the narrative structure of *Avatar*.

Killing or domesticating animals does, of course, imply a semiotic system in which we assign different meanings to non-human animals—meanings that justify and even lend spiritual value to the activities in question. It is tempting to fall back on the naturalistic fallacy to defend killing (i.e., hunting) or domesticating non-human animals, resorting to an "Eywa knows best" explanation: since the bond works, it is an expression of spiritual harmony despite the apparent violence. Back on Earth, far from the fictional utopian world of *Avatar*, we must still come to terms with the killing and domestication of non-human animals. While a sustained moral analysis is beyond the scope of my analysis here, suffice it to say that history and evolution matter. Humans evolved as animals that killed and ate non-human animals and that domesticated non-human animals as well as plants. We also evolved as spiritual animals that, as part of our existence, mystified actions such as killing and domestication. A semiotic analysis helps us to explain such narratives, but it does not tell us whether such narratives *ought* to have a place in a better, possible, postmodern future—what Bron Taylor (2010) calls "dark green religion."

On the real evolved world of Earth, wild horses fight each other fiercely to establish their place in the herd's dominance structure. Wolves act similarly, at times even killing an aged leader of the pack. In the natural world, violence and subjugation are part of life. As humans or Na'vi enter into a material-semiotic bond with wild animals, they may have to struggle with the non-human animal on its own terms. The spiritual hunter or animist accepts this struggle, along with the pain or even death that comes with it, as something that gives meaning to life. Although the spiritual hunter might kill a hexapede or elk today, the same hunter might become a meal for a *toruk* or grizzly bear tomorrow. This is not a modernist, hierarchical semiotics of "man over nature." Instead, in a levelled semiotic structure, the Na'vi and *toruk*—or spiritual hunter and grizzly—are all in it together.

Conclusion

Humans evolved not just as hunters but as hunted. Despite the ascendance of "man the hunter" theories in an era when male anthropologists dominated the field, recent anthropological discussion is just as likely to be about the evolution of man-the-hunted (Hart and Sussman 2008). At a cultural and biological level, humans are fascinated by large, fierce predators, whether we identify with them as fellow hunters or fear them as dangerous enemies (Kruuk 2002). As spiritual hunters, the Na'vi accept that there are large, fierce critters in the forest that can and will eat them if they are not careful. Still, they recognize a deep kinship with other predators. This kinship ranges from the tender scene in which Neytiri and Sully watch a viperwolf with pups to the Na'vi warrior's bond with a banshee. In exploring the social dynamics of large-carnivore conservation in North America, Kellert et al. (1996) identify predator traits that contribute to species charisma for both contemporary society and indigenous cultures. These traits are based largely on perceived power and intelligence and on resemblance to human physicality and social structure. For reasons like these, wolves and bears (particularly grizzly bears) are the most popular non-human animals in native legends and contemporary culture. Interestingly, an Internet search and hit count for Pandoran animals support Kellert's analysis: the *toruk* is far and away the most popular, followed by the banshee, thanator, direhorse, viperwolf, hammerhead titanothere, and hexapede. Clearly, predators outscore prey on the Google-hit scale of charisma, and when it comes to predators, the larger and fiercer the better.[14]

The restoration of predators such as wolves and grizzly bears, Kellert et al. argue, indicates an increasing sense of respect for the natural world. Similarly, the popularity of *Avatar* seemingly indicates this growing respect, as well as the emergence of spiritual animism. Wolves are, to quote Kellert et al. (1996, 980), "a powerful barometer of changing attitudes toward the natural world. Many North Americans now view wilderness as the expression of a delicate and even divine handiwork, and wilderness species, especially large carnivores, as vital components of a complex, quasi-living structure." Many people are coming to realize the harm caused to our world by modernism's nature/culture divide. Although we cannot recover the Edenic world of Edgar Rice Burroughs (1914) where humans and other animals live in harmony, perhaps we can draw on imagination and our innate biophilia to develop a postmodern spiritual engagement with nature. *Avatar*, and sympathetic scholarship like that in this volume, may be a step in that direction.

Notes

Special thanks to Bron Taylor and the anonymous reviewers for their valuable suggestions and to Emma MacKenzie for our many thought-provoking conversations. Their help improved my analysis and saved me from some embarrassing errors.

1 On Haraway's phrase "humans and other animals," see Schneider (2005, 77–86).

2 As a prime example of Crist's criticism, see Cronon (1996). For a favourable view of how a social constructivist approach might heal the nature/culture divide, see Eder (1996).

3 See Kulchyski (2007). In advocating for traditional hunting cultures, Brody instantiates arguments by Shepard (1973).

4 See Kellert and Wilson (1995) on the biophilia hypothesis, which undergirds much of Petersen's and Kellert's spiritual hunting argument.

3 On structuralism, see, for example, De Saussure (1983) and Lévi-Strauss (1963).

4 See Jameson (1972, 124, 167–68).

5 Note that, technically, objective things that can be seen or otherwise sensed are sign-vehicles and not signs per se. Following Peirce (1991) and Deely (2004), the sign is constructed through vehicle–object–interpretant relationship.

6 In a more narrow sense, language—as linguistic communication—evolved in humans as a powerful modelling system and a highly specialized Innenwelt. See Deely (2004).

9 The *Leatherstocking Tales* took their name from the protagonist Natty Bumppo's original nickname and consist of a series of Cooper's novels, including *The Last of the Mohicans* (1826) and *The Deerslayer* (1841).

10 See song "Tssik Tssik Tsá" (Tony Bird 1990). Sadly, this way of life may be passing away. A recent ethnographer reported that even though some Ju|'hoansi practise traditional hunting, they were Christianized, and many denied traditional beliefs such as the existence of an animal-spirit world (Taylor 2008).

11 According to the Avatar shooting script and James Cameron, a deleted scene of ten-plus minutes further emphasized Na'vi hunting and possibly the rite of passage from hunter to warrior. See Rosenberg (2009) and Brennan (2010). Note also that the film does not depict scenes of the dead hexapede being butchered or eaten, perhaps to assuage the appetites of American film audiences uncomfortable with the eating habits of indigenous peoples.

12 Mann's film differs significantly from Cooper's novel in this regard, for the film depicts Hawkeye as a bold lover.

13 Despite Rebecca Keegan's (2009) *Vanity Fair* essay about James Cameron as a closet feminist, *Avatar* does not seem to stand as a feminist film: Neytiri's choice of Jake as a mate, the relative lack of female Na'vi in the rite-of-passage scenes, and the story as told from Jake's point of view all argue against a strong feminist interpretation; see Conrad (2011).

14 Search performed using Google on 15 June 2010. For each animal, the English search term was used combined with the word "avatar" to reduce irrelevant hits for terms such as *banshee*. The number of hits were as follows: *toruk* 2.810 million; *banshee* 836,000; *thanator* 263,000; *direhorse* 79,800; *viperwolf* 51,100; *hammerhead titanothere* 40,800; *hexapede* 17,900; and *sturmbeest* 11,100. Only for *yerik* (26,800) did the Na'vi term score more hits than the English.

References

Biesele, Megan, and Steve Barclay. 2001. "Ju|'hoan Women's Tracking Knowledge and Its Contribution to Their Husband's Hunting Success." *African Study Monographs*, Suppl. 26: 67–84.

Bird, Tony. 1990. *Sorry Africa*. CD. Cambridge, MA: Rounder Records.

Bodenhorn, Barbara. 1990. "I Am Not the Great Hunter—My Wife Is: Inupiat and Anthropological Models of Gender." *Études/Inuit/Studies* 14(1–2): 55–74.

Brennan, David. 2010. "The Avatar Screenplay: Alterations, Deletions, and Analysis." http://jamescameron.blogspot.com/2010/avatar-screenplay-alterations-deletions.html (site discontinued).

Brody, Hugh. 2001. *The Other Side of Eden.* New York: North Point Press.

Burroughs, Edgar Rice. 1914. *Tarzan of the Apes.* Chicago: A. C. McClurg.

Callahan, David. 2005. "Containing Manhood in James Fenimore Cooper's *The Deerslayer.*" In *Viagens pela Palavra: Livro de Homenagem á Professora Maria Laura Bettencourt Pires,* edited by Mário Avelar, 75–90. Lisbon: Universidade Alberta.

Chung, Ling. 2005. "Gary Snyder's American-Asian Shamanism." *The Comparatist* 29: 38–62.

Conrad, Dean. 2011. "Femmes Futures: One Hundred Years of Female Representation in SF Cinema." *Science Fiction Film and Television* 4 (Spring): 79–99.

Crist, Eileen. 2004. "Against the Social Construction of Nature and Wilderness." *Environmental Ethics* 26 (Spring): 5–24.

Cronon, William, ed. 1996. *Uncommon Ground: Toward Reinventing Nature.* New York: W. W. Norton.

Deely, John. 2004. "Semiotics and Jakob von Uexküll's Concept of *Umwel.*" *Sign Systems Studies* 32(1–2): 11–34.

De Saussure, Ferdinand. 1983. *Course in General Linguistics.* Translated by Roy Harris. Illinois: Open Court.

Eder, Klaus. 1996. *The Social Construction of Nature: A Sociology of Ecological Enlightenment.* London: Sage.

Estioko-Griffin, Agnes, and P. Bion Griffin. 1981. "Woman the Hunter: The Agta." In *Woman the Gatherer,* edited by Frances Dahlberg, 121–40. New Haven, CT: Yale University Press.

Fitzgerald, Amy J. 2005. "The Emergence of the Figure of 'Woman-the-Hunter': Equality or Complicity in Oppression?" *Women's Studies Quarterly* 33: 86–104.

Greimas, Algirdas. 1987. *On Meaning: Selected Writings in Semiotic Theory.* Translated by Paul J. Perron and Frank H. Collins. London: Frances Pinter.

Haraway, Donna. 1997. *Modest_Witness@Second_Millenium.FemaleMan©_Meets_Oncomouse: Feminism and Technoscience™.* New York: Routledge.

———. 2003. *The Companion Species Manifesto: Dogs, People, and Significant Otherness.* Chicago: Prickly Paradigm Press.

———. 2008. *When Species Meet.* Minneapolis: University of Minnesota Press.

Hart, Donna L., and Robert W. Sussman. 2008. *Man the Hunted: Primates, Predators, and Human Evolution.* Boulder CO: Westview Press.

Heinrich, Bernd. 1999. *Mind of the Raven: Investigations and Adventures with Wolf-Birds.* New York: HarperCollins.

Hillis, Ken. 2009. "From Capital to Karma: James Cameron's *Avatar.*" *Postmodern Culture* 19(3). http://pmc.iath.virginia.edu/text-only/issue.509/19.3contents.html.

Ingram, David. 2004. *Green Screen: Environmentalism and Hollywood Cinema.* Exeter, UK: University of Exeter Press.

Jameson, Frederic. 1972. *The Prison House of Language*. Princeton, NJ: Princeton University Press.

Keegan, Rebecca. 2009. "James Cameron: Closet Feminist." *Vanity Fair: The Hollywood Blog*, 15 December. http://www.vanityfair.com/online/oscars/2009/12/james-cameron-closet-feminist.html.

Kellert, Stephen R. 1978. "Attitudes and Characteristics of Hunters and Anti-hunters and Related Policy Suggestions." *Transactions of the North American Wildlife and Natural Resources Conference* 43: 412–23.

———. 2005. *Building for Life: Designing and Understanding the Human–Nature Connection*. Washington, DC: Island Press.

Kellert, Stephen R., and Edward O. Wilson, eds. 1995. *The Biophilia Hypothesis*. Washington, DC: Island Press.

Kellert, Stephen R., Matthew Black, Colleen Reid Rush, and Alistair J. Bath. 1996. "Human Culture and Large Carnivore Conservation in North America." *Conservation Biology* 10: 977–90.

Kheel, Marti. 1995. "License to Kill: An Ecofeminist Critique of Hunters' Discourse." In *Animals and Women: Feminist Theoretical Explanations*, edited by Carol J. Adams and Josephine Donovan, 85–125. Durham, NC: Duke University Press.

Kolodny, Annette. 1975. *The Lay of the Land: Metaphor as Experience and History in American Life and Letters*. Chapel Hill, NC: University of North Carolina Press.

Kruuk, Hans. 2002. *Hunter and Hunted: Relationships between Carnivores and People*. Cambridge: Cambridge University Press.

Kulchyski, Peter. 2007. "Hunting Stories." In *The Culture of Hunting in Canada*, edited by Jean L. Manore and Dale G. Miner, 25–41. Vancouver: University of British Columbia Press.

Leverenz, David. 1991. "The Last Real Man: From Natty Bumppo to Batman." *American Literary History* 3: 753–81.

Lévi-Strauss, Claude. 1963. *Structural Anthropology*. Translated by Claire Jacobson and Brooke Grundfest Schoepf. New York: Doubleday.

———. 1963. *Totemism*. Boston: Beacon Press.

Lewis-Williams, J. D., and M. Biesele. 1978. "Eland Hunting Rituals among Northern and Southern San Groups: Striking Similarities." *Africa* 48: 117–34.

Louv, Richard. 2005. *Last Child in the Woods: Saving Our Children from Nature-Deficit Disorder*. Chapel Hill, NC: Algonquin Books.

Malamud, Randy. 2010. "Animals on Film: The Ethics of the Human Gaze." http://www.english.gsu.edu/pdf/Spring.pdf.

Mann, Barbara. 1998. "Man with a Cross: Hawkeye Was a 'Half-Breed.'" *James Fenimore Cooper Society Miscellaneous Papers No. 10*, August.

Marzluff, John M., and Tony Angell. 2005. *In the Company of Crows and Ravens*. New Haven, CT: Yale University Press.

Merchant, Carolyn. 1980. *The Death of Nature: Women, Ecology and the Scientific Revolution*. San Francisco: HarperCollins.

Nash, Roderick. 1967. *Wilderness and the American Mind*. New Haven, CT: Yale University Press.

Nelson, Richard K. 1983. *Make Prayers to the Raven: A Koyukon View of the Northern Forest*. Chicago: University of Chicago Press.

————. 1996. "Introduction: Finding Common Ground." In *Hunter's Heart: Honest Essays on Blood Sport*, edited by David Petersen, 1–10. New York: Henry Holt.

Peirce, Charles Sanders. 1991. *Peirce on Signs: Writings on Semiotic by Charles Sanders Peirce*. Edited by James Hoopes. Chapel Hill: University of North Carolina Press.

Petersen, David. 2000. *Heartsblood: Hunting, Spirituality, and Wildness in America*. Boulder, CO: Johnson Books.

Petrilli, Susan, and Augusto Ponzio. 2001. *Thomas Sebeok and the Signs of Life*. Cambridge: Icon Books.

Radomska, Marietta. 2001. "Zoosemiotics as a New Perspective." *Homo communicativus* 1: 71–77.

Roepstorff, Andreas. 2001. "Thinking with Animals." *Signs Systems Studies* 29(1): 203–15.

Rosenberg, Adam. 2009. "James Cameron Details One of His 'Avatar' Deleted Scenes, Featuring Sam Worthington and an Unseen Beast." http://moviesblog .mtv.com/2009/12/18/james-cameron-details-one-of-his-avatar-deleted -scenes-featuring-sam-worthington-and-an-unseen-beast/.

Schneider, Joseph. 2005. *Donna Haraway: Live Theory*. New York: Continuum International.

Sebeok, Thomas A. 2001. *Global Semiotics*. Bloomington: Indiana University Press.

Shepard, Paul. 1973. *The Tender Carnivore*. Athens: University of Georgia Press.

————. 1982. *Nature and Madness*. Athens: University of Georgia Press.

Slotkin, Richard. 2000. *Regeneration through Violence: The Mythology of the American Frontier, 1600–1860*. Norman: University of Oklahoma Press.

Snyder, Gary. 1969. *Earth House Hold: Technical Notes and Queries to Fellow Dharma Revolutionaries*. New York: New Directions.

Stange, Mary Zeiss. 1997. *Woman the Hunter*. Boston: Beacon Press.

Swan, James A. 1995. *In Defense of Hunting*. New York: HarperCollins.

Taylor, Bron. 2010. *Dark Green Religion: Nature Spirituality and the Planetary Future*. Berkeley: University of California Press.

Taylor, Robert H. 2008. "Hunting with the Bushmen of Namibia." *The Old Ways*. http://www.jelldragon.com/theoldways/dewpost.htm.

Van der Post, Laurens. 1961. *The Heart of the Hunter*. London: Harcourt Brace.

Williams, Ted. 1991. "Open Season on Endangered Species." *Audubon* (January): 26–35.

Calling the Na'vi: Evolutionary Jungian Psychology and Nature Spirits

BRUCE MACLENNAN

Avatar evokes many archetypal themes that have contemporary relevance, including the Great Mother, Dame Nature, Mother Earth, the World Tree, the Wise Old Woman, the Hunter, the Innocent Child, Resurrection and Rebirth, and the Hero's Journey.[1] These are relevant not only to our relation to nature and Earth but also to the wider role of spiritual experience in twenty-first-century Western culture. This archetypal richness is part of the reason why the movie has captivated audiences. However, *Avatar* is more than simply an evocative story or a modern myth, for if we understand the archetypal themes that it embodies, we can discover in it a way toward a deeper connection with nature and a more meaningful life.

I will argue for this thesis within the explanatory framework of evolutionary Jungian psychology, which combines study of the evolved neuropsychological adaptations of humans (pursued by evolutionary psychology) with experiential investigation of the archetypes (the unconscious psychological structures common to all humans), which are investigated by Jungian psychologists (MacLennan 2006). Evolutionary psychology has its defenders (e.g., Barkow, Cosmides, and Tooby 1992; Buss 2005, 2012) and its critics (e.g., Buller 2005; Richardson 2007), and Jungian psychology also evokes skepticism (e.g., Nagy 1991). Although a defence of these major movements in psychology is beyond the scope of this chapter, I contend that, on the whole, evolutionary psychology has strengthened the scientific basis of Jungian psychology. Moreover, I believe that these movements in

combination provide exceptional insights into human nature, both neurophysiological and psychological, and its relation to the rest of nature;
this double perspective illuminates the impact that the film *Avatar* has on
viewers. To advance this argument, however, I need to explain some of the
less well-known aspects of Jung's theory of the archetypes.

Archetypes

According to Jung, the archetypes are the psychological correlates of phylogenetic neurophysiological structures that regulate human motivation,
affect, perception, and behaviour.[2] That is, our species, like all others, has
characteristic ways of interacting with its environment that are rooted in
our shared biological structure; these are commonly called "instincts,"
which are defined as evolved behavioural adaptations to an environment.[3]
Usually, instincts are studied from the "outside" by investigating the
observable behavioural patterns and physiological responses characteristic of a species. When the subject is human instincts, however, we can
also investigate them from the "inside": that is, in terms of their effect on
our mental state—moods, feelings, emotions, motivations, perceptions,
impulses to act, and so forth. Jung used the term *archetype* to refer to the
psychological aspect of an instinct. He wrote, for example, "Just as his
instincts compel man to a specifically human mode of existence, so the
archetypes force his ways of perception and apprehension into specifically
human patterns. The instincts and the archetypes together form the 'collective unconscious'" (Jung 1967–78, 8:270).[4]

The archetypes reside in the collective unconscious because they are
characteristic of our species (hence, collective) and because they do not
manifest consciously until they have been released by a triggering cir-
cumstance (hence, they are usually unconscious). Like other unconscious
structures, they cannot be observed introspectively; they are known only
through their effects on the conscious mental state and overt behaviour
when they have been activated by some innate or learned releasing mechanism. As Jung (1967–78, 9, pt. 1:155) put it, "The existence of the instincts
can no more be proved than the existence of the archetypes, so long as they
do not manifest themselves concretely." The unconscious mind also contains personal structures, such as "complexes" woven from unconscious
associations and dispositions acquired during an individual's life.

The archetypes correspond to patterns of relating to each other and to
our environment that are adaptive: that is, that have contributed to the
survival of *Homo sapiens* and its ancestor species. Light is being shed on
these adaptations by evolutionary psychology, which seeks to understand
human psychology in terms of its adaptive function and by comparison

to other species, especially our nearest relations. There is evidence that, among other things, instincts condition sexual relations (Buss 2005, chaps. 9–14), child care (chaps. 16–17), dominance and status relationships (chap. 23), and emotional dispositions to other species, such as attraction to juvenile mammals (Eibl-Eibesfeldt 1970; Lorenz 1971), and fear of snakes and spiders (Buss 2005, chap. 7). Separating the effects of genetic and cultural evolution, especially in the face of gene-culture co-evolution, is a continuing complex empirical investigation, but we may draw a few general conclusions.[5]

The Na'vi as Ideal Humans

Overall, it is reasonable to assume that our instincts have facilitated human survival in our "environment of evolutionary adaptedness" (EEA): that is, in the environment in which our species evolved and to which it is coupled through natural selection. But what is this environment? Modern humans have existed for approximately two hundred thousand years, and for 95 per cent or more of that time, we have been foragers who survived primarily by means of gathering food and hunting. Indeed, we were foragers before we became *Homo sapiens*, so our foraging history is much longer, perhaps two million years (Wilson 1978, 34, 84; 1993, 32). Therefore, foraging is our EEA; it is to this environment that we should look to understand the specific adaptations of *Homo sapiens*.

Paleogeneticists have been surprised at how little our genome has changed over the past three hundred thousand years (Gibbons 2010, 680, 684): E. O. Wilson (1978, 87–88) notes that a quarter of a million years ago, when *Homo sapiens* emerged, the brain stopped increasing in size, and since then, genetic evolution has had a decreasing influence compared to cultural evolution. Therefore, in spite of gene-culture co-evolution, our genome has not changed very much over the two hundred thousand or so years that modern humans have existed, and even less over the approximately ten thousand years since agriculture was invented and many humans adopted a more settled way of life. For these many millennia, the instincts have provided a largely stable foundation for rapid cultural evolution. Therefore, since the instincts encoded in our genome are little changed from those of our foraging ancestors, the archetypes—which, according to Jung, are the psychological correlates of those instincts—are, for the most part, those of foragers, a conclusion defended by Jungian psychologists Anthony Stevens and Meredith Sabini, and indeed, by Jung himself (Jung 1967–78, 10:104–47; 2003, 99–118; Sabini 2000; Stevens 1993, 63–67).

Given that our behavioural adaptations are those of foragers, what can we conclude about the corresponding archetypes, understood as the psychological expressions of those adaptations? Stevens (1993, 2003) argues that we can learn much by looking at contemporary foraging cultures and by studying our close primate relatives. If we do so, we conclude that our ancestors were probably adapted to living in clans of a few dozen loosely related individuals of all ages, not unlike the Omaticaya clan, which occupies Hometree in *Avatar* (Wilhelm and Mathison 2009, 34). The information about our behavioural adaptations provided by cultural anthropology and evolutionary psychology has been supplemented by the empirical research of Jung and other depth psychologists who have investigated the archetypes through analytical psychology, which uses introspective, dialectical, and other techniques to explore unconscious psychological structures. An extensive, expanding Jungian literature contains reports of these (primarily clinical) investigations and interpretations of their results (Dyer 1991, vii–viii).

Jung (1967–78, 8:253) stressed that both archetypes and complexes behave like autonomous personalities. The archetypes in particular, since they correspond to instincts, have their own phylogenetic agendas (such as procreation, child care, and establishment of dominance), which may diverge from conscious purpose. They correspond to behavioural "programs" that are somewhat independent of each other but are nevertheless parts or aspects of the complete innate human behavioural repertoire, which we may call the "archetypal human." Jung called this ideal human the "Self" (with a capital "S"), and I will call it the archetypal or higher self. It is the phylogenetic human psyche, which is encoded in the genes of every person.

The higher self and the archetypes it comprises can be considered an ideal human, but it is *ideal* only in the sense of being a transpersonal dynamic form; it is not ideal in any moral sense. The archetypes are psychobehavioural programs implemented in human neurophysiology, which is encoded in the genome shared by all humans (hence, transpersonal). They can be called "good" only insofar as they are adaptive: that is, they have promoted our survival as a species in our environment of evolutionary adaptedness.

The archetypes correspond to the gods, nature spirits, and so on of polytheistic religions and animistic perceptions, although, of course, the archetypes are overlaid with cultural characteristics. When an archetype is activated by some external or internal releasing stimulus, it conditions motivation, affect, perception, and action to serve some evolutionary function. The conscious mind may experience the influence of this autonomous personality as a kind of possession (Von Franz 1980; Jung 1967–78, 8:204; 9, pt. 1:220–24, 621; Stevens 2003, 68–69). Even short of full-scale possession, a stimulus that partially activates an archetype may be experienced as numinous, spiritually potent, charged with existential significance (as it is). In particular, natural phenomena can evoke archetypal spiritual responses (Stevens 1999, 99–116, 332–91).

I think that the Na'vi have captured the imagination of *Avatar*'s audiences because they represent ideal humans, not in the sense of romantic "noble savages" but in the sense of archetypes: our innate psychodynamic models of phylogenetically normal human behaviour. As I have argued above, the archetypal human is a forager, not unlike the Na'vi, whose "technology is Neolithic...bows and spears, clay pots, animal skins, that sort of thing" (Cameron 1994, 29).[6] Therefore, like the figures of myth, the Na'vi are literally evocative because they activate our ancestral archetypes, making them psychologically present as forces moving in our psyches, which is one reason why the movie is so compelling.

The word avatar comes from the Sanskrit word *avatāra*, "descent," which refers to an incarnation of divinity. Thus, in the movie, human "drivers" incarnate into the avatars, which are otherwise non-sentient beings created by humans. The Na'vi call the humans *Tawtute*, "Sky People," because they descended from the heavens and incarnate into the avatars. As Jung observed, in our culture, spacecraft have assumed the role of the chariots and other vehicles of the gods that were prevalent in earlier cultures (1967–78, 10:589–90, 608–11, 614, 621, 624). Reinforcing the incarnation theme is Dr. Grace Augustine's remark in the scriptment, "Time to take flesh and walk the earth" (Cameron 1994, 61).[7] From a different perspective, however, the Na'vi themselves are avatars, for as physical inhabitants of Pandora, they are physical incarnations of our archetypal gods. The movie invites viewers to project human archetypes onto the Na'vi, thus activating the archetypes within themselves.

Jake Sully's first contact with the Na'vi is with Neytiri, who both saves his life and begins his orientation to an alien world. Clearly, she is what Jungians call an "Anima figure," for the Anima in a man, which conditions his relation to women, is the archetype closest to a man's conscious mind and is therefore the archetype most likely to serve as a guide and mentor in the archetypal realms (Jacobi 1973, 118). (Similarly, the Animus in a woman's psyche regulates her relation to men and serves as her archetypal guide.)[8]

The Psychological and the Physical

As the unconscious psychological correlates of the instincts, the archetypes provide a nexus between, on the one hand, a spiritual realm occupied by gods and ancestral spirits and, on the other hand, neurophysiologic structures that are grounded in nature and our evolutionary history. That is, by virtue of the latter, the archetypes are physical, but by virtue of their intervention in consciousness, they are psychological. Hence, as Jung (1967–78,

14:767) stressed, the physical and the psychological must be understood as two aspects of a single underlying reality, the *unus mundus*, or "one world": "Undoubtedly the idea of the *unus mundus* is founded on the assumption that the multiplicity of the empirical world rests on an underlying unity, and that not two or more fundamentally different worlds exist side by side or are mingled with one another." Therefore, the archetypes are central to understanding the role of human consciousness in nature; they are the articulation points between the preconscious channels of our conscious experience and human neurophysiology grounded in natural history. Hence, archetypal figures, as perceived spiritual beings grounded in nature, contribute to our understanding of human perception of the sacredness of nature.

In their psychological impact, the Na'vi are spiritual beings and Pandora is a spiritual realm, but in the film, they were manifestly physical: natural, not supernatural. Although we experience them as archetypal figures arising from the collective unconscious, dwellers in an archetypal Garden (Stevens 1999, 200–209), in the context of the movie, they are physical beings inhabiting a physical place (a moon orbiting a planet in the Alpha Centauri system). Humans reach the Na'vi by physical means—an interstellar cruiser—and interact with them by means of physical avatars controlled by sophisticated technology. As a consequence, the Na'vi and their world are appealing to those viewers who are suspicious of dualistic conceptions of spiritual phenomena. Most of our contemporaries have difficulty taking seriously gods, nymphs, satyrs, and so forth, but a generation raised on space stations and shuttles and on video games and virtual reality finds it easier to believe in an expedition to a distant world and technologically controlled avatars: "Anything that looks technological goes down without difficulty with modern man" (Jung 1967–78, 10:624). The technological setting, therefore, reinforces a view that nature spirits reside in physical nature, not elsewhere.

Evolutionary Jungian psychology is similarly non-dualistic, seeing the physical and psychological realms as two aspects of a single underlying reality, the *unus mundus*. These two realms are addressed by the evolutionary and Jungian approaches, respectively. First, through comparative studies of related species, evolutionary psychology seeks to understand human neurophysiology as an adaptive mechanism in our environment of evolutionary adaptedness. Thus, this mechanism is thoroughly grounded in nature, experienced from the outside as an *object* of empirical investigation. Second, nature, and in particular human nature, is also experienced from the inside, or as *subject*, when the psyche is explored through phenomenology, which is the systematic empirical investigation of the

structure of consciousness. Jung's clinical work and his personal phenomenological research, for example, led to his description of the archetypes as
phylogenetic psychodynamic structures. Therefore, evolutionary Jungian
psychology addresses human nature from both sides, the physical and the
psychological, putting both in their natural context. In particular, from a
Jungian perspective, the Na'vi—or beings very much like them—*are* real,
but not in the Alpha Centauri system. Rather, they exist simultaneously in
the objective structure of the human genome and in the equally objective
species-specific structure of human psychospiritual experience.

Biophilia

On Pandora, we find not just archetypal people but also archetypal plants
and animals. These are species and larger genera that evoke characteristic psychological responses from people. These responses correspond to
innate behavioural patterns that have proved adaptive in the evolution of
Homo sapiens, especially during our long foraging phase. (An example is
a startle reaction to snakes [Buss 2012, 92–97].) As a consequence, many
plants and animals function as symbols capable of activating archetypal
patterns of motivation, emotion, perception, and action.

In 1984, Edward O. Wilson coined the term *biophilia* for the "innate
tendency to focus on life and lifelike processes" (1984, 1). This tendency is
unlikely to be encoded directly in the genome: "Biophilia, like other patterns of complex behavior, is likely to be mediated by rules of prepared and
counterprepared learning—the tendency to learn or to resist learning certain responses as opposed to others.... The feelings molded by the learning
rules fall along several emotional spectra: from attraction to aversion, from
awe to indifference, from peacefulness to fear-driven anxiety" (Wilson
1993, 31). Biophilia thus comprises the whole array of evolved adaptive
responses to living things. Stephen R. Kellert (1993, table 2-1), for instance,
describes nine different innate responses to nature, each with characteristic
adaptive functions: utilitarian (physical survival), naturalistic (curiosity,
outdoor skills), ecologistic-scientific (observation, knowledge), aesthetic
(environmental vitality, security), symbolic (enriched communication),
humanistic (bonding, nurturing care, co-operation, altruism), moralistic
(conservation, feelings of well-being), dominationistic (physical prowess),
and negativistic (safety). These "biophilia values" are all components of a
broad biophilia hypothesis, but there is evidence supporting each of them.
Kellert observes that all these values have "both the capacity for functional
advantage as well as exaggerated distortion and self-defeating manifestation" (56). Similarly, Jung (1967–78, 8:590n9) stressed that the archetypes
are ambivalent in moral valence.

From the perspective of archetypal psychology, these biophilia values are phylogenetic patterns of human response to nature (in particular, to our environment of evolutionary adaptedness), and they have both innate and learned triggering stimuli. The designers of Pandora's flora and fauna made expert use of these stimuli to evoke feelings of fear, awe, tenderness, wonder, and so on. Given the space constraints that preclude a comprehensive analysis of the symbolism of Pandoran life, I will discuss just two examples: dragons and trees.

Pandora hosts several species of winged reptiles, which are effectively dragons: *toruk*, the "last shadow"; *ikran*, the mountain banshee; *ikranay*, the forest banshee; *riti*, the stingbat; and *tetrapteron*, the four-winged flamingo-like bird. Symbolically, dragons combine wings, which establish a connection to the heavens (Stevens 1999, 630), with reptilian elements, which evoke the "more primitive, atavistic, and compulsive forms of human behaviour" (340). More broadly, the dragon combines the ability to soar to the heights with the ambivalent depths of nature, the unity of spirit and matter (128). Furthermore, Sully's perilous bonding with his *ikran* and especially his climactic bonding with *toruk*—both of which have their rookeries high in the Hallelujah Mountains (Wilhelm and Mathison 2009, 61, 79)—have the character of an archetypal Dragon-Battle, a type of the hero's "supreme ordeal" by which he obtains the "boon" (Campbell 1968, 245–46; Stevens 1999, 210). Sully's subsequent flights on the *ikran* and *toruk* also resemble the "soul flight" typical of shamanism (Winkelman 2002; 2010, 119–20).

Pandora

The moon Pandora is the body of Eywa, who is "the Great Mother. The goddess made up of all living things" (Cameron 2007, 53). As the coordinating process of all life on Pandora, Eywa is both physical and psychological, dual aspects of the *unus mundus*. "Some believe interconnectedness, which on Earth is often considered a spiritual concept, exists in a physical and tangible way on Pandora" (Wilhelm and Mathison 2009, 186). This interconnection is manifest in bioluminescence, which is one of the most characteristic features of Pandoran life and one of the most beautiful. It captivates the characters in the movie and the audiences who view it. It seems to be common to most, if not all, Pandoran life forms, and the bioluminescent network is even visible from space, revealing the energetic web that interconnects the entire living moon (Cameron 2007, 150).

This light resembles what Jung (1967–78, 8:388–96) called "scintillae," or soul-sparks, which appear in dreams and visions as points of light or eyes in the darkness: for example, the starry firmament, stars reflecting off the surface of the sea, myriad fish eyes in the sea's dark depths, flecks of gold sprinkled on dark sand, iridescent eyes on a peacock's tail, or even a nighttime regatta decorated with lanterns. Psychologically, the scintillae represent points of partial consciousness in the unconscious mind, the archetypal beings in the collective unconscious projected onto nature: that is, emerging consciousness of the spirits in nature (8:392). Jung quoted the seventeenth-century alchemist Heinrich Khunrath, who recognized scintillae as the "fiery sparks of the soul of the world" (8:388), the pure essential forms of a universally animated world. Jung explained: "These *formae* correspond to the Platonic Ideas, from which one could equate the *scintillae* with the archetypes.... One would have to conclude from these alchemical visions that the archetypes have about them a certain effulgence or quasi-consciousness, and that numinosity entails luminosity" (8:388). The scintillae attract conscious attention and focus the imagination (Mogenson 2006, 48); thus, they establish a resonance or symbolic link between activated archetypes and their projections in nature. According to archetypal psychologists, they reveal visually the numinous significance of the stimulus that has awakened the archetype, and they draw our attention to it, allowing its greater manifestation in consciousness. In their totality—as the myriad eyes of nature—they reveal the pervasiveness of meaning and the sacred in our environment.

The scintillae are incomplete manifestations of the *Lumen Naturae* or "Light of Nature," which is the complete web of symbolic connections, but repeated attention to the scintillae strengthens observers' "mental eyes" until they can experience full illumination (Jung 1967–78, 8:389), a holistic grasp of the symbolic network of meaning in nature, for "the light of nature is an intuitive apprehension of the facts, a kind of illumination" (13:148). According to Paracelsus, quoted in translation from Latin by Jung (13:148n6), the wise ones of old "derived their knowledge from the Light of Nature. This they nurtured in themselves.... It comes from nature which contains its manner of activity within itself. It is active during sleep and hence things must be used when dormant and not awake—sleep is waking for such arts—for things have a spirit which is active for them in sleep." Here, we see the same ambiguity between the dreaming and waking states that Sully experienced. As a "dreamwalker" (Cameron 2007, 45), he could perceive the luminous and numinous connections among all things. Sleep is waking for such arts. Paracelsus also said that the Light of Nature "is in the World and the whole edifice of the World is beautifully adorned and will be naturally preserved by it" (quoted in Jung 1967–78, 12:356), a perfect description of bioluminescence on Pandora.

Archetypal Trees

Besides animals, human biophilia encompasses the plant world and the landscape at large (Heerwagen and Orians 1993), both of which are exploited impressively in *Avatar*. In particular, trees are central to the symbolism of the movie and are an important archetypal image. Jung (1967–78, 13:350) summarized its symbolic range in "The Philosophical Tree": "Taken on average, the commonest associations to its meaning are growth, life, unfolding of form in a physical and spiritual sense, development, growth from below upwards and from above downwards, the maternal aspect (protection, shade, shelter, nourishing fruits, source of life, solidity, permanence, firm-rootedness, but also being 'rooted to the spot'), old age, personality, and finally death and rebirth." Many of these associations apply to the significant trees of *Avatar*.

In Jungian psychology, the tree, like the dragon, symbolizes a union of opposites (Earth and heaven, human and divine, conscious and unconscious), which is necessary for psychological integration (Stevens 1999, 253). Thus, the philosophical tree is closely associated with the alchemical philosopher's stone, which symbolizes this state of integration. It is not surprising, then, that Hometree and other sacred sites on Pandora are located over large unobtanium deposits (Wilhelm and Mathison 2009, 34).

Much of the action in *Avatar* revolves around *Kelutral* (Hometree), only one of many "great trees," where some of the Na'vi clans dwell (Cameron 2007, 44). These clans correspond closely in size and organization to the probable social groups of our foraging ancestors (Fox 1989; Stevens 1993, 67; Wilhelm and Mathison 2009, 34; Wilson 1978, 82–88). The Hometree of a clan may symbolize the group's organic integration, nurturing protection, integrity, stability, and permanence: the "maternal aspect." Cameron (2007, 45) describes Hometree's interior as "a living cathedral," as befits the dwelling place of archetypal spirits. Each clan has its wise woman, called a *tsahìk*, whom Augustine describes as "a kind of shaman," the spiritual leader who interprets the will of Eywa, the Great Mother "made up of all living things" (46, 53). In the Omaticaya clan, which Sully joins, the *tsahìk* is Mo'at, the mother of Neytiri, who is Sully's Anima-psychopomp (soulguide) and will be the next *tsahìk* (96). Serving a different function are the *Utraya Mokri* (Trees of Voices), which stand in the sacred groves. Looking something like willows, their tendrils can interface directly with the Na'vi's neural queues, which permits the Na'vi to upload their experiences into the Pandoran neural network and to download ancestral wisdom from it (89, 101). In the same way, shamans "plug into" the ancestral wisdom of the collective unconscious.

According to Mircea Eliade and others, the World Tree is a common feature of many shamanic cosmologies (Butterworth 1970, chap. 1; Eliade 1964, 269–74; Ryan 2002, 188–92). It is the *Axis Mundi*, or world axis, which the shaman ascends to contact celestial spirits or descends to contact chthonic spirits. Perhaps most like the shamanic World Tree is the Mother Tree, an ancient Pandoran "willow" that stands at the centre of *Vitraya Ramunong* (the Well of Souls), which is the fountainhead of Pandora's conscious energy vortex (Cameron 2007, 115–16). Joined with the other "willows" ringing the caldera, it forms "a braided mat resembling the surface of a brain" (116). Indeed, as Augustine explains, the trees of Pandora form a vast global neural network, each of the trillion trees acting like a neuron connected through their root tendrils to ten thousand other trees (101).

From a Jungian perspective, the Mother Tree, like the shamanic World Tree, is a powerful symbol of the *unus mundus* and of the relation of individual human psyches to the collective unconscious. Jung (1967–78, 10:53) said the archetypes are like "roots psyche has sunk into the earth... the most effective means conceivable of instinctive adaptation.... The chthonic portion of the psyche... in which its link with the earth and the world appears at its most tangible." The tree trunk represents the phylogenetic psyche common to all humans and encoded in the human genome. The tree ramifies, like our individual family trees, representing patterns of genetic relationship between our individual genotypes. From a Jungian perspective, this all reflects unconscious ancestral wisdom. Sometimes the shamanic World Tree has "soul-flowers" blooming at the periphery of its branches (Jung 1967–78, 9, pt. 1:596, 604; Ryan 2002, 44–46, 53, 58, 186). These represent the conscious minds of individual people. This symbol appears in *Avatar* both as the tendrils of the "willows," which interface with conscious Na'vi, and as the Na'vi sleeping in Hometree.

An important, related symbol is the *atokirina'* or woodsprites, the seed-pods of the Mother Tree (and the other Trees of Voices), which Neytiri describes as "very pure spirits" (Cameron 2007, 43): that is, they are soul-flowers. Swarming, as they do around Sully when he is anointed by them (Cameron 1994, 58), they also resemble Jungian scintillae, or soul-sparks. The two symbols merge if we understand them as points of incipient consciousness in the collective unconscious: "Though not coinciding with the ego, which Jung defines as the center of consciousness, these sparks of partial consciousness in the unconscious appear to us outwardly as the things of the world that attract our attention, compel our reveries, and stir the imagination" (Mogenson 2006, 47–48).

Connecting with the Archetypes

The Na'vi use their neural queues to connect to each other, to other animals, and to the Pandoran neural network in order to access "the collective wisdom of all Pandoran life" (Wilhelm and Mathison 2009, 28–29). This bond is presented as a physical connection, but in the archetypal world of Pandora, it is also spiritual, for the Na'vi are archetypal figures, evocative of the ideal human. The neural queue represents the spiritual connection with nature, which most contemporary people have lost, for "the Na'vi do not see themselves as separate from nature, but rather an integral part of it. Humans had a similar interconnectedness with nature long ago" (Wilhelm and Mathison 2009, 29).

Avatar shows this bond being used in two different ways. First, it is used to connect the individual Na'vi to the Pandoran collective intelligence, as when Sully bonds with the Tree of Voices. Second, it is used to connect one individual to another, as riders bond with their direhorses or *ikrans* (mountain banshees), or when two Na'vi join together in love (as do Sully and Neytiri). In Jungian psychological terms, the first is a connection between an archetype or complex and the undifferentiated ground of all archetypes; the second is an interaction between two distinct archetypes, with some coordination and perhaps contamination of content. Since the archetypes are just differentiated aspects of a unified collective unconscious and the complexes are just unconscious individual elaborations of them, such connections are common. Furthermore, since the archetypes and complexes are psychological in substance, there is no barrier to their communicating or coordinating psychological content, as represented by the neural connections of the Na'vi.

If we understand individual Na'vi as archetypes, then when they connect with Eywa through a Tree of Voices, they are drawing strength and inspiration from the undifferentiated unconscious archetypal self, of which they are but parts. When Na'vi die, they return to Eywa and contribute to the ancestral voices. We may see these as metaphors, respectively, for the genome's contribution to individual behavioural adaptations and for these behaviours' contributions to the genome's future evolution. The various human instincts (of which the archetypes are the psychological expressions), through their greater or lesser adaptation to the environment, contribute to the evolution of the human genome, which defines our species both physically and psychologically.

When avatar-Sully, who represents Sully's conscious ego interacting with the archetypal realm, connects his neural queue with Neytiri's or an animal's, he is establishing intimate contact with that archetype. In an analogous way, the ego can negotiate its relations with the archetypes, learn from them, draw strength from them, and work toward integration of the psyche. According to Jung (1967–78, 9, pt. 1:620), "This is the answer to the great question of our day: How can consciousness, our most recent acquisition, which has bounded ahead, be linked up again with the oldest, the unconscious, which has lagged behind? The oldest of all is the instinctual foundation." And how can we, who do not have the avatar technology, journey to Pandora and contact the Na'vi?

Visiting Pandora

In the movie, Pandora is a physical place, a moon of a planet in the Alpha Centauri system, but it has the characteristics of a spiritual realm. Its geography, flora, and fauna are numinous, perhaps more typical of fairy tales than science fiction. Superconductivity and intense magnetic fields create subtle forces and mysterious, awe-inspiring effects, such as the levitating Hallelujah Mountains—among which is Mons Veritatis, the "Mountain of Truth" (Cameron 2007, 70; Wilhelm and Mathison 2009, 21–23). The gravity is low, and the avatars felt freer, less embodied, less physical than they do in their Earthly bodies (Cameron 1994, 25; 2007, 24, 80). This spiritual character is reinforced by Pandora's atmosphere: a dense air lower in pressure than Earth's and breathable by its archetypal inhabitants but unable to sustain human life (Cameron 2007, 8; Wilhelm and Mathison 2009, 6, 8–9). Likewise, the Pandoran plant life is inedible by humans (Wilhelm and Mathison 2009, 5). Pandora is a magical place but not a human realm. It is significant that humans can live their avatar lives for only limited amounts of time. They have to return to the human world, leaving their "psionic link units" to eat and, presumably, to take care of the other necessities of human embodiment.[9] Pandora is manifestly a sort of Garden of Eden, at least for the Na'vi, a paradise to which the humans are seeking re-entry, if only to exploit its abundant resources.[10] By means of the avatar technology, people can walk once again in the archetypal Garden, but human nature prevents them from residing there permanently. As Augustine pointedly reminds Sully, "Our life out there takes millions of dollars of machinery to sustain. You visit—and you *leave*" (Cameron 2007, 84).

Likewise shamans, so long as they are alive, cannot remain in the spirit world indefinitely. Their presence there is maintained by a technology—drumming, chanting, psychoactive substances, and so on—but they must return because they are human and because it is their duty to bring the fruits of their journey back to their community (Walsh 1990, 31–32; Winkelman 2010, 57–58). A recurring motif in folklore and mythology is the temptation to refuse the return, to remain in the ecstatic dream (Campbell 1968, 193–96, 218). Sully expresses the common dilemma: "Everything is backwards now. Like out there is the true world, and in here is the dream," a feeling common among the avatar "drivers" (Cameron 2007, 66; 1994, 29).

The Innocent Child

Sully is typical of shamanic initiates who, according to some scholars, begin their path to shamanism through some trauma that brings them to the brink of death, leaving them broken in mind as well as body (Eliade 1964, 25–32; Ryan 2002, 90; Walsh 1990, 39–41; Winkelman 2010, 49, 52–53).[11] Sully subsequently hears an irresistible call to the realm of archetypal spirits, where he undergoes incredible trials, including the *uniltaron*, or "dream hunt," which is a formal "vision quest" (Eliade 1964, 36–38, 53–56; Ryan 2002, 107–10; Winkelman 2010, 57–58). He is consequently accepted into the community of spirits and becomes a sort of ambassador between the spirit world and our own—metaphorically, through the Pandoran story—thus becoming able to bring its wisdom and healing power back to our world (Walsh 1990, 31–32). Like some mythological heroes, he eventually achieves apotheosis, leaving his human body behind and joining the ranks of the archetypal spirits, symbolized in the movie by the Na'vi, who resurrect him with a subtle, luminous, incorruptible, spirit-body, the traditional dwelling place for the true self, uniting mind and nature, the conscious and the unconscious (e.g., Eliade 1969, 274, 283; Jung 1967–78, 13:29–30, 68–69, 76, 392).

Sully's childlike emptiness is stressed. Neytiri tells him, for example, "You are like a baby" (Cameron 2007, 40), and when Sully asks Neytiri why she saved him, she answers, "You have a strong heart. No fear. *But stupid!* Ignorant like a child!" (40–41). Augustine has already expressed her dismay at his lack of scientific training, but this turns out to be an advantage. Mo'at observes that it is difficult to teach humans—because "it is hard to fill a cup which is already full"—and Sully replies, "My cup is empty, trust me. Just ask Doctor Augustine. I'm no scientist" (47). As Cameron (1994, 75) explains, eventually Sully "embraced the animistic forest, which is alive with invisible dynamic forces, spirits. Things which he doesn't understand, but accepts, in a way a scientist could not without taking it apart and finding out how it worked. He deeply respects these primal people who are in touch with forces we no longer see and feel." Sully is psychologically prepared for contact with archetypal spirits. Aside from his somewhat fragile psychological condition, he is unburdened with complex theories and unaccustomed to extensive rational analysis; therefore, he is susceptible to an intrusion of unconscious forces. The conscious, rational ego, which wants to be in control, must be passivated to contact the archetypal world. This is achieved by *adaptive regression*, or *regression in service of the ego*:

that is, the ego abdicates conscious control to permit entry (and even possession) by subconscious forces (Rosegrant 1980, 1987; Stein 1974, 91–93; Wild 1965). This involves a lowered level of arousal, defocused attention, and a shift from "secondary process" rational cognition to more instinctual "primary process" non-rational thought (Martindale 1999; Mednick 1962; Mendelsohn 1976). Shamanic techniques for achieving a trance state include drumming, chanting, dancing, fasting, sleep deprivation, and the use of certain mind-altering substances (Walsh 1990, chap. 12; Winkelman 2010, chap. 4). Even in the more technological context of *Avatar*, when Sully enters the link unit for his first experience as an avatar, Augustine instructs him, "Relax and let your mind go blank. That shouldn't be hard for you" (Cameron 2007, 18). In this way Sully, the empty vessel, the innocent child, is prepared for his eventual rebirth as one of the Na'vi.

Rediscovering Our Place in Nature

How can we apply the insights of *Avatar* to our own situation? Although the avatar technology of the movie is more acceptable to contemporary people than archaic shamanic techniques are, there is nothing supernatural about the latter, for shamans use their understanding of neurophysiology and potent cultural symbols to facilitate conscious engagement with the unconscious archetypes (Winkelman 2002; 2010, 38, 113, 214–15). Furthermore, modern psychoanalytic techniques, such as active imagination, and modern incarnations of archaic techniques, such as dream incubation and shamanic journeying, permit contemporary Westerners to engage these archetypal forces (Harner 1980; Ingerman 1991; Jung 1997; Johnson 1986, pt. 3; LaBerge and Rheingold 1990; Meier 2009; Walsh 1990).

The goal of these techniques is psychological integration (Winkelman 2010, 4–6), especially between an often detached and calculating conscious ego and a deeper, more instinctual psyche, which is rooted in, and ultimately continuous with, nature. Jung (1967–78, 7:266; 9, pt. 1:490) called this practice of integrating our conscious and unconscious lives in order to discover our true selves "individuation," because its goal is a psyche that is undivided (Latin: *individuus*).

When Sully enters the world of the Na'vi, ultimately becoming one of them, he discovers the relation of archetypal humans to their environment. We can do the same, not through "psionic link units" and avatars but through ancient and modern psychospiritual practices, possibly enhanced by technology, including 3-D motion pictures. In this way, we can consciously integrate the archetypal human and its relation to nature into our contemporary lives. By these means, we may explore the archetypal landscape, as Sully and the others explore Pandora, coming to know this common, unconscious substrate of human experience, which will help us to discover how to relate to nature in a way consistent with human nature and human thriving. (I believe this would result in a more reverential attitude toward nature, mitigating environmental degradation.) Also by these means, we may engage the higher self in dialogue, bringing it into the light of consciousness in order that we may live in better accord with human nature.

Although science has not finished unravelling the complex interdependencies of genes and culture, I think it is clear that the archetypal human is fundamentally a paleolithic forager. Moreover, the pace of evolution is slow, so our biological nature cannot change quickly, but this conclusion does not imply that we should attempt an atavistic return to a paleolithic lifestyle. On the contrary, human nature also includes the capacities for learning, language, cultural evolution, and a highly differentiated conscious ego, so a return to the past would be contrary to human nature. Rather, our task is to strive for a rapprochement between our collective consciousness (as reflected in contemporary culture) and the collective unconscious (deriving from our biological nature). By using new and updated ancient practices, we can discover the nature, needs, and potentials of the human higher self and address them consciously in a contemporary context, thus improving the quality of life.

Jung was very sensitive to the dynamic tension between nature and culture. He concluded, "Nature *must not* win the game, but she *cannot* lose" (1967–78, 13:229). I believe that this statement is both wise and accurate (MacLennan 2007). On the one hand, nature must not win; that is, we should not allow her to win, if by that we mean a decline of civilization and a regression to a less differentiated state of conscious awareness. Indeed, such regression would be a denial of human nature, which is wired for cultural development. On the other hand, it is not possible for her to lose, because human nature is part of nature, and whatever we do, we must play by nature's rules. This could be interpreted as an irresolvable dilemma—Freud's "discontents of civilization"—but it is better to see it as a marriage, a *coniunctio oppositorum*, between collective consciousness (culture) and the collective unconscious (nature). Rather than fighting the Na'vi (nature spirits and archetypal ancestors), we should be seeking co-operation for mutual benefit.

Notes

1 There is no comprehensive list of Jungian archetypes, since they are somewhat fluid manifestations of a unitary collective unconscious, which emerge differently in differing cultural contexts. The archetypes mentioned here have been discussed by Jungian psychologists and are relevant to *Avatar* but are not all addressed in this essay.

2 "Phylogenetic" refers to the development of a species or other class of organisms, as opposed to "ontogenetic," which refers to the development of individual organisms.

3 Oversimplified definitions of *instinct* are treacherous, but for convenience, I will use the word. Our instincts "(1) are complexly specialized for solving an adaptive problem, (2) reliably develop in all normal human beings, (3) develop without any conscious effort and in the absence of formal instruction, (4) are applied without any awareness of their underlying logic, and (5) are distinct from more general abilities to process information or behave intelligently" (Buss 2005, 18). See McFarland (1987, 309–10) for a brief overview of the history and present understanding of instincts; Stevens (2003, chap. 4) addresses the definition of *instinct* in the context of the archetypes.

4 Jung (1967–78) refers to Jung's *Collected Works*, which will be cited by volume and paragraph number. Volume 8 is especially relevant to the present discussion. Jung devotes volume 9, part 1, paragraphs 87–110 to the collective unconscious.

5 "Gene-culture co-evolution" refers to the mutual influence of genetic evolution and cultural evolution on each other (Lumsden and Wilson 1983, 19–21, 170–71).

6 This is the 114-page "scriptment" (Cameron's term) of *Avatar*. Its pages are unnumbered, so for purposes of citation, I have counted them from the beginning, numbering the title page "1." The scriptment is sometimes more explicit about Cameron's intentions than the script (Cameron 2007), but, of course, we must beware of changes in Cameron's conception over the thirteen intervening years.

7 In the scriptment, Grace Augustine is called Grace Shipley and Jake Sully is called Josh Sully.

8 In the scriptment, Augustine has a corresponding Animus figure, N'deh, her mentor and guide in the world of the Na'vi (Cameron 1994, 29–31, 74, 87–88).

9 Sully remains on Pandora, but in his apotheosized Na'vi form. Presumably, the other avatar controllers who stay behind will survive in the same way.

10 In the scriptment, Sully tells the other controllers, "Pandora is not Hell, it is Eden" (Cameron 1994, 80). Interestingly, this garden seems to contain no serpents.

11 *Shaman* is, of course, a contested term. Here, I accept the principal characteristics of shamans identified by the empirical studies by Winkelman (1992), which were later summarized and discussed in Winkelman (2010, chap. 2).

References

Barkow, Jerome H., Leda Cosmides, and John Tooby, eds. 1992. *The Adapted Mind: Evolutionary Psychology and the Generation of Culture*. New York: Oxford University Press.

Buller, David J. 2005. *Adapting Minds: Evolutionary Psychology and the Persistent Quest for Human Nature*. Cambridge: MIT Press.

Buss, David M., ed. 2005. *The Handbook of Evolutionary Psychology*. Hoboken, NJ: Wiley.

———. 2012. *Evolutionary Psychology: The New Science of the Mind*. 4th ed. Boston: Allyn and Bacon.

Butterworth, E.A.S. 1970. *The Tree at the Navel of the Earth*. Berlin: Walter De Gruyter.

Cameron, James. 1994. *Avatar*. Scriptment. http://sfy.ru/?script=avatar.

———. 2007. *Avatar*. Screenplay. Twentieth Century Fox. http://web.archive .org/web/20100525105437/http://www.foxscreenings.com/media/pdf/ JamesCameronAVATAR.pdf

Campbell, Joseph. 1968. *The Hero with a Thousand Faces*. 2nd ed. Princeton, NJ: Princeton University Press.

Dyer, Donald R. 1991. *Cross-Currents of Jungian Thought: An Annotated Bibliography*. Boston: Shambhala.

Eibl-Eibesfeldt, Irenäus. 1970. *Ethology: The Biology of Behavior*. New York: Holt, Reinhart and Winston.

Eliade, Mircea. 1964. *Shamanism: Archaic Techniques of Ecstasy*. Translated by Willard R. Trask. Princeton, NJ: Princeton University Press.

———. 1969. *Yoga: Immortality and Freedom*. Translated by Willard R. Trask. Princeton, NJ: Princeton University Press.

Fox, Robin. 1989. *The Search for Society*. New Brunswick, NJ: Rutgers University Press.

Gibbons, Ann. 2010. "Close Encounters of the Prehistoric Kind." *Science* 328: 680–84.

Harner, Michael. 1980. *The Way of the Shaman: A Guide to Power and Healing*. San Francisco: Harper and Row.

Heerwagen, Judith H., and Gordon H. Orians. 1993. "Humans, Habitats, and Aesthetics." In *The Biophilia Hypothesis*, edited by S. R. Kellert and E. O. Wilson, 138–72. Washington, DC: Island Press.

Ingerman, Sandra. 1991. *Soul Retrieval: Mending the Fragmented Self*. New York: HarperCollins.

Jacobi, Jolande. 1973. *The Psychology of C. G. Jung: An Introduction with Illustrations*. Translated by Ralph Manheim. New Haven, CT: Yale University Press.

Johnson, Robert A. 1986. *Inner Work: Using Dreams and Active Imagination for Personal Growth*. New York: Harper and Row.

Jung, Carl G. 1967–78. *The Collected Works of C. G. Jung*. Translated by R. F. C. Hull. Princeton, NJ: Princeton University Press.

———. 1997. *Jung on Active Imagination*. Edited and introduction by Joan Chodorow. Princeton, NJ: Princeton University Press.

———. 2003. *The Earth Has a Soul: The Nature Writings of C. G. Jung*. Edited by Meredith Sabini. Berkeley, CA: North Atlantic Books.

Kellert, Stephen R. 1993. "The Biological Basis for Human Values of Nature." In *The Biophilia Hypothesis*, edited by S. R. Kellert and E. O. Wilson, 42–69. Washington, DC: Island Press.

LaBerge, Stephen, and Howard Rheingold. 1990. *Exploring the World of Lucid Dreaming*. New York: Ballantine Books.

Lorenz, Konrad. 1971. "Part and Parcel in Animal and Human Societies." In *Studies in Animal and Human Behaviour*, vol. 2, 115–95. Cambridge, MA: Harvard University Press.

Lumsden, Charles J., and Edward O. Wilson. 1983. *Promethean Fire: Reflections on the Origin of Mind.* Cambridge, MA: Harvard University Press.

MacLennan, Bruce. 2006. "Evolutionary Jungian Psychology." *Psychological Perspectives* 49(1): 9–28.

———. 2007. "Evolutionary Psychology, Complex Systems, and Social Theory." *Soundings: An Interdisciplinary Journal* 90(3–4): 169–89.

Martindale, C. 1999. "Biological Bases of Creativity." In *Handbook of Creativity*, edited by R. J. Sternberg, 137–52. Cambridge: Cambridge University Press.

McFarland, David, ed. 1987. *The Oxford Companion to Animal Behavior.* Oxford: Oxford University Press.

Mednick, S. A. 1962. "The Associative Basis of the Creative Process." *Psychological Review* 69: 220–32.

Meier, Carl A. 2009. *Healing Dream and Ritual: Ancient Incubation and Modern Psychotherapy.* 4th ed. Einsiedeln, Switzerland: Daimon Verlag.

Mendelsohn, G. A. 1976. "Associative and Attentional Processes in Creative Performance." *Journal of Personality* 44: 341–69.

Mogenson, Greg. 2006. "The Eyes of the Background: Nature, Spirit, and Fireside Psychoanalysis." *Spring* 75: 43–67.

Nagy, Marilyn. 1991. *Philosophical Issues in the Psychology of C. G. Jung.* New York: State University of New York Press.

Richardson, Robert C. 2007. *Evolutionary Psychology as Maladapted Psychology.* Cambridge: MIT Press.

Rosegrant, J. 1980. "Adaptive Regression of Two Types." *Journal of Personality Assessment* 6: 592–99.

———. 1987. "A Reconceptualization of Adaptive Regression." *Psychoanalytic Psychology* 4(2): 115–30.

Ryan, Robert E. 2002. *Shamanism and the Psychology of C. G. Jung: The Great Circle.* London: Vega.

Sabini, Meredith. 2000. "The Bones in the Cave: Phylogenetic Foundations of Analytical Psychology." *Journal of Jungian Theory and Practice* 2 (Fall): 17–33.

Stein, M. I. 1974. *Individual Procedures.* Vol. 1 of *Stimulating Creativity.* New York: Academic Press.

Stevens, Anthony. 1993. *The Two-Million-Year-Old Self.* College Station: Texas A&M University Press.

———. 1999. *Ariadne's Clue: A Guide to the Symbols of Humankind.* Princeton, NJ: Princeton University Press.

———. 2003. *Archetype Revisited: An Updated Natural History of the Self.* Toronto: Inner City Books.

Von Franz, Marie-Louise. 1980. *Projection and Re-Collection in Jungian Psychology: Reflections of the Soul.* La Salle, IL: Open Court.

Walsh, Roger N. 1990. *The Spirit of Shamanism.* Los Angeles: Tarcher.

Wild, C. 1965. "Creativity and Adaptive Regression." *Journal of Personality and Social Psychology* 2: 161–69.

Wilhelm, Maria, and Dirk Mathison. 2009. *James Cameron's* Avatar*: An Activist Survival Guide.* New York: HarperCollins.

Wilson, Edward O. 1978. *On Human Nature.* Cambridge, MA: Harvard University Press.

———. 1984. *Biophilia: The Human Bond with Other Species.* Cambridge, MA: Harvard University Press.

———. 1993. "Biophilia and the Conservation Ethic." In *The Biophilia Hypothesis,* edited by S. R. Kellert and E. O. Wilson, 31–41. Washington, DC: Island Press.

Winkelman, Michael. 1992. "Shamans, Priests, and Witches: A Cross-Cultural Study of Magico-Religious Practitioners." *Anthropological Research Papers* #44. Tempe: Arizona State University.

———. 2002. "Shamanism as Neurotheology and Evolutionary Psychology." *American Behavioral Scientist* 45(12): 1873–85.

———. 2010. *Shamanism: A Biopsychosocial Paradigm of Consciousness and Healing.* 2nd ed. Santa Barbara: Praeger.

Avatar and Artemis: Indigenous Narratives as Neo-Romantic Environmental Ethics

JOY H. GREENBERG

Since its origins during the past quarter century, environmental ethics has morphed into a multidisciplinary field, largely because of an increased awareness of our planetary eco-crisis combined with what many perceive as the failure of unitary disciplines to engage and adequately address the associated concerns. Clearly, a new discourse is needed: one that not only is informed by multidisciplinary approaches, including psychology, but also unifies the collective while pointing toward a more responsible treatment of nature and each other. Because stories are critical for establishing self and community identity, many have argued that an effective discourse of environmental ethics must be in narrative form. Along this line, geologian Thomas Berry (1988, 123) asserts, "It's all a question of story. We are in trouble just now because we do not have a good story." Like many, Berry found "the old story, the account of how the world came to be and how we fit into it," no longer practical. By "old story," Berry meant the Bible, which served its followers well until the so-called Enlightenment, which caused many to question the validity of its religious claims about the cosmos.[1]

Many indigenous "old" stories, however, continue to retain their cultural influence and to attract non-natives. Berry (1988, 184) suggests that this is because native myths, unlike those of non-indigenous groups, articulate an innate connection to a sanctified environment that stipulates each natural entity's place in the cosmos: "Awareness of a numinous presence throughout the entire cosmic order establishes among [native] peoples one of the most integral forms of spirituality known." For in many indigenous traditions, the "cosmic, human, and divine are present to one another in a way that is unique" and this mode of experience "might simply be called a nature mysticism" (ibid.). It is precisely this "nature mysticism" that is readily apparent in the 2009 film, *Avatar*, whose indigenous characters (the Na'vi) inhabit a setting replete with archetypal motifs such as inversion, personification, and transmorphism.[2] On the aptly named Pandora, mountains float in space seemingly of their own accord, and luminous tentacled particles resembling dancing jellyfish (*atokirina'*, the seeds of Eywa, the Great Mother) display the "energy that flows through all living things." All of this is further enhanced by 3-D technology, which allows the viewer, in effect, to become not only part of the story but part of the placescape. But *Avatar*'s nature mysticism did not arise in a vacuum: such an ethos has been present for millennia in one form or another in western indigenous traditions as well. In particular, a prototypical environmental ethic may be recognized in myths about the ancient nature goddess Artemis. An ecopsychological discussion of what I call "Artemisian spirituality" and *Avatar* will support the contention herein that both embody an eco-ethical perspective that is found in many indigenous hunting traditions.[3] *Avatar* and Artemis myths thus demonstrate the potential for neo-romantic narratives with worldviews that inspire eco-ethical action—what religion historians Bron Taylor (2010) and Roger S. Gottlieb (2006) call "dark green religion" and "religious environmentalism," respectively.

The Emergence of Artemis

One of the earliest records of Artemis in classical Greek myth is found in Hesiod's *Theogony* from the eighth century BCE, in which she is identified as the "archeress Artemis," a daughter of Zeus and Leto, and Apollo's twin (Caldwell 1987, 30). According to literary historian Robert P. Harrison (1993, 29–30), Artemis apparently originated as "the noumenal spirit of the forests which gives birth to a multiplicity of species (forms) that preserve their originary kinship within the forests' network of material interdependence." This concept of "originary kinship" associated with Artemis speaks to a primal, cosmic unity experienced by ancient Greeks. Her marginal status within the Olympic pantheon supports the theory that Artemis represented a prehistoric nature religion.

According to historian J. Donald Hughes (1990, 191), Artemis came from the transformation of a universal form that had existed for thousands of years: the goddess of the hunt, who was thought to protect wild animals and to exact retribution from hunters for disrespect, improper injury, or needless killing. Such a characterization seems logical given hunting's primacy as a means of sustenance for paleolithic peoples, who developed oral traditions, myths, and rituals that survived in folk culture, influenced art and literature, and actively inhibited exploitation of wildlife. From these may be deduced an unwritten Artemisian "hunters' code" that demanded respect for animals and plants and allowed the slaying of game only for human nourishment (194). Such a hunters' code is evident in *Avatar* and, in fact, still exists in many native hunting traditions.[4]

As an indigenous hunters' religion, Artemis's cult preserved beliefs and practices of the Greeks' early forebears. In addition to her prowess as a hunter, the two Homeric Hymns invoking her identify Artemis as a "virgin archer" and "the sacred virgin" (*Homeric Hymns* 2006, 4, 5). Apparently, Artemis functioned to encourage the Greeks to value their "un-erotic," or virginal, sides, as well as their hunting ability (xi). In this way, virginity became linked to purity and innocence and deserved protection. Possibly because of these archaic associations between Artemis and virginity, her domain came to be defined as chaste as well.[5] In psychological parlance, Artemis was "the projection of whatever it is in the human psyche that finds the sacred and the inviolable in nature" (Hughes 1990, 193).

The environmental relevance of Artemis's virginity was that everything within her domain—animals, forests, mountains, rivers, and the sea—was sacrosanct and therefore warranted protection. In this way, sacred groves with initially undefined borders became dedicated to her, and experience of the divine, metaphorized as rituals, sanctified the settings where these experiences took place. By staying the hunter's hand and preserving wilderness areas from habitat destruction, the worship of Artemis is credited with saving sizable portions of the Greek landscape from desecration for centuries (Hughes 1990, 196).

Artemis's protective influence should not be underestimated, for the ancient forests were not always safeguarded, as many have pointed out. Neolithic humans exploited and harvested their woods extensively, which is perhaps why the goddess came to be assigned dominion over "those dark and inaccessible regions where wild animals enjoyed sanctuary" (Harrison 1993, 23). While veneration of Artemis and her groves did not prevent all anti-environmental activity, it seems to have slowed it down considerably. However, once Artemis was stripped of her divine stature by the Greek philosophers, the groves fell into a state of neglect, ultimately disappearing with the "mindless deforestation of the Mediterranean" (55).

By the fourth century BCE, Plato was recalling nostalgically a time when much of Attica was still covered by forests. In *Critias* he observes about the hills surrounding Athens: "In comparison of what then was, there are remaining only the bones of the wasted body" where once there had been forests (Plato 360 BCE). What Plato did not acknowledge was his role, along with the other early philosophers, in contributing to the "bones

of the wasted body," which may be read with a dual meaning: Plato's barren scene evokes images not only of environmental expiration but of the
death of Artemis and all her mythic cohorts. For in deracinating myths
from their spirituality, Homer and Plato desanctified the sacred groves
dedicated to Artemis and the other pagan deities. Once the myths were
rendered virtually meaningless, the established taboos and protective legislation became so as well, resulting in the collective abandonment of formerly ingrained moral and ethical truths. The desanctification of myths
combined with Plato's formerly abundant but now denuded Athenian hill-
sides seem to symbolize Artemis's similar fate as she slowly morphed into
a formless *anima mundi*, the all-encompassing World Soul envisioned in
Timaeus (Plato 360 BCE).[6]

Clearly, deforestation was a problem in ancient Greece, although it had
not yet achieved the calamitous proportions evident in contemporary
Greece, the result of twenty-five hundred more years of environmental
exploitation (Dillon 1997, 127). The demise of Artemisian spirituality and,
with it, her inherent environmental ethic ultimately came about when
her faithful followers stopped believing her stories. The bare "bones" of
Attica may now be understood to represent both Artemis's denuding by
Actaeon—who, in Ovid's account, dared to watch the goddess bathing in
a spring—and Actaeon's being skinned alive by his hunting dogs as part of
her retaliation (Ovid 1993, 82–86).

Artemisian Spirituality and *Avatar*

When understood as a form of environmentalism, Artemisian spirituality
conveys a cultural, political, ethical, and religious stance similar to the one
exemplified by the indigenous Na'vi in *Avatar*. Just as there seems to have
been a "hunter's code" in Ancient Greece, so do the Na'vi demonstrate a
reverence for life and a desire to heal the breach provoked by its taking.
For instance, when alien-cum-native Jake Sully thanks Neytiri, an Omaticaya clan princess of the Na'vi, for saving his life by killing the ferocious
viperwolf that attacked him, she reprimands him: "You do not thank for
this! This is sad." She is not pleased to have taken the beast's life for a reason other than food procurement. It thus becomes apparent that, as with
Artemis's cults, needless killing and injury are forbidden on Pandora, the
mythical planetary setting for *Avatar*. Indeed, Neytiri strongly resembles
Artemis throughout the above scene, particularly when she leaps through
the air with bow and arrow poised to shoot the viperwolf.

Neytiri's Artemisian quality also becomes apparent when she begins
teaching Sully's avatar how to live as a Na'vi member. One of his first lessons
is the correct way to take the life of an animal. Just as the ancient Greeks

participated in rites associated with hunting, fishing, and gathering that embodied an implicit ethic of respect for other forms of life (Hughes 1990, 194), the Na'vi perform similar rituals following animal and plant life-taking in which they "bless" the dead and pray: "Your spirit goes with Eywa." In this way, the Na'vi affirm their reverence for Eywa, their "Great Mother," a Gaia figure of whom Artemis is an aspect. Bron Taylor and Adrian Ivakhiv (2010, 386) note this implicit ethic of reverence for others that the Na'vi reveal throughout *Avatar*, calling this sensibility a "holistic ecological spirituality." As with Artemisian spirituality, this ecological ethos may be seen not only in the Na'vi obligatory respect toward prey noted above but also in the close relationship the clans believe is possible with other species. Conversely, such respect for "mother" wisdom contrasts sharply with the apparently masculinist, non-indigenous, "sullied" society of Jake Sully before he is "reborn" as a member of the Na'vi.

Because of their awareness of and appreciation for the environment, the Na'vi belief system, like that of many other indigenous mythologies, may be seen as a repository of "traditional ecological knowledge," or TEK, as environmental anthropologist Fikret Berkes calls such wisdom (1999). Indeed, *Avatar* director James Cameron has acknowledged the "specific indigenous knowledge" from which contemporary society can benefit (Suozzi 2010). Such knowledge inspires a *"sacred ecology"* (Berkes 1999, 163, emphasis in original). Moreover, this connection between environmental knowledge and spirituality is noted in religion researcher Jon P. Bloch's (1998, 65) study, which found that attaining environmental knowledge was "important in adopting a spiritual worldview" among those who felt alienated from organized religions. In *Avatar*, TEK can be recognized in the scenes depicting Neytiri teaching Sully the Na'vi language and way of life and showing him how to hunt and use his "queue" to enable the bonding that occurs between hunters and their direhorses and *ikran*, the flying pterodactyl-like banshees that the Na'vi tame and ride by linking their hair braids to tails extending from the creatures' ears. Neytiri also explains to Sully how to use his queue to connect with the branch ends of the Tree of Souls, enabling communication with Eywa and connection to Pandora's "network of energy."

This focus on Na'vi traditional knowledge iterates the unity with nature expressed by indigenous cultures that is generally lacking in non-natives and without which the latter may be powerless to alter their attitudes toward the environment. Sully demonstrates his woeful lack of TEK when he wanders into the Pandoran forest against orders and confronts a vicious thanator that almost kills him in a scene not unlike Actaeon's encounter with Artemis. Thus, although contemporary ecological problems may derive from the human estrangement from nature that has enabled her mistreatment, as postulated by many theorists, indigenous epistemologies like those portrayed in *Avatar* may inform new narratives that cohere with more pro-environmental attitudes. That such an environmental ethic is critical for Earth and human survival is the message that Cameron seems to be implying, for when the environment is sanctified, people feel more compelled to defend it, just as the Na'vi act to save Pandora. Indeed, several religion research studies have shown that belief in the inviolability of nature may be integral for an eco-ethical attitude (Bloch 1998; Tarakeshwar et al. 2001).

Because of Amerindian attachment to and reverence for Earth, it has been suggested that non-indigenous Americans might look to their native predecessors as potential guides for eco-ethical reindigenization. As Dakota Sioux historian Vine Deloria Jr. points out, "Indians experience and relate to a living universe, whereas western people—especially scientists—reduce all things, living or not, to objects" (quoted in Bernstein 2005, 121). This objectification has allowed Westerners to manipulate and exploit their environment, expediting their ability to "destroy the world while attempting to control it" (ibid.). Deloria saw Westerners through the eyes of one whose people's culture was manipulated, exploited, and destroyed by Euro-Americans, enabling him to understand the meaning of displacement and alienation. It also enabled him to comprehend the paradoxical quality of Western culture, which has succeeded masterfully on the ability of its collective consciousness to achieve while at the same time has failed generally to comprehend "nature as a source of spiritual and psychological life" (Deloria 2009, 2). Deloria believed that indigenous cultures like that of the pre-contact Sioux contained "certain understandings that can help us rethink and redress this lack" of environmental awareness (ibid.). Integral to the Sioux worldview was its holism, meaning that unlike many Westerners, "the Sioux did not separate their thoughts into categories and disciplines. Everything was practical, economic, political and religious all at once," just as in Greek mythology (7).

The sanctification of nature is readily apparent in *Avatar* as well. The Tree of Souls is so sacred that the Na'vi are ultimately moved to defend it. *Avatar* thus exemplifies cinematically an essential feature of what may be called "ethopoietic narratives of place": celebrations of natural environments with inherent spiritual value that motivates activism for their protection, an example of Gottlieb's (2006) "religious environmentalism." Sully's initiation, or indigenization, therefore reflects his transformation from someone with a modern Western perspective into someone with a native, Eywa-Artemisian ethos. Sully further demonstrates this indigenization with his speech: "Look at the world they [Sky People] come from. There is no green there. They killed their mother [Earth]." Sully's choice of pronoun ("they" instead of "we") clearly confirms his dissociation from the invaders and his indigenous "rebirth." As the nefarious Colonel Quaritch sneers, Sully has "gone native."

Avatar and the Romantic Polemic

Sully's altruistic actions to save the Na'vi, however, are neither universally accepted nor appreciated by viewers. Indeed, much controversy has erupted over the meaning of the Na'vi's violent resistance and Sully's role in inciting it. Some critics have suggested that by organizing the Na'vi to defend themselves against the imperialistic Sky People, Sully actually feeds into the "white messiah" stereotype. As such, he represents the Eurocentric attitude that colonizers are not so much exploiting the indigenes and their natural environment as helping "primitives" to become more "civilized." Viewed this way, Sully is the "white messiah" or "saviour" of the Na'vi, who are believed to be incapable of saving themselves, a clearly racist perspective. Cameron denies this analysis, however, pointing out that the general response to the film by indigenous people has been "overwhelmingly positive" (Suozzi 2010). In fact, native viewers seem to have fewer issues with the film's representation of them than do non-natives.[7]

Because of concerns about the portrayal of native people in films, Cherokee indigenous traditions scholar Daniel Heath Justice acknowledges that he and his cohorts viewed Avatar with low expectations, but their actual "responses ranged from guarded optimism...to thoughtful frustration" (2010). Justice is critical of Avatar for its missed narrative opportunities. He especially finds fault with the selection of Sully, "the least interesting and most consistently obtuse figure," as the "point-of-view character." Here, Justice is spot on: Avatar's narrative is its weakest element. In fact, the storyline is a blatant pilfering of several previous films, including FernGully: The Last Rainforest (1992) and Pocahontas (1995), as many have noted in online essays and blogs.[8] Even so, those who characterize Sully as a "white messiah" forget that it is not the white Sully who "saves" the Na'vi homeland—it is the blue Sully in his avatar body and Na'vi spirit who galvanizes them into saving themselves. Only after Sully is "reborn" as an Omaticaya clan member does he become impassioned sufficiently to rally the Na'vi to defend Pandora. In this way his "rebirth"—his indigenization—resembles a religious conversion, which in many ways it is.

Linked to complaints about Sully's "white messiah" stereotyping are claims that Avatar also represents a "noble savage" narrative that is distinguished by a main character from an advanced civilization (Sully) who "goes native" after immersion in a pre-technological tribe—an action, according to science historian Adam Frank (2009), that allows Sully to see that "only in the more natural state of the hunter-gathering tribe" was a "pure connection with the world" retained. *Avatar* is different, however, from previous "noble savage" stories in that it adds "a significant ecological theme" (ibid.). In this way, says Frank, Cameron relates "a newer story" about how science can lead to "pantheistic spiritual sensibilities." Such sensibilities are demonstrated by the Na'vi recognition of an interconnecting dynamic among all living things on Pandora that replicates the "network of material interdependence" and "originary kinship" associated with Artemis, as discussed above. Indeed, this connection is shown empirically in the film by the data recorded on the scientists' instruments when they are studying the Pandoran forest. By asking his audience to attend to the environment in all its visible and invisible forms and patterns, Cameron suggests that science can help forge stronger cosmic connections, allowing "a means of seeing more deeply and responding more authentically" to the world (Frank 2009).

The "white messiah" and "noble savage" references are related to the persistent accusations of romanticism made whenever non-native people are perceived as idealizing native cultures.[9] Such idealism is deemed naive, or worse, by some who suggest that it symbolizes impossible yearnings for a return to Eden, Arcadia, or the Golden Age. The implication is that such nostalgia is immature escapism, and many skeptics have emerged to discredit the idea of Westerners turning to, for instance, Native American traditions looking for an exemplary environmental ethic. These commentators disparage such idealizing of indigenous traditions as disingenuous: "neo-romantic hogwash, just...noble-savage nonsense with a new environmental spin," according to environmental philosophers J. Baird Callicott and Michael P. Nelson (2004, 132–33), who argue against this derogation and attempt to show the positive qualities of Native American environmental ethics.

Callicott, in particular, has endured disparagement of his theories about Native American environmental ethics by radical ecologist Mick Smith (2001, 6, 35), who claims that the former's "Arcadian romanticism" extends to Callicott's belief in human interconnectedness with nature at the quantum level. Callicott's argument is problematic for Smith "because humans do not operate ethically at the level of quanta. The fact that we are one with nature at this level gives us no ethical guidance at all" (35). However, by assuming that what is true for him must be so for everyone, does not Smith commit the scholar's "crime" of essentialism? It seems that Smith has failed to consider the positive emotional response connected to the experience of oneness with nature, which has been reported by many. It stands to reason that if human functioning is affected by visible as well as invisible forces like those posited in quantum physics and if ethics formation is a human function, then invisible quanta may, indeed, influence ethics. Moreover, Smith apparently misses Callicott's point, which seems to be that human-nature holism can and does lend ethical guidance by transforming attitudes, as suggested by the Bloch (1998) and Tarakeshwar et al. (2001) studies. Smith concludes that in articulating a case for cosmic wholeness, Callicott's "holistic extensionism," as Smith calls it, is about humans *behaving* as if they do not feel isolated from nature, when Callicott's idea seems to be rather about humans *feeling* that they are a part of the environment, which inspires them to treat it deferentially.

In my reading, Callicott's human-nature holism is not about the elimination of human-nature dualism; it is about the awareness of it. Awareness leads to greater empathy for the "Other" in this opposition and precedes attitudinal transformation. Many say that when in nature, whether hiking or surfing or enjoying being outside in some other way, they do feel a sense of unity, which manifests as reverence. As a result of this awareness, they report being more inclined to believe that one way to increase the likelihood of re-creating this experience is to preserve the place for future visits. In so doing, they are expressing Artemisian spirituality. By invoking Artemis, however unconsciously, a concept that she represents—the ethical treatment of the environment—is made conscious. In this way, environmental ethics arguably becomes psychically embedded, eliciting eco-ethical behaviour that is *felt* to be right as opposed to that which has been coerced. The problem for Smith and his fellow anti-romantics appears to be their discomfort with non-rationalist discourse, but how else to discuss human feelings?

Callicott and Nelson (2004, 134) have responded to the romanticism critique by noting that while proponents of indigenous eco-ethics stress attitude, "skeptics offer behavioral evidence." By focusing on what some Amerindians "did (and do) in and to nonhuman natural entities and nature as a whole," these critics fail to see that such behavioural evidence is only marginally relevant "to the existence of traditional American Indian environmental ethics," which is a cognitive as well as behavioural phenomenon (134, 135). For imputing to all indigenous Americans the actions of a few tribes serves to perpetuate the essentializing, racist stereotyping of all Indians. As Callicott (1994) puts it, "The debate over whether or not an environmental ethic was part of the cognitive cultures indigenous to North America has largely proceeded *a priori*—that is, without benefit of reference to specific Native American intellectual traditions" (130). In

other words, critics of Native American environmental ethics have gener-
alized the anti-environmental activities of a few tribes to all while failing to
acknowledge the possibility for eco-ethical conduct in unstudied subjects.
More importantly, Callicott insists that when compared to those whose
beliefs are "preserved in cultural materials" like the Bible, an innate Native
American environmental ethic is, indeed, confirmed (130–31).[10]

Yes, Native American groups have committed what might be considered
anti-environmental behaviour, but many of the actions occurred following the mass invasion of Europeans and reflect the resulting disintegration
of native cultures and not necessarily their former attitudes or conduct
toward nature. Moreover, "in any culture, actual human behavior will
never measure up to the moral norms or ideals envisioned by its worldview
and ethos, but in striving toward them,... some overall movement in the
direction of those norms and ideals will have been achieved" (Callicott and
Nelson 2004, 134–35). This is why, when all is said and done, Amerindians,
on the whole, "probably treated nature better because of their environmental ethics than otherwise they might have" (135). With this in mind, might
it not behoove those attempting to address the eco-crisis at least to consult,
if not plumb, indigenous narratives?

Healing Fictions

For psychologist Renee A. Lertzman (2010, 41), *Avatar* demonstrates how
"green fantasy lends itself to a splitting up of the world—and arguably our
psyche—in our desire to return to a more primitive, innocent mode of
existence." She argues that through this infantilization, watching *Avatar*
allows a "safe and culturally sanctioned context" to experience "the deepest longings we have for the return to the Mother." In this way, Eden and
Mother are idealized into an "image of nature before the Fall itself: the
fantasy of returning to the Garden that continues to plague most of us with
any form of environmental consciousness" (42). Lertzman refers to the
depth psychological view that the "paradise age" represents a primordial
time when humans were "still in union with the gods" (Edinger 1992, 8).
During this period, the ego was "as yet unborn, not yet separated from the
womb of the unconscious and hence still partaking of the divine fullness
and totality" (ibid.). For ancient humans, consciousness-ego had not yet
detached from the unconscious-psyche, which contributed to the perception of oneness with their environment. While Lertzman's linking of Eden,
Earth, and Mother as metaphors of loss and longing are consistent with
Jungian theory, she presumes that "most of us" who are environmentally
conscious share this intense nostalgia for a perfect, pristine nature. However, many who profess "environmental consciousness" do not claim to be

"plagued" by "the fantasy of returning to the Garden" (Lertzman 2010, 42). Rather, they appear more interested in preventing what environmental complexity and resiliency remains from being further destroyed or degraded.[11]

In addition, while longing for paradise represents for psychologists an archetypal condition of humanity, Lertzman's contention that such yearning is unrealizable and hence, pathological, ignores the potential for healing afforded by such feelings. As eco-poet Gary Snyder (1995, 240) writes, "There is no 'original condition' that once altered can never be redeemed." Snyder understands original nature "in terms of the myth of the 'pool of Artemis'" visited by the goddess to renew her virginity: "the wild has—nay, is—a kind of hip, renewable virginity" (ibid.). Snyder speaks to the uniquely human ability to travel anywhere that pleases, if only in imagination—something that seems not to have occurred to Lertzman. Even if her premise that "most" environmentalists "share this intense nostalgia" for primal return were accurate, Lertzman's argument that to reach "psychic maturity" one must eschew such edenic longing seems ill-founded (2010, 42). In fact, such longing represents a universal mytheme: the desire to "return" to primordial unity because "going back" is part of the archetypal journey of the hero, of self-realization, undertaken throughout the course of life and over which we have scant conscious control.

Rather than pathological, as Lertzman would have us believe, the awareness of such longing may be experienced as healing, or, as ecopsychologist James Hillman (2005, 2006) says, "soul-making." Indeed, pathology is indispensable for healing. Without a wounding, there can be no change. Without longing, there is no paradise. The environment is simply the collective projection. For these reasons, Hillman (2006, 73) argues that romanticism is also soul-making, for "ensouling *the world* was a crucial part of their [the romantics'] program" (emphasis in original). The romantics "recognized the traps of narcissistic subjectivity in their vision. Hence, they sought the spirit in physical nature...and a return to the classic Gods and Goddesses, attempting to revivify the soul of the world with pantheism" (73–74). Instead of disdaining romanticism, as many postmodern theorists do, might we not cultivate it as a healing response to the global eco-crisis?

Despite its derogation, the romantic longing for return endures. Psychotherapist Jerome Bernstein (2005, 81) believes that such persistence stems from the Western ego being thrust into a "reconnection with nature by an evolutionary process in the name of species preservation—if not the preservation of all of life as we know it." To put it bluntly, survival of not only humans but all life depends upon remaking the bond—or queue, in *Avatar*—with the environment. Bernstein emphasizes that this "'reconnection' is *not* a regression." It is rather a "*dimension of existence*, as a *life form*, as a *reality principle*, different from that to which we have accustomed ourselves, integrating with it. The major impact of this reconnection on the western ego is psychological and spiritual" (ibid.; emphasis in original). Bernstein disputes the anti-romantic contention that the environmentalist impulse to reconnect with nature is psychologically regressive. In fact, this yearning reflects the recursiveness of nature—both inner and outer—and nature's ongoing drive to return, to regain, and to restore what already enjoys a certain familiar place in memory.

Not coincidentally, recursiveness also defines the narrative form, which is the key to a postmodern eco-ethic that reconnects people with nature, as argued herein.[12] This argument has merit because one of the functions of stories is to provide worldview. Environmental attitude is thus determined by the stories absorbed from one's culture. But not just any story is ethopoietic, or ethos-making. In order to empower attitudinal change, a story must be mythopoeic. Myths resonate ecopsychologically because, according to Hillman, "the entire narrative of a human life, the characters that we are and the dreams we enter, are structured by the selective logic of a profound *mythos* in the psyche" (2005, 11; emphasis in original). In other words, myths are plots, and the "basic answers to why in a story are to be discovered in myths" (ibid.). Here is where *mythos* meets *poiesis*, which Hillman takes as "making by imagination into words" (4). Mythopoiesis thus means "the persuasive power of imagining in words, and artfulness in speaking and hearing, writing and reading" (ibid.): in other words, myth making.

Just as dreaming, speaking, hearing, writing, and reading mythopoeic narratives can be transformational, so can watching them. In this way, film—particularly 3-D film, as was *Avatar*—may be experienced like the Greeks did their tragedies. According to Hillman (1992, 38), "Healing begins when we move out of the audience and onto the stage of the psyche, become characters in a fiction... and as the drama intensifies, the catharsis occurs; we are purged from attachments to literal destinies, find freedom in playing parts, partial, dismembered, Dionysian, never *being* whole but *participating in* the whole of the play" (emphasis in original). Here Hillman alludes to the "participation mystique" (a term coined by Rudolf Otto [1958]) that occurs during gatherings perceived as sacred, an experience felt to be collectively transformational. Because films are often viewed in large theatres, their potential for facilitating participation mystique experiences seems evident.

Through mythopoeic stories, people connect with others not only on an *inter*personal level, as they identify with the teller-protagonist, but on an *intra*personal level: that is, psychically. Such a feeling of "uniting" and "convincing" through myth suggests that the coming together for a common cause like environmentalism can only take place when there exists an embedded ethos within a guiding narrative that is recognized and internalized within a community. The uprising of the Na'vi to defend Pandora in *Avatar* clearly demonstrates this phenomenon.[13]

Conclusion

Mythic narratives are essential to cultures because they help individuals to make sense of life, as philosopher Charles Taylor argues (1989). Identity requires "an orientation to the good," which has to be woven into an understanding of "life as an unfolding story" (Taylor 1989, 47). Accordingly, a "basic condition of making sense of ourselves [is] that we grasp our lives in a *narrative*" (ibid.; emphasis in original). Making sense of life as a story is absolutely obligatory, because in order to have a sense of self, one must have a notion of how one has become and of where one is going. By the same token, ethics—"an orientation to the good"—must be embedded in mythopoeic stories in order to reach the collective. The problem for environmental ethics, according to Buddhism scholar and eco-critic Graham Parkes (1997, 124), is how to generate "an experiential realization" of the cogency of such concepts in the urbanized, many of whose lives are devoid of the natural. He concludes that imparting environmental ethics through myths and literacy education is critical, but because the people most needing their perspectives changed do not read much anymore, film is an optimal medium for the dissemination of these ideas (124–25). Parkes's advocacy for cinematic narratives as environmental ethics makes sense given the screen-addiction that is characteristic of contemporary life.

Bernstein (2005, xviii) extends this notion by noting that unlike the past, when the arts, poetry, drama, troubadours, and literature were "primary carriers of archetypal awareness," film has now become a "primary mode of incarnating and communicating collective consciousness and evolution." Film's emergence as a "major vehicle and harbinger of society's psychic evolution" has made it possible to see "mythological and archetypal themes and changes happening in our midst" (ibid.). In this way, film can be a "graphic confrontation with emerging positive and negative social consciousness as well as new psychic realities" (ibid.). Because of its mass accessibility, film facilitates the mythopoeic revisioning of narratives, expediting changes in the collective consciousness.

In the context of the above articulation of the significance of stories, *Avatar*'s narrative deficiencies become more glaring. Nevertheless, the film illustrates that by embodying cultural worldviews, indigenous myths may inspire ethical attitudes and behaviour toward nature. No one forces or even advises the formerly apathetic Sully to defend Hometree; he simply does it, as if in response to an inner directive. As explained by psychologist Lionel Corbett (2001, 84), "When the myth in which we live is unconscious, we are like...fish in water." The myth "creates the atmosphere in which we live and is taken for granted. Our fundamental attitudes are then derived from it." Articulated here is the innate sense of "doing the right thing" when one is guided by an ethopoietic narrative that situates ethics within a "cognitive context" (Callicott 1994, 26).

Analyzing *Avatar* ecopsychologically allows the comprehension of its "evolutionary-ecological environmental ethic," which is complemented by indigenous eco-ethics providing images, metaphors, and myths to advance the process of ethopoiesis (Callicott 1994, 192). By exemplifying indigenous eco-ethics, the film evokes Artemisian spirituality—an androgynous perspective, which, like Hillman's (2005, 102) psychic hermaphroditism, "holds juxtapositions without feeling them as oppositions." The recognition that oppositions like human-nature exist on a continuum in syzygy rather than as separated polarities frees the imagination and facilitates changes in attitude.[14] With an Artemisian outlook, as with psychic hermaphroditism, "nature is transformed by imaginative deformation, *physis* by *poiesis*" (ibid.; emphasis in original). This transformation promotes inner—and, by extension, environmental—healing. For when we heal ourselves, we heal the world, according to ecopsychological theory (Hillman 2006).

If imagination is the key to transformation, then creative people are potential sources of new myths. Psychologically, "such individuals are being prompted by archetypal forces, which as they evolve emerge...into collective consciousness" (Corbett 2001, 93). It is a process not unlike the revisioning and recording of indigenous stories by Homer and Hesiod. Admittedly, however, this evolution in consciousness will not happen soon. This is because, as Callicott (1994, 192) acknowledges, the "process of worldview poiesis is gradual, cumulative, and ongoing." C. G. Jung (1983, 401) concurred, saying the spiritual transformation of humanity "follows the slow tread of the centuries and cannot be hurried or held up by any rational process of reflection, let alone brought to fruition in one generation." Nevertheless, what *is* possible now is the transformation in individuals who create opportunities to influence others of like mind. But such change will not happen "by persuading or preaching" (ibid.). It will come about through self-reflection, because those who have insight into their own actions, and have thus, in Jung's words, "found access to the unconscious," involuntarily influence their environment (ibid.). Jung was saying that self-reflection enables self-change, which in turn transforms the environment in a manner not unlike Callicott's holism above. In other words, a transformed psyche projects a transformed environment. Gottlieb (2006, 30) puts it like this: "Getting a rational and moral sense of what is responsible treatment of the earth depends on our getting a responsible and moral sense of what it means to be human and of how we ought to treat each other as well as the rest of the earth." The way we relate to nature is not just about marvelling at the external and visible. It is also about the inner and invisible: ourselves.

Such a rapprochement between humans and nature is plausible, Hillman suggests, because the individual *anima* (soul) coheres with the *anima mundi* (World Soul). Accordingly, and in line with Jung's above insight, any "alteration in the human psyche resonates with a change in the psyche of the world," transforming the collective consciousness in the process (Hillman 2006, 35). All of this seems to indicate that, like the ancient myths that once communicated moral behaviour and values, the discourse of environmental ethics will be most effective when the symbolic, non-rational language of poetry is rejoined with science, which was extracted from mythology by Greek philosophy. Mythology will then be restored to its archaic function of providing individuals and communities with TEK-packed narratives that help them make sense of their lives and that enable indigenization, thereby instilling a desire to care for the environment and each other. Yes, "it's all a question of story," or, hopefully, stories: neo-romantic, mythopoeic, eco-ethical stories. And like the last "gift" in Pandora's basket, hope may be all we have left.

Notes

1 See Greenberg (2010) for a discussion of ways in which Christians have been revisioning Genesis to be more eco-friendly. See also Gottlieb (2006, 22–31) on eco-theological responses.

2 Bron Taylor (2010, 14–22) calls this form of nature worship "spiritual animism."

3 Ecopsychology posits that the psyche is "rooted inside a greater intelligence once known as the *anima mundi*" (Roszak 1995, 16; see also Hillman 2006, 27–49).

4 For more on the primacy of hunting culture, see Munday (this volume).

5 Indeed, the description of the Artemisian grove in Euripides's *Hippolytus* works as a metaphor for Hippolytus's own virtuous life of dedication to the goddess, making this Greek tragedy the first narrative to equate virginal nature with chastity (Parry 1964, 281).

6 Nor is this phenomenon unique to Greece—it may be seen in West Africa, where fundamentalist Christian sects and population pressures have challenged traditional sacred groves by fishing, hunting, clearcutting, and building farms in them (Chérif and Greenberg, forthcoming, 2013). For a study of the indigenous Hawaiian affinity with *Avatar*, see Gould, Ardoin, and Hashimoto (2010, and this volume), and for a study of the interaction among religious faith, social location, and environmental degradation, see Haluza-Delay, Ferber, and Wiebe-Neufeld (this volume).

7   Although some viewers decried the film's violence (e.g., see Klassen, this volume), David Landis Barnhill notes that in *Avatar*, "violence was not contrary to but rather a natural outgrowth of the warrior culture" (2010, 405, and this volume).

8   Dozens of parallels between *Avatar* and *Pocahontas* may be viewed online, including the parody *Avahontas or Pohatar*, which overdubs parts of the *Pocahontas* soundtrack onto *Avatar* scenes: https://www.youtube.com/watch?v=W0J9yxBzwWw.

9   See, for example, Chris Klassen (this volume).

10   Relying upon behavioural evidence also fails to take into account that conduct does not always evince attitude. One might have environmental concern, but that does not always translate into eco-ethical action. More to the point, actions do not always manifest cultural identity, known by many Native American groups as "The Indian Way." The Sioux word for this holistic worldview is "*wounicage*, which simply means 'our way of doing things'" (Deloria 2009, 7, emphasis in original). Deviation from The Indian Way is interpreted to be a spiritual problem resulting from westernization that conflicts with native cultural identity. Re-establishing identity is thus seen as a remedy for behavioural problems. For this reason, sociologists have theorized that identity guides behaviour and founds one's worldview (Stets and Biga 2003; Hand and Van Liere 1984).

11   For a Jungian analysis of *Avatar*, see MacLennan (this volume).

12   For more on the need for a universal eco-ethical story, see Freya Mathews (2011).

13   Gottlieb (2006) calls such spiritual action "religious environmentalism"; Hillman (2006, 332) names it "responsive environmentalism." Lisa H. Sideris (2010, 471, and this volume) considers empathy to be the "dominant theme of the film" and believes that it "has enormous potential as an environmental value." Matthew Holtmeier (2010, 415, and this volume) dubs the phenomenon observed in depressed fans who complain because they do not live on Pandora "*Post-Pandoran Depression*" (emphasis in original). Britt Istoft (2010, 412, and this volume) observes that the "sacredness of Eywa/Earth influences fans' environmental practices because they come to believe that one way to venerate Eywa is by living ecologically."

14   Syzygy represents a connected pair of *related* but not necessarily *opposite* entities, much like conjoined twins that are an embodied oxymoron: at once the same but different. Syzygy, then, is another form of opposition resolution expressed in myths. Primordial peoples experienced life as a syzygy of oppositions in which subject-object sometimes merged, outer world became inner world, and vice versa.

References

Avatar. 2009. Directed by James Cameron. DVD. Twentieth Century Fox.

Barnhill, David Landis. 2010. "Spirituality and Resistance: Ursula Le Guin's *The Word for World Is Forest* and the Film *Avatar*." *Journal for the Study of Religion, Nature, and Culture* 4(4): 478–98.

Berkes, Fikret. 1999. *Sacred Ecology: Traditional Ecological Knowledge and Resource Management.* Philadelphia: Taylor and Francis.

Bernstein, Jerome S. 2005. *Living in the Borderland: The Evolution of Consciousness and the Challenge of Healing Trauma.* London: Routledge.

Berry, Thomas. 1988. *The Dream of the Earth.* San Francisco: Sierra Club.

Bloch, Jon P. 1998. "Alternative Spirituality and Environmentalism." *Review of Religious Research* 40(1): 55–73.

Caldwell, Richard S. 1987. *Hesiod's Theogony.* Cambridge, MA: Focus Information Group.

Callicott, J. Baird. 1994. *Earth's Insights: A Multicultural Survey of Ecological Ethics from the Mediterranean Basin to the Australian Outback.* Berkeley: University of California Press.

Callicott, J. Baird, and Michael P. Nelson. 2004. *American Indian Environmental Ethics: An Ojibwa Case Study.* Upper Saddle River, NJ: Pearson.

Chérif, Sadia, and Joy H. Greenberg. Forthcoming, 2013. "Religious Perspectives on Climate Change in the West Ivoirian Mountainous Region." In *How the World's Religions Are Responding to Climate Change: Social Scientific Investigations,* edited by Randolph Haluza-DeLay, Andrew Szasz, and Robin Globus. New York: Routledge.

Corbett, Lionel. 2001. *The Religious Function of the Psyche.* East Sussex, UK: Brunner-Routledge.

Deloria, Vine Jr. 2009. *C. G. Jung and the Sioux Traditions: Dreams, Visions, Nature, and the Primitive.* Edited by Philip J. Deloria and Jerome S. Bernstein. New Orleans: Spring.

Dillon, Matthew P. J. 1997. "The Ecology of the Greek Sanctuary." *Zeitschrift für Papyrologie und Epigraphik Bd.* 118: 113–27.

Edinger, Edward F. 1992. *Ego and Archetype: Individuation and the Religious Function of the Psyche.* Boston: Shambhala.

Euripides. N.d. *Hippolytus.* Translated by E. P. Coleridge. Internet Classics Archive. http://classics.mit.edu/Euripides/hippolytus.pl.txt.

Frank, Adam. 2009. "Avatar: Science, Civilization and the Noble Savage in Space." *NPR,* 22 December. http://www.npr.org/blogs/13.7/2009/12/avatar _movie_post.html.

Gottlieb, Roger S. 2006. *A Greener Faith: Religious Environmentalism and Our Planet's Future.* Oxford: Oxford University Press.

Gould, Rachelle K., Nicole M. Ardoin, and Jennifer Kamakanipakolonahe'okekai Hashimoto. 2010. "'Mālama the 'āina, Mālama the people on the 'āina': The Reaction to *Avatar* in Hawai'i." *Journal for the Study of Religion, Nature, and Culture* 4(4): 425–56.

Greenberg, Joy H. 2010. "In the Beginning Was the Image: Revisioning Christianity as Mythopoetic Environmental Ethics." Presented at the AAR Mid-Atlantic Regional Conference, New Brunswick, NJ.

Hand, Carl M., and Kent D. Van Liere. 1984. "Religion, Mastery-over-Nature, and Environmental Concern." *Social Forces* 63(2): 555–70.

Harrison, Robert Pogue. 1993. *Forests: The Shadow of Civilization.* Chicago: University of Chicago Press.

Hillman, James. 1992. *Re-Visioning Psychology.* New York: Harper Perennial.

———. 2005. *Healing Fiction.* Putnam, CT: Spring.

———. 2006. *City and Soul.* Putnam, CT: Spring.

Holtmeier, Matthew. 2010. "Post-Pandoran Depression or Na'vi Sympathy: *Avatar*, Affect, and Audience Reception." *Journal for the Study of Religion, Nature, and Culture* 4(4): 414–24.

The Homeric Hymns. 2006. Translated by Charles Boer. Kingston, RI: Asphodel.

Hughes, J. Donald. 1990. "Artemis: Goddess of Conservation." *Forest and Conservation History* 34(4): 191–97.

Istoft, Britt. 2010. "*Avatar* Fandom as Nature-Religious Expression?" *Journal for the Study of Religion, Nature, and Culture* 4(4): 394–413.

Jung, C. G. 1983. "The Undiscovered Self." In *The Essential Jung: Selected Writings*, edited by Anthony Storr, 348–403. Princeton, NJ: Princeton University Press.

Justice, Daniel Heath. 2010. "James Cameron's *Avatar*: Missed Opportunities." *First People's New Directions*, 20 January. http://firstpeoplesnewdirections .org/blog/?p=169.

Lertzman, Renee A. 2010. "Desire, Longing and the Return to the Garden: Reflections on *Avatar*." *Ecopsychology* 2(1): 41–43.

Mathews, Freya. 2011. "The Eco-Genesis of Ethics and Religion." *Journal for the Study of Religion, Nature, and Culture* 5(3): 263–83.

Otto, Rudolf. 1958. *The Idea of the Holy.* Translated by John W. Harvey. London: Oxford University Press.

Ovid. 1993. *The Metamorphoses of Ovid.* Translated by Allen Mandelbaum. San Diego: Harcourt.

Parkes, Graham. 1997. "Voices of Mountains, Trees, and Rivers: Kūkai, Dōgen, and a Deeper Ecology." In *Buddhism and Ecology: The Interconnection of Dharma and Deeds*, edited by Mary E. Tucker and Duncan R. Williams, 112–28. Cambridge, MA: Harvard University Press.

Parry, Hugh. 1964. "Ovid's *Metamorphoses*: Violence in a Pastoral Landscape." *Transactions and Proceedings of the American Philological Association* 95: 268–82.

Plato. 360 BCE. *Critias.* Translated by Benjamin Jowett. *Internet Classics Archive.* http://classics.mit.edu/Plato/critias.html.

———. 360 BCE. *Timaeus.* Translated by Benjamin Jowett. *Internet Classics Archive.* http://classics.mit.edu/Plato/timaeus.html.

Roszak, Theodore. 1995. "Where Psyche Meets Gaia." In *Ecopsychology: Restoring the Earth—Healing the Mind*, edited by Theodore Roszak, Mary E. Gomes, and Allen D. Kanner, 1–17. San Francisco: Sierra Club.

Sideris, Lisa H. 2010. "I See You: Interspecies Empathy and *Avatar*." *Journal for the Study of Religion, Nature, and Culture* 4(4): 457–77.

Smith, Mick. 2001. *An Ethics of Place: Radical Ecology, Postmodernity, and Social Theory.* Albany, NY: State University of New York Press.

Snyder, Gary. 1995. *A Place in Space: Ethics, Aesthetics, and Watersheds.* New York: Counterpoint.

Stets, Jan E., and Chris F. Biga. 2003. "Bringing Identity Theory into Environmental Sociology." *Sociological Theory* 21(4): 398–423.

Suozzi, Marguerite A. 2010. "*Avatar* in the Real World: James Cameron on Indigenous Struggles." *Pulse*, 4 May. http://pulsemedia.org/2010/05/04/avatar-in-the-real-world-james-cameron-on-indigenous-struggles/.

Tarakeshwar, Nalini, Aaron B. Swank, Kenneth I. Pargament, and Annette Mahoney. 2001. "The Sanctification of Nature and Theological Conservatism: A Study of Opposing Religious Correlates of Environmentalism." *Review of Religious Research* 42(4): 387–404.

Taylor, Bron. 2010. *Dark Green Religion: Nature Spirituality and the Planetary Future*. Berkeley: University of California Press.

Taylor, Bron, and Adrian Ivakhiv. 2010. "Opening Pandora's Film." *Journal for the Study of Religion, Nature, and Culture* 4(4): 384–93.

Taylor, Charles. 1989. *Sources of the Self: The Making of the Modern Identity*. Cambridge, MA: Harvard University Press.

Spirituality and Resistance: *Avatar* and Ursula Le Guin's *The Word for World Is Forest*

DAVID LANDIS BARNHILL

Imagine this fictional scenario.

Earth is an environmental ruin, with essential resources desperately scarce. A distant planet is colonized for resource extraction, and in the process, the local environment is savaged and the indigenous peoples are oppressed. A few Earthlings, including an ecologist and anthropologist, are sympathetic toward the natives and critical of the colonial practices, and one in particular cultivates a close relationship with one of the natives. However, tension between the two groups leads to a final confrontation. In preparation for the battle, the local tribe recruits participation from other clans in order to mount a massive force against their technologically advanced enemy. In the end, the indigenes prevail, and the colonists from Earth are removed from the planet.

The native society is primarily based on hunting, and women are included among the hunters. The indigenous peoples have a religious reverence for the natural world, and culture and nature are closely interwoven. Spirituality involves animistic relations with individual spiritual presences as well as an intimate connection to the sacred as a Gaia-like whole.

★ ★ ★

This scenario, of course, describes the basic contours and structure of the film *Avatar*. But it is, at the same time, a summary of *The Word for World*

Is Forest, a short novel by Ursula K. Le Guin originally published in 1972. The degree of similarity in narrative, theme, tone, and perspective is striking, and both works are simultaneously dystopian and utopian and venture into apocalypticism. Both works present the indigenous culture in a strongly positive light. Both works, written while the United States was at war, offer withering criticism of racism toward indigenous people, rampant militarism, and the ecological destructiveness and social injustice of corporate capitalism. Indeed, in both works, the natives consider the invaders to be insane. Yet there are also very substantial differences between the two works. A comparison highlights the distinctive character of each work and its artistic, ecological, political, and spiritual strengths and weaknesses. In exploring these two works, I will assume the reader is familiar with *Avatar* and not with *The Word for World Is Forest*, so I begin with a review of Le Guin's novel.

Nature in *The Word for World Is Forest*

The Word for World Is Forest was written during the winter of 1968 when Le Guin was sojourning in England.[1] Enraged by the brutality and waste of the Vietnam War, she spent the winter composing this impassioned novel. She has said that although writing for her is usually hard but enjoyable work, this book was easy to write but disagreeable (1979, 152). When the narrative begins, Terrans (colonizers from Earth) have been on the planet of Athshe for nearly five years. Earth's environment has been impoverished and its forests erased. In the words of Captain Don Davidson, a particularly aggressive and arrogant military officer, the Terrans arrived in this deeply forested world in order to "turn the tree-jumble into clean sawn planks, more prized on Earth than gold" (Le Guin 1976, 7). But then there were those inconvenient natives. Although the indigenous inhabitants are green and furry and about half as tall as Terrans, they are humans, although some in each culture doubt whether those in the other culture are really human after all.

To expedite the extractive process, the Athsheans have been made slaves ("voluntary labor"); they are victims in part because their culture is nonviolent. Eventually, one Athshean, Selver, comes to the realization that the only way for his people to remain sane and survive is for them to eradicate the invaders.[2] This realization is fuelled in part by the fact that his wife was raped by Davidson and died as a result. Selver subsequently visits many villages, teaching a "new thing": group enmity and the willingness to kill. He leads a raid on a Terran camp that is nothing short of a massacre. Representatives of the colonial administration, who happen to be nearby after dropping off supplies (which includes several hundred young women), decide to hold an inquest into what happened and why. The why is particu-larly puzzling, since Captain Raj Lyubov, the anthropologist who knows the Athsheans well (and has befriended Selver), claimed that they were incapable of mass violence. The result of the inquest is the freeing of all the natives held in captivity and an insistence that they be left alone. Then the ship departs for another planet, scheduled to return three years later.

Davidson responds to the inquest by secretly slaughtering all Athsheans in a nearby village. In revenge, Selver mounts a massive raid on the central compound, an attack that kills hundreds (including all the women and, unintentionally, his friend Lyubov). The defeated Terrans capitulate to Selver's demand that, until the ship returns and can take them away, they live without contact with the Athsheans in a restricted area that they previ-ously logged—an ironic allusion to Indian reservations. The narrative in the final chapter takes place three years later, when one of the officers on the returning ship promises, in the name of a newly formed interplanetary League of Worlds, that no one will come to Athshe for five generations, and even then, only with the Athsheans' permission will a small party be permitted to come and learn about their culture.

Le Guin presents the forest world of Athshe in a complex way, with alternating narrative frameworks (and chapters) involving the three main characters—Davidson, Selver, and Lyubov. The book begins with a pre-sentation of Davidson's human arrogance and an oppressively hierarchical worldview based on anthropocentrism and the logic of domination. When the Terrans arrive, all they see is darkness and chaos, which to them is a kind of emptiness: "When they came here there had been nothing. Trees. A dark huddle and jumble and tangle of trees, endless, meaningless" (7). Not only value but also meaning comes only when humans—more specifically, Terrans—mix their labour with the land. Wild nature is waste, but it can be conquered, and in the contest between people and nature, Davidson crows, "it's Man that wins, every time. The old Conquistador" (6). The for-est world of Athshe can and should be turned into a man-made paradise, he believes, and indeed the colony is called New Tahiti. "Cleaned up and cleaned out," Davidson muses, adding, "the dark forests cut down for open fields of grain, the primeval murk and savagery and ignorance wiped out, it would be a paradise, a real Eden" (3).

The native Athshean perspective on nature is, of course, quite differ-ent. In the Selver chapters, *The Word for World Is Forest* provides a richly ecological narrative. The Athsheans consider the forest a sacred place alive with spirits. In one of Selver's dreams, for instance, "the Ash spirit walked in front of him, taller than Lyubov or any yumen [Terran humans], tall as a tree, not turning its white mask to him" (118). As the gesture of the Ash spirit *not* turning toward people suggests, the natural world is not merely animate but also sentient, and it exhibits independent subjecthood. The ash-tree has its own songs that the Athsheans learn to sing, and nature communicates with them: "the river Menend, the master river of Sornol, spoke ceaselessly in the world and in the dream" (126). The Athsheans and the non-human organisms interact as subjects sharing the same community. And the depth of the indigenous identification with their forest habitat can be seen as well in the very title of the book.

The third view of nature expressed in the book is that of the anthropologist Lyubov, which develops slowly after his arrival on the planet. Coming from Earth, which is barren of trees, the forest of Athshe is at first befuddling to him, but it eventually becomes home: "The mass and jumble of various competitive lives all pushing and swelling outwards and upwards towards light, the silence made up of many little meaningless noises, the total vegetable indifference to the presence of mind, all this troubled him, and like the others he had kept to clearings and to the beach. But little by little he had begun to like it...and now after four years of it he was completely at home under the trees, more so perhaps than anywhere else" (88–89). Although Lyubov's view of nature is not as strongly or richly ecological as that of the Athsheans, he develops a respect for the forest and a sense of belonging there, and he learns to recognize the value of the deeply ecological perspective that is common among the Athsheans. Lyubov seeks to mediate the two opposing forces of natives and invaders, not only in his attempts to defend the Athsheans from the colonial rulers but also in struggling to deal with the moral corruption in which he is thoroughly enmeshed. American readers inheriting the legacy of slavery, the genocide of Native Americans, and the Vietnam War can easily identify with him.

These three views of nature alternate and interact throughout the book. In addition, the narrator has a distinct perspective. The most telling depiction can be found in the opening of the first Selver chapter: "No way was clear, no light unbroken, in the forest. Into wind, water, sunlight, starlight, there always entered leaf and branch, bole and root, the shadowy, the complex. Little paths ran under the branches, around the boles, over the roots; they did not go straight, but yielded to every obstacle, devious as nerves" (25). The narrative in *The Word for World Is Forest* thus presents the natural world as fundamentally interrelated, but there is actually little discussion of this quality besides a statement about the "collaboration of living things with the long, elaborate death of leaves and trees, and from that rich graveyard grew ninety-foot trees, and tiny mushrooms that sprouted in circles half an inch across" (25).

In terms of spirituality, the forest is viewed not so much as the locus of the sacred but as the sacred world itself. As Lyubov notes to his military superiors at the inquest, "the word for *world* is also the word for *forest*" (72). In this regard, we could say that *The Word for World Is Forest* exemplifies Gaian qualities in Bron Taylor's sense of the term *Gaian*, although the focus is terrestrial: the vast, unbroken forest rather than the entire planet with its encompassing seas.[3] Indeed, the Athsheans are organically integrated into their forest world, for it is a "living forest of which the town was one element" (40). Even their dwellings suggest this imbrication: "the timber houses were three-quarters sunk, fitted in among tree-roots like badgers' setts" (39–40).

In Le Guin's tale, animism complements this Gaian spirituality.[4] While the Athsheans live in and as part of the forest, they also live *with* the spirits of the rivers and trees. As part of the Ash clan, for instance, Selver communicates and interacts with the Ash spirit (118, 168). Singing the songs of the Ash spirit is an important spiritual practice. When Selver is near insanity after the final raid, he is incapable of singing, but others sing Ash songs for him, helping him heal (127). At the conclusion of the narrative, Selver is shaken by the way the face of the Lepennon, an emissary from Hain, reminds him of the mask of the Ash spirit.

Two dimensions of reality, called "world-time" and "dream-time," are additional and crucial aspects of Athshean religiosity. The former refers to the phenomenal world, but for Athsheans there is another, equally important—and equally real—dimension, which is accessed through dreams. Dreaming is not simply what happens during sleep. It is a spiritual art that requires training (27, 34). When it is well cultivated, Athsheans dream while awake and are able to, in the words of a Great Dreamer named Coro Mena, "weave and shape, direct and follow, start and cease [their dreams] at will" (32). The ideal is to balance one's sanity "not on the razor's edge of reason but on the double support, the fine balance, of reason and dream" (99). For the Athsheans, therefore, dreaming is connected with the "springs of reality" (38). The inability of Terrans both to dream while awake and to control their dreams not only manifests a failure to comprehend the fullness of reality; it is also a sign of a dangerous spiritual sickness. Selver believes that this incapacity to dream explains why the Terrans can so easily "go about in torment killing and destroying" (45).

Nature in *Avatar*

Turning now to *Avatar*, we also see nature given profound significance, although with some important differences. Unlike Le Guin's novel, in which nature is either a peaceable and pleasant home for the Athsheans or the passive recipient of the exploitation of Terran colonialism, *Avatar* presents nature as highly active and dangerous. In his first venture into the forest, avatar Jake Sully is confronted by an angry hammerhead, attacked by a ferocious thanator, and then besieged by a pack of viperwolves. The perils of the planet are emphasized by the military commander, Colonel Miles Quaritch, when, near the beginning of the film, he addresses new arrivals: "Out beyond that fence every living thing that crawls, flies or squats in the mud wants to kill you and eat your eyes for jujubes" (Cameron 2007, 9).[5] This danger of nature in the film gives it a vitality and presence that is not found in *The Word for World Is Forest*. But while danger is emphasized, Cameron also adds to the complexity of his portrait of nature when, later in the film, Neytiri shows Jake a viperwolf that is a loving mother, "bringing meat to her cubs, which frisk around her legs. She licks their faces" (63).

That vitality is accentuated by the prominence of animals in *Avatar*, in contrast to the largely botanical world of *The Word for World Is Forest*. Although the Athsheans are hunters, Le Guin depicts no actual hunts. In *Avatar*, however, the hunting of animals is a central part of the culture and an essential aspect of Jake's training in learning the ways of the Na'vi. In addition, animals are not simply the hunted; they too are active predators, with humans as one of their prey species. However, there is more to the relation between the Na'vi and animals than the two-sided predator–prey relation. Some animals are part of their cultural activities and are treated as kin. This is most clearly exemplified by the direhorses and banshees, with which Na'vi hunters achieve an active and intimate relationship through the interconnection of their queues, lengths of hair that both Na'vi and animals have. Affection, particularly with the banshees, flows both ways. The integration of nature and culture is therefore more interactive in *Avatar* than in *The Word for World Is Forest*.

Na'vi culture is clearly characterized by animism, although in a somewhat different way than in Athshean culture. In *Avatar*, animals have spirits, something not found in *The Word for World Is Forest*. After Neytiri attacks the viperwolves that are about to overwhelm Jake, she speaks to the spirit of a wolf she is putting to death: "Forgive me. May your spirit run with the Great Mother" (38). Plants are also animated. When Jake makes his first trip out of Hell's Gate, the forest, in the words of the screenplay, is "more alive than any on Earth, with plants that react and move like animals" (28).

In addition to the spirits of individual living things, the principal and universal spirit is, of course, Eywa, the Great Mother. While she is a personal spirit, she is also "made up of all living things" (52), indicating Gaian qualities in the Na'vi view of nature. Eywa also suggests a pantheism that is theistic (in the form of a goddess) in a way that is not characteristic of Athshean culture. This anthropomorphic imagery of the goddess is complemented, if not subtly contradicted, by the more modern description of the "network of energy that flows through all living things" (78). The scientific language of network and the anthropomorphic imagery of the goddess are (to a degree) brought together by the fact that this network is sentient. Dr. Grace Augustine, the chief scientist on Pandora, tries in vain to explain this web of world-consciousness to the corporate boss, Parker Selfridge: "It's a network—a global network. And the Na'vi can access it—they can upload and download data—memories—at sites like the one you destroyed" (100).[6]

One additional point is worth making here about the differences in nature spirituality between the two works. The narrative of *Avatar* is rich in the notion of sacred place. The Tree of Voices and, especially, the Tree of Souls are classic examples of a specific site that has special spiritual power and meaning. In *The Word for World Is Forest*, however, there is virtually no sense of sacred place. Sacred places give additional richness to the nature spirituality of Pandora, but the absence of these in Le Guin's novel underscores the point that the entire forest is itself the sacred.[7]

Political Critique in *The Word for World Is Forest* and *Avatar*

In addition to presenting a rich view of nature and nature spirituality, the two works also present a ringing eco-social critique. In both books, colonialism leads to ecological devastation. In the very first page of *The Word for World Is Forest*, Davidson acknowledges that there are some limits even for the old Conquistador:

> The report from Dump Island of crop failures, massive erosion, a wipe-out.... It looked like that bigdome Kees was right and you had to leave a lot of trees standing where you planned to put farms. But he still couldn't see why a soybean farm needed to waste a lot of space on trees if the land was managed really scientifically. It wasn't like that in Ohio; if you wanted corn you grew corn, and no space wasted on trees and stuff. But then Earth was a tamed planet and New Tahiti wasn't. That's what he was here for: to tame it. If Dump Island was just rocks and gullies now, then scratch it; start over on a new island and do better. Can't keep us down, we're Men. (Le Guin 1976, 1–2)

The gender reference is revealing, for here as elsewhere, Davidson's attitude is intensely patriarchal. Indeed, this passage is preceded by Davidson's thoughts about the arrival of "the second batch of breeding females for the New Tahiti Colony, all sound and clean, 212 head of prime human stock" (1)—women as sexual cattle.

The ecological devastation, of course, is felt most keenly by the Athsheans. Chapter 2 begins with an exhausted Selver stumbling through the forest far from home after he and others, desperate after years of brutal occupation, have attacked a Terran outpost and killed all its inhabitants. Chancing upon the lodge of Coro Mena, Selver is given a place to sleep. Coro Mena then enters dream-time, where he senses the destructiveness of the tall invaders even though he has not met or even heard of them: "Coro Mena felt unreasoning fear press upon him, and slipped into dream to find the reason for the fear; for he was an old man, and long adept. In the dream the giants walked, heavy and dire. Their dry scaly limbs were swathed in cloths; their eyes were little and light, like tin beads. Behind them crawled huge moving things made of polished iron. The trees fell down in front of them" (28). When Selver awakes, he tells of what he has done: "My city was destroyed by the yumens when they cut down the trees in that region.... I left Sornol, where no town is safe from the yumens now, and came here to the North Isle.... There presently the yumens came and began to cut down the world. They destroyed a city there, Penle.... I watched the trees fall and saw the world cut open and left to rot" (30). The yumens are not merely cutting down trees but cutting down the world; not only the forest but also the Athshean city is destroyed. While the slaughter clearly suggests the Vietnam War, the reference to the world "left to rot" recalls bison carcasses rotting on the American plains after white hunters killed them for their hides and tongues.

The extent of the devastation wrought by the Terrans is recognized by Lyubov. At an official inquest concerning the Athshean attack, Lyubov testifies, "We've been here four years. I don't know if the native human culture will survive four more. As for the total land ecology...we've irrecoverably wrecked the native life-systems on one large island, have done great damage on this subcontinent Sornol, and if we go on logging at the present rate, may reduce the major habitable lands to desert within ten years" (71). Nevertheless, the extraction of natural resources is allowed to continue, although the colonists are ordered to free all indigenous workers and leave the native people alone—an order that Davidson disobeys with disastrous results.

The political critique in *The Word for World Is Forest* is just as sweeping as the ecological one. Davidson embodies the logic of domination with a vengeance. The patriarchal thrust of his violence is obvious: he believes that "the only time a man is really and entirely a man is when he's just had a woman or just killed another man" (81). Obvious also is his racist imperialism. He is convinced that his fellow Terrans will "realize that getting rid of the creechies [is] going to be the only way to make this world safe for the Terran way of life" (83). It is, after all, manifest destiny: "They're going to get rubbed out sooner or later, and it might as well be sooner. It's just how things happen to be. Primitive races always have to give way to civilized ones" (12).[8] Lyubov, however, testifies at the inquest, "We have ignored the responses, the rights and obligations, of non-violence. We have killed, raped, dispersed, and enslaved the native humans, destroyed their communities, and cut down their forests. It wouldn't be surprising if they'd decided that we are not human" (62). After the hearing, the League representatives impose constraints on the operation. When violence breaks out again near the end of the novel, the League abandons the operation altogether as intolerable and unsalvageable.

The book's critique is not limited to ideology or behaviour. Ecological psychology merges with political and ecological criticism. Selver sees his oppressors as psychologically impoverished and concludes that this is the root of their violence. "If the yumens are men," he tells a Head-woman of another tribe, "they are men unfit or untaught to dream and to act as men. Therefore they go about in torment killing and destroying, driven by the gods within, whom they will not set free but try to uproot and deny. If they are men they are evil men, having denied their own gods, afraid to see their own faces in the dark" (45). Immediately following the massacre of Terrans by Selver and his followers, the ecologist Gosse angrily confronts Selver. Selver replies that Terrans are insane and thus unacceptably dangerous: "A realist is a man who knows both the world and his own dreams. You're not sane: there's not one man in a thousand of you who knows how to dream. Not even Lyubov and he was the best among you. You sleep, you wake and forget your dreams, you sleep again and wake again, and so you spend your whole lives, and you think that is being, life, reality! You are not children, you are grown men, but insane. And that's why we had to kill you, before you drove us mad" (125). Ignoring the reality and significance of dreams, Terrans are like a contagious mental disease.

While the Vietnam War was the catalyst for the novel, the book's critique has a much broader scope, including the long history of Western imperialism, from its ideological and psychological roots to its catastrophic effects. The "creechies" are reminiscent not only of the villagers of Vietnam but also of Native Americans, African slaves, and Indian coolies. In addition, the book criticizes the even longer history of sexism. *The Word for World Is Forest* is a radical critique because it exposes a fundamental way of thinking and system of values that has dominated the world for centuries.

The environmental and social critique in *Avatar* is similar to the one in *The Word for World Is Forest*, but there are notable differences. The film does not portray the strong sense of sexism that is found in Le Guin's novel. The security forces show no difficulty with the helicopter pilot Trudy Chacon being a combat leader, and neither Selfridge nor Quaritch display obvious sexist attitudes.[9] *Avatar*'s critique is also more sharply focused on corporations. In the film, the corporation's central role is stressed, and a corporate executive is in control. In *The Word for World Is Forest*, those in charge are military figures. This difference, I suggest, is reflective of our contemporary historical period, when the global power of corporations has increased and people are more aware of their rapacity.[10]

Environmental despoliation is a central element in the two works, but their ecological critiques are different in at least two ways. In *The Word for World Is Forest*, the worst case of environmental destruction has already occurred. We are told about it on the first page of the novel, and even David-son acknowledges (for practical reasons only) that they have to find ways to be less destructive. In *Avatar*, the major environmental depredation occurs before our eyes and thus feels more painful. In addition, the corporation targets certain sites that have deep cultural meaning for the Na'vi: Home-tree and the sacred sites of the Tree of Voices and the Tree of Souls. The obliteration of the Tree of Voices is intended to provoke the Na'vi to armed resistance. In the screenplay, Augustine says of the attack on the Tree of Voices, "They bulldozed a sacred site on purpose, to trigger a response. They're fabricating this war to get what they want" (Cameron 2007, 102). After Hometree has fallen, Quaritch tells his troops that they will destroy the Tree of Souls because such a cultural devastation would cause the Na'vi to give up and abandon resistance: "This mountain stronghold is suppos-edly protected by their...deity," he says mockingly and the troops laugh. "When we destroy it, we will blast a crater in their racial memory so deep they won't come within a thousand klicks of this place" (123), something that would give RDA unimpeded access to mineral wealth. Combining environmental ruin with religious desecration sharpens for the audience the sense of the evil involved.

Dystopia and Apocalypse in *The Word for World Is Forest* and *Avatar*

We can gain a deeper understanding of *The Word for World Is Forest* and *Avatar* by applying to them three related terms: utopia, dystopia, and apoc-alypse. Both works contain these elements, although in different ways and to different degrees. These terms, however, need clarification, as they have been used in divergent and even conflicting ways. The basic meaning of *utopia* is an ideal place that does not exist. Thomas More, who coined the term in writing his famous book *Utopia* (1516), created a pun, combining *u-topia* (Greek for "no-place") and *eu-topia* ("good-place"). Utopia is often thought of in terms of a fantasy that presents a blueprint for perfection. Such an ideal is usually dismissed as dreamy wish-fulfillment that has no significant relation to the real world, its limits, and its problems, and thus is not only irrelevant but also a diversion from the productive social analysis and action that is sorely needed.

Over the last several decades, however, utopian theorists have fashioned more sophisticated notions of utopia, linked in part to creative developments in science fiction. Perhaps the most important notion is that of "critical utopia," a utopia that critiques both contemporary society and itself. It presents an imperfect ideal that is open-ended, contested, and in process. It articulates not a blueprint but a horizon and an orientation. A related term is "concrete utopia," one that is not airy fantasy but is discerning about the ills of current society while drawing on utopian elements in contemporary culture. We can also speak of "transformational utopia," for critical utopian writers and theorists seek to transgress the current hegemony and transform society to one that is closer to the ideal. Utopian thought is necessary, it is argued, to counter the ideology that "there is no alternative" to the current social system: we need the subversive social dreaming of utopianism.[11] Le Guin's *The Dispossessed: An Ambiguous Utopia* is often considered a foundational text in the development of critical utopianism.

Dystopias, in contrast, are worlds that are substantially worse than the ones we live in. George Orwell's *Nineteen Eighty-Four* (1949) is a classic example. Social critique is obviously central, both in terms of the nature of society today and the direction in which it is heading. But in the parlance of utopian theory, dystopias can be utopian or anti-utopian. The term *anti-utopian* refers to texts that present no utopian possibilities, a closed world that we can neither transgress nor transform. A grim dystopia, however, can actually be utopian in its stance if it points toward the possibility of fundamental change that can turn society toward a utopian horizon (see Sargent 1967 and Moylan 1986).

The notion of apocalypse is closely tied to Biblical thought, in particular the Book of Revelation, which imagines a cataclysmic end to history and the coming of the millennium, a divine order brought to Earthly life (and, lest we forget, the eternal damnation of the unrighteous). More generally, the fundamental meaning of apocalypse is a catastrophic event that creates a radical break in (or end to) history. In a religious context, that rent in history is usually perceived as ultimately positive—often called "millennial apocalypticism"—but an apocalypse can be dystopian, with the cataclysm leading to a wretched, fearful world. In fact, secular literature and, especially, films often present a post-apocalyptic nightmare, following, say, nuclear war or ecological collapse, as in the *Mad Max, Matrix,* and *Terminator* films.

The Word for World Is Forest is clearly a dystopian novel. Actually, the novel presents accounts of two instances of dystopia: Earth and Athshe.[12]

Athsheans are experiencing dystopia because Terrans have previously created one on Earth. Earth is "worn-out," a "desert of cement," where the only remaining wild animals are rats, and because deer had vanished, hunters are forced to search out "robodeer" (Le Guin 1976, 3, 5, 6) In addition, human society has been ravaged by several famines. When the Athshean resistance succeeds in bringing an end to dystopia on their planet, they sent the Terrans back to their home planet, which would probably remain dystopian for the indefinite future. This doubling of dystopia, even if Athshean dystopia is temporary, intensifies and extends Le Guin's critique. The ecological ruin on Athshe is not an isolated event; it is something we have already done to our own planet. This yields a dark picture of our tendency to ravage both people and planet.

If this dystopian novel is apocalyptic, it is so only in a muted and unusual way. It is unusual because the catastrophic event is not what has been done to them: colonialist oppression. That cruelty creates the dystopia. If there is an apocalypse, it is in the merciless violence perpetrated by the Athsheans against their oppressors. Selver, we are repeatedly told, is a "god" in the sense of one who has brought to the world something entirely new, something that did not issue forth from anything in their own culture. Group enmity has never been experienced before, and the slaughter of hundreds—on two occasions—runs counter to their basic ethos. Unlike the horrors that they have endured, their butchery of the Terrans is a *cultural* cataclysm, one that Selver and Coro Mena recognize as evil, however necessary and successful it might have been. The question is whether this new thing will pass away once the oppressors have gone. After the first attack by the Athsheans, Lyubov comes to a troubling realization: "That which seemed to rise from the root of his [Selver's] own suffering and express his own changed being, might in fact be an infection, a foreign plague, which would not make a new people of his race, but would destroy them" (107). Concerning this possibility, Le Guin leaves us in uncertainty. At the end of the book, Lepennon tells Selver, "We shall go. Within two days we shall be gone. All of us. Forever. Then the forests of Athshe will be as they were before." But Selver replies, "Maybe after I die people will be as they were before I was born, and before you came. But I do not think they will" (169). What has been the cultural cost of the liberatory violence? The reader does not know if there has been an apocalyptic break in the Athsheans' cultural history or a momentary breach that will be healed. However, the calm discernment of Selver at the end suggests that even if this new, horrible thing that Selver initiated has become part of their culture, there will be enough cultural continuity to mitigate this Terran disease.

Avatar also has dystopian, apocalyptic, and utopian dimensions. Unlike Le Guin's novel, the film is more apocalyptic than dystopian. When the narrative begins, environmental degradation has occurred in the process of mining. Our first sight of the "Sky People's" compound comes after we fly over the sensuous beauty of Pandora. "Suddenly the carpet of virgin Rainforest gives way to—an open-pit mine. A lifeless crater—as if a giant cookie cutter took a chunk out of the world. Down among the terraces are excavators and trucks the size of three story buildings" (Cameron 2007, 5). And then there is a deadly episode that causes the school that Augustine started to be shut down. The film gives us little clue of what occurred, but according to the screenplay, one of Augustine's brightest students, Neytiri's older sister Sylwanin, became angry about the clear-cutting and helped set a bulldozer on fire. When the troopers pursued her, she ran to the school. The troopers shot and killed her—right in the doorway to the schoolhouse and in front of Neytiri—and then shot other children and wounded Augustine (67). However, despite this grievous violation, there is no subjugation or forced labour as in *The Word for World Is Forest*, and the Na'vi continue to practise their culture largely free of (but highly wary of) intrusion by the Sky People. Then, of course, things change, cataclysmically.

The sense of apocalypse deepens in stages. First, a gigantic bulldozer demolishes the sacred Tree of Voices, and its link to the ancestors is lost. The forest in the area is razed in a way that suggests scenes of rainforest destruction. The Na'vi then realize that their world, including their spirituality, is now under attack. Far more catastrophic is the next stage, the demolition of Hometree. The physical and spiritual home of the Omaticaya for countless generations, the tree is the centre of their life. But it also stands atop an exceptionally rich deposit of unobtanium, and Selfridge insists on access to it: "They're fly-bitten savages who live in a tree! Look around—I don't know about you but I see a lot of trees. They can move" (103). When Quaritch mounts a massive attack, the enormous tree is finally torched and oh-so-slowly toppled. The Omaticaya watch in horror and, importantly, disbelief. The screenplay describes the scene this way: "Hometree hits the ground *like the end of the world*, raising a great cloud of dust and pulverized debris" (108, my emphasis).

But there is a final stage of apocalypse: the destruction of the Tree of Souls. This is the Omaticaya's most sacred place and appears to be the hub in the spiritual network of energy and consciousness. After Hometree is levelled, the Na'vi converge at the Tree of Souls. It is clear to all that the obliteration of the Tree of Souls would amount to deicide and would precipitate the end to the Omaticaya world. Quaritch makes this point explicitly when he rouses his troops to battle, pledging, "We will blast a crater in their racial memory" (123). In a thinly veiled reference to George W. Bush's invasion of Iraq, he adds, "Our only security lies in preemptive attack. We will fight terror with terror." However, it is more than terror; it is the annihilation of the Na'vi's cultural and spiritual world. The sympathetic Earthlings realize this too. When they are informed of the imminent attack, Norm tells Jake and Trudy, "If he takes out the Tree of Souls—it's over. It's their main line to Eywa, to their ancestors—it'll destroy them" (125).

When the confrontation begins, the Na'vi fight fiercely and heroically, but eventually, the battle turns into a rout. Neytiri's banshee is shot down, leaving her on the ground close to RDA's advancing forces. Overhead, Trudy is shot out of the sky, and the warrior Tsu'tey is killed in an attack on the *Valkyrie*, the airship loaded with an enormous bomb intended for the Tree of Souls. Below, the native ground forces are being slaughtered, a scene described in the screenplay this way: "At ground level it is an apocalypse. Running Na'vi are blasted out of existence by fire and shock waves" (131). The apocalyptic atmosphere culminates in a haunting vision of a direhorse, wholly aflame, running through a forest of fire. With death at hand, Neytiri, hiding behind a tree trunk, radios Jake that they are about to be overrun, and she prepares to face her enemy and deliver one final arrow.

To emphasize the apocalyptic dimension to these scenes, Cameron has crafted a complex allusion centreing on fire and horses. The Bible's Book of Revelation includes a series of horse imagery: the four horses of the apocalypse near the beginning and, near the end, the white horse that bolts down from heaven, upon which is a rider with eyes "as a flame of fire" (Revelation 19:12, KJV). But more relevant to the film is Richard Wagner's *Götterdämmerung*, the last of the four operas in his *Der Ring des Niebelungen*. The opera draws on Norse mythology, including the story of Brünnhilde, a daughter of Odin. The four-opera sequence climaxes in a fiery scene. A web of intrigue, deception, and death has made Brünnhilde's world crumble. She orders a huge pyre lit and mounts her horse, and they ride into the conflagration—the "immolation scene," as it is known. The apocalypse is total, for Valhalla and the gods themselves are consumed in the inferno— hence, the title of the last opera, which means "The Twilight of the Gods." Neytiri does not ride a horse into a pyre, but, surrounded by fire and with direhorses aflame, she is about to turn boldly to her death.

If linking *Avatar* to Wagner seems a stretch, it should be noted that Brünnhilde is a Valkyrie, a female figure in Norse mythology who chooses to die in battle and thus gain entrance to Valhalla. Invoked in ironic fashion in *Avatar*, *Valkyrie* is the name of the airship that is about to drop death onto the Tree of Souls. This mechanical Valkyrie chooses the Na'vi for death, but they will not be transported to any spiritual abode, for that will have been destroyed in the process.

Cameron's apocalyptic allusion to Wagner has another dimension. In a famous scene in a celebrated anti-war film, Lt. Colonel Bill Killgore— played magnificently by Robert Duvall—is the commanding officer of US forces that are facing resistance from the Viet Cong. He orders an airstrike to incinerate the jungle where the enemy is hiding. As American airships scream by and flames engulf the trees, Killgore effuses, "I love the smell of napalm in the morning." The triumphant music famously being played during this scene is Wagner's "The Ride of the Valkyries" from *Götterdämmerung*. The film is *Apocalypse Now* (1979). *Avatar* is thus linked to both Wagner's dark tragedy and Francis Ford Coppola's black comic scene, both of which refer to the notion of apocalypse.

But while Cameron strongly invokes the idea of apocalypse, in *Avatar*, a complete and final cataclysm is averted. As Neytiri is about to turn to face her destroyers and with the *Valkyrie* about to obliterate the Tree of Souls, in true Hollywood fashion, the cavalry come to the rescue. But here the cavalry are the animals of Pandora, sent by Eywa to save the day, bringing the Na'vi and their spiritual culture back from the brink of apocalypse. Such theatrics are part of what has made *Avatar* such a commercial success.

Cameron also makes effective use of well-worn Hollywood narrative structures: boy gets girl, boy loses girl, boy gets girl. In addition, there is old-fashioned heroic violence, intensified by bringing the good guys to the brink of destruction and then snatching victory from the jaws of apocalypse. Two other themes deepen the appeal of the storyline, but they are controversial. There is the Great White Messiah figure, who comes to the natives and brings them a victory they cannot accomplish by themselves, and the Great White Fantasy—leaving behind the constraints of civilization and becoming indigenous.[13] This fantasy in fact involves a parallel to the boy gets girl storyline: boy becomes part of the native tribe, boy gets tossed out, boy is made permanent member (in fact, the heir apparent to the leadership of the tribe). These narrative elements appeal to many viewers, but they exemplify a major lacuna in *Avatar:* the ambiguity and nuanced self-reflexiveness that characterizes critical utopias such as *The Word for World Is Forest*.

It is noteworthy that none of these attractive elements occur in *The Word for World Is Forest*. There is no love story. Violence is evil, even when—or especially when—committed by the oppressed with whom we sympathize. There is no White Messiah: the natives, led by the new god, Selver, achieve victory by themselves, and the sympathetic Lyubov is largely impotent. There is no White Fantasy of going native on Athshe. It's safe to say that Le

Guin's novel could not become a billion-dollar film, but it provides more sophisticated and complex utopian thinking.

Conclusion

We can review and extend this comparative analysis by reflecting on the nature and role of violence in these two works and how the different portraits of violence are related to the depictions of nature and the historical context of the two works. For instance, in *The Word for World Is Forest*, although the Athsheans are said to be hunters, their peacefulness and even passivity is emphasized. Similarly, in the largely botanical world of Athshe, there are no real predators: nature is essentially gentle. So too, violence is contrary to the culture of the Athsheans. Violence, even though it successfully rids them of the Terran menace, is presented as evil and corrupting, possibly permanently so. The immediate historical context for writing the book, as noted before, was the Vietnam War. It was a time when opposition to the military itself was strong, and there was considerable opposition to war and violence in general, particularly with Dr. Martin Luther King's non-violent campaign fresh in the cultural memory. Non-violence, as they say, was in the air.

In *Avatar*, however, violence is not contrary to the Na'vi's warrior culture but a natural outgrowth of it. Similarly, the violence of predator–prey relations is characteristic of the natural world on Pandora. Like Le Guin's novel, *Avatar* was written during and in part as a response to a war. But public anger (at least until 2008) seemed to be aimed at different targets than during the Vietnam conflict: the Bush administration, related corporations (especially Halliburton, where Vice-President Cheney had previously been the CEO), and private security forces such as Blackwater. Even the scandal of prisoner abuse at Abu Ghraib did not generate the anti-military sentiment of "baby-killers" that arose during the Vietnam War. In addition, the last ten years has seen no significant pacifist movement in the United States similar to that in the 1960s. However, with use of ecotage since the 1980s by Earth First! and, beginning in 1992, the Earth Liberation Front, some environmentalists have seen violence, at least sabotage of property and machinery, as possibly playing a constructive role (Taylor 2005). Indeed, as mentioned previously, ecotage by the Na'vi is depicted in the screenplay.

Thus, the different roles and characteristics of violence in *The Word for World Is Forest* and *Avatar* may reflect the historical contexts of creation of the two works. But in terms of *Avatar*, a stronger influence may simply have been the long Hollywood tradition of redemptive violence and the popular appeal of the good guys putting down the bad guys.

We can review and extend our analysis by reflecting on these two works in terms of optimism and pessimism. *The Word for World Is Forest* is optimistic in several important ways. It is possible for humans to sympathize with a different race and overcome the hegemonic view that the indigenous peoples are inferior. It is possible for a colonial administration to be concerned about justice and to terminate operations if injustice cannot be eliminated. The natives are able to overcome their oppressors without a White Messiah or even any aid from outsiders. However, the novel portrays the gulf between the two races as largely unbridgeable beyond a certain sympathetic concern. Not only is it apparently impossible for an outsider to become a member of the indigenous culture, but the outsiders are incapable of establishing an enduring humane relationship with the natives—the only humane act is to leave. But even here, optimism is at least suggested: at the end of the novel, Lepennon demonstrates true respect for the Athsheans, and another attempt at humane interchange might be possible after five generations. The book ends, though, with reference to the most deeply pessimistic aspect of the story: the Athsheans have learned, adopted, and employed the hate and violence of their oppressors, and there is no certainty that this evil will simply disappear.

Avatar, of course, is upliftingly optimistic. As in Le Guin's novel, some Earthlings can become deeply sympathetic with those whom their own culture is oppressing, even to the point of being willing to put their lives at risk (something not seen in *The Word for World Is Forest*). As in Le Guin's novel, Goliath can be overthrown, in this case through heroic action. And it is possible for the civilized not only to sympathize with but actually to become indigenous. Still, the film is pessimistic in ways that may not be apparent. There are, of course, huge losses in the climactic battle, but this pain is easily laid aside in a Hollywood production (as it is all too often in our very real wars). More importantly, the natives require not only the assistance of outsiders; victory is also dependent upon the leadership of someone originally from outside of their tribe and race. And even the natives and their new leader cannot succeed without the unexpected assistance from the animals sent by Eywa. Of course, that the animals come to their aid, that Eywa cares to intervene for their welfare, that the difference between humans and other animals is minor compared to the chasm between human oppressors and the oppressed: these also make the film heartwarmingly optimistic.

We can press the optimism issue by considering the two works in terms of utopia, focusing in particular on the possible relevance of the two indigenous societies to our own.

Do the Athshean and Na'vi cultures represent a utopian ideal, one that we can at least move toward? If we conclude that in our society and historical period we *cannot* emulate or even approach these types of cultures, then for us they are impossible utopias. If we believe that we *should* not, then their societies are actually false utopias.

Certainly, many would claim that these cultures are false utopias: that is, they do not represent an ideal that we should strive toward. But I would argue that this ideal of a small, decentralized, and egalitarian community in intimate relation to and harmony with the natural world is exactly the kind of society we should pursue, however far away from that ideal we may be. And if we have any hope of moving in that direction, fictional depictions of such a horizon can be inspirational and suggest some directions, even if they cannot provide blueprints. Unfortunately, although I am relatively confident in arguing that these are not false utopias, it is far more difficult, given contemporary society and its relation to the natural world, to refute the position that they are impossible utopias.

But we should keep in mind that utopias, as I am using the term, are not blueprints for us to try to put into practice. Rather, they delineate basic qualities of what we can and should work toward. And this is possible because they are, in fact, concrete utopias. The ideals of these societies are reflected, at least in part, in current social, environmental, and intellectual movements: bioregionalism, anti-globalization, the Zapatistas, social ecology, the Quakers, and writers such as Le Guin and Kim Stanley Robinson, to name just a few. For me, these movements—and, importantly, their variety—suggest that there is a degree of connection between these utopias and our rather dystopian world today. There are aspects of our contemporary culture that can be drawn on to move us in the direction of the utopian ideals presented in *Avatar* and *The Word for World Is Forest*.

Notes

1 Le Guin's *The Word for World Is Forest* was first published in 1972 as a novella in an anthology of science fiction. It was republished as a separate book in 1976, and my page references are to that edition.

2 The narrative gives no indication that Selver has any special role or characteristics before the narrative begins to suggest that he would be capable of his radical transformation into a "god." Selver is apparently his full Athshean name, the only one used in the narrative except for "Sam," as he was called when he was working as a servant to Terrans.

3 Bron Taylor (2010, 16) characterizes Gaian Earth religion as an organicist view: that is, the biosphere is an "energetic, interdependent, living system" that is "alive and conscious" and is the most fundamental spiritual reality.

4 According to Taylor (2010, 15), animism refers to beliefs that natural entities have a vital life force, spirit, personhood, or consciousness.

5 Quotations from the film are taken from the James Cameron screenplay that is published online (Cameron 2007). However, the film departs from that screenplay at various points. A detailed comparison between the screenplay and the film would be welcome.

6 The screenplay refers explicitly to the notion of world-consciousness. Unlike in the film, in the screenplay, Tsu'tey is not merely killed in an attack, he is captured and his queue is cut off. In the screenplay, "Tsu'tey screams in agony, his nervous system exploding on overload. Grinning, Lyle holds up the queue—Tsu'tey's only connection to the world-consciousness which is his life" (Cameron 2007, 135).

7 Some environmental philosophers, nature writers, and eco-critics, such John Elder, have warned that any sense of sacred place could imply that other places are not worthy of our concern. "The love of nature must be comprehensive" (Elder 1993, 150).

8 Le Guin conceded that in the outrage she felt in the "bitter year" of 1968, she created Davidson as pure evil, even though she does not believe that purely evil people exist. By contrast, "neither Lyubov nor Selver is mere Virtue Triumphant; moral and psychological complexity was salvaged, at least, in those characters" (1979, 151–52).

9 While Selfridge is dismissive of Augustine, that seems to be the result less of sexism than of his indifference to science and his contempt for her respectful attitude toward the culture and spirituality of the native population—combined, of course, with his clear priority of creating profit for his corporation.

10 For an argument that there has been a shift from the nation-state as the primary problem to the "more pervasive tyranny of the corporation," see Moylan (2003, 135–36).

11 "There is no alternative" is a phrase made infamous by former British prime minister Margaret Thatcher.

12 She also does this in *The Dispossessed*, where, at the end of the novel, an emissary arrives from an environmentally ruined and (as a result) a politically repressive Earth.

13 The issues involved in the criticisms of the messiah complex and the "going native" theme are complex, although actual criticisms are often superficial. For criticisms, especially of the white messiah complex, see Yee (2010), Newitz (2009), Brook (2010), and Podhoretz (2009). For a nuanced rebuttal, see Bill the Lizard (2009).

References

Bill the Lizard. 2009. "What Does *Avatar* Tell Us about Masculinity and Disability?" *Open Salon*, 23 December. http://open.salon.com/blog/chauncey_devega/2009/12/23/what_does_avatar_tell_us_about_masculinity_and_disability.

Brook, David. 2010. "The Messiah Complex." *New York Times*, 8 January. http://www.nytimes.com/2010/01/08/opinion/08brooks.html.

Cameron, James. 2007. *Avatar*. Screenplay. Twentieth Century Fox. http://www.scribd.com/doc/25009954/James-Cameron-original-screenplay-for-Avatar.

Elder, John. 1993. *Following the Brush: An American Encounter with Classical Japanese Culture*. Boston: Beacon Press.

Le Guin, Ursula K. 1974. *The Dispossessed: An Ambiguous Utopia*. New York: Harper and Row.

———. 1976. *The Word for World Is Forest*. New York: Berkley Medallion.

————. 1979. *The Language of the Night: Essays on Fantasy and Science Fiction.* New York: G. P. Putnam's Sons.

Moylan, Tom. 1986. *Demand the Impossible: Science Fiction and the Utopian Imagination.* New York: Methuen.

————. 2003. "'The Moment Is Here...And It's Important': State, Agency, and Dystopia in Kim Stanley Robinson's *Antarctica* and Ursula K. Le Guin's *The Telling.*" In *Dark Horizons: Science Fiction and the Utopian Imagination*, edited by Raffarella Baccolini and Tom Moylan, 135–53. New York: Routledge.

Newitz, Annalee. 2009. "When Will White People Stop Making Movies Like 'Avatar'?" io9: We Come from the Future, 18 December. http://io9.com/5422666/when-will-white-people-stop-making-movies-like-avatar.

Podhoretz, John. 2009. "Avatarocious: Another Spectacle Hits an Iceberg and Sinks." *Weekly Standard* 15(15), 28 December. http://www.weeklystandard.com/Content/Public/Articles/000/000/017/350fozta.asp.

Sargent, Lyman Tower. 1967. "The Three Faces of Utopianism." *Minnesota Review* 7(3): 222–30.

Taylor, Bron. 2005. "Earth First! and the Earth Liberation Front." In *Encyclopedia of Religion and Nature*, edited by Bron Taylor, 518–24. London: Continuum International. http://www.religionandnature.com/ern/sample/Taylor--EF!and ELF.pdf.

————. 2010. *Dark Green Religion: Nature Spirituality and the Planetary Future.* Berkeley: University of California Press.

Yee, Andy. 2010. "China: Bloggers' Reviews of Avatar." *Global Voices*, 11 January. http://globalvoicesonline.org/2010/01/11/china-bloggers-reviews-of-avatar/.

I See You:
Interspecies Empathy and *Avatar*

LISA H. SIDERIS

Carl Sagan once predicted that if Earth were ever visited by alien life forms, humans would have little to fear and much to learn from them, science fiction and film depictions of aliens notwithstanding. Sagan's argument went roughly as follows: any civilization with the technology required to visit our planet from remote space would necessarily be much more advanced than our own; that would also mean that they would have passed through the critical, perilous stage in their technological development when they realized the possibility of self-annihilation by global nuclear war. Having survived its technological "adolescence," Sagan reasoned, such a civilization would be unlikely to wage unprovoked war against another civilization. They would have long ago learned the art of peaceful coexistence. A message from extraterrestrials should inspire profound hope, not fear, Sagan believed, for it would signal that "someone has learned to live with high technology" (1980, 302). Although Sagan did not put it in quite these terms, such a message would also mark the dawn of an unprecedented era of empathy between the most disparate life forms and civilizations imaginable.

Unfortunately, the prospect of encountering alien forms of life (including unfamiliar or strange inhabitants of our own planet) is more often greeted with fear or revulsion than with hope. In the film *Contact* (1997), based on Sagan's further musings about human-alien encounters, the advanced alien civilization seeks to mitigate such fear by having the emissary from their world greet the Earthling space traveller, Ellie, in the familiar form of her beloved and long-deceased father. In that instant, Ellie's emotions—her childhood memories and longing for her father—are comprehended but also manipulated (in largely benign ways) by the superior alien civilization. In James Cameron's film *Avatar*, a similar arrangement occurs between the Earthlings who have colonized an Earth-like moon called Pandora and the Na'vi, Pandora's native inhabitants. To interact with the Na'vi, humans take on an avatar form that resembles the Na'vi outwardly but is an engineered hybrid between human and Na'vi genetic material. By appearing in familiar form to the natives, the humans hope to gain their trust—*and* (for some, at least) their valuable natural resources. Unlike the technologically advanced races envisioned by Sagan, the humans on Pandora in the year 2154 have mastered a full range of biotechnologies, as well as space travel, without having made the ethical breakthrough that Sagan optimistically predicted.

Reflecting upon scenarios such as Sagan's and Cameron's, we begin to discern some of the moral ambiguity that attends empathy and the uses to which it is put. What, for example, are the limits of human empathic capacities? (Does empathy depend upon sameness and familiarity?) What are the ethically appropriate and inappropriate uses of empathy? (When does empathy qualify as a virtue?) *Avatar*, as I interpret it, is replete with themes of empathy and empathic bonding, as well as spiritual and physical interconnection. In many ways, *Avatar* is a tale of moral awakening, focused on the character of Jake Sully, a paraplegic Marine who infiltrates and is ultimately absorbed into the Na'vi world. As I hope to show, a number of Sully's characteristics, and his situation generally, make him an almost ideal candidate for empathic conversion. To say that Sully is ideally disposed toward empathy (or well positioned for empathic education), however, is not to say that his behaviour is always ideal in an ethical sense. Sully's behaviour and other aspects of the plot serve to illustrate some potential abuses of empathy, as well as empathy's enormous potential as a basis for humanitarian (or whatever the equivalent term—inclusive of aliens—might be) and environmental virtue.

There are, of course, many (sometimes incompatible) definitions of empathy.[1] I touch upon only a subset of these definitions and debates about what constitutes empathy. My discussion focuses especially on normative claims about empathy and owes much to Nancy Sherman (1998), who proposes that empathic imagination entails an often imperfect but salutary struggle to see the world from the perspective of others who are really alien to us.

Empathy: A Brief Overview

It is common to hear empathy touted as a virtue, and a flurry of writing has recently emerged on the moral necessity of empathy in the modern world.[2] The notion that empathy is unambiguously good is a function of empathy's close association with sympathy, which suggests feelings of compassion, solidarity, concern, fellow-feeling, or (somewhat less positively) pity. But these are dispositions that may or may not resemble or be engendered by empathy. Indeed, the term *empathy* emerged much more recently than *sympathy*.[3] The earliest usage of the word *empathy* had to do with human encounters with aesthetic objects. The word first appeared in English as a translation of the German *Einfühlung*, a term meant to convey the sense of projecting oneself into an object of beauty (Wispé 1987, 18). In 1909, as Wispé notes, psychologist Edward Titchener translated *Einfühlung* as *empathy*, drawing upon the Greek *empatheia*, literally, "in-suffering" (ibid.). A useful, if not terribly nuanced, distinction commonly drawn between empathy and sympathy is that the latter term suggests feeling *for* another, while empathy entails feeling into another, imagining oneself in, or projecting oneself into another's situation. If I see that you are distressed and feel distressed as well, I am empathizing; but if I feel sorry for you in your distress, that response is more in line with sympathy. A number of theorists define two basic types (or dimensions) of empathy: cognitive and affective. Cognitive empathy entails awareness of another's state of mind and is associated with role- or perspective-taking—imaginative attempts to step into another's shoes.[4] Affective empathy refers to a shared (or matched, or mirrored) emotional response.

Moral philosophers are often interested in the question of whether empathy can or ought to allow one to leave behind entirely one's self and perspective or interests—what Sherman (1998) calls the "home base"—in the act of empathizing. Some theorists draw a distinction between empathic projection in which one imagines *oneself* in the position of the other (how one would feel in another's place) as opposed to imagining how another's situation is experienced *by that person*. The first form, sometimes referred to as "self-focused role-taking" may lead to "egoistic drift," where one becomes lost in egoistic concern, including concern with one's own empathic distress (Hoffman 2000, 56). In the second form, empathy resembles what a good character actor does: "We do not pretend to be the characters we are acting, we become those characters. This is not a transfer, but a transformation" (Sherman 1998, 101). Transformation requires relinquishing—temporarily—the home base, and it is not easily accomplished, particularly for those of us who are not character actors. Sherman suggests that transformational empathy be viewed as "an ideal to aim for"—a state rarely, if ever, achieved perfectly and one that can radically challenge us to imagine the experiences of others whom we find truly "alien" (101–2).

As one considers the nature of the relationship between the self and others with whom we empathize, two problematics present themselves. One possibility is that the self and its perspective remain dominant, perhaps to the extent that the other's feelings and perspective are grossly distorted by one's own lenses. A second possibility is that one may radically, even irrevocably, lose oneself, one's sense of identity or objectivity, in the other's perspective or emotional state (as with Stockholm syndrome and other forms of traumatic bonding where return to sense of self is severely jeopardized). If the first extreme suggests the problem of parochiality—the difficulty of breaking out of the biases and boundaries of our own perspectives—the second underscores the perils of becoming overly enmeshed in another's psychic reality. Genuinely helpful and compassionate responses to others demand "that we navigate between the Scylla of self-absorption and the Charybdis of vicarious possession" and that we remain alert to "unhealthy fortifications or transgressions of the boundaries of the self" (Piper 1991, 251). Examples of the first pole, or something approaching it, can be discerned in the storyline of *Avatar*. It is more difficult to find evidence in the film that vicarious possession—erosion of the self's boundaries or of one's critical stance—is understood as a danger of empathy. By recognizing these different types, we can see that the film portrays empathy in largely positive ways, as a transformative step toward enlightenment.[5]

A related concern regarding the self and its relation to the other has to do with the motives behind empathy. Here, the danger is that one may feel oneself into another's perspective only to manipulate or betray another in the pursuit of one's own ends. Empathy, after all, can be fully consistent with sadism, narcissism, or other sociopathic tendencies. "It all depends on why one is interested in the other's perspective" (Darwall 1998, 261). Empathy "need not yield prosocial behavior" (Decety and Meyer 2008, 1069). Illuminated in these ways, the capacity for empathy is a morally neutral "method of gathering data" (Wispé 1987, 32). Empathizing may or may not lead to a moral response, such as by expressing sympathetic concern or providing concrete assistance. These possibilities are also represented in *Avatar*.

Our ability to modulate and direct empathic responses may be partly under our control but our basic capacity for empathy appears to be innate. Research in a variety of disciplines points to the conclusion that from the time we are infants, "we see through others' eyes, take on others' emotions, imagine what others believe" (Sherman 1998, 83). For example, infants engage in motor mimicry—imitating movements and facial expressions of caregivers—almost from birth (Decety and Meyer 2008). Day-old infants cry in response to other infants crying, and infants and their mothers readily synchronize their emotions (ibid., 1056–57). Neuro-imaging studies have focused on mirror neurons in the brain, which are activated during a given motor action—say, smiling or reaching for an object—*and* when observing the same action done by another person. These neurons appear to play an important role in social cognition; defects in this system correspond to empathy deficits seen in a variety of disorders such as autism.

Empathy and Role-Taking: Sully's Empathic Education

Jake Sully's identity may be ambiguous and in transition, but his personality consistently demonstrates mental strength, resourcefulness, and adaptability. All of these features make him a good candidate for empathic cultivation, but we also see in the story of Sully's transformation hints of empathy's darker side. Sully inhabits a variety of worlds, belonging fully to none. First and foremost, his identity is mingled with that of his deceased twin brother, Tommy, a scientist selected to work for the avatar program. The program is overseen by Dr. Grace Augustine, whose team of botanists study Pandora's flora and fauna in order to understand the mysterious "network" of communication pervading the planet. These researchers have developed genuine sympathy and admiration for the Na'vi and their understandings of Pandora's living world. Despite his lack of scientific training, Sully is hired to take his brother's place—much to the dismay of Augustine and her team. He likewise transitions regularly between human and Na'vi identities (via his avatar form), and, as a paraplegic Marine, he is marginalized in the highly aggressive world of his fellow Marines, whose epithets for him—"meat" or "meals on wheels"—objectify Sully and liken him to an animal to be consumed.

Because Sully is an identical twin, he can readily link with the avatar originally designed with and for his brother's genetic material. When Sully joins the science team and assumes his avatar form, he thus surrenders his own (or parts of his own) identity. His mission is explained to him in terms immediately evocative of empathy: "since your genome is identical, you could step into his shoes, so to speak." Sully becomes (at least temporarily) a dual hybrid of sorts, *both* with his twin and with the Na'vi genetic material. At the same time, he joyously recovers the freedom of movement not possible in his own partially paralyzed body.

As Sully's masculinity is assailed by the Marines, his intelligence is routinely derided by the scientists who (reluctantly) put him to work in their lab. When he introduces himself to Augustine, she responds flatly, "I need your brother" and, shortly thereafter, dismisses him to others as a "jarhead."

"Try to use big words," one of the scientists advises, although he clearly doubts that Sully can do so. The Na'vi are equally unimpressed. Once in his avatar body, Sully finds himself again castigated, this time by the Na'vi as a "moron" and a "baby" for his inability to instantly absorb their language and customs, although for the most part, he maintains admirable equanimity throughout.

The one Marine who recognizes Sully's usefulness is the man in charge of the military operation, Colonel Quaritch. Quaritch secretly attempts to persuade Sully to give up "intel" on the Na'vi in exchange for a promise that Sully will receive an operation to restore his legs at the completion of his mission. Quaritch's instructions point to yet another layer of Sully's multiple identities. He coaches Sully to assume two false identities at once as the most effective way of accomplishing his mission. He must blend in with the Na'vi—"learn these savages from the inside"—in the guise of a scientist (whom the Na'vi distrust somewhat less than the Marines), while keeping his mission a secret from the team to which he is officially assigned. "You walk like one of her [Augustine's] science pukes, you quack like one," Quaritch instructs, "but you report to me" (Cameron 2007, 25). Now Sully has stepped into not one but several sets of shoes. He has taken on his brother's role among the scientists (and the avatar hybrid designed for him); with his avatar form, he hopes to pass more easily as a member, or at least a friend, of the Na'vi people. All the while—assuming he accepts Quaritch's mission—he is a soldier mimicking a scientist (trying to pass as a Na'vi), carrying out a mission that may restore his (compromised) status as a respected member of the Marine Corps. Throughout much, if not most, of the film, Sully's identity and loyalties remain obscure and contested.

What does this have to do with empathy? It is clear that Sully is learning—or being coerced—to view the world from multiple, and alien, perspectives, and this is an important step in developing empathy. For most of us, imaginatively taking on the role of another is more difficult the more different from us they are, but, as some researchers argue, there may be great benefits to doing so: "We increase in self-awareness through comparison and contrast with those we encounter empathically.... We must stretch to connect empathically with such diverse experience, and we are creatively 'enlarged' as a result of this enrichment" (Everding and Huffaker 1998, 423). An increasingly common method of cultivating empathy, in both children and adults, is through role-taking exercises. Experiments in psychology have demonstrated that "taking the perspective of another person increases empathic arousal" (Sherman 1998, 111). With the express goal of instilling empathy, a number of international NGOs have established immersion programs, such as a village immersion program that allows international staff to spend several days living with poor families in developing countries, helping with household tasks and experiencing daily life from their perspective (Krznaric 2008, 5). Participants in such programs often report enhanced ability to empathize. Sully's mission essentially lands him in one such immersion program.

Psychologists have also noted an association between the capacity for empathic arousal and what is sometimes called "ego resilience." Resilience assesses "flexible, adaptive behavior across broad social and behavioral domains" and "such adaptive behavior is facilitated by understanding others' feelings and points of view" (Strayer and Roberts 1989, 227). Individuals with resilient egos can more easily change places with others (imaginatively), in part because they do not feel overly threatened when confronted by difference. In other words, resilient individuals are more able to consider different points of view, and that allows them to better understand others' perspectives, which further increases their adaptability in times of stress or in unfamiliar settings. Resilience is particularly strong in individuals who have experienced major physical or psychological trauma and who have a strong sense of themselves as survivors. "Characteristics of survivor personality traits are quite similar to the attributes of ego-resiliency" and include flexibility, sociability, confidence, and curiosity, among others (Wilson 2005, 389–90).

Sully fits the profile of a highly resilient and potentially empathic individual. His identity may be in flux, but the one constant in his character throughout his many transformations is what the Na'vi princess Neytiri immediately identifies (despite her initial distrust and dislike of him) as a "strong heart." Not only has Sully sustained major trauma in the past, but, as noted above, he is routinely marginalized and ridiculed by every subculture he encounters during his mission, whether scientists, fellow Marines, or the Na'vi. Despite this treatment, he survives and perseveres in the midst of extreme mental and physical adversity. As the plot progresses, we learn that the qualities that Neytiri discerns in him will make him a great warrior (according to Na'vi, if not also American warrior paradigms), as well as an individual marked for spiritual excellence. Sully turns out to be the sixth in a succession of spiritual leaders/warriors known as Toruk Makto—a rare breed of individuals known for their ability to bond with and tame one of Pandora's top predators, an enormous birdlike creature; more significantly, the Toruk Makto has the ability to unite the many clans that inhabit Pandora, and near the conclusion of the story, Sully does precisely this. So effective does Sully become as a trans-species communicator that under his leadership, even Pandora's wild animals join forces with the Na'vi in the final battle against humans.

For much of the film, Sully appears inscrutable: it is not clear what his intentions are with regard to his conflicting orders, or where, if anywhere, his loyalties lie. Sully must decide what he will do with the bonds of trust and empathy he is able to forge. Is he simply gathering "intel" or is his bond with the Na'vi genuine? Will he use his connection to the Na'vi to betray them, as Quaritch requests? Within this suspenseful element of the story, we see a nod to the idea that empathy, as a means of gathering data, can be used for good or for ill. Insofar as he follows Quaritch's orders, Sully demonstrates precisely how empathic connection is readily abused. For their own part, the Na'vi, too, may glean information from Sully in order to outwit their human colonizers. "We must understand these Sky People if we are to drive them out," Neytiri's father observes (Cameron 2007, 49).

Embodiment and Empathy

The act of assuming a Na'vi form has an immediate and heady effect on Sully. Upon first awakening in a Na'vi body, he wreaks havoc in the hospital-like setting, overturning furniture and equipment as he races outside to enjoy the sensation of being not just able bodied but preternaturally strong and agile. Interestingly, studies that use virtual reality headsets to create the illusion of body transfer suggest that people adapt their behaviour to fit their appearance *and* that subjects feel a strong connection to their virtual body even after leaving it. One study found that subjects behaved more aggressively when given virtual avatar bodies taller than the bodies of other avatars around them (Biever 2006). While body transfers that increase aggression may not bode well for cultivation of empathy, other studies with virtual body transfers indicate that subjects feel a strong sense of ownership of their avatar bodies and retain some degree of identification with their avatar body once they have "returned" to their own body. Men who were given the virtual body of a ten-year-old girl, for example, reported feeling that the girl's body was their own (Zukerman 2010). More surprising was that when these subjects (no longer in the perspective of the girl's body) watched the girl being slapped, their physiological reactions such as heart rate were similar to those of individuals who feel themselves threatened. We might venture, then, that an individual in Sully's position would feel a strong sense of connection with his Na'vi avatar— and perhaps some degree of identification with other Na'vi as well, who resemble his avatar form.[6] Sully does increasingly identify with the plight of the Na'vi and comes to view their human enemies as his own. And like subjects in virtual reality studies, he reports in his videolog that he can no longer clearly distinguish reality from unreality as a result of repeated body transfers.

Initially, Sully does not take on these various roles and perspectives completely voluntarily; insofar as he does so of necessity, he is not exercising empathy as a virtuous disposition. But changes in his perspective pull him along and begin to transform him, almost against his will. His moral progress is marked by particular rites of passage as he is inducted into the Na'vi community, as well as by moments of empathic bonding with other creatures and, especially, with Neytiri.

Empathic Bonding, Eye Contact, and Spiritual Awakening in *Avatar*

Like Quaritch (although for different reasons), Augustine orders Sully to listen closely to Neytiri, to learn the Na'vi customs, and especially to "see the forest through her [Neytiri's] eyes." References to what Sully sees—and to the act of seeing in general—recur throughout *Avatar*. He implores Neytiri, "Teach me to see," but he is ridiculed by a Na'vi warrior who observes that "a rock sees more" than Sully does. The traditional greeting among the Na'vi (and the title of the film's theme song) is the phrase "I see you." To say "I see you" to another can simply convey that I recognize or acknowledge you, much as a brief hello or wave might do. But as the story unfolds, it becomes clear that the phrase contains a more profound range of meanings, including something akin to "I love you" and allusions to the transformation of one's perspective that may occur through love. "I see you" is also associated with gaining an accurate apprehension of another: in one scene, as a member of Augustine's team coaches Sully to use the phrase in appropriate contexts and with proper intonation, he stresses its core meaning as "I see into you, I understand you." This expression (particularly as fleshed out in the theme song's lyrics) also suggests seeing through another's eyes and seeing oneself through the other's eyes, both of which are important dimensions of empathy since "we learn about ourselves through others' intimate understanding of us" (Sherman 1998, 84). Lyrics to the theme song make these meanings explicit: "I see you.../ I see me through your eyes," "Now I live through you and you through me," and, perhaps most dramatically, "I offer my life as a sacrifice / I live through your love."

Visually, *Avatar* places great emphasis upon the act of seeing as well. The film's characters—and to some extent, viewers who see the film in 3-D—have the opportunity to experience the world through different eyes, to experience a new reality. There is little doubt that the 3-D technology in *Avatar* has created renewed interest in 3-D cinematography, yet much of the commentary on *Avatar* fails to treat the use of 3-D as more than an impressive technological feat or visual treat.[7] The immersive experience of 3-D is, however, not peripheral but integral to the film's message about the importance of enhanced perception through immersion in other perspectives. In a variety of ways, *Avatar* suggests that the eyes play a crucial role in spiritual transformation. *Avatar* begins with a shot of Sully's eyes popping open, after a long journey to Pandora in a cryo-vault. The film similarly ends with his eyes opening wide to a new life and new world after he experiences "rebirth" into a Na'vi form. In scenes depicting Sully moving in and out of his avatar body—a transformation, incidentally, that takes place in a "link unit" remarkably similar to an MRI machine—the focus is always on his eyes.[8]

Eye contact is critically important in experiences of empathy between humans and between humans and other species, so it is no surprise that *Avatar* places much emphasis upon eyes as a symbol of meaningful connection. Non-verbal forms of communication may add far more to the process of communication than verbal forms, and proper eye contact is crucial for developing empathy and trustworthiness (Morrison 2009). Where verbal communication is not possible—as with human-animal interactions or (we might imagine) human-alien encounters—non-verbal cues become profoundly meaningful.[9] The significance of eye-focused forms of communication is affirmed (although largely anecdotally) by numerous encounters in the field between humans and animals. Ethologists and primatologists such as Mark Bekoff and Jane Goodall believe that the primary means of communication for many animals is through the eyes: "In many species eyes reflect feelings, whether wide open in glee or sunken in despair," writes Bekoff (2007, 49–50), adding, "There is no more direct animal-to-animal communication than staring deeply into another's eyes." In his writing about human-animal encounters and animistic perceptions of the natural world, Bron Taylor (2010) refers to such encounters as eye-to-eye epiphanies—moments when locking eyes with another being conveys more information and greater depth of feeling than words can communicate. The belief that humans can enter imaginatively into the world of non-human life forms through the experience of eye-focused communication, as well as other ancient forms of non-verbal communion, is common among nature writers, ethologists, and environmentalists generally. At the heart of this belief, Taylor writes, "there is at work a kind of empathetic and animistic moral imagination" (26).

Yet another way in which *Avatar* emphasizes eyes as symbolic of spiritual transformation is in the frequent references to waking and sleeping. The imperative to "wake up" is voiced by various characters in the film and in a variety of contexts; often the phrase is exchanged by characters with different agendas regarding the Na'vi and with radically divergent views of reality in general. At a point in the film when Sully is ostracized by the

Na'vi, who perceive him as a traitor, he finds himself "in the place the eye does not see." For their own part, the Na'vi refer to the engineered avatar forms as "dreamwalkers," and as Sully comes to identify with the Na'vi and with the world he experiences as an avatar, he is no longer certain which life is "real" and which merely a "dream."[10] At the end of the film, his dream existence as a Na'vi, as a dreamwalker in their world, becomes the reality.

Waking up thus signifies awareness of a higher consciousness or a more ultimate reality. This is most clearly seen at the end of the film when Sully participates in the sacred ritual that permanently transfers him to a Na'vi body and perspective.[11] Here, we have an example, one might say, of empathic identification so complete that the former self is eclipsed. The film's theme song refers to sacrifices, and the scene resembles a sacrifice, with Sully's human and Na'vi forms laid out at the foot of a profoundly sacred site. The ritual has little of the solemnity of death because Sully will be reborn as a more enlightened being. The text of the screenplay, however, portrays Sully's relentless identification with the Na'vi, culminating in his complete transformation, as a dangerous and potentially self-destructive obsession. Omitted from the film, for example, are Augustine's warnings that Sully is getting in "way too deep" and her efforts to call him back to his identity: "no matter what you prove out there, *you* are still in here" (Cameron 2007, 83).[12] As Sully gets in deeper and deeper, he utterly neglects his physical health, and the screenplay increasingly likens his link unit to a "coffin." The Na'vi rite of passage that marks him as a clan member is depicted in the screenplay as a suicidal "vision quest" that Sully almost hopes he will not survive: "It's okay. Mo'at [Neytiri's mother] says an alien mind probably can't survive the Dream Hunt anyway" (ibid., 85). The most dramatic difference is apparent in the ceremony that permanently installs Sully in his avatar form. Described in the film as Sully's "birthday party," it is characterized in the screenplay as a funeral. "There's a funeral tonight," Sully records in his final videolog. "It was someone very close to me"; when the transfer is complete, Neytiri "gently closes his dead eyes" (ibid., 151).

The more sombre tone of the screenplay and its explicit references to Sully's death suggest a degree of ambivalence about his radical transformation. In the film, however, empathic identification shades into spiritual rebirth and a welcome and celebrated end to the former self—an ideal that finds resonance in many religious traditions. Empathy implies the possibility of oneness, of dissolution of boundaries between self and other; seen in this light, it shows affinities with ideals of spiritual communion, non-duality, or the essential oneness of reality.[13] Because *Avatar* unambiguously depicts the Na'vi worldview as superior to that of humans (who have destroyed their own world), there is nothing to fear or lament in Sully casting off the vestiges of his former self. We sense that, from the filmmaker's point of view, the Na'vi's world and way of being *is* the superior reality and mode of existence. Indeed, there is an unmistakable empirical dimension to the Na'vi worldview that leaves little doubt about the truth of their beliefs. Empathic connection is depicted most dramatically—and quite literally—in a bonding ritual that the Na'vi initiate with animal companions trained for labour and transport. Na'vi tradition maintains that animals choose their masters and that only animals that have voluntarily bonded will assent to training. The bonding ritual involves actually plugging into the animal by means of a long braid worn by the Na'vi. The braid connects with a similar cluster of (presumably) nerves in the animal's body; at the moment the connection is made, the camera zooms in on the dilated pupils and widened eyes of the bonded animal whose perception of the world is now attuned to its master's. With this bonding, a kind of neural interface occurs between the Na'vi rider and his or her steed; the rider now feels what the animal feels and synchronizes perfectly with its movements and thoughts (although with the rider in control).

A symbiotic relationship between the Na'vi and animals is depicted in other ways as well—not infrequently, in ways that borrow from practices and beliefs commonly attributed to native peoples. Killing of animals is permitted only when done with an attitude of reverence. In one scene, Neytiri demonstrates to Sully the proper method of killing, which involves reciting a prayer of thanks and a quick kill with a sharp and carefully aimed knife. Sully's first clean kill constitutes a rite of passage to manhood, according to Na'vi custom. Yet it seems to me (and perhaps others) that Sully is rather mechanically mimicking behaviours of reverence and compassion as modelled by Neytiri. In fact, Sully appears to botch some sacred rites, voicing what seem to be shallow, inappropriate or disingenuous sentiments, as though just going through the motions. When it is Sully's turn to demonstrate his "readiness" and understanding of the Na'vi hunt, for example, he appears to rush through the prayer and eagerly plunge the knife in, as a hungry child might mechanically mumble a prayer before eating. In another scene depicting an important rite of passage, Sully tames one of the large dragon-bird creatures that the Na'vi use as transports.[14] Although viewers are apprised of the Na'vi belief that the animal chooses its rider—and then bonds exclusively with him or her for life—Sully's enactment of this rite appears anything but reverential (or voluntary on the part of the non-human animal). Having finally wrestled the thrashing animal to the ground, Sully forces the bond, while muttering, "That's right. You're mine." His remark and his enjoyment of dominance over this creature are what we might expect from a Marine but not from the enlightened Na'vi warrior he is supposed to have become. We would expect that, were his empathic transformation genuine, or complete, so would be his expressions of compassion, reverence, and gratitude.[15] What makes the Na'vi admirable, after all, is not just their capacity for empathy but the way in which their empathic abilities predispose them toward a whole host of (other-regarding) virtues. Put differently, becoming a Na'vi entails not just understanding the world from their perspective but understanding that their perspective *is also* the perspective of the animal being hunted or tamed. Sully appears to get it wrong.

On the one hand, that Sully seems at certain points to revert back to a "jarhead" mentality can be read as a flaw in the film itself (or in Cameron's view of what constitutes moral progress or harmony between species).[16] On the other hand, such moments illustrate that Sully's transformation and empathic education remain imperfect and incomplete. Nancy Sherman (1998, 102) notes that the process of transformation to a wholly different perspective is bound to be halting and at times deeply flawed. The transformative model of empathy "serves as an ideal to aim for, though one, typically, only imperfectly achieved and that never fully escapes some residue of the home base." Early on in the film, Sully verbalizes doubts about his capacity for radical change: "There's no such thing as an ex-Marine. You never lose the attitude." Rather than interpret Sully's regressive behaviour as a flaw in the film, we might read it as an illustration of the challenge of inhabiting (fully, emotively, and cognitively) alien perspectives and values. It remains incumbent upon all of us to "hone and refine our empathic skills so that we can be appropriately sensitive to the emotional needs of others" (Snow 2000, 75).

Conclusion: Empathy, Education, and Environmentalism

Avatar has been identified by viewers and critics as an environmental film because it upholds common environmental themes and values such as understanding the land as sacred and life forms as intricately interconnected and innately valuable; the film also rejects the duality of the physical and the spiritual and casts doubt on the idea of technological advance as synonymous with progress. The Na'vi, as we have seen, exhibit attitudes of reverence and ideals of symbiosis in their dealings with the land and animals. In all of these ways, *Avatar* affirms values held (in varying degrees) by those who consider themselves environmentalists. But I want to stress that empathy—arguably, the dominant theme of the film—has enormous potential as an environmental value as well, and it is integral to the environmental message of the film.

It might appear that *empathy* is a current buzzword, but the history of environmentalism is bound up with cultivation of the empathic imagination. In the first half of the twentieth century, the American conservationist and founder of land ethics Aldo Leopold famously urged readers to "think like a mountain"—to step outside of limited human perspectives, to imagine ecological and evolutionary time frames. Doing so will enhance appreciation of the role played by predators in an ecosystem, as well as other forms of life that humans fear and sometimes vilify, if not hate. Leopold's phrase has since been adopted by environmentalists of many varieties as a way of expressing their rejection of anthropocentrism and their respect for difference. Writing both contemporaneously and then after Leopold, Rachel Carson similarly emphasized empathy, as, for example, in her writings about the sea, which evocatively transport readers into ocean worlds inhabited by strange and unfamiliar creatures. Engaging the empathic imagination was a primary objective of Carson's narrative style. Because most popular works on the sea take the human perspective, Carson (1998, 55–56) set out "to avoid this human bias as much as possible.... I wanted my readers to feel that they were, for a time, actually living the lives of sea creatures. To bring this about I had first, of course, to think myself into the role of an animal that lives in the sea."

Many environmentalists can pinpoint a kind of conversion experience, a moment of awakening when they first comprehended that humans inhabit a world filled with wonderfully strange life forms—creatures whose values and perceptions are independent of human values and perceptions. Think again of Leopold, who, as he watched the "fierce green fire" dying in the eyes of a wolf gunned down by foresters, sensed that a unique and valuable perspective on the world, an alien form of knowing, lay behind those eyes. "I realized then, and have known ever since, that there was something new to me in those eyes—something known only to her and to the mountain" (1949, 130). What Leopold glimpsed was the world as seen through the eyes of the Other—the wolf, the mountain, the alien. As Lucas Johnston (2010, 19) notes, moments of awakened consciousness to the affinity of all life can lead individuals to discern a broader set of moral concerns, the outlines of a "biophilic ethic, manifest in new forms of "empathetic engagement." Leopold's story resembles Sully's story.

Recent developments in the global environmental crisis present further challenges to our empathic imaginations. How do we generate concern for environments and creatures with which most humans have little direct experience, such as marine ecologies that remain distant and inaccessible to us? How might we persuade current generations of humans that they have moral obligations to future generations—persons unknown to us— who will bear the full brunt of our fossil fuel addiction? Here, empathy is key. Climate change, for example, challenges us to feel ourselves into the situation of individuals remote from us both in space and time—future generations as well as distant communities hit hard by its effects. Roman Krznaric refers to this challenge as one of "outrospection."[17] "Generating empathy both across space and through time," he writes, "is one of the most powerful ways we have of closing the gap between knowledge and action, and for tackling the climate crisis" (2008, 2). Krznaric particularly endorses perspective-taking or cognitive forms of empathy (encouraged through workshops, immersive programs, and other means) as highly susceptible to intentional cultivation. "Taking the perspective of others through a leap of the empathetic imagination erodes our ability to dehumanise strangers and treat them as being of less worth than ourselves" (4).

We can be fairly certain that humans have innate, evolutionarily based capacities for empathy; we know, too, that this capacity may find expression in ways that actually benefit other humans and the biosphere generally. In our evolutionary past, however, empathy probably did not extend beyond one's family or group, but "with the growth of civilization and human cognitive abilities, humans have gained the ability to familiarize themselves with increasingly diverse and distant cultural groups" (Chismar 1988, 263). Education and exposure to diversity and difference can thus expand empathy's range. But is such familiarity actually conducive to empathic engagement? Does our constant bombardment with images of suffering, disaster, and injustice inure us, leading to what experts call empathy or compassion "fatigue" (Moeller 1999)? Perhaps. It makes sense, after all, that the same evolutionary processes that established empathic capacities would also circumscribe them, setting minimum thresholds and outer limits to empathic expression so as to safeguard its adaptive function (Rifkin 2009, 124). As environmentalists often worry, bombarding the public with bad news and predictions of environmental disaster—oil spills, global warming, species extinction—may engender despair and apathy, even anger, rather than motivate action; moreover, doing so fosters a stereotype (frequently voiced by climate change deniers) of environmentalists as preoccupied with end-of-the-world scenarios.

Clearly, there are no simple solutions or easy answers to problems such as these, but I remain largely persuaded by those such as Rifkin who see education for empathy, with all its caveats, as part of the solution. I am particularly heartened by environmental education for children that (explicitly or implicitly) incorporates empathic education.[18] Many educators and environmentalists are returning to the idea that children need to form an emotional, visceral bond with the natural world and with non-human forms of life *before* learning the dispiriting details of the environmental crisis (Louv 2005).[19] Empathy's scope—as *Avatar* illustrates so well—is not limited to "negative" emotions such as distress but is strongly implicated in positive feelings of identification, wonder, and attachment.[20] Empathic environmental education should not begin with or focus upon negative emotional responses as a way of motivating action. Some of the objectives of nature-study movements from a century ago remain relevant here and are discernible in current programs aimed at empathy. A kind of revolt against formal science and mechanical memorization, nature study aimed to teach not facts but "spirit"—"a point of view, a means of contact" with the natural world (Bailey 1911, 18).[21]

Early attachment to the natural world can form the basis for ethical engagement later in life, as writers ranging from Rachel Carson to Richard Louv have understood. Sociobiological interpretations of children's innate attachment to nature, notably the biophilia hypothesis first developed by E. O. Wilson (1984), suggest that young children are particularly predisposed to empathic engagement, curiosity, and attraction to the natural world. Assuming that the "fundamental development of any biologically rooted tendency [such as biophilia] is likely to occur during childhood" (Kellert 2005, 64), education should target early childhood as the "age of empathy," a time to encourage live animal contact, sensory engagement, and nature-based storytelling (White 2001). For older children and adults, the sort of perspective-taking exercises and empathy workshops described by Krznaric and Rifkin may be highly effective, particularly those that encourage participants to make connections between their own lifestyle choices, on the one hand, and impacts on the natural world and on the lifeways and communities of distant people, on the other. We inhabit a world in which network concepts are almost second nature and in which systems thinking is increasingly the norm, yet we fail to make the most important connections. "If we can harness holistic thinking to a new global ethics that recognizes and acts to harmonize the many relationships that make up the life-sustaining forces of the planet," Rifkin (2009, 600) argues, "we will have crossed the divide into a near-climax world economy and biosphere consciousness."

Avatar gives us a glimpse into just such a world. On Pandora, systems thinking, network relationships, and biosphere consciousness are one and the same. As the story ends, all life on Pandora has joined together in solidarity against a common threat emanating from the far more technologically advanced (but spiritually impoverished) "Sky People" of Earth. Sagan's prediction that technologically advanced civilizations would encounter less advanced worlds in a spirit of peace and understanding is not borne out by this scenario. But his belief that citizens of a planet can join together in common cause against a threat to their continued survival remains relevant. On Pandora, the threat is from an alien civilization; here on Earth, we have created threats for ourselves—not only the threat of global nuclear annihilation but the nightmare of catastrophic biosphere destruction, which may prove more difficult to avert because, to many on Earth, it does not yet seem real. Sooner or later, to paraphrase Sully, we will have to wake up.

Notes

1 See for example Batson (2009), who identifies eight distinct phenomena referred to as empathy in scholarly literature.

2 See, for example, Jeremy Rifkin's recent encyclopedic work, *The Empathic Civilization: The Race to Global Consciousness in a World in Crisis* (2009).

3 Adding to the confusion is the fact that what some philosophers, notably Hume, call "sympathy" is probably more accurately labelled "empathy" (Cohon 2010).

4 More fundamentally, cognitive empathy entails awareness that the other *has* a mind, as it is closely connected to what philosophers and psychologists refer to as theory of mind.

5 The film departs from the screenplay in subtle and interesting ways regarding Jake Sully's empathic loss of self, as I discuss below.

6 This is speculation, of course, as I know of no studies of this sort using alien—non-human—bodies as avatars and/or measuring subjects' reactions to aggression against other bodies that *resemble* their virtual body.

7 At least one critic (Cohen 2009) makes this connection between the technology and the film's message.

8 The resemblance to an MRI unit is explicit in the screenplay, which describes link units as a cross between a "coffin" and an "MRI." MRI units offer the possibility of "seeing into" others' mental and emotional states. Characters in the film comment on (and are surprised by) the impressive—"gorgeous"—activity of Sully's brain as seen through the machine, particularly since they had judged him a simpleton.

9 Staring openly is perceived to be a threat by many social animals, including humans. (The tendency to avoid eye contact altogether is a pervasive trait among autistic individuals.) Fear of certain types of eye contact may have to do with the manner in which predators stare fixedly at prey—and may explain why many species, such as butterflies, have evolved eye-like spots to ward off their enemies (Midgley 1995, 11).

10 The term *dreamwalker* occurs in the screenplay (Cameron 2007, 46, 48).

11 We might say that Sully's soul or spirit is transferred to Na'vi form, although by this time, Sully has undergone such radical transformation—physically, mentally, and emotionally—that it is difficult to pinpoint an "essence" that remains of his former self, other than those qualities Neytiri recognizes in him.

12 On the other hand, Augustine later regrets having "held back" and commends Sully for giving the Na'vi his "heart" (also omitted from the film).

13 Some theorists would reject this interpretation of empathy as suggesting that we are blurred selves or part of an ontological whole (as, I think, *Avatar* does). Snow (2000), for example, insists that empathy involves numerically distinct states held individually by separate persons.

14 It is significant that the creatures chosen for 'bonding are (in more than one instance) hybrids as well (like Sully) and, in particular, a hybrid of bird and reptile, a creature that in mythological literature often symbolizes a unity of heaven and earth or spirit and body.

15 The screenplay states that during his first clean kill, Jake speaks the customary Na'vi words "haltingly, but with feeling" (Cameron 2007, 66).

16 In my mind, these problematic scenes are so glaring as to seem deliberate; on the other hand, subtlety is not among Cameron's chief strengths as a filmmaker.

17 See Krznaric's very thoughtful weblog on empathy at http://www.romankrznaric .com/empathy.

18 For examples, see the Children and Nature Network, http://www.childrenand nature.org/, and a white paper titled "Helping Children Learn to Love the Earth before We Ask Them to Save It," http://www.worldforumfoundation.org/wf/ wf2006_nature/pdf/lovetheearth.pdf.

19 The idea is not new. The nature-study movement of the early twentieth century had precisely such objectives, instilling what it termed "nature-sympathy"—more accurately called "empathy"—for nature and animals, as part of a child's daily education away from the confines of the classroom and distinct from science education. Nature-study advocates worried that children who did not form sympathetic bonds with nature would suffer from developmental problems—mental, physical, and emotional—much as Richard Louv (2005) recently argued.

20 Some studies suggest that in young children, affective or emotive empathy occurs prior to development of cognitive forms of empathy that entail awareness of other minds. See Hoffman (2000) and Snow (2000).

21 Rifkin (2009, 608) similarly endorses teaching children what he calls "empathic science" in lieu of mechanistic models that portray the world as "a cold, uncaring place, devoid of awe, compassion, or a sense of purpose."

References

Bailey, Liberty Hyde. 1911. *The Nature-Study Idea*. 4th ed. New York: Macmillan.

Batson, C. Daniel. 2009. "These Things Called Empathy: Eight Related but Distinct Phenomena." In *The Social Neuroscience of Empathy*, edited by Jean Decety and William Ickes, 2–15. Cambridge, MA: MIT Press.

Bekoff, Mark. 2007. *The Emotional Lives of Animals: A Leading Scientist Explores Animal Joy, Sorrow, and Empathy—And Why They Matter*. Novato, CA: New World Library.

Biever, Celeste. 2006. "For a New Personality, Click Here." *New Scientist*, 25 February.

Cameron, James. 2007. *Avatar*. Screenplay. Twentieth Century Fox. http://www .scribd.com/doc/25009954/James-Cameron-original-screenplay-for-Avatar.

Carson, Rachel. 1998. "Memo to Mrs. Eales on *Under the Sea-Wind*." In *Lost Woods: The Discovered Writing of Rachel Carson*, edited by Linda Lear, 53–62. Boston: Beacon Press.

Chismar, Douglas. 1988. "Empathy and Sympathy: The Important Difference." *Journal of Value Inquiry* 22(4): 257–66.

Cohen, Adam. 2009. "Next Generation 3-D Medium of 'Avatar' Underscores Its Message." New York Times, 25 December. http://www.nytimes.com/2009/12/26/opinion/26sat4.html.

Cohon, Rachel. 2010. "Hume's Moral Philosophy." In *The Stanford Encyclopedia of Philosophy*, edited by Edward N. Zalta. http://plato.stanford.edu/archives/fall2010/entries/hume-moral/.

Darwall, Stephen. 1998. "Sympathy, Empathy, Care." *Philosophical Studies* 89: 261–82.

Decety, Jean, and Meghan Meyer. 2008. "From Emotion Resonance to Empathic Understanding: A Social Developmental Neuroscience Account." *Development and Psychopathology* 20: 1053–80.

Everding, H. Edward, and Lucinda A. Huffaker. 1998. "Educating Adults for Empathy: Implications of Cognitive Role-Taking and Identity Formation." *Religious Education* 93(4): 413–30.

Hoffman, Martin L. 2000. *Empathy and Moral Development*. New York: Cambridge University Press.

Johnston, Lucas F. 2010. "From Biophilia to Cosmophilia: The Role of Biological and Physical Sciences in Promoting Sustainability." *Journal for the Study of Religion, Nature, and Culture* 4(1): 7–23.

Kellert, Stephen 2005. *Building for Life: Designing and Understanding the Human-Nature Connection*. Chicago: Island Press.

Krznaric, Roman. 2008. "Empathy and Climate Change: Proposals for a Revolution of Human Relationships." http://www.romankrznaric.com/wp-content/uploads/2011/12/Empathy%20and%20Climate%20Change%20Krznaric.pdf.

Leopold, Aldo. 1949. *A Sand County Almanac and Sketches Here and There*. New York: Oxford University Press.

Louv, Richard. 2005. *Last Child in the Woods: Saving Our Children from Nature-Deficit Disorder*. Chapel Hill, NC: Algonquin.

Midgley, Mary. 1995. *Beast and Man: The Roots of Human Nature*. Rev. ed. New York: Routledge.

Moeller, Susan. 1999. *Compassion Fatigue: How the Media Sell Disease, Famine, War, and Death*. New York: Routledge.

Morrison, Rodger. 2009. "Empathy from Avatars: Propositions for Improving Trust Development in Pseudo-Social Relationships with Avatars." *European Journal of Social Sciences* 12(2): 298–309.

Piper, Adrian M. S. 1991. "Impartiality, Compassion, and Modal Imagination." *Ethics* 101: 726–57.

Rifkin, Jeremy. 2009. *The Empathic Civilization: The Race to Global Consciousness in a World Crisis*. New York: Tarcher/Penguin.

Sagan, Carl. 1980. *Cosmos*. New York: Random House.

Sherman, Nancy. 1998. "Empathy and Imagination." *Midwest Studies in Philosophy* 22: 82–119.

Snow, Nancy. 2000. "Empathy." *American Philosophical Quarterly* 37(1): 65–78.

Strayer, Janet, and William Roberts. 1989. "Children's Empathy and Role Taking: Child and Parental Factors, and Relations to Prosocial Behavior." *Journal of Applied Developmental Psychology* 10: 227–39.

Taylor, Bron. 2010. *Dark Green Religion: Nature Spirituality and the Planetary Future*. Berkeley: University of California Press.

Wilson, John P. 2005. *The Posttraumatic Self: Restoring Meaning and Wholeness to Personality*. New York: Routledge.

Wispé, Lauren. 1987. "History of the Concept of Empathy." In *Empathy and Its Development*, edited by Nancy Eisenberg and Janet Strayer, 17–37. New York: Cambridge University Press.

White, Randy. 2001. "Moving from Biophobia to Biophilia: Developmentally Appropriate Environmental Education for Children." White Hutchinson Leisure and Learning Group. http://www.whitehutchinson.com/children/articles/biophilia.shtml.

Wilson, Edward O. 1984. *Biophilia*. Cambridge, MA: Harvard University Press.

Zukerman, Wendy. 2010. "The Real Avatar: Body Transfer Turns Men into Girls." *New Scientist*, 13 May. http://www.newscientist.com/article/dn18896-the-real-avatar-body-transfer-turns-men-into-girls.html.

Knowing Pandora in Sound:
Acoustemology and Ecomusicological Imagination
in Cameron's *Avatar*

MICHAEL B. MACDONALD

The sound of this little hand drum is filling the entire universe. Lonnie, my musical mentor, and I sit around a smoky ceremonial fire, each of us playing and singing a Mi'kmaq honour song.[1] This has become a regular, almost weekly ritual. We hike out into the forest, prepare a fire, and sing the songs we have learned from Mi'kmaq elders. The words of the songs are powerful even if I do not really understand many of them. I know a phrase here and there. Mostly, I am uttering foreign and beautiful sounds. But with each singing, the song becomes more familiar.

The song has ended. The entire universe is holding its breath as the resonance from the last drumbeat contracts, folding in along the edges of my universe-filling beats. I am returning to myself on the tides of my drumbeat. I feel myself filling my body again—hearing the birds and the crackle of a dry stick exploding into flames.

Mi'kmaq elders say that the drumbeat is our first encounter with our mother. The great beat of our mother's heart fills our newly emerging ears. I am ceremonially returning to this first experience. The elders explain our relationship to Earth and to life through our primal relationship with our biological mother. We are born into the world twice when we hear that sound. I was born both a son and a human.

I exhale. My eyes open as if attached to my lungs. The leaves of the surrounding trees appear a little greener. The fire seems to warm my face just a little bit more than I remember. The cloudy sky may be richer. Everything seems just a little bit more vibrant. This is the experience I look forward to each week. It is as if I have plugged into a more complex world.

I reach into a leather pouch. I plunge my fingers into tobacco and feel the soft coolness. My imagination surges back through time, exploring nooks of my memory. I am exploring my subjective world like a dockworker flipping through a newly arrived ship's manifest.[2] I am ritually inspecting my most recent stowage. I am patrolling for a long-forgotten container left unnoticed, and unopened, or perhaps shelved too hastily. The tobacco, as well as the songs and fire, provide me with a method to review my life and its accompanying emotional baggage.

I feel the moist ball of tobacco in my hand. I press it with my fingers and reflect. I focus my energy on this newly noticed concern and feel its energy drain from somewhere in my subjective world. I can actually feel energy moving down my arm and into this little tobacco ball. I feel like opening my hand just to see if the tobacco has actually changed shape, but I resist. The download has finished.

The fire burns brightly. I drop my little tobacco package of immaterial tension, made material, into the open arms of the small ritual fire. I watch as the tobacco burns. I feel the release of tension as the tobacco is burned. The burning is another transformation. It is now smoke. Something that just minutes ago was a troubling territory in my subjectivity is now filtering up through the green canopy overhead on its way to another territory. The eagle, as messenger of the Great Spirit, now has access to my concerns. It's his job to ferry them to the Creator. As the ritual draws to a close, my healing begins, and so does my transformation.

Lonnie and I light cigarettes and sit casually around our fire. The world slowly returns to normal. But I feel that something in me will not return to the same shape it was before. I have been transformed, just a little, but enough. Perhaps more than I know.

Early the next morning, Lonnie and I are again together. But this time, we are on our way to a standoff with a mining company. The local government has succumbed to pressure from mining executives and has allowed for a development on public land. We have not considered the possibility that our ritual the day before could be connected to our attendance at this protest. We are attending because this is a great hiking area, not because we are spiritually connected to the land. Or are we? I am forced to re-evaluate when we arrive at the protest to find that we are two of very few European-Canadians in attendance. The Mi'kmaq elder raises an eagle wing overhead and dedicates our actions to the Creator. This time the honour song has many drums and many voices. Again, I am transformed. I have joined a "home culture" protecting our land.

Home Culture Music

My emergence into this home culture was a personal moment of potent political transformation. I began to see myself as an environmental activist and to lobby the government to protect this land, my home. We were successful. In the years that followed, I was part of a number of environmental causes, struggling against industrial development and working toward environmental cleanup. In all these struggles, I worked alongside indigenous and non-indigenous allies from a variety of ethnic groups. It seemed that we were all motivated by a shared and deep connection to this place, by what might be summed up as a feeling of home. In the introduction to *At Home on the Earth: Becoming Native to Our Place*, David Landis Barnhill (1999, 3) writes:

> For a heavenly vision of nature we have substituted one that is not earthy but commercial, and the enormous power of this perspective resides in its blindness to the earth and to our embeddedness in nature. There is another kind of vision. The eyes feel the curve and slope of the earth as it flows, following the water to the sea. The mind follows as well, wondering what creek lies below, what stream below that, what river. It is a geographical vision. What is here does not end here; all is unbroken. Place molds the sensual mind.

In some cases, home culture has been conflated with indigeneity, but it seems important to resist this kind of reduction. My opening example illustrates that there are categories where home might be shared beyond race and ethnicity. I am strategically resisting the application of indigenous and settler culture tropes (e.g., Starn 2011; Simpson 2011). As my discussion illustrates, it is possible to join a home culture as an ally. I did not become indigenous, in the ethnic sense, but I did join a home culture as an active participant who felt a responsibility. I joined a home culture as a neighbour might join a community, taking on the responsibilities of place and space. In my example, the gateway to home culture was music education provided by elders. My environmental responsibility *emerged* as a property of belonging to this home culture, and this belonging emerged following a sound-oriented epistemology—a way of knowing (epistemology) that occurs through sound (acoustics) and music and that Steven Feld (2003, 223) has named "acoustemology." Feld argues that "soundscapes, no less than landscapes, are not just physical exteriors, spatially surrounding or apart from human activity. Soundscapes are perceived and interpreted by human actors who attend to them as a way of making their place in and through the world" (226). Building upon this notion, I will suggest that acoustemology is a way to connect with the world experienced as home culture.

Home culture, since at least J. W. Herder's work in Western philosophy, has also been the root of folk culture (Hayes 1927, 720). But when folk culture is used as the basis of the colonial nation-state, a break emerges between indigeneity and the folk. Both indigeneity and the folk become racially marked. Folk culture is the home culture of "whites," and indigeneity the home culture of non-white, and often colonized, peoples. This racialized slip and obfuscation of home culture within the history of anthropological discourse continues to impact music scholarship. Often there is little or no connection between folk music scholarship and indigenous music scholarship, even though both may be more productively understood as home culture musics. Folk music has been completely digested by global systems of music capital (i.e., the music industry), and this process is also evident in the world music economy, which has impacted musical indigeneity. Arguing for home culture as a replacement for folk and indigenous culture will, I am sure, have its own problems, but it also seems to be an interesting idea to explore. My interest in home culture, as the above story illustrates, emerges from my experience of local people of different "ethnic" communities working together to protect "their" land from outside industrial interests. It is from this perspective that I view James Cameron's *Avatar* (2009), which I will use as the basis for a thought experiment to illustrate how an understanding of home culture music might allow for a richer understanding of the important role that music plays in supporting environmental awareness.

An Ethnomusicologist Views *Avatar*

A surface analysis of the music production process in James Cameron's *Avatar* is enough to illustrate that the music score contradicts and undermines the storyline of the film. The dramatic thrust of *Avatar* warns against the destructive impacts of unwelcome mining of indigenous lands. Cameron clearly draws inspiration from plenty of real world cases. One need only look to the documentaries *Crude* (2009) or *The Pipe* (2010), or follow the ongoing dispute over the direction of proposed pipelines that will carry bitumen from the Alberta oil sands. Environmentalists such as David Suzuki, Bill McKibben, and Al Gore have been warning about the environmental impact of unregulated resource extraction for decades. Their arguments have linked the root of environmental degradation to a culture of racist dislocation of indigenous peoples. Cameron draws upon what David Harvey (2005) calls "accumulation by dispossession" to inform *Avatar*'s conflict, so it is perhaps surprising that this ethic does not inform the production of music in the film. In fact, James Horner, Cameron's long-time composer, mines and then processes "indigenous" music in the same way in which the antagonist in his film mines the commodity resource unobtanium. The contemporary ethnomusicologist is in a related position.

Ethnomusicologist Wanda Bryant was hired by Cameron to assist James Horner in the production of the *Avatar* soundtrack.[3] Bryant was charged with finding sound resources for Horner. A dutiful researcher, Bryant explored recording archives to compile raw resources, which Horner then electronically manipulated. The sounds were combined, layered, stretched, and mutated to produce an "authentically indigenous" soundscape. Sounds were mined by an ethnomusicologist for the economic profit of a global entertainment company. In this way, the production of the soundtrack works against the ethical core of the film.[4]

The history of anthropology, like industry and environmentalism, is tied up with colonization. In the film, human anthropologists use avatars to study the Na'vi in a project funded by an intergalactic mining company. Presumably, the anthropologists try to naively "game the system" to generate legitimate documentation of Pandora's indigenous peoples, but unsurprisingly, the research gets used against both the Na'vi and the (questionably) innocent anthropologists. The "evil" company executives—who presumably promised to deal with the indigenous peoples in a fair and equitable way when hiring academic researchers in the first place—eventually dismiss the researchers when "negotiation" with the indigenous landowners fails. The industry response to failed negotiation, unsurprisingly, is to unleash a private military brought along "for security." The anthropologists struggle in vain to negotiate an ethical position vis-à-vis an impossibly compromised position familiar to all first-year anthropology students.

This critique needs to be added to the mounting criticism that Cameron made *Dances with Wolves in Space* as a white saviour discourse that assists colonialist audiences in creating psychological distance between the viewer in the Global North and the actions of our colonial ancestors, while also shielding contemporary actors from their roles in global resource exploitation. Everyone gets to be Jake Sully, the broken soldier of capitalism who becomes freed from his disability by the magic of indigeneity. *Avatar* needs to face this criticism.

Acoustemology and Ecomusicological Imagination

Given that Cameron needed to have a soundtrack for a film about indigenous subjects and that the only current model available for composing a soundtrack is a compositional method that is not anthropologically sensitive, what could be done? I suggest an anthropologically sensitive compositional practice that would require thinking ecologically to develop an "ecomusicological imagination." While this suggestion might sound theoretically outrageous, I would like to point out that it is precisely this process that I have outlined in the opening of this paper. My opening account illustrates that home culture may be experienced as an emergent property of a network of music, community, and environment. While ethical and environmental concerns might seem distant to most composers, these are not distant concerns for ethnomusicologists and filmmakers. Anthropologically sensitive composition might lead to a different form of film music. Instead of an ethnomusicologist assisting a composer by supplying sound resources (what could be called a "colonial model"), an ethnomusicologist might assist the composer to develop connection between sound resources and acoustemology (possibly a "post-colonial model") in the formation of a space-based ecomusicological imagination.

I will illustrate how this might have been done for James Horner in the preparation of the score for *Avatar*. I will draw upon four famous anthropological/ethnomusicological case studies, all of which illustrate aspects of home culture acoustemology that are seen, but not necessarily heard, in *Avatar*. Had Wanda Bryant brought these examples to James Horner, how might the musical score sounded, and what might its impact have been on the audience?

Musical Emergence

An ecomusicological perspective requires an understanding of musical emergence. Emergence in art is the idea that musical practices and musical subjects arise from a scaffolding of complex interconnections. Emergence, as a term, can be traced to nineteenth-century physical, chemical, and biological studies.[5] Darwin, for instance, discussed emergence in his description of the riverbank, wherein complex interconnections may be viewed as "ecology."[6] More recently, Gilles Deleuze and Felix Guattari (1983, 1987) extended emergence in their discussion of "becoming" within a rhizome. The rhizome, like Darwin's riverbank, is a model in which complex interactions produce the basis for the emergence of an assemblage—in this case, an ecology. Assemblages have emergent properties: for example, the complex interactions of synapses in the brain allow for the emergence of the mind, the complex interactions of the mind allow for the emergence of subjectivity, the complex interactions of subjectivities allow for the emergence of culture, and from culture come works of art.[7]

Cameron's fictional world, Pandora, is a rhizome, with its complexities and interconnections. We discover that the Na'vi are an emergent property of the Pandora ecology. The Na'vi are able to biologically plug into the energies that flow through their environment. They connect themselves to the animals they ride and the trees through which they hear the voices of their ancestors. It is genius to see how the Na'vi are immersed within the rhizome, the non-centralized connections that permeate all strata of life! *Musical* emergence then—music as an emergent property of the rhizome—is not far-fetched.

Transversality and the Rhizome

Subjectivity might be understood as an emergent property of a society. Subjectivity is a much more expansive terrain than notions of identity: "Information and communication operate at the heart of human subjectivity, not only within its memory and intelligence, but within its sensibility, affects and unconscious fantasm" (Guattari 1995, 4). For instance, the transformation that Sully undergoes behind the eyes of his avatar occurs within subjective space. It is not simply that Sully's identity changes. Technology might have provided an opportunity for Sully to experience new worlds of experience, new possibilities of life, but it is Sully's understanding of his connection to Pandora and the Na'vi that ultimately changes. Guattari (1995) calls this movement between possible subjective worlds "transversality." Transversality is a type of subjective movement. Kaluli and Suyá compositions, in the discussions below, are an emergent property of this form of motion. A human transforming into a Muni bird or a deer or a soul communicating from another place is a musical expression of transversality. Transversality might also be a source of Na'vi musicality. The film composer might find music that allows for connection with the rhizome and that facilitates musical emergence, even if from a fictional world. But where would one look for examples of ways of doing this? I have illustrated what might be emergent musical properties of transversal movement, but how might a composer understand imaginative travel?

We need to understand transversality to be able to answer this question. In Guattari's (1995) model, subjectivity is not fixed. It is an auto-developing experience of self that "belongs to the processual subject's engendering of an existential territory and self-transportation beyond it" (Genosko 2002, 55).[8] Guattari based this idea, in part, upon Bateson's *Steps to an Ecology of Mind* (1972), which itself emerged from already circulating notions of the need to expand Western philosophy.[9] Guattari's ideas have an ecological element probably drawn from Arne Naess's work in deep ecology and ecosophy (Naess 1973). Fictionalized musical emergence, which uses new pathways of subjective travel as a way of knowing the world through sound, might assist in the creation of film music that works to make sense of the world of the film rather than, as it currently stands, an external application of romantic conventions (e.g., sweeping strings and orchestral platitudes).

As I illustrated in the opening of this chapter, music might be a type of knowing-through-sound (acoustemology), which requires simultaneous travel and transformation. What is the pathway that leads the soul of the

Suyá to the land of bees or the pathway to the muni bird, which the young Kaluli travels? Guattari (1995) suggests that this travel, transversality, is the becoming of a subject. This is a different sort of thinking about motion, motion as becoming, and becoming as travel through space. In the following examples, "musicians" travel *somewhere* by becoming something else, just as space changes as it intersects with an informed subjectivity in motion.

If we begin to look around at the lifeways of indigenous peoples on Earth, with an eye for music as a form of subjective travel, we find examples that resemble the Na'vi. There are accounts of indigenous peoples who maintain a relationship with what we call "nature" in a way that is at least as sophisticated as the Na'vi.[10] In *Avatar*, the Na'vi can use music as a method of transversal movement through ecological universes of experience. This travel might occur through flows of energies along pathways between all things. A rhizome exists in the film. The sum total of this collective energy is given the name of Eywa by the Na'vi. Eywa, an emergent property of Pandora, does not appear as an individual character but is experienced in signs interpreted by the Na'vi. This emergence is captured in the Cree notion of "Mistabeo," an ancient animating energy moving through the world that "manifests himself in the material world by his actions, influencing events or providing knowledge (as in what we call good or bad luck), in sorcery's illnesses, in cures, in predicting the future, and in explanations of the past" (Preston 2002, 127).

Recognizing music as an emergent property and as subjective travel, however, does not—by itself, anyway—assist a composer in the development of the ecomusicological imagination. Recognizing that *knowing* the physical world through sound (acoustemology) helps create home culture might assist us in *hearing* the Na'vi's connection to the rhizome of Pandora. Guidance in this process might be drawn from anthropological and ethnomusicological literature. What follows are sketches of ecomusicological imagination drawn from existing ethnomusicology literature, which, while not claiming to be exhaustive, present some examples of acoustemology. My suggestion is that we can learn something about the connection between the development of subjectivity and musicality that might inform deeper ecological thinking about music and imagination.

The Kaluli of Papua New Guinea[11]

In an important Kaluli myth, a boy and his sister go fishing for crayfish and they call each other *ade*. After the sister catches many crayfish, the brother demands to have one. The sister says no repeatedly and the brother begins to weep. In his weeping, he loses the power of speech and turns into a muni bird. The boy flies away, leaving the sister calling after him. This story illustrates the relationship between the Kaluli and birds. It is this connection that ethnomusicologist Stephen Feld (1982) built into a sophisticated ecologically oriented Kaluli musicology. The story illustrates that "becoming a bird is the core Kaluli aesthetic metaphor. Understanding that metaphor is an exercise in how cultural and semantic fields are organized in myth, language, expressive codes, and behaviors" (217). For the Kaluli, the singing of the muni bird is the singing of ancestors.

In Feld's very personal ethnographic account of his research, he admits having problems trying to figure out an aspect of a particular taxonomy when his Kaluli partner responded, "Listen—to you they are birds, to me they are voices in the forest." Feld writes, "I was startled by this, not because it was so direct (Kaluli tend to be very direct, even confrontative, in face-to-face interaction) but because it so thoroughly expressed the necessity of approaching Kaluli natural history as part of a cultural system" (45).

The relationship between the Kaluli and ornithology illustrates that "birds become a metaphoric human society, and their sounds come to stand for particular forms of sentiment and ethos" (31). Birds are, therefore, not just birds. Understanding Kaluli lifeways required, for Feld, an "essential unity of natural history and symbolism"; it required seeing "Kaluli feelings about birds as a complex and many-layered cultural configuration that intersected with other areas of thought and action." Feld saw a need to avoid "trying to separate zoology and myth as distinct and neatly bounded modes of observation and deduction" (45). One might choose to see this as an ecomusicological practice. Drawing from R. Murray Schafer's *The Soundscape: Our Sonic Environment and the Tuning of the World* (1977), Feld (2003, 225) synthesized acoustic ecology and soundscape studies in his work with the Kaluli and recognized that "the mediation between this rainforest ecology and Bosavi music turned out to be cosmological, for Kaluli consider birds not just singers but spirits of their dead. Birds appear to one another and speak as people, and to the living their presence is a constant reminder of histories of human loss, an absence made present in sound and motion."

It is impossible to discuss the Kaluli and birds as separate elements. They are interconnected parts of a complex whole (rhizome) and music is an emergent property that "communicates the most deeply felt sentiments in Kaluli social life" (Feld 1982, 217–18). This might be a model for Na'vi song—music as an emergent property of the rhizome and the planetary energy of Pandora. Na'vi music might connect to the central energy flows of the moon Pandora. The film composer might consider musical ideas that illustrate the interconnections that the Na'vi have with the Hometree, the voices of the ancestors, and the voices of the animals to which they connect their queues. Indeed, this seems to be suggested when group Na'vi singing assists the migration of Dr. Augustine's human body energy into the body of Eywa.

The Suyá of the Brazilian Rainforest[12]

Anthony Seeger studied the musical practice of the Suyá in Brazil and focused on compositional practice. In *Why Suyá Sing* (2004), he illustrates three ways in which songs are composed. I will describe two of these that might be useful for rethinking Na'vi home culture music.

People without souls compose the first form. Witches among the Suyá are responsible for a great deal of magic. They are also responsible for nearly all sickness and death. Sometimes this sickness is caused by jealousy. This occurs when a hunter is particularly successful in a hunt, in fishing, or in collecting honey. Witches may become jealous with this success and transform themselves into nighttime creatures, sneak into the offending person's home while he sleeps, and steal his soul. The soul is then carried away. If the hunter dies, it is because the soul is carried to the place of the dead. But often the sorcerers will leave the soul in a land associated with their particular jealousy. For instance, as Seeger recounts, if the jealousy was due to a successful day of fishing, the soul may be left in the world of the fishes, in the river. Or if it was due to an abundant harvest of honey, the soul may be left in the land of the bees. In either case, once the soul is taken, the now soulless person will become very sick. If the person recovers, he or she will continue with life but now in conversation with his or her now displaced soul. This is where songs come from among the Suyá: they are the communications of a trapped soul. Seeger (2004, 53, brackets in original) recounts this story, told to him by Takuti, an older Suyá man:

> [A witch takes a man's spirit] to the birds. He has convulsions and lies in his hammock for a long time. He lies in his hammock while his spirit is with the birds. A vulture takes the man's spirit flying with him in the sky, and the man has convulsions. Then he sees himself [discovers that his spirit is with the birds in a dream or delirium vision].... Then the man begins to hear the birds' shout songs (*akia*), and the birds' unison songs (*ngére*). He hears the birds singing about themselves. His health improves and he lives as before.

The second type of song comes from people who, outside of the village, are transformed into animals (69). For instance, "a man who was slowly turning into a large deer sang a song that has since always been sung in the Savannah Deer Ceremony; a man who became a wild pig/person sang a song that became the Wild Pig Ceremony for the initiation of young boys" (52). Musical emergence for the Na'vi might emerge from moving through spaces of interconnection within the rhizome. This might be understood in terms of transversal subjectivity.

The Cree of Central and Western Canada[13]

For the Cree, "men are only one kind of person in a world populated by many kinds of persons" (Preston 2002, 210). The Cree attribute to animals human qualities, such as logical thought, dreams, and emotions (203), and these qualities appear in the characters of the animals as represented in dreams, and in songs that "link images in the dream world to animals in the real world" (Whidden 2007, 51). For the Eastern Cree hunter, this relationship involves a "sincere belief in a reciprocal attitude of love between men and animals" (Preston 2002, 199). The Cree hunter has two ways of communicating with the natural world. The first way is his relationship with the ancient spirit Mistabeo (210); the second is through song. Both of these are interrelated and will help us conceptualize Pandora-as-rhizome. Ritual communication with Mistabeo, about whom there are many myths, aids the Cree hunter in his life in the world. Mistabeo flows through all life and blurs the distinction between the material and non-material worlds.[14]

Lynn Whidden (2007, 49) suggests that Cree song should be understood as traditional ecological knowledge (TEK): that is, a "holistic way of knowing, specific to a place and to a people, and generally different in form from other types of knowledge." Cree songs have words that are "more esoteric than secret, where understanding is acquired through the experience of hearing songs *and* of participating in the environmental, social, and emotional milieu that the songs express" (Preston 2002, 198). Just as we have seen in the other examples, music is an emergent property of the rhizome. Eywa, like Mistabeo, is understood by experience. Sully becomes Na'vi through a coming-into-awareness of Eywa. This process occurs, in part, through the soundworld of Pandora; it is Sully's acoustemology. In a brief example of ritual music, we see how the Na'vi connect with Eywa both through biological connections (their queues) and sound connections (singing). A sound approach may also be seen in the lifeways of the Achuar of Ecuador.

The Achuar of Ecuador[15]

Philippe Descola (1994) writes that for the Achuar, the world is marked by a network of highly diversified spatiotemporal coordinates. These include "astronomical and climatic cycles, seasonal periodicity of various types of natural resources, landmark systems, and the organization of the universe into layers as defined in mythic thought" (62). For the Achuar, the world is an interconnected set of planes experienced at a variety of registers, a rhizome.

The everyday act of identifying cardinal directions illustrates this. The passage of the sun (which is broken down into periods) and the flow of rivers (downstream-upstream) relate to two directions (sun=east-to-west and river=west-to-east), illustrating the way the Earthly disc is connected to the heavens. Descola notes that for the Achuar, the "terraqueous disk and the celestial hemisphere are joined by a band of water, the source of all rivers and their final destination" (67).

Humans and animals are also connected in continuum. There is no disconnect between human life and "nature." The natural is no more real than the supernatural (93), and in a myth that relates the transformation of a human being into an animal of the same name, the change of status is often marked by the loss of spoken language and the acquisition of a specific call (83). All of "nature's beings have some features in common with mankind, and the laws they go by are more or less the same as those governing civil society. Humans and most plants, animals, and meteors are persons (*aents*) with a soul (*wakan*) and an individual life" (93).

As Descola recounts:

> In mythical times, nature's beings had a human appearance too, and only their names contained the idea of what they would later become. If these human-looking animals were already potentially possessed of their future animal destiny in their name, this is because their common predicate as nature's beings is not man as species, but humankind as condition. When they lost their human form, they also, *ipso facto*, lost their speech organs and therefore the capacity to express themselves in spoken language; they did retain several features of their former state, however, to wit, consciousness—of which dreams are the most direct manifestation—and, for certain species, a social life organized according to the rules of the world of "complete persons." (93)

Since all living things are essentially persons, the faculty of speech is useful for communication. But speech does not come from the mouth but from the soul, which "transcends all linguistic barriers and transforms every plant and animal into a subject capable of producing meaning.... Normally humans speak to plants and animals by means of incantations, which are supposed to go straight to the heart of whoever [*sic*] they are addressed to" (99). These incantations are another example of a form of musical emergence from the home culture rhizome.

Conclusion

I have used the music of James Cameron's *Avatar* to reflect upon a way of knowing-through-sound called acoustemology. Drawing upon four ethnomusicological case studies to illustrate how musical emergence and ecomusicological imagination might point the direction to a *sound* approach to "knowing," I have illustrated how James Horner, assisted by ethnomusicologist Wanda Bryant, produced a film score for *Avatar* that did not draw upon indigenous acoustemology. My interest is to point out how ethnomusicologists, like colonial anthropologists of the past, risk becoming complicit in the very thing that *Avatar* criticizes. This presents an interesting challenge for thinking about film music. Film music, which seeks to represent indigenous people, might need to explore anthropological and ethnomusicological literature for instances of how music is used by indigenous people, not just how it sounds. Anthropologically sensitive composers might begin to practise acoustemology as they attempt to compose film music to assist viewers in their transversal travel through the fictional rhizome that they musically characterize. If James Horner had considered Pandora acoustemologically, *Avatar*'s soundscape might have been as captivating, imaginative, and immersive as its visual images.

Notes

1 The Mik'maq are a Canadian First Nation whose traditional territory includes western Newfoundland, Nova Scotia, New Brunswick, and northern Maine.

2 I use the concept of "subjectivity" as understood in Strozier's *Foucault, Subjectivity, and Identity* (2002).

3 For an interview with Dr. Bryant that explains her working relationship with James Horner, please see http://www.youtube.com/watch?v=9WI3kJIObHE.

4 From an interview with Dr. Bryant about the process, this is quite obvious:

> Some of the examples I brought in were from a woman named Susanne Rosenberg who does these beautiful Swedish cattle herding calls that are phenomenally gorgeous. I took in South African mining songs, girls' greeting songs from Burundi, Bolivian aerophones, singing from Comoros Islands (between Madagascar and Mozambique), Värttinä, which is a Finnish female singing group, voices from the Naga culture in Northeast India.... I would just play examples. I would hit track one, and James would sit there with his eyes closed. After five or ten seconds he would say, "No. I'd go next track. No...no...aww, I like that. I like that. What is that? Where's that from? Save that one."

Access the full interview, "LA Ethnomusicologist Brings Otherworldly Sounds to Biggest Motion Picture of All Time," at http://www.music.ucla.edu/blog/2010/02/02/avatar_ethnomusicology.

5 More on the history of the term *emergence* can be found in Jon McCormack and Alan Dorin (2001).

6 For more on this and its role for twenty-first-century ecology, see Morton (2011).

7 While emergence is beginning to become established in philosophy with some Deleuzian scholars writing about music and art, little musicology identifies emergence in music practice.

8 I will suggest here, however, that our theoretical imagination needs to expand beyond the linear model of progress at the core of neo-liberalism and beyond the dialectical materialism of the various Marxisms. Guattari's (2008) model of ecosophy and the "three ecologies," developed upon Gregory Bateson's influential *Steps to an Ecology of Mind* (1972), may provide the starting point for a re-evaluation of existing anthropological writings.

9 This movement can be seen in Wilhelm Dupre's *Religion in Primitive Cultures: A Study of Ethnophilosophy* (1975). Ethnophilosophy developed from themes included in some anthropology and psychology of the period. A brief list would include Freud's *Totem and Taboo* (1950) and Lévi-Strauss's *The Savage Mind* (1966) and *Myth and Meaning* (1978).

10 There are also some indicators that this process is occurring within Western philosophy. Perhaps the development of New Age literature suggests that there is a connection between the natural and physical worlds that people in industrialized culture still feel. Michael Harner (1980, 57) suggests that "millennia before Charles Darwin, people in shamanic cultures were convinced that humans and animals were related. In their myths, for example, the animal characters were commonly portrayed as essentially human in physical form." Bron Taylor (2010, 197), picking up on this theme, describes "the traits typical of dark green religion—such as a stress on ecological interdependence, an affective connection to the earth as home and to nonhuman organisms as kin, and the overturning of anthropocentric hubris—are unlikely to promote either the suppression of others or lead to cultural homogenization, let alone virulent strains of nationalism." Taylor suggests that "what matters is whether people are moved and inspired when they encounter such [green] spirituality. What matters is whether they find meaning and value in its beliefs and practices, whether they identify with it and are drawn to others engaged in it, whether it will spread and influence the way people relate to, live from, and change the biosphere" (220).

11 For musical examples, please see "Voices of the Rainforest," *Smithsonian Folkways*, http://www.folkways.si.edu/albumdetails.aspx?itemid=3295.

12 For musical examples, please see "Anthology of Brazilian Indian Music," *Smithsonian Folkways*, http://www.folkways.si.edu/albumdetails.aspx?itemid=760.

13 For musical examples, please see "Music of the Algonkians," *Smithsonian Folkways*, http://www.folkways.si.edu/albumdetails.aspx?itemid=735.

14 Guattari's (2008) focus on the in-between fluxes of the three ecologies closely approximates the flows for which Mistabeo is a sign. Living ecosophy, in the language developed by Deleuze and Guattari (1983; 1987), is to live in the fluxes and flows of the becoming-in-between.

15 As of the writing of this paper, I have not been able to identify any online recordings of Achuar songs. But the short video "The Achuar and Occidental Petroleum," about the struggle between the Achuar and oil industries in Peru uses home culture music in the introduction: http://www.youtube.com/watch?v=qg2v5sabLFc.

References

Barnhill, David Landis. 1999. *At Home on the Earth: Becoming Native to Our Place*. Berkeley: University of California Press.

Bateson, Gregory. 1972. *Steps to an Ecology of Mind.* San Francisco: Chandler.

Deleuze, Gilles, and Felix Guattari. 1983. *Anti-Oedipus: Capitalism and Schizophrenia.* Translated by Robert Hurley, Mark Seem, and Helen R. Lane. Minneapolis: University of Minnesota Press.

———. 1987. *A Thousand Plateaus: Capitalism and Schizophrenia.* Translated by Brian Massumi. Minneapolis: University of Minnesota Press.

Descola, Philippe. 1981. "From Scattered to Nucleated Settlements: A Process of Socio-Economic Change among the Achuar." In *Cultural Transformations and Ethnicity in Modern Ecuador,* edited by Norman E. Whitten Jr, 614–46. Chicago: University of Illinois Press.

———. 1994. *In the Society of Nature: A Native Ecology in Amazonia.* New York: Cambridge University Press.

Dupre, Wilhelm. 1975. *Religion in Primitive Cultures: A Study in Ethnophilosophy.* Berlin: de Gruyter.

Feld, Steven. 1982. *Sound and Sentiment: Birds, Weeping, Poetics, and Song in Kaluli Expression.* 2nd ed. Philadelphia: University of Pennsylvania Press.

———. 2003. "A Rainforest Acoustemology." In *The Auditory Culture Reader,* edited by Michael Bull and Les Back, 223–39. New York: Berg.

Freud, Sigmund. 1950. *Totem and Taboo.* London, UK: Routledge and Kegan Paul.

Genosko, Gary. 2002. *Felix Guattari: An Aberrant Introduction.* New York: Continuum.

Guattari, Felix. 1995. *Chaosmosis: An Ethico-Aesthetic Paradigm.* Translated by Paul and Julian Pefanis Bains. Bloomington: Indiana University Press.

———. 2008. *The Three Ecologies.* Translated by Ian and Paul Sutton Pindar. New York: Continuum.

Guattari, Felix, and Antonio Negri. 2010. *New Lines of Alliance, New Spaces of Liberty.* Brooklyn, NY: Autonomedia.

Harner, Michael. 1980. *The Way of the Shaman.* San Francisco: HarperCollins.

Harvey, David. 2005. *A Brief History of Neoliberalism.* New York: Oxford University Press.

Hayes, J. H. 1927. "Contributions of Herder to the Doctrine of Nationalism." *American Historical Review* 32(4): 719–36

Lévi-Strauss, Claude. 1966. *The Savage Mind.* Chicago: University of Chicago Press.

———. 1978. *Myth and Meaning.* London, UK: Routledge and Kegan Paul.

McCormack, Jon, and Alan Dorin. 2001. "Art, Emergence, and the Computational Sublime." In *Second Iteration: A Conference on Generative Systems in the Electronic Arts,* edited by Alan Dorin, 67–81. Melbourne, Australia: CEMA.

Morton, Timothy. 2011. "The Mesh." In *Environmental Criticism for the Twenty-First Century,* edited by Stephanie LeMenager, Teresa Shewry, and Ken Hiltner, 19–30. New York: Routledge.

Næss, Arne. 1973. "The Shallow and the Deep, Long-Range Ecology Movement. A Summary." *Inquiry* 16(1): 95–100.

Preston, Richard J. 2002. *Cree Narrative: Expressing the Personal Meanings of Events.* Montreal and Kingston: McGill-Queen's University Press.

Schafer, R. Murray. 1977. *The Soundscape: Our Sonic Environment and the Tuning of the World*. Rochester, VT: Destiny Books.

Seeger, Anthony. 2004. *Why Suyá Sing: A Musical Anthropology of an Amazonian People*. Chicago: University of Illinois Press.

Simpson, Audra. 2011. "Settlement's Secret." *Cultural Anthropology* 26(2): 205–17.

Starn, Orin. 2011. "Here Come the Anthros (Again): The Strange Marriage of Anthropology and Native America." *Cultural Anthropology* 26(2): 179–204.

Strozier, Robert M. 2002. *Foucault, Subjectivity, and Identity: Historical Constructions of Subjects and Self*. Detroit: Wayne State University.

Taylor, Bron. 2010. *Dark Green Religion: Nature Spirituality and the Planetary Future*. Berkeley: University of California Press.

Whidden, Lynn. 2007. *Essential Song: Three Decades of Northern Cree Music*. Waterloo, ON: Wilfrid Laurier University Press.

Works of Doubt and Leaps of Faith:
An Augustinian Challenge to Planetary Resilience

JACOB VON HELAND

SVERKER SÖRLIN

I. GRACE [AUGUSTINE]
I'm not talking about pagan voodoo here—I'm talking about something
real and measurable in the biology of the forest.

II. GRACE...takes a tiny sample using a needle-like probe. Norm uses a
digital DEVICE to scan the roots.

III. GRACE
Parker, it's their ancestral home. They've lived there since before human
history began. You can spare them a few more weeks.

IV. GRACE
I—always held back. But you gave them your heart. I'm proud of you,
Jake.... Help them. You do whatever it takes. You hear me?[1]

In James Cameron's *Avatar* (2009), accelerated climate change and loss
of ecosystem functioning from human activities have tipped the Earth's
system to a state where it can no longer support life. As one of the film's
protagonists states, Earth has been killed and has no green left. This scenario holds aspects of real concern among prominent climate and Earth
system scientists, who, consequently, in their roles as knowledge providers
and state advisors, advocate policy frameworks for globally coordinated

environmental politics (e.g., Millennium Ecosystem Assessment 2005 and IPCC 2007).

Of particular, related interest, is a recent project referred to as "planetary boundaries" (hereafter PB), launched under the expansive and loosely defined sustainability science known as "resilience thinking" (Walker and Salt 2006; Folke 2006; Libby 2012).[2] Resilience in this sort of analysis refers to a system's ability to function well while continuing to develop, even during dramatic times of change (Folke et al. 2010). The PB project can be seen as a first attempt at a framework for resilience management of the planet as a living system and for operationalizing a safe space in which social subsystems (e.g., states and economies) can develop without risking irreversible and degrading changes to the biogeophysical system as a whole. The motivation for this task is purported to lie in the self-interest of humanity. Human-centred and utilitarian abstractions of the world as a living and interdependent system that emphasize the need to sustain ecological functions for human well-being are not new to systems ecology, of course, but devising a policy framework to operationalize such a global management system is, and, considering the professed urgency and the potentially enormous impact of environmental policies, the framing, translation, and representation of such policies deserve careful attention.

In this regard, the film *Avatar* emerges as timely and "good to think" (Lévi-Strauss 1963, 89). Following the box office records across the world, the story about how humans have left Earth and started colonization and mineral extraction on the distant moon Pandora is well known and lends itself to becoming a surface for thought-experiments that test the imagination. *Avatar* and its astounding reception seem to support the sense of urgency found in resilience research to establish some form of globally coordinated environmental politics, or at least to acknowledge that boundaries exist for the human enterprise on Earth and that humanity may already have started the era of those boundaries' transgression, which the film captures in a sadly advanced stage.

In this article, we first present resilience thinking about indigenous knowledge, as well as what we term the "extended resilience enterprise," including ideas about social-ecological systems and the grand design of planetary boundaries. We then look for similarities and differences between resilience thinking within a PB framework and the approach taken by Dr. Grace Augustine in the film to create a protective story for the Hometree and the entire moon Pandora. We use the concept of "protective story" to focus analysis on the ways in which users and actor groups articulate and build values around environments through practice-based construction of narrative (Sörlin 1998; Ernstson and Sörlin 2009). We will also refer to David Turnbull's sociology of scientific knowledge, where difference and similarity between knowledge traditions (in our case, between Western technoscientific knowledge, on the one hand, and indigenous traditional ecological knowledge [TEK], on the other) can be understood by paying attention to how knowledge is negotiated and assembled in what Turnbull (2000, 38–39) calls "knowledge spaces": "some traditions move it [knowledge] and assemble it through art, ceremony and ritual, whilst science does it through forming disciplinary societies, building instruments, standardising techniques and writing articles." On Pandora, Earthlings and Pandorans come in contact, with their knowledge traditions engaging the same space, resulting in tension. One seems bound to overrule the other unless a new protective story can be woven to change the fatal outcome of the encounter.

Traditional Ecological Knowledge and Resilience Thinking

Resilience thinking widely subscribes to a complex-adaptive-systems understanding of the world as comprising societies and ecosystems that are entangled and dynamic, and thus, that also change in non-linear and surprising ways (Levin 1999; Gunderson and Holling 2002; Folke et al. 2010). Ecological resilience refers to the ability of an ecosystem to handle disturbance and change while retaining its key processes and identity (Holling 1973; Carpenter et al. 2001). Maintaining resilience of Earth's ecosystems in desired states is considered a foundation for human well-being (Millennium Ecosystem Assessment 2005), and "adaptive management" is proposed to nurture ecosystem resilience in a changing world. Societies should arrange process-based forms of management, resilience scientists argue, where humans are seen as part of the environment and where applying a diversity of knowledge increases the chances of understanding complexity and successfully handling uncertainty and surprise. Resilience scientists also commonly endorse traditional ecological knowledge (TEK), but only partly for its intrinsic socio-cultural value; they propose that traditional societies have a right to exist with their own cultures and belief systems (Berkes, Folke, and Gadgil 1995, 282). More important to resilience thinking is a functionalist rationale: traditional knowledge systems often contain sophisticated knowledge about ecosystem dynamics and are therefore useful in environmental management, and indigenous institutions have proven capable of protecting species or habitats that are important by scientific standards (Colding and Folke 2001).

These belief-knowledge-practice complexes have, since the 1990s, enjoyed a significant presence in the total body of resilience literature that explicitly or implicitly integrates TEK in its analyses. A standard feature of this literature is the claim that local communities have—through ongoing, adaptive learning and through co-evolution—discovered key mechanisms of local ecosystems, thus forming functional and resilient social-ecological systems (SESs). These SESs seem to be found wherever resilience scientists choose to set up a case study, and reference to them is frequent in resilience literature (Berkes and Folke 1998; Berkes 1999; Olsson and Folke 2001; Olsson, Folke, and Berkes 2004; Barthel, Sörlin, and Ljungkvist 2010). This literature also has affinity with the case-based approaches in Elinor Ostrom's (1990) common pool resources database at Indiana University. Civic management of resources, in a commons governance structure, can readily be interpreted in the resilience literature as evidence of resilient SESs based on TEK in various parts of the world (Berkes, Colding, and Folke 2000; Berkes and Turner 2006; Armitage, Berkes, and Doubleday 2007; Chapin et al. 2009).

While we do not contest the claims in the resilience literature that TEK is important for sustainable resource management, we have observed, as have some critical commentators of resilience thinking (Armitage 2006; Leach 2008; Nadasdy 2007; Hornborg 2009), that resilience displays a general ambiguity with regard to explicit and formal political institutions and structures and different and conflicting interests. TEK, however, seems attractive since it does appear as the result of co-evolution rather than "politics" or "power" in the conventional sense, and it does not favour any particular social group or political strand. Thus, the resilience literature, at least implicitly, displays a high level of confidence in a kind of governance that might be called "pre-political" (Ruttan and Mulder 1999; Nadasdy 1999, 2007): that is to say, governance that does not rest on complex forms of social participation and negotiation but rather on a certain form of authority that is based on (pre-scientific) knowledge and its co-evolution between humans and nature over time, which is also one of many signs that resilience has its roots in ecology proper. We argue that part of the attraction of TEK to resilience science lies in precisely this presumption of a primordial knowledge authority on which successful management could be based.

Here lies a key point of departure for our reading of *Avatar*: the approach proposed by resilience science for contemporary global environmental policy—that is, planetary boundaries—bears a structural similarity with TEK insofar as it also presupposes a functionally superior knowledge-based authority for resource management that can be equally positioned as indifferent to various social interests and other social and political ramifications that are linked to the resource use. This symmetry between certain properties of TEK and those of the planetary boundaries is further reinforced if observed through the literature of what we could call the "post-political paradigm" (Swyngedouw 2009): that is, the growing tendency since the 1980s to manage public concerns, be they environmental or social, in ways that lie primarily outside of democratic structures and considerations of issues like fairness, justice, or equity and instead relate to concepts like efficiency, accountability, and measurability. In short, there is a movement toward a new public management, or NPM (Kjaer 2004, chap. 2; Pollitt and Bouckaert 2011, chap. 1), version of management that is justified on metrics and purportedly objective, even "scientific," grounds rather than based on values or collective decision-making, or negotiated in relation to conflicting societal interests and needs.

To sum up, in the perspective we have chosen for this analysis, we have emphasized tendencies in contemporary resilience thinking that privilege science as a supreme policy authority for the purported welfare of the planet and, at the same time, that are unwilling to include in their schemes underlying issues to do with values, justice, power, and other dimensions of politics.

Adding the Planetary Boundaries

The most noteworthy example of how the extended resilience enterprise can appear in a multi-scalar context was presented as a multi-authored and often cited article on planetary boundaries (PBs) published in *Nature* in September 2009 (Rockström et al. 2009b).[3] Perhaps surprisingly, this article does not contain a single reference to TEK, nor does it make active use of any TEK knowledge. It also aligns very well with the post-political paradigm in that it is an attempt to squeeze all social values and collective decision-making out of the argument and replace them with a solely science-based framework for global management.

The article argues that it is possible to scientifically define boundaries of a "safe operational space" for humanity within the Earth system. These boundaries are proposed for nine dimensions, including, for example, atmospheric CO_2, atmospheric nitrogen, biodiversity, ocean acidity, cultivable land, and soil erosion. The claim that the boundaries are not arbitrary is sustained by another proposal: namely, that during the Holocene (the period after the latest Ice Age, ca. 10,000 years before present) most, if not all, known Earth system parameters have been comparatively stable, and it is within this time frame that human culture and civilization as we know it has emerged and, as it is phrased in the article, has "flourished."

There is, thus, an anthropocentric core to PB reasoning. Linked to this argument is the notion of the Anthropocene, which suggests that humanity during the present era of globalized industrialism has become the single most important factor impacting on Earth system dynamics

(Crutzen 2002; Steffen, Crutzen, and McNeill 2007). It is, therefore, highly urgent to impose PB as a measure to ensure that human impact is not allowed to erode this stable and desirable ten-thousand-year state and tip the Earth's environment—that is, its nine environmental indicators—into degraded states that would threaten the welfare of humanity. The Anthropocene should, in other words, be managed so that it functions like the Holocene *on the global scale*, which can be achieved, apparently without any loss of welfare or wealth (categories that are not problematized at all in the article, let alone their global distribution), because as long as the planetary boundaries are not crossed, "humanity has the freedom to pursue long-term social and economic development" (Rockström et al. 2009b, 475).

Perhaps the most striking feature of this already iconic (judging from citation data) and highly influential contribution to the field of resilience and global change science is that it assumes global relevance. In other words, it claims at least indirect significance for each and every one of the world's local ecosystems. This is why it is worth noting that there is no mention of TEK. This seems even more ironic since the group of authors contains several members who have influentially argued the need to make visible the important albeit often "invisible" role that TEK has in "local resource management" (Colding and Folke 2001).[4] Here, when global resource management is discussed, TEK is completely invisible.

Admittedly, the *Nature* article (Rockström et al. 2009b) is only a very general and early draft of an idea that realistically needs much more elaboration (and has already drawn some tentative and quite foreseeable criticism; see Schmidt 2013; Carpenter and Bennett 2011; Townsend and Porder 2011), but if we share—like most people on the planet, surely—the overall concern of the PB argument—to have a sustainable Earth—it seems inevitable that the question of scale will be raised. Is there a link between global resilience and the welfare and fate of thousands of local cultures and the human diversity they represent? Or do they belong to the kinds of casualties we should be prepared to accept if we wish to survive as an increasingly economically efficient and flourishing "humanity" on a vulnerable planet? Our analysis of *Avatar* speaks precisely to questions like these, and if there is any truth in the idea of planetary boundaries, which we earnestly believe is an interesting possibility, these are urgent questions that should be discussed. Preservation and rights of traditional local cultures, with their knowledge and belief systems, are certainly not new issues, but what is new is their appearance in dilemmas of Earth system governance.

Dr. Augustine Navigates Knowledge Authority from Her Scientific Space

Avatar is set in the year 2154 CE at a time when the human societies on Earth are, because of their copious energy consumption, dependent on an alien mineral fuel called "unobtanium," which exists on the moon Pandora. Humanity has sent science-supported vanguard troops to collect the mineral in a massive, military-led manoeuvre that is met by fierce local resistance from the people of Pandora, the Na'vi. The whole operation resembles European colonization projects on continents overseas, or—in structure, spirit, technology, costume, style, and language—more recent US-led military operations in foreign lands.

Avatar presents, on the surface, what seems to be a conventional relation between different knowledge traditions: the modern, represented by the colonizing human civilization, and the traditional, represented by the Na'vi. During the film, however, this seemingly simple and straightforward relation becomes increasingly complex and filled with paradoxes. The traditional knowledge proves to be at least as advanced as the modern, and the clearly defined camps of colonizers and colonized break up as the complexity of the Pandoran world becomes clear. A viewer who initially identifies with the intrepid humans will soon recognize the goodness, sophistication, and stunning beauty of Pandora and her people. As "knowledge" thus becomes ambiguous, the viewer is made to realize, much in the spirit of modern science and technology studies, that science is a social enterprise, always related to interests, filled with moral and political judgments, and facing dilemmas and decisions from which the scientists cannot escape, no matter how hard they try (Hess 2007).

Much of the plot in *Avatar* revolves around Dr. Grace Augustine, the chief scientist in the human camp, who is in charge of the Avatar program—to make and operate avatars, which give humans Na'vi bodies to safely and efficiently explore the planet. Augustine has also written *the* book on Pandora's botany. She is, thus, the authority among the colonizers on how life works on Pandora. In this regard, Augustine resembles an ethnobiologist striving to make academic contributions (e.g., reports and publications) in line with conventional conceptions of science as naturalistic, precise, and experiment-based. There is even some similarity between Augustine's work and the kind of research on social-ecological systems that the resilience community pursues: they are both trying to find out how the finer mechanisms between the human and non-human worlds operate in a local setting.

As a member of the mining mission, however, Augustine is continuously forced to relate her work to the political situation on both Pandora and Earth. To justify the high costs of the Avatar program, Dr. Augustine and her team are expected, first and foremost, to be useful to the mission. The chief administrator, Parker Selfridge, who is responsible for the profits and success of the enterprise, asks Augustine to inform him how to win the hearts and the minds of the Na'vi: "Find me a carrot to get them to move, or it's going to have to be all stick" (Cameron 2007, 53). Likewise, Colonel Quaritch demands that her student Jake Sully, a former Marine soldier, gather intelligence on the Na'vi to find out how to best "force their cooperation, or hit 'em hard if they don't" (26).

In this power landscape, Augustine plays the role of a hard and elitist natural scientist. But when she tells Sully that she once ran a Na'vi school, she reveals a caring and emotional side of her personality. One day, she says, a group of children sabotaged a mining company bulldozer and came to hide in the school, thinking she could protect them, but the mining company's troops pursued and killed them. Augustine draws on this story as she instructs Sully to respect the divide between human and Na'vi societies—to learn what he can while living with the Na'vi but to refrain from becoming emotionally attached: "It is not our world, Jake. And we can't stop what's coming" (49). Indeed, Selfridge, the head of the mining activities, reminds Sully about *their* world and about the fact that Augustine can be sent back to Earth if she disobeys orders. "Unobtanium is what pays for your science," says Selfridge. "Comprendo?" (16).

Dr. Augustine Translates TEK to Science and Maintains Divides

But even though Augustine feels she can not "stop" the colonial exploitation, she does not passively obey. She is clearly sympathetic to the Na'vi's TEK, based on her admiration for the subtlety and beauty in their way of life as well as their non-scientific knowledge space. She is therefore excited that her student Sully has *gotten in* with the Hometree clan and offers him classic ethnographic advice: try to see the world the way the Na'vi do. Consequently, layer after layer of their sophisticated biotech knowledge system is revealed. The divide between scientific and indigenous knowledge established by conventional Western rationality, however, creates a wicked zero-sum game for Augustine (cf. Hornborg 2003), wherein to officially recognize TEK would question the experimental standards in Augustine's own knowledge space built on the authority of science and its legacy. Augustine already has a weak position (vis-à-vis economic and military reasoning) for influencing the politics of the mining enterprise. Therefore, rather than voice sympathy for TEK, she seems to translate some of its core aspects into biological experiments, hoping to establish scientifically valid facts and thereby increase the value of Pandora's living trees. But like most science based on tree and soil samples taken manually with needles and calibrated instruments, Augustine's work is painstakingly slow and the results unpredictable.

When it is finally decided that the mining mission will, through a de facto military operation, destroy the Na'vi's Hometree in order to access a particularly rich deposit of unobtanium, Dr. Augustine and the entire movie arrive at a turning point. Her previous attempts to create a protective story using authoritative and universal arguments based on field observation, the standard scientific way, has apparently broken down and she comes to experience *august* (venerable and revered) concern about her own role and position. Her strategy of "organized skepticism" having failed, she now rapidly begins to question her own role as a scientist and even as a member of "humanity."[5]

To begin with, Augustine openly admits her moral conviction that it is wrong to destroy the Hometree, thereby demonstrating to herself that, at the deepest level, her position is not, after all, predicated on science. Before this, science was her inner conscience. Now, lacking the full scientific answer, she turns to Selfridge and describes the forest as the site where the copious intergenerational Na'vi bio-cyber-cultural memory is stored.[6] Selfridge, part of an objectivist-materialist discourse in which trees are non-conscious organic matter, just laughs: "What the hell have you people been smoking out there? They're just Goddamn Trees" (Cameron 2007, 100–101). The crucial point here is that Selfridge's discourse until this point has been Augustine's own. But from this moment, she rejects the universality of this form of reasoning, having experienced Na'vi wisdom. Augustine begins to argue for their rhizomatic relationalism, an understanding that is typical of TEK.

For Augustine, this insight is not nostalgic or backward but, on the contrary, points the direction forward for a wayward humanity that has already demonstrated its incompetence in managing resources on Earth and is repeating the same mistakes on Pandora. In fact, appreciating Na'vi wisdom holds out far more marvellous riches *for all* than any primitive mining operation *for a few* can harvest: "You need to wake up, Parker," warns Augustine. "The wealth of this world isn't in the ground—it's all around us. The Na'vi know that, and they're fighting to defend it. If you want to share this world with them, you need to understand them" (ibid.). Accordingly, when the mining operation still proceeds according to plan and the attack on Hometree is launched, Augustine puts aside the last of her remaining doubts and joins the Na'vi resistance.

Works of Doubt, Leaps of Faith: Augustine Is Morally Compelled to Ignore Divides and Leave the Scientific Space

Having witnessed the Hometree massacre, when the gigantic tree is destroyed, Augustine has to accept her failure at constructing a science-based preservation narrative. She has entertained a utopian, yet quite conventional, confidence in science, believing that it is capable of translating TEK into formulaic language and thus forge a "window of opportunity" (Olsson, Folke, and Hughes 2008) for a new hybrid understanding between scientific and traditional ecological knowledge. Instead, she has reified the Eurocentric dualism: hypermodern versus primitive culture. Even worse, Augustine's research has exacerbated the situation, because the results are now used as military intelligence to justify and plan the attack. Western knowledge, refracted through the righteous soul of Augustine, only takes her so far in her quest to support what she, through experience and the workings of her conscience, has known from the outset was right.

Consequently, after a period of doubt, Augustine leaves her old life and stature as the chief scientist. She becomes a righteous outlaw on a moon that she has learned to love but whose environment she can never adapt to or become a natural part of. While it comes across to the spectators of the film as "doing the right thing," Augustine's behaviour remains absurd from the rationale of Western science, from the profit-seeking logic of the economic administrator Selfridge, and from the perspective of the military operations leader, Colonel Quaritch, in whose limited understanding Sully, the avatar ethnographer, can be nothing but a "traitor." Augustine's decision can be understood only as a fundamental change of values and logic, a deeper insight about the problematic entanglement of science with a path of development that must be abandoned (regardless of the functionality and formal correctness of the scientific method itself).

The faith that Augustine placed in science's ability to "do good" is shattered. In our reading, her experience has an affinity with what Sören Kierkegaard, in his book *Fear and Trembling* ([1843] 2006, 46), calls the "teleological suspension of the ethical." Teleology is of central concern for existential philosophy, according to which every person is unique and finite, and therefore unable to know anything with finality (Gillespie 2006, 533). A life unfolds, people need to make world-altering decisions, and these can only be based on provisional knowledge-beliefs. Every important decision is thus tied to "existential doubt" concerning its unforeseeable consequences. In Hannah Arendt's political philosophy, it is this doubt— "the ceaseless and restless activity of questioning that which we encounter"—that makes people human and saves them from participating in evil deeds, even when these deeds seem normal to everyone else (Yar 2005).

This existential doubt with uncertain outcomes is also present in decisions made by scientists, and it imposes on them a burden of reflecting ethical concern and truthfulness to informants and themselves. Dr. Augustine
is no exception; her decision to resist comes when a higher and truer order
demands her attention in a way that cannot be disregarded.[7] Kierkegaard
believed that such moments demand leaps of faith. Augustine has come
to know enough, despite how absurd it appears from the standpoint of
her own culture's understanding, to take a leap of faith in an entirely new
direction based on sympathy for a different worldview.

We Have Never Been Baconian

We may view the presence of Dr. Augustine and the scientific team on Pandora as reflecting, in the opening parts of the film, an essentially Western
perspective, an extra-planetary extension of Francis Bacon's centuries-old
legacy for science as important for the progress of modern societies. As we
know, Bacon encouraged natural philosophers to probe nature through
systematic interrogation and "vexations" and thereby derive objective, certain, and true facts (Merchant 1982, 2008). But as we also know, the universal authority claims of Baconian science, predicated on its perceived ability
to reveal facts independently of the investigator, have become increasingly
problematic in late modern epistemology, in which nature is regarded as
non-linear, entangled, and ever emerging (Latour 1993; Prigogine 1997)
and the observer is part of the observed. Of this epistemology, more akin
to the Na'vi worldview, there was nothing in the original Augustinian science before her "fall."

We could thus rephrase her fundamental change of mind and say that
she has come to realize that a belief in conventional Western science, based
on "vexation" and the detached observer, will never bring Pandora, or
indeed the Na'vi, any closer to a desired state. The Earthly paradise, held
in promise by Baconian method as a future attainment, is a deception—
because paradise is already here and lived by the Na'vi. The actual and
frightening performance of the Earthly science-military-industrial complex on Pandora moves Augustine beyond doubt to a paradoxical certainty
that her current way of knowing is not leading to the solution. So, in her
"leap," Augustine embodies a critique of the modern faith that science
is intrinsically good. By the same token, translating Na'vi wisdom, their
TEK, into formulaic modern science is also, while not presented as ultimately unattainable in the film, ruled out as a practical possibility during
the politically relevant time frame. Her own experience of representing
the Na'vi as their translator has proven it to be futile. Moreover, the reliance on Western (Earth) science masks reasons for preserving Hometree

that are already known to the Na'vi. The deeper meaning of Hometree is that through conscience and compassion, more insight can be found than through the assembly of many, but partial, scientific facts.

In our view, then, the film concludes that when science has proven insufficient for the purpose of protecting real values (the Na'vi and their "paradise"), there must exist more appropriate ways of giving voice to people and landscapes. In a way that coheres with some of the most reflexive voices in current science and technology studies literature, *Avatar* leaves the viewer with a deep imprint of doubt as to the usefulness of the modern scientific enterprise to live up to its claims of doing good in the world. Science, the film seems to suggest, must not stand in the way of conscience, ethics, or politics on behalf of protecting vulnerable species and cultures—and when it does, the best decision may be to represent and act on the understandings of people without modern scientific means (Turnbull 2009). This is the disturbing undercurrent of the film, which might also explain its massive, yet subtle appeal, as if a global audience has already realized that the reason the world is facing ever-growing environmental and sustainability challenges may not be the absence of science. After all, has there ever been more of it? The film voices a nagging suspicion that the saviour who professes to rescue us is part of the problem. Extending Baconian science into every corner of human decision-making will, the film implies, increase the level of peril we are facing. In some sense, "we" (who live with open eyes in this world) already knew this, and therefore, with good reason, we can claim, paraphrasing Bruno Latour (1993), that "we have never been Baconian."

Augustine as Honest Broker

Having argued above that part of the appeal of *Avatar* has to do with the way the film articulates doubt in the ethical and political trustworthiness of the modern scientific project, we turn to the argument that another explanation of the film's appeal can be found in its way of articulating a new relation between science and policy. After all, Dr. Augustine is not only a kind of ethnobiologist; she also serves as a science advisor in the hunt for unobtanium.

It is, in our reading, essential to observe that Dr. Augustine wants to understand and support actions that are both factually accurate and morally correct. She considers the economic value of the extractive mining activities as well as the biological value of the trees. She also recognizes the value of the forest as a whole, as perceived by the Na'vi, through her efforts at intercultural communication with them. It is not by privileging only one of these knowledge spaces but by taking all of them into account that

Augustine (significantly aided by her pre-scientific conscience) comes to her subjective truth about which is more important, the forest or the mine. Her insight emerges as she draws on a diversity of knowledge traditions.

This speaks directly to the relation of resilience research and traditional knowledge. Officially, as we have seen, resilience research respects both mainstream science and TEK. But the motto "think globally, act locally" (cf. Clark and Munn 1987, chap. 1) has now shifted to "both think and act globally," and planetary boundaries can be seen as a way to realize this shift of spatial attention (Steffen, Rockström, and Costanza 2011), implying a wish to universalize the human predicament in relation to Earth. Thinking in terms of planetary boundaries also expands the boundaries in time to encompass the Holocene as a stable era, humanity's fortunate time of grace. Before her "fall," Augustine uses the Baconian vision of science to promote her scientific protection story for Pandora's forests, just as the planetary boundary scale, we would argue, has been built using conventional science. In both cases, local knowledge is not important enough to count as relevant.

This should not surprise us. Science policy has had, for a long time, very little to offer to the preservation of local cultures or indeed of any form of diversity. The enterprise of science policy has instead been built around the interests of the state in terms of security or economic performance. Consequently, science policy alliances have disregarded non-Western knowledge traditions and entire ways of life in nature (Visvanathan 2002, 98–99). The ideal science advisor has been, much like Dr. Augustine at the beginning of the film, the "pure scientist" who does the science, presents the facts, and lets others take care of the moral and political judgments.

Increasingly, however, this image of the science advisor has been challenged in ways that resemble the Dr. Augustine who reacts with her conscience and with a scientific intuition that has not yet been corroborated by evidence. Alternative incarnations of the science advisor, it has been suggested, should include the "science advocate," who uses scientific results to try and achieve certain policy goals, and the "honest broker," who presents the facts and actively uses knowledge to broker a reasonable position among conflicting outcomes (Pielke 2007). While not fitting perfectly any of these ideal types, but rather borrowing elements of both, *Avatar's* depiction of Dr. Augustine as science advisor is moving away from a detached "pure scientist" position in the direction of one who seeks to align (an always imperfect) science with responsibility for larger values and entities—in this case, the future of Pandora and its original inhabitants, the Na'vi.

Resilience Science and Other Local Knowledge Traditions

Dr. Augustine's character presents a role of the scientist with which resilience research, planetary boundaries style, does not sit well. On its face, this may seem counterintuitive. As already suggested, exploring environmental governance that stresses complexity, non-linearity, and diversity has been a long-standing theme in resilience thinking. But the discipline's objectivist perspective is also very strong and firmly grounded in systems theory. There is, thus, an internal epistemological tension built into resilience thinking that is likely to become more acute as the resilience enterprise extends into planetary boundaries. This tension was not as visible in the early years, when resilience was still largely a theory within ecology in support of local and experience-based knowledge and had lesser pretentions about integrated systems thinking and comprehensive governance of societal as well as natural phenomena. With this internal tension, it now seems as if scientistic systems thinking is gaining the upper hand at the cost of properties closer to local communities and their interests, even though this latter theme is recurrent in recent critiques of resilience (Armitage 2006; Leach 2008; Nadasdy 2007; Hornborg 2009). This would imply that critical reflection on the relations among scaling, resilience knowledge, values, and beliefs runs the risk of becoming problematically absent in resilience science if it is pursued exclusively in a systems-oriented manner.

These are complex and entangled relations, but they are essential if we want to be serious about how to enhance sustainability in the world. As Dr. Augustine becomes aware, it is almost impossible to disentangle knowledge from beliefs and ethics in situations of serious judgment, and if it is hard in science-conscious modern societies, it may be even more difficult in traditional societies. Indeed, several scholars have contended that social and religious values in most traditional societies are inseparable from ecological factors (Gadgil, Berkes, and Folke 1993, 155; Berkes, Folke, and Gadgil 1995, 283), and although it is obviously often a good idea to separate these factors to gain knowledge, respect for TEK demands that the very process of producing knowledge that is also useful for sustainability must take the integrative character of traditional knowledge seriously. Resilience scholars Fikret and Mina Berkes (2009, 11) argue that "indigenous knowledge is a challenge to the positivist-reductionist paradigm and to the essential question of what constitutes knowledge." For support, they cite David Turnbull (1997, 560): "When local knowledge is probed deeply 'in no case does it come out looking like the standard Western notion of information'; rather, it tends to be a 'blend of knowledge, practice, trusted authority, spiritual values, and local social and cultural organization: a knowledge space.'" Nowhere, however, do Berkes and Berkes mention that, for Turnbull, "deep" descriptions of knowledge *also* apply to scientific knowledge. Actually, Turnbull's 1997 article is entitled "Reframing Science *and Other Local Knowledge Traditions*" (our emphasis). Turnbull's foremost aim is to problematize the modern idea that science is such a very different kind of knowledge, to show how it too is value-laden and situated, never objective or universal (Turnbull 2000). We would add that this could also go for its special variety called resilience science.

It is against this backdrop that it becomes interesting to understand the way the extended resilience enterprise has conducted the giant and impressive translation work necessary to move science-based knowledge from countless local sites, implied by the importance of TEK, into the almost Benthamian panopticon required to monitor planetary boundaries. Having used *Avatar* in this thought-experiment fashion, a set of hypothetical and ethical questions emerges with seeming relevance for our Earthling reality. Could Augustine, if a planetary boundaries regime had been installed on Earth, be certain that such a regime would protect a Hometree and its forest? When would sacrificing a Hometree tip the world over to the wrong side of any of the nine boundaries? How should a Dr. Augustine, under a planetary boundaries regime, argue her case for cultural diversity? What could she say to the defence of, for example, the Mikea on Madagascar, the Lamalera in Eastern Indonesia, and the Arctic Saami in Scandinavia when the authorities governing planet Earth let it be known that it is in the interest of humanity and its freedom to pursue long-term social and economic development that local people, and the habitats on which they depend, give way to large-scale, supposedly more eco-efficient ways of enhancing well-being?

The answer is that Augustine cannot be certain, for planetary boundaries thinking, in its current form, seems not to be construed with the *local* peoples on Earth in mind, a criticism that has been repeatedly made in relation to previous totalizing attempts to link the planet to humanity, neglecting local voices and situatedness of experience and, in particular, the geographical distribution of environmental stress (Mendelsohn, Dinar, and Williams 2006; Kende-Robb and Van Wicklin 2008; Karlsson 2010, 21–22). Even if such absolute boundaries could be agreed on (a difficult challenge that is as much political as scientific), such boundaries would provide no answer as to who, among the growing numbers of Earth's inhabitants, must adapt the most. Nor would agreement about these boundaries protect Earth's many small-scale and indigenous cultures, cultures represented metaphorically by the Na'vi in *Avatar*. "The 'global view' cannot adequately depict environmental problems because the impacts of these problems vary with class, gender, age, and race" (Litfin 1997, 38).

Conclusion

In a world full of serious challenges, science engenders hope and expectations. It is considered able to tell those in power what they should do to ensure the survival of humanity and Earth's ecosystems. Such hopes have been especially raised vis-à-vis strands of the environmental sciences—not the least being systems ecology—and the now vital and expansive subfield of resilience. We question, however, whether what we have called "the extended resilience enterprise," including the study of social-ecological systems and the concept of planetary boundaries, can live up to these expectations in a way that has affinity with critiques of the actual position of resilience science in matters concerning power, minorities, and resource politics (Armitage 2006; Leach 2008; Nadasdy 2007; Hornborg 2009). But these criticisms have yet to offer a comprehensive language or common understanding of what resilience is or purports to be.

We have emphasized that resilience research has a history of recognizing the value of many knowledge traditions to address complexity. It has also sought to represent indigenous interests by recognizing the value of TEK and by trying to align TEK with mainstream science. To rely so heavily on natural sciences when extending the resilience enterprise to policy formation on the global scale, as is done in the quest for demarcating planetary boundaries, requires explanation.

We have highlighted and described the pattern of the problem through a Kierkegaardian reading of the film *Avatar*. Our analysis is reflected in the fate of Dr. Augustine and her attempt to build a protective story to help preserve the local Na'vi. In the film, she loses faith in the progressivist narrative she has inherited from Western/Baconian science. Furthermore, she realizes that as long as she keeps refining her knowledge of the social-ecological interface on Pandora, she will, through her scientific practice, be complicit in an unfolding disaster. Her self-defined role, also as advisor, is in line with that of the stereotypical "pure scientist," although she entertains a private hope that her science will one day prove capable of supporting with facts the Na'vi knowledge and sustainable way of life. Augustine's protective story does not fail because it is based on an insufficient science but because it lacks other actors and social support. This analysis coheres with what we know about successful contemporary conservation efforts, which are made possible by encouraging the participation of multiple actors and groups, building influence through networks, and establishing a common narrative in which the protected areas themselves play a prominent role (Walker 2007; Ernstson and Sörlin 2009).

Our reading of Avatar suggests that conservation science demands humility and doubt, like that at which Augustine arrives as disaster looms over the Na'vi forest. The film and Augustine's role in it point to one of the most central features of contemporary societies around the world: the tendency to reduce to scientifically definable quantities issues involving real living humans and environmental systems, and all the complex values they represent. The film seems to suggest that it is precisely when values, in order to cross scales, are transformed into metrics—be they energy equivalents or, most commonly, money—that societies make lethal and immoral decisions.

This tendency, in an increasing number of social arenas, to replace collective decision-making with various forms of accountability or efficiency measures—including marketization, sometimes summarized as "new public management"—has consequently grown into a major feature of ongoing analysis in many social science disciplines. Few would dispute that this trend diminishes the role of politics as a form of democratic common decision-making; it has even been described as the main component of the post-political age (Swyngedouw 2009, 2010). The extended resilience enterprise, on the trajectory of building measurable and comparable Earth science indicators, displays elements that we see as akin to those of the post-political state.

Our reading of *Avatar* suggests that resilience thinking may soon reach the very bifurcation point that Augustine's dilemma illustrates. Taking TEK seriously has been for some time a key element of understanding social-ecological systems (SESs). At the same time, SES and resilience thinking has needed to mainstream its knowledge to serve urgent and legitimate policy demands, mostly on larger scales. The actual usage of local SESs has, in that process, rather disregarded TEK and its closely related cultural values and has instead privileged, and possibly overstated, the self-governing, systems properties of local societies. This has created a somewhat unlikely, perhaps unholy (and probably unhappy) marriage between strands of resilience thinking and the current, supposedly post-political management tendencies. It is, for example, already a long-standing part of resilience thinking to look for ways to express the values of ecosystems in monetary terms (Daily 1997; Ring et al. 2010). Despite the mounting critique against this as a scientifically narrow and politically hazardous "complexity blinder" (Norgaard 2010), quantification and monetarization seem likely, inevitable directions for resilience science and policy if it continues on its present trajectory.

This is where *Avatar* suggests a bifurcation point. While it is very easy to see (and we do) the virtues, scientifically and otherwise, of an enterprise like planetary boundaries—a global "level playing field" with boundaries set by science—Augustine helps us also to see the potential pitfalls and shortcomings of such an approach. Reading planetary boundaries through the doubts of Augustine, we can sense that on Pandora, much is lost before planetary boundaries are transgressed. We can refine the economics of ecosystem services and calibrate the acceptable degree of global warming, but if we take Augustine's self-probing position seriously, we must also see how real values—cultural as well as natural—are threatened as we go about our putatively neutral calculations. SESs and planetary boundaries, and a corresponding business-as-usual environmental politics, run the risk of serving as an excuse to pass over the situated ethics and politics of the marginalized, the poor, and the local communities, which suffer disproportionately under global change.

Put simply, Augustine forces resilience up against the wall. She contends: your quest may have been noble, but, like me, you have come to a point when you will have to consider whether your attempted transgression of scales, and your current epistemic enterprise, is capable of linking the local to the global and to address major issues of resilience and well-being in social-ecological systems around the world, as your science claims it is able to do. To its credit, resilience research has provided strong evidence that local communities and the ways in which they manage natural resources are often both efficient and sustainable. But it has also, paradoxically, failed to appreciate that in most of these communities, the state of nature is worsening, not because there is too much politics but because the politics are wrong. If that is the case, more science—even resilience science—is an anemic prescription.

Notes

1 The quotations from the *Avatar* screenplay (Cameron 2007, 100, 31, 81, 120–21) illustrate Dr. Grace Augustine's broadened identification with knowledge traditions: from a scientific representation of the world through the experimental science production of "facts" (I, II), to expressing understanding and concern with traditional ecological knowledge (III), to confession of doubt, solidarity and action (IV).

2 See the website established by the Stockholm Resilience Centre, which introduces and focuses on PB analysis: http://www.stockholmresilience.org/planetary-boundaries.

3 The *Nature* feature was coordinated with the publication of a longer and peer-reviewed article on planetary boundaries by the same authors (Rockström et al. 2009a), in the journal *Ecology and Society* of the Resilience Alliance (http://www .ecologyandsociety.org).

4 This article was cited internationally to suggest a general need to increase attention for TEK and other non-scientific knowledge traditions on multiple scales of adaptive ecosystem management, conservation, and governance; see, for instance, Folke et al. (2002), Moller et al. (2004), Drew (2005), Bhagwat et al. (2005), Cinner and Aswani (2007), Jones, Andrimarovolona, and Hockney (2008), Berkes and Berkes (2009), and Tengö and von Heland (2011).

5 The phrase "organized skepticism" famously originated in the last two letters of Robert K. Merton's CUDOS norms of science (Merton [1942] 1973).
6 Incidentally, Dr. Augustine here comes close to descriptions in the resilience literature of what has there been called "social-ecological memory" (Barthel 2008; Barthel, Sörlin and Ljungkvist 2010), thus further underlining the kinship between her work and that of an early, community-oriented resilience research.
7 Kierkegaard saw the highest truth as faith, a subjective amalgam, not something that one has (facts), but a truth that one is, not of the intellect (moral) but of the whole person (Barrett 1958, 152).

References

Armitage, Derek. 2006. "Resilience Management or Resilient Management? A Political Ecology of Adaptive, Multi-Level Governance." Paper presented at "Survival of the Commons: Mounting Challenges and New Realities," Eleventh Conference of the International Association for the Study of Common Property, Bali, Indonesia, 19–23 June.

Armitage, Derek, Fikret Berkes, and Nancy Doubleday, eds. 2007. *Adaptive Co-Management: Collaboration, Learning, and Multi-Level Governance.* Vancouver: University of British Columbia Press.

Barrett, William. 1958. *Irrational Man: A Study in Existential Philosophy.* New York: Random House.

Barthel, Stephan. 2008. *Recalling Urban Nature: Linking City People to Ecosystem Services.* Stockholm: Department of Systems Ecology, Stockholm University.

Barthel, Stephan, Sverker Sörlin, and John Ljungkvist. 2010. "Innovative Memory and Resilient Cities: Echoes from Ancient Constantinople." In *The Urban Mind: Cultural and Environmental Dynamics*, edited by Paul Sinclair, Gullög Nordquist, Frands Herschend, and Christian Isendahl, 391–405. Uppsala, Sweden: Department of Archaeology and Ancient History, Uppsala University.

Berkes, Fikret. 1999. *Sacred Ecology: Traditional Ecological Knowledge and Management Systems.* Philadelphia: Routledge.

Berkes, Fikret, and Mina Kislalioglu Berkes. 2009. "Ecological Complexity, Fuzzy Logic, and Holism in Indigenous Knowledge." *Futures* 41(1): 6–12.

Berkes, Fikret, Johan Colding, and Carl Folke. 2000. "Rediscovery of Traditional Ecological Knowledge as Adaptive Management." *Ecological Applications* 10(5): 1251–62.

Berkes, Fikret, and Carl Folke, eds. 1998. *Linking Social and Ecological Systems: Management Practices and Social Mechanisms for Building Resilience.* Cambridge: Cambridge University Press.

Berkes, Fikret, Carl Folke, and Madhav Gadgil. 1995. "Traditional Ecological Knowledge, Biodiversity, Resilience and Sustainability." In *Biodiversity Conservation: Policy Issues and Options*, edited by Charles Perrings, Karl-Göran Mäler, Carl Folke, Crawford Stanley Holling, and Bengt-Owe Jansson, 281–99. Dordrecht: Kluwer Academic Publishers.

Berkes, Fikret, and Nancy J. Turner. 2006. "Knowledge, Learning and the Evolution of Conservation Practice for Social-Ecological System Resilience." *Human Ecology* 34(4): 479–94.

Bhagwat, Shonil A., Cheppudira G. Kushalappa, Paul H. Williams, and Nick D. Brown. 2005. "The Role of Informal Protected Areas in Maintaining Biodiversity in the Western Ghats of India." *Ecology and Society* 10(1).

Cameron, James. 2007. *Avatar.* Screenplay. Los Angeles: Twentieth Century Fox. http://www.scribd.com/doc/25009954/James-Cameron-original-screenplay -for-Avatar.

Carpenter, Stephen R., and Elena Bennett. 2011. "Reconsideration of the Planetary Boundary for Phosphorus." *Environmental Research Letters* 6(1): 014009.

Carpenter, Stephen R., Brian Walker, J. Marty Anderies, and Nick Abel. 2001. "From Metaphor to Measurement: Resilience of What to What?" *Ecosystems* 4(8): 765–81.

Chapin, F. Stuart III, Gary P. Kofinas, Carl Folke, Stephen R. Carpenter, Per Olsson, Nick Abel, Reinette Biggs, Rosamund L. Naylor, Evelyn Pinkerton, D. Mark Stafford-Smith, Will Steffen, Brian Walker, and Oran R. Young. 2009. "Resilience-Based Stewardship: Strategies for Navigating Sustainable Pathways in a Changing World." In *Principles of Ecosystem Stewardship: Resilience-Based Natural Resource Management in a Changing World*, edited by F. Stuart Chapin III, Gary P. Kofinas, and Carl Folke, 319–37. Amsterdam: Springer Verlag.

Cinner, J. E., and S. Aswani. 2007. "Integrating Customary Management into Marine Conservation." *Biological Conservation* 140(3–4): 201–16.

Clark, William C., and R. E. Munn, eds. 1987. *Sustainable Development of the Biosphere.* Cambridge: Cambridge University Press.

Colding, Johan, and Carl Folke. 2001. "Social Taboos: 'Invisible' Systems of Local Resource Management and Biological Conservation." *Ecological Applications* 11(2): 584–600.

Crutzen, Paul J. 2002. "Geology of Mankind." *Nature* 415(6867): 23.

Daily, Gretchen C., ed. 1997. *Nature's Services.* Washington, DC: Island Press.

Drew, Joshua A. 2005. "Use of Traditional Ecological Knowledge in Marine Conservation." *Conservation Biology* 19(4): 1286–93.

Ernstson, Henrik, and Sverker Sörlin. 2009. "Weaving Protective Stories: Connective Practices to Articulate Holistic Values in the Stockholm National Urban Park." *Environment and Planning A* 41(6): 1460–79.

Folke, Carl. 2006. "Resilience: The Emergence of a Perspective for Social-Ecological Systems Analyses." *Global Environmental Change* 16(3): 253–67.

Folke, Carl, Stephen R. Carpenter, Thomas Elmqvist, Lance Gunderson, Crawford S. Holling, and B. Walker. 2002. "Resilience and Sustainable Development: Building Adaptive Capacity in a World of Transformations." *Ambio: A Journal of the Human Environment* 31(5): 437–40.

Folke, Carl, Stephen Carpenter, Brian Walker, Martin Scheffer, F. Stuart Chapin III, and Johan Rockström. 2010. "Resilience Thinking: Integrating Resilience, Adaptability and Transformability." *Ecology and Society* 15(4): 20.

Gadgil, Madhav, Fikret Berkes, and Carl Folke. 1993. "Indigenous Knowledge for Biodiversity Conservation." *Ambio: A Journal of the Human Environment* 22(2–3): 151–56.

Gillespie, Michael Allen. 2006. "The Search for Immediacy and the Problem of Political Life in Existentialism and Phenomenology." In *A Companion to Phenomenology and Existentialism*, edited by Hubert L. Dreyfus and Mark A. Wrathall, 531–45. Oxford: Wiley-Blackwell.

Gunderson, Lance, and Crawford S. Holling, eds. 2002. *Panarchy: Understanding Transformations in Human and Natural Systems*. Washington, DC: Island Press.

Hess, David. 2007. "Ethnography and the Development of Science and Technology Studies." In *Handbook of Ethnography*, edited by Paul Atkinson, Amanda Coffey, Sara Delamont, John Lofland, and Lyn Lofland, 234–35. London: Sage.

Holling, Crawford S. 1973. "Resilience and Stability of Ecological Systems." *Annual Review of Ecology and Systematics* 4: 1–23.

Hornborg, Alf. 2003. "Cornucopia or Zero-Sum Game? The Epistemology of Sustainability." *Journal of World-Systems Research* 9(2): 205–16.

———. 2009. "Zero-Sum World: Challenges in Conceptualizing Environmental Load Displacement and Ecologically Unequal Exchange in the World -System." *International Journal of Comparative Sociology* 50(3–4): 237–62.

IPCC. 2007. *Impacts, Adaptation and Vulnerability. Contribution of Working Group II to the Fourth Assessment Report of the Intergovernmental Panel on Climate Change*. Edited by Martin Parry, Osvaldo Canziani, Jean Palutikof, Paul van der Linden, and, Clair Hanson. Cambridge: Cambridge University Press.

Jones, Julia P. G., Mijasoa M. Andrimarovolona, and Neal Hockley. 2008. "The Importance of Local Taboos and Social Norms to Conservation in Madagascar." *Conservation Biology* 22(4): 976–86.

Karlsson, Rasmus. 2010. *Three Essays on Our Planetary Future*. Lund, Sweden: Lund University, Lund Political Studies 162.

Kende-Robb, Caroline, and Warren A. van Wicklin. 2008. "Giving the Most Vulnerable a Voice." In *Strategic Environmental Assessment for Policies: An Instrument for Good Governance*, edited by Kulsum Ahmed and Ernesto Sanchez-Triana, 95–122. Washington, DC: World Bank.

Kierkegaard, Soren. (1843) 2006. *Fear and Trembling*. Edited by C. Stephen Evans and Sylvia Walsh. Translated by Sylvia Walsh. Cambridge: Cambridge University Press.

Kjaer, Anne Mette. 2004. *Governance*. Cambridge: Polity.

Latour, Bruno. 1993. *We Have Never Been Modern*. Translated by Catherine Porter. Cambridge: Harvard University Press.

Leach, Melissa, ed. 2008. *Re-Framing Resilience: A Symposium Report*. Brighton, UK: Steps.

Lévi-Strauss, Claude. 1963. *Totemism*. Translated by R. Needham. Boston: Beacon Press.

Levin, Simon. 1999. *Fragile Dominion: Complexity and the Commons*. Cambridge: Helix Perseus Books.

Libby, Robin. 2012. "Resilience: A Geography and History of an Ecological Concept in Global Change Science." Keynote address, "Rethinking Invasion Ecologies: Natures, Cultures and Societies in the age of the Anthropocene," Mellon Foundation Conference, University of Sydney, 17–18 June 2012.

Litfin, Karen. T. 1997. "The Gendered Eye in the Sky: A Feminist Perspective on Earth Observation Satellites." *Frontiers: A Journal of Women Studies* 18(2): 26–47.

Mendelsohn, Robert, Ariel Dinar, and Larry Williams. 2006. "The Distributional Impact of Climate Change on Rich and Poor Countries." *Environment and Development Economics* 11: 159–78.

Merchant, Carolyn. 1982. *The Death of Nature: Women, Ecology, and the Scientific Revolution.* San Francisco: Harper.

———. 2008. "Secrets of Nature: The Bacon Debates Revisited." *Journal of the History of Ideas* 69(1): 147–62.

Merton, Robert K. (1942) 1973. "The Normative Structure of Science." In *The Sociology of Science: Theoretical and Empirical Investigations,* 267–80. Chicago: University of Chicago Press.

Millennium Ecosystem Assessment. 2005. *Ecosystems and Human Well-Being: General Synthesis.* Washington, DC: Island Press.

Moller, Henrik, Fikret Berkes, Philip O'Brian Lyver, and Mina Kislalioglu. 2004. "Combining Science and Traditional Ecological Knowledge: Monitoring Populations for Co-Management." *Ecology and Society* 9(3): 2.

Nadasdy, Paul. 1999. "The Politics of TEK: Power and the 'Integration' of Knowledge." *Arctic Anthropology* 36(1–2): 1–18.

———. 2007. "Adaptive Co-Management and the Gospel of Resilience." In *Adaptive Co-Management: Collaboration, Learning and Multi-Level Governance,* edited by Derek Armitage, Fikret Berkes, and Nancy Doubleday, 208–27. Vancouver: University of British Columbia Press.

Norgaard, Richard B. 2010. "Ecosystem Services: From Eye-Opening Metaphor to Complexity Blinder." *Ecological Economics* 69(6): 1219–27.

Olsson, Per, and Carl Folke. 2001. "Local Ecological Knowledge and Institutional Dynamics for Ecosystem Management: A Study of Lake Racken Watershed, Sweden." *Ecosystems* 4(2): 85–104.

Olsson, Per, Carl Folke, and Fikret Berkes. 2004. "Adaptive Co-Management for Building Resilience in Social-Ecological Systems." *Environmental Management* 34(1): 75–90.

Olsson, Per, Carl Folke, and Terry P. Hughes. 2008. "Navigating the Transition to Ecosystem-Based Management of the Great Barrier Reef, Australia." *Proceedings of the National Academy of Sciences of the United States of America* 105(28): 9489–94.

Ostrom, Elinor. 1990. *Governing the Commons: The Evolution of Institutions for Collective Action.* Cambridge: Cambridge University Press.

Pielke, Roger A. Jr. 2007. *The Honest Broker: Making Sense of Science in Policy and Politics.* Cambridge: Cambridge University Press.

Pollitt, Christopher, and Geert Bouckaert. 2011. *Public Management Reform: A Comparative Analysis: New Public Management, Governance, and the Neo-Weberian State.* 3rd ed. Oxford: Oxford University Press.

Prigogine, Ilya. 1997. *The End of Certainty.* New York: Free Press.

Ring, Irene, Bernd Hansjürgens, Thomas Elmqvist, Heidi Wittmer, and Pavan Sukhdev. 2010. "Challenges in Framing the Economics of Ecosystems and Biodiversity: The TEEB Initiative." *Current Opinion in Environmental Sustainability* 2(1–2): 15–26.

Rockström, Johan, Will Steffen, Kevin Noone, Åsa Persson, F. Stuart Chapin III, Eric F. Lambin, Timothy M. Lenton et al. 2009a. "Planetary Boundaries: Exploring the Safe Operating Space for Humanity." *Ecology and Society* 14(2): 32.

Rockström, Johan, Will Steffen, Kevin Noone, Åsa Persson, F. Stuart Chapin III, Eric F. Lambin, Timothy M. Lenton et al. 2009b. "A Safe Operating Space for Humanity." *Nature* 461(7263): 472–75.

Ruttan, Lore M., and Monique Borgerhoff Mulder. 1999. "Are East African Pastoralists Truly Conservationists?" *Current Anthropology* 40(5): 621–52.

Schmidt, Falk. 2013. "Governing Planetary Boundaries: Limiting or Enabling Conditions for Transitions towards Sustainability." In *Transgovernance*, edited by Louis Meuleman, 215–34. Berlin: Springer.

Sörlin, Sverker. 1998. "Monument and Memory: Landscape Imagery and the Articulation of Territory." *Worldviews: Environment, Culture, Religion* 2(4): 269–79.

Steffen, Will, Paul J. Crutzen, and John R. McNeill. 2007. "The Anthropocene: Are Humans Now Overwhelming the Great Forces of Nature?" *Ambio: A Journal of the Human Environment* 36(8): 614–21.

Steffen, Will, Johan Rockström, and Robert Costanza. 2011. "How Defining Planetary Boundaries Can Transform Our Approach to Growth." *Solutions* 2(3). http://www.thesolutionsjournal.com/node/935.

Swyngedouw, Eric. 2009. "The Antinomies of the Postpolitical City: In Search of a Democratic Politics of Environmental Production." *International Journal of Urban and Regional Research* 33(3): 601–20.

———. 2010. "Impossible Sustainability and the Post-Political Condition." *Urban and Landscape Perspectives* 9(2): 185–205.

Tengö, Maria, and Jacob von Heland. "Adaptive Capacity of Local Indigenous Institutions: The Case of the Taboo Forests in Southern Madagascar." In *Governing Social-Ecological Transformation: Adapting to the Challenge of Global Environmental Change*, edited by Emily Boyd and Carl Folke, 37–74. Cambridge: Cambridge University Press.

Townsend, Alan R., and Stephen Porder. 2011. "Boundary Issues." *Environmental Research Letters* 6: 1–3.

Turnbull, David. 1997. "Reframing Science and Other Local Knowledge Traditions." *Futures* 29(6): 551–62.

———. 2000. *Masons, Tricksters and Cartographers: Comparative Studies in the Sociology of Scientific and Indigenous Knowledge.* London: Routledge.

————. 2009. "Futures for Indigenous Knowledges." *Futures* 40(1): 1–5.

Visvanathan, Shiv. 2002. "The Future of Science Studies." *Futures* 34(1): 91–101.

Walker, Brian, and David Salt. 2006. *Resilience Thinking: Sustaining Ecosystems and People in a Changing World*. Washington, DC: Island Press.

Walker, Richard. 2007. *The Country in the City: An Environmental History of the San Francisco Bay Area*. Seattle: University of Washington Press.

Yar, Majid. 2005. "Arendt, Hannah (1906–1975)." *The Internet Encyclopedia of Philosophy*. http://www.iep.utm.edu/arendt/.

Epilogue: Truth and Fiction in *Avatar*'s Cosmogony and Nature Religion

BRON TAYLOR

Entwined in a complex mix of historical, aesthetic, spiritual, and ideological presuppositions, the ferment over *Avatar* has been diverse and contentious. This should not be surprising, since *Avatar* metaphorically attacks all martial, colonial, and expansionist histories, which have occurred at the expense of the world's indigenous peoples and Earth's biocomplexity. Both implicitly, through the film's narrative, and explicitly, in statements made about it, James Cameron has also challenged the materialism—and thus, the lifeways and aspirations—of the vast majority of people today. He has even implicitly challenged the world's predominant religions by offering as an alternative spiritualities of belonging and connection to nature and animistic ethics of kinship and reciprocity with the entire chorus of life, all of which could be understood either religiously (as the goddess Eywa, the divine source and expression of life) or scientifically (as an interconnected and mutually dependent environmental system). Critics quite naturally arose to defend histories, worldviews, lifeways, ideologies, and religions that they concluded Cameron had challenged in his film, contending as well that the views promoted in *Avatar* were misguided, if not dangerous.

Conservative Responses
Some of the strongest criticisms came from monotheists who felt that the film promoted a spiritually perilous paganism or pantheism. Typical of this response was the reaction of the Vatican's official newspaper, which

complained that that the film promotes "spiritualism linked to the worship of nature." Vatican Radio commented that the film "cleverly winks at all those pseudo-doctrines that turn ecology into the religion of the millennium," and asserted that in *Avatar*, "nature is no longer a creation to defend, but a divinity to worship" (Rizzo 2010). A Vatican spokesman confirmed that these reviews were consistent with Pope Benedict's views about the danger of "turning nature into a 'new divinity'" (ibid.). Evangelical Christians affiliated with the Cornwall Alliance felt similarly, releasing a twelve-part DVD series titled "The False World View of the Green Movement" and a subsequent segment, "From Captain Planet to *Avatar*: The Seduction of Our Youth," which attacked these and other programs and films as threats to the Christian faith.[1] But these attacks are moderate compared to those posted at jesus-is-savior.com, where David Stewart, while agreeing that *Avatar* teaches a demonic, false gospel, asserts that according to the Bible (which he quotes), Cameron and the film's actors will be "cursed" for promoting a false gospel. Stewart also criticizes the evangelical magazine *Christianity Today* for recommending the film.[2]

Whatever their differences, these reactions from conservative Christians reflect fears that their youth are being seduced by pagan and environmentalist spiritualities and that such heterodox spiritualities are growing within Christian churches.[3] Such fears were even expressed in the pages of the *New York Times* by staff columnist Ross Douthat (2010), who perceives in Cameron's films a "long apologia for pantheism—a faith that equates God with Nature, and calls humanity into religious communion with the natural world." Douthat even seems to share a key part of Stewart's critique, claiming that "pantheism has been Hollywood's religion of choice for a generation now." Douthat expresses a clear preference for the orthodox Christian hope of divine rescue from this world, concluding, "Nature *is* suffering and death.... And human societies that hew closest to the natural order aren't the shining Edens of James Cameron's fond imaginings. They're places where existence tends to be nasty, brutish and short" (emphasis in original). As we have seen in this volume, however, especially in the case study on the response of Canadian Christians (Haluza-Delay, Ferber, and Wiebe-Neufeld), some churchgoers are much more positive about the film than these critics. This may be surprising to those who only read the conservative critics or who do not know how plural and internally conflicted Christianity has become, with regard to both worldviews at variance with traditional doctrines and environmental concerns and spiritualities (e.g., Taylor 2005, esp. 1:301–82, and cross references).

The reactions of conservative political pundits held other surprises. David Boaz (2010) of the libertarian Cato Institute, for example, after acknowledging that most conservatives consider *Avatar* to be "anti-American, anti-military and...anti-capitalist," contends that the central evil depicted in the film is the Resource Development Administration's "stark violation of property rights," which are "the foundation of the free market and indeed of civilization." He concludes that rather than vilify the film, "conservatives should appreciate a rare defense of property rights coming out of Hollywood."

A dramatically different sort of conservative, the neo-con pundit Ann Marlowe (2009), contends that *Avatar* promotes universal values that Americans cherish, even asserting that it could be the most neo-conservative movie ever because it advances "the point we neo-cons made in Iraq: that American blood is not worth more than the blood of others, and that others' freedom is not worth less than American freedom." She even suggests that, although "*Avatar* has been charged with 'pantheism' its mythos is just as deeply Christian," reasoning that "the metaphor where one figure entered the skin of another" is akin to the incarnation of God in human form in Christian theology. Finally, she wonders, "Since when is flattening nature a conservative position, anyway? Are we supposed to be 'against' nature just because lefties are 'for' it?"

US Military Responses

Boaz is correct, of course, that many conservatives, including in the US Military, consider the film anti-military and un-American. The Marine Corps director of public affairs, Colonel Bryan Salas, for example, charged that the film did "a disservice" to the Marine Corps, which, he averred "prides itself on understanding host country narratives and sensitivities in complex climes and places" ("Core Official" 2010). A barrage of responses followed on the *Military Times* forum, however, showing greater diversity of opinion in the military than many would assume. Retired Marine Corps Colonel Victor Bianchini wondered if the public relations officer even watched the movie, noting (as did a number of other forum participants) that the RDA forces were "not in the service of their country, but mercenaries of a mega-corporation." "The true heroes of the film," he added, were former Marines, "the paraplegic Jake Sully and the heroic female helicopter pilot Trudy Chacon." Bianchini added other details, including, "Jim Cameron is a friend of the Marine Corps, has portrayed Marines positively in many of his films and has a brother, of whom he is very proud, who served in the Corps." Bianchini concluded his discussion by noting that "many films convey morality metaphors that are often only intended to appeal to the 'better angels of our nature,' and this one is no exception."[4] Most of the forum participants responding to the film viewed the film positively (many explicitly agreeing with Bianchini) and thought that the true Marine spirit was represented honourably; many of the positive comments were from armed service members who described themselves as politically conservative. "Gabe078" even contended that the real hero was Trudy Chacon, "who behaved how a Marine should—standing up for what is right and helping those who cannot help themselves." In a subsequent comment, he added praise for Jake Sully, and then, in a statement that many postcolonial critics would probably find surprising coming from a US military serviceman, he declared: "The real enemy was... colonization of a people and land for profit, greed, asserting a will and dominance on a 'nation of people' (an alien species in this case) who were given no choice." In an environmental ethics class that I taught the semester after the film was released, students from military families (more than a dozen) were highly positive about the film and said their families were too; none of them thought the film was anti-American. One young man among them said that he and his buddies had been drawn to the film because of the promised special effects, and he and his friends began their discussion afterward by speaking enthusiastically about these effects. Soon, however, and hesitantly at first because they were afraid of how the others might react, he and his friends began talking about the beauty of Pandora, how much they loved being outdoors (often while hunting or fishing), and how the film reminded them of the beauty of Earth.

Of course, some service members were harshly critical of the film. One veteran who commented online wrote that "portraying our military as fanatical crazed killers who have joined a military mercenary force to destroy a civilization so that corporations can capitalize on some rare commodity prized by earthlings is disrespectful to our soldiers, especially in this time of war." He added, "Knowing that 90% of 'Hollywood' is liberal... only confirms the anti military theme of this movie" (Treese 2010).[5] Another online commentator wrote an anonymous post titled "Avatar Made Me Want to Throw Up," arguing that Sully and Chacon committed treason, murdering "their fellow soldiers and American comrades." After a number of respondents countered that Sully and Chacon behaved honourably, faulting the writer for failing to recognize that the RDA's forces were mercenaries, not Marines, the anonymous author responded by defending the invaders even more vehemently:

> The "Sky People" never once made the first move without due warning. They wanted the tree and so they took it. Eminent domain. I am sure the resources provided under that tree could be used to help save many American lives— why else would it be so valuable. The natives were being greedy. They did not have to die and they did not have to retaliate. If they wanted to retaliate, that

is fine, but do not expect sympathy. If all had gone according to plan, NO ONE would have died and who knows what benefits would have come.[6]

He concluded that the Na'vi were "not even humans" and that, although he volunteers at an animal shelter, "you better believe I will put my human life over" that of dogs or other non-humans. These comments were met with incredulity by some of the respondents.

Which, if any, of the views expressed by current or former US military personnel will be surprising will depend on one's preconceptions about military subcultures. The same dynamic occurs with regard to views supposedly promoted by "Hollywood."

Responses from Left-Wing Radicals

Pre-existing cognitive frames seem to be no less important to the understandings of left-wing thinkers. For those acquainted with certain intellectual schools, for example, it is unsurprising that leftist, postmodern, and post-colonial theorists would criticize Cameron for promoting what they view as a destructive stereotype of the "ecologically noble savage" and for the film's implication that the liberation of oppressed peoples depends on a "white messiah" and other saviours from the ranks of the oppressors.[7] Some feminists condemn what they consider the film's misogyny. Some of these positions are presented in previous chapters of this volume, but some of the more extreme critics remain to be explored.

One of the most extreme voices is that of the Marxist philosopher Slavoj Žižek. He contends that, contrary to the film's "politically correct themes," *Avatar* presents "an array of brutal racist motifs: a paraplegic outcast from earth is good enough to get the hand of a beautiful local princess, and to help the natives win the decisive battle. The film teaches us that the only choice the aborigines have is to be saved by the human beings or to be destroyed by them. In other words, they can choose either to be the victim of imperialist reality, or to play their allotted role in the white man's fantasy." Thus, the film enables viewers to sympathize "with the idealised aborigines while rejecting their actual struggle" (Žižek 2010a). Yet Žižek does not explain why these binaries are the only possible interpretations of the film, nor does he provide any evidence that the film promotes sympathy but not solidarity with the actual struggle of indigenous peoples. Instead, he expresses a view held by some progressives and probably the majority of leftist radicals: that the film does little if anything to promote anti-capitalist action and solidarity with indigenous peoples, let alone revolutionary class consciousness. Žižek's apparent antipathy toward contemporary environmentalism, and especially environmental spirituality, may help illuminate his hostility to *Avatar*.[8] In a YouTube video, for example, he denounces "ecology as religion," calling it a mystifying ideology and "the new opium of the masses" (2010b). According to Žižek, this ideology—with its diagnosis of "alienation from nature" as the root of our current predicaments and its prescription for healing (namely, seeing ourselves as rooted in and belonging to nature)—is deeply conservative. Instead of trying to return to some supposed natural balance that hubristic humans have disturbed, he contends, we must sever our roots in nature and embrace artificiality, including by transforming nature through genetic engineering. He concludes by admiring a pile of trash and arguing that we need to love and embrace the real world, not an idealized one. Clearly, for such radicals, Prometheus lives!

Radical environmentalists, however, who advance a worldview akin to what Žižek criticizes, usually see more to praise than to criticize in *Avatar*. Long-term radical environmental activist Harold Linde (2010), for example, considers the film a stunning work of radical environmentalist propaganda that promotes a Gaian worldview as well as the view that "destroying the rain forest for profit is morally and spiritually wrong." For other radical environmentalists, however, the capitalist motivation for making the film and the immense expense of it (including the supposed costs to the non-human world from all such filmmaking) is sufficient to reject any claim that the film has value. Some of these radicals share the previously mentioned criticism that the film is rooted in regressive ideas such as the supposed white saviour theme.[9]

Anarcho-primitivists, a subset of radical environmentalists who seek to reharmonize humans with nature through a return to pre-agricultural foraging lifeways, seem to be especially receptive to the film.[10] Layla AbdelRahim, a Canadian citizen born in Moscow and of mixed Somali and Russian ancestry, for example, praised the film on her blog and on "Anarchy Radio," which is hosted by the best-known primitivist theorist, John Zerzan.[11] She contends, "The film is an overt commentary on the historical and present-day place of anthropologists in imperialist expeditions and of the role the hard sciences play in, both, elaborating the philosophy of imperialism and in providing the necessary information for its execution. As Col. Quaritch makes clear, the scientist is the carrot and the military is the stick" (AbdelRahim 2009). In another post, she directly counters the view (commonly expressed by left-wing critics) that *Avatar* is sexist or racist, arguing that "by presenting the Human as part of the animal world," Cameron attacks both speciesism and humanism, which "furnishes the philosophical foundation for all 'isms': sexism, racism, animalism, etc." (ibid.).

In two ways, AbdelRahim's commentary is noteworthy. First, it suggests that at least some of those who have affinity with anti-authoritarian and biocentric ethics may be more likely than others to approve of *Avatar*. (For a contrary view from another anarchist critic, see John Clark's scathing critique in an essay published under his pseudonym, Max Cafard [2010].) Second, AbdelRahim highlights the pernicious role that anthropologists (and other scientists) have played in the subjugation of indigenous peoples and their deracination from and the destruction of their habitats. Cameron himself has stressed that the scientist Augustine is "on the wrong side, she's one of the invaders," even though she eventually comes to love the Na'vi people and tries to help them (Dunham 2012, 191).

Most contemporary anthropologists, of course, understand and attempt to distance themselves from this history, including through efforts to support aboriginal peoples in their struggles against further threats to their cultures and homelands (Starn 2011; Clifford 2011). Part of this effort includes criticism of ideas they consider to be overtly or covertly colonialist. This helps to explain the strong criticism of *Avatar* by those who think that it promotes an image of indigenous peoples as "noble savages" and that the plot in which turncoat American soldiers successfully defend the Na'vi obscures history and is rooted in colonialist attitudes (Simpson 2011).[12] What at least some in the anarchist tradition are doing, however, is extending their critique of authoritarianism to the exploitation and subjugation of non-human living beings, even identifying humanism (and its leftist variants) as part of the global problem. This helps explain why radical environmentalists, including the anarchists among them, have for the most part found more to praise than criticize in *Avatar*.

Evaluating the Evaluations

My own perceptions have been enhanced and complicated by the diverse commentaries about *Avatar*, including the preceding essays in this volume. This is one reason why I welcomed the widest range possible of perspectives about the film and its significance when issuing a call for critical reflections about *Avatar*. It is also why I have been especially interested in the views of those who typically do not express themselves in print and thus pursued analyses based on fieldwork that would seek out such views and voices. The fieldwork-based articles and those that analyze the many, increasingly open forums on the Internet, show how insightful and nuanced are the views of individuals who are rarely asked for their opinions.

I have, up to this point, held in abeyance my own judgments, in part because I wanted to consider carefully the diverse views precipitated by the film and possibly modify my initial views of the film as a result. While still in an analytical mode, working back and forth between sometimes competing perspectives, I will now weave in my own views about Cameron, his film, and its significance. These views have been shaped by over three decades as a scholar and activist trying to understand what leads people to participate in movements that seek to protect Earth's biological and cultural diversity. I have been especially focused on how the affective and spiritual (or religious) dimensions of human experience might relate to such mobilization. These are some of the lenses through which I examine nature-related social phenomena, which I provide because, to evaluate my analyses, readers quite understandably may want to know something about what shapes my perspective.

Is *Avatar* (and Cameron) Misogynist, Colonialist, or Racist?

In my view, if by *misogyny* we mean the hatred of women (and girls), the criticism that *Avatar* (and, by implication, Cameron) is misogynist can be quickly dismissed, for it appears to be based on weak, if any, evidence, as well as upon a remarkable ability to ignore evidence to the contrary.[13] Cameron is properly recognized, to evidence a counter-argument, for creating powerful heroines, unlike most Hollywood directors (Keegan 2009, 225, 227).[14] A number of articles written or co-authored by indigenous scholars, however, have raised more poignant observations and criticisms. These express both appreciation for and disappointment with the film.

John James and Tom Ute (2011), for example, strongly criticize *Avatar* and several other films that have taken up colonial themes, contending that despite their efforts to criticize colonial repression, these films "actually reaffirm the colonial prejudices they seek to challenge" (187).[15] For evidence, they note that in *Avatar*, Sully prevails over Omaticaya natives in athletic events. This positions Sully, in their view, "not only as an unlikely Savior of the Na'vi, but as a self-indulgent one for the average theatergoer" (190). Because James and Ute do nothing to explain or provide evidence for their claim that this theme is "self-indulgent," I do not find that point compelling. But this observation gives me pause: why *does* the Sully character have to be superior to the tribals in their own sports and martial arts and with the animals they customarily use in those activities? This hardly seems necessary and may provide an example of how difficult it is, as many have argued, for the beneficiaries of colonialism to "decolonize" their minds. James and Ute, and some other critics of *Avatar*, seem to be arguing that in making Sully superior in some ways to some of the Na'vi, Cameron has revealed a moral blind spot, an assumed sense of superiority. As have many others, James and Ute directly criticize what they perceive to be the "white messiah" theme, asserting that "the film only reaffirms the colonial, social, and economic paradigms that it seeks to undermine by suggesting the natives' inability to liberate themselves from the forces of oppression...thereby conferring power to a privileged colonizer, in this case, a white American male" (191; for similar critiques see Simpson 2011; Clifford 2011; and Douthat 2010). James and Ute conclude that filmmakers such as Cameron should stop congratulating audiences "for their pseudo-cognizant effort" and instead "hold them actively accountable for their actions" (197).

I have no idea what these critics mean by "pseudo-cognizant effort," nor do I understand how a popular theatrical filmmaker (let alone a didactic documentarian) is supposed to "hold audiences responsible" for any action, let alone for the ways in which audiences might benefit from, or be complicit in, the exploitation of indigenous populations and nature. This is only one of many examples in which critics set an impossibly high ethical bar for a filmmaker to vault. Moreover, I think it is important to ask: Through what other means has the violent deracination of indigenous peoples by imperial forces ever been presented *to a global mass public*? One would think that this would draw praise, not such sharp criticism, from those who would like to raise global awareness of this long history and resistance to its continuing process.

For many critics, of course, reaching a mass audience with a pro-indigenous and reverence-for-life message is far from enough. Columbia University anthropologist and Kahnawá:ke/Mohawk scholar Audra Simpson, who is one of many who criticize the supposed "white messiah" theme, also offers a unique argument: after noting that spectacles like *Avatar* do political work, she argues that in settler, colonialist societies, such spectacles "redirect emotions, histories, and possibilities" in a way that obscures the genocidal dynamics and law-based justifications of "dispossession, disenfranchisement, and containment" (2011, 207). She finds it difficult to see how a spectacle like *Avatar* could be, in any sense, helpful to native peoples. Nevertheless, she adds in a footnote that she appreciates one aspect of the film: "Cameron's surprise," she writes, was to "reimagine...the familiar period in U.S. history known as 'the Indian Wars'" as one in which the settlers are repulsed and their occupation fails. In this singular aspect, she writes, *Avatar* is "optimistic, uplifting, and perhaps absolving" (212–13n1). By "absolving," she probably means that Cameron can therefore be forgiven for the film's flaws, but clearly, Simpson finds something inspiring in *Avatar*: namely, the possibility of indigenous victory and of constructing a flourishing new world.[16]

Of the indigenous analysts of the film, I found the reflections of Daniel Heath Justice and Julia Good Fox especially nuanced and insightful. Using an approach that complements the fieldwork-based studies in this volume, Justice (2010) notes that people in his own indigenous and intellectual circles, who are deeply engaged with issues of "indigenous sovereignty and spirituality, colonization and decolonization, other-than-human kinship, traditional ecological knowledge and environmental destruction," have had complicated responses to the film. Given the "blistering critique online and in print from both the right and the left," Justice expected his friends and colleagues to express "substantial indignation" if not also "sweeping dismissal" of the film. "That's not how it turned out, not even for me," he writes. "Our responses ranged from guarded optimism...to thoughtful frustration (it's powerful in so many ways, but why do we need yet another story about Indigenous struggle told through a non-Native's voice and per-spective?), but no one dismissed it. On the whole, the overwhelming sense was, 'Well, it's flawed, but at least it's getting people talking.'" Justice con-tinues, "That there's so much commentary in the blogosphere on the film's underlying current of 'white guilt' indicates to me that *something* is happen-ing with audiences and critics" (emphasis in original). He then surmises, "There's probably a good opportunity here to engage an audience on Indig-enous issues that might not otherwise have been interested or receptive."

As for the film itself, however, Justice is more critical, arguing that by creating simplistic characters that are either purely good or evil, Cameron's protagonists are so obviously unreal that audiences can not relate to them. Justice mentions, for example, that he knows many native and non-native soldiers, adding thoughtfully that military service is very complicated for Native Americans and that it is simplistic to characterize soldiers "as brutes and bigots." The result of these simplistic characterizations, Justice con-tends, is that audience members do not see themselves as part of the his-tory, or current reality, that the film metaphorically depicts. Consequently, "the potential for *actual* critical commentary is diminished, and the audi-ence is left with a self-congratulatory feeling of having grappled with major issues without having actually dealt with any of the *real* complexities of colonialism, militarism, reverence for the living world, or environmental destruction" (emphasis in original).

Even though I consider such claims about the affective states of audi-ence members to be unduly speculative, I do think that Justice's argument is plausible, that overly simplistic characters might hinder people from making connections between their own histories and actions and the deracination of indigenous peoples from their lands and the destruction of those lands. The skepticism expressed by Justice (and others) about the film's ability to produce understanding and evoke sympathy and solidarity with indigenous peoples is certainly understandable.

Unlike the more strident critics, however, Justice acknowledges that the film has some "narrative brilliance," as when Neytiri scolds Sully for "his casual response to the destruction of life his rescue required; the soul-crushing horror of Hometree's destruction and the survivors' disorientation and exile; and the adoption ceremony that remakes Jake into a full Na'vi, with both the rights and responsibilities that such a ceremony necessitates, and his subsequent betrayal of the Na'vi and Neytiri's anguished response." He is also forthcoming about his own emotional response to the film, reporting that in places he found it moving, although he subsequently indicates that neither this nor the filmmaker's good intentions are enough: "For all its good intentions, for all its visual spectacle and effecting sentiment (yes, I got teary-eyed a couple of times), it's still ultimately a story about 'those bad guys who aren't us.' Sadly, as we know from example after example in the past, distant and immediate, the bad guys, all too often, *are* us" (emphasis in original).

Julia Good Fox also understands well any cynicism about the film in light of the long history of filmmaking serving imperial interests and the ideology of manifest destiny. Moreover, she expresses frustration at seeing yet another cinematic expression of the "non-Tribal man's fantasy that an Indigenous woman will find him more desirable than she does all other Tribal men" (Good Fox 2010).[17] Nevertheless, she argues that "it is a willful oversimplification" to reduce the film to "going native" or "white-saviour" themes. She insightfully notes that all of Cameron's films wrestle with difficult, "cross-cultural intersections that occur in improbable circumstances," where "representative individuals and cultures misconnect, disconnect, shun connection, abuse connection, and, of course, connect." She cites indigenous studies professor Taiaiake Alfred (from the University of Victoria, British Columbia), who has observed that one of the shared traits of Native American peoples has been "the ability to appreciate and recognize multidimensional relationships," a notion found "in such translated phrases as 'all my relations.'" Good Fox suggests that in *Avatar*, the phrase "I see you" coheres with such an understanding. This notion, she writes, refers not merely to "a glance or a gaze, but rather [to] an accurate and encompassing recognition, an insightful and respectful acknowledgment." It expresses the idea that "I comprehend our connection, our relatedness." For Good Fox, *Avatar* represents a valuable exploration of what makes possible, and hinders, authentic recognition of relatedness. Moreover, contrary to many of the critics, according to Good Fox, because it is sometimes easier to communicate such realities indirectly "through the use of analogies," the film has a chance of countering manifest destiny, "the de facto ideology of the United States."[18]

With regard to the "white-saviour" critique, Good Fox observes that Sully's transformation required "the assistance and mentoring" of four women, "Neytiri, Mo'at, Dr. Grace Augustine, and Trudy Chacon." Good Fox also insightfully notes that two of Sully's female mentors (Augustine and Mo'at) are maternal figures: Mo'at plays a particularly powerful role as "the moral anchor of the film," at one point denying the request from the Na'vi men to kill Sully, an intervention that gives him "a second chance at life" and makes it possible for him "to reemerge as a new man on Pandora."[19]

Good Fox makes another striking observation, which is all the more notable since it would have been easy for her to miss given her frustration with certain aspects of the love story between Sully and Neytiri. She comments that, despite its problematic aspects, the love story "goes beyond white people's desire to be the object of beauty and erotic attraction for Indigenous Peoples. Colonizers also want to be forgiven for the damage they (and their ancestors) have wrought. This is most strongly suggested in the Pietà scene near the film's end, when Neytiri holds Scully's human form and the audience is presented with a visual of the perceived redemptive power of Native love for the non-Native." This struck me, in part because it reminded me of one November evening in 1995 when Walter Bresette, an Ojibwe activist who fought for Indian treaty rights and against various mining projects, hijacked a conference on ecological resistance movements that I had orchestrated at the University of Wisconsin.[20] Bresette and the Scottish author/bard and land-rights activist Alastair McIntosh used the term "hijack" when they interrupted the panel, declaring that it was improper that a conference dealing with indigenous land rights and environmental issues had no prayer or ceremony. After giving the approximately two hundred audience members time to flee if they wished (few, if any, did), Bresette led what he called a "welcome ceremony" for the nonindigenous conference participants. His stated motivation was, essentially, that if the latecomers did not feel at home, if they did not feel that they belonged to this continent, then they would continue to treat badly its Aboriginal peoples and the land itself.[21]

For the purpose of this analysis, the details of the ceremony are less important than its emotional dimensions. Some Americans with European ancestry are aware of the devastating impact on native peoples and on the continent's environmental systems that followed their arrival, feel guilty as a result, and would like to atone as best they can. But reconciliation can only really be achieved through the generosity of native peoples. After the ceremony, Bresette told me that it was a difficult thing to do emotionally, to welcome the descendants of the original invaders, but he considered this sort of ritual to be essential bridge building in the cause of protecting native rights and the continent's land and waters. Good Fox observes, it seems to me, an important parallel moment in *Avatar* that symbolizes the possibility (despite fraught histories and human frailties) that cross-cultural respect and reciprocity can be developed. Perhaps *Avatar* goes even further, suggesting that against all odds, grievances can be forgiven and respect and even love might emerge when colonial peoples acknowledge the injustices and work to change the dominant society's course. Here, it seems to me, Good Fox illuminates important mythic and religious themes in the film, including those of repentance, redress, forgiveness, and reconciliation.

As we have seen, Daniel Heath Justice is more pessimistic than Good Fox about the film precipitating respect for and solidarity with indigenous peoples, let alone kinship feelings toward our Earthly non-human co-inhabitants. Soon after the release of the film, Justice nevertheless wrote that the "jury was still out" with regard to the impact of the film. For my part, during many interviews with environmental activists over more than two decades, I have learned that no small number of them trace their activist vocations to, or at least note important influences of, artistic productions that explore and evoke outrage and sympathies regarding injustices toward people and the wider natural world. Some have cited J.R.R. Tolkien's fantasy trilogy *The Lord of the Rings*, for example, while others have mentioned animated motion pictures such as *FernGully* and *The Lion King*, or television programs, such as the Gaia-themed cartoon series *Captain Planet* (Taylor 2010, 127–55). As a result of such testimonies, I am more inclined to expect that a film like *Avatar* will inspire some viewers to become activists or to deepen such commitments, if they are already present. Moreover, while I think Justice's concern that the exaggerated good-versus-evil characters in *Avatar* could preclude some from connecting the film to trends and events in their own histories and worlds, I doubt that this is usually the case. Many statements that audience members have made about the film, including those reported in this volume, indicate that they recognize that the film is a melodrama that exaggerates characters to get audiences rooting for one side over the other. I doubt, therefore, that its oversimplifications would significantly reduce the extent to which audiences would draw the messages the filmmaker intended to convey.

Cameron's Intentions, Strategy, and Affinity with "Dark Green" Nature Spirituality

Unlike most critics of the film, I think it is important (and a matter of fairness) to consider what Cameron has said about his intentions for the film and to note his rejoinders to the most prevalent criticisms of it.

In the prologue to this volume, I noted Cameron's intention to use *Avatar* to help people appreciate the "miracle of the world that we have right here" and to understand that all living things are interconnected and mutually dependent (Associated Press 2010). I noted also Cameron's biocentric sentiments, expressed in public statements of concern about anthropogenic species extinctions.[22] These sentiments were also shown in Cameron's delight that many of *Avatar*'s viewers took the side of nature against the destructive forces of an expansionist human civilization, even expressing support for those engaged in direct action resistance to such forces here on Earth and, on many occasions, calling for more people to become "warriors for Mother Earth."[23] Moreover, in his 1994 *Avatar* scriptment, Cameron expresses the respect he has for indigenous peoples and their often animistic spiritualities, lending credence to such spiritual perceptions through his character Jake Sully, who comes to respect the Na'vi people and their own perceptual horizons, including their belief that the forest "is alive with invisible dynamic forces" (Cameron 1994). In an official *Confidential Report on the Biological and Social History of Pandora*, also subtitled *An Activist Survival Guide*, these and related themes are also expressed, from the need to celebrate the "magic and mystery" and "interconnectedness" of nature to the recognition of biotic kinship (symbolized in the movie by the neural "queue" at the end of the Na'vi's braids). Readers are also urged to "Fight for the Earth!" (Wilhelm and Mathison 2009a, xiii, xv, xiv, 72, 31).

All of these themes are characteristic of what I have called "dark green religion" and provide evidence that Cameron has affinities with at least the non-theistic forms of such spirituality. (Cameron has forthrightly stated that he is an atheist.)[24] Additional characteristics typical of such spirituality include feelings of awe and wonder at the mysteries of the universe, peace and contentment when in the midst of relatively healthy environmental systems, and humility rooted in an understanding that like all other organisms, sooner or later, we are all part of the food chain. Cameron has expressed just such feelings and views, as, for example, when describing the peace he feels in the ocean, especially when underwater, where no one "knows who you are. You're just part of the food chain" (Keegan 2009, 212). For many who have affinity with dark green spirituality, understanding that death is the necessary wellspring of new life also eliminates the fear of death. Cameron imputes just such a perspective to the Na'vi, who "are brave and unafraid of death because they know it is part of a greater cycle" (254).

Indeed, at the very heart of dark green spirituality are *feelings* of belonging and connection to nature—and the *recognition* that all living things belong to nature, for they all emerge from, depend upon, and return to

Earth. Cameron has often and directly expressed such feelings, as when responding to an interviewer who asked him whether changes in the natural world that he had witnessed had influenced his creation of *Avatar*. Cameron answered that his "sense of a connection to nature" leads him to want to halt the widespread destruction of the natural world and that since he is a filmmaker, he tries to make a difference through the cinematic arts (Suozzi 2010). Cameron's often-expressed affirmation of the importance of connecting with nature was probably part of his motivation in making *Aliens of the Deep* (co-directed with Steven Quale in 2005), a documentary that introduces viewers to the wonders of the ocean's depths. More evidence about his desire to help people connect to nature can be discerned in his response to a question about the meaning of *Avatar*. He replied that in the movie, he tried to address critical questions about our relationships to other people and other cultures, and "our relationship with the natural world at a time of nature-deficit disorder" (in Louv 2010). The phrase "nature-deficit disorder," coined by Richard Louv (2005), reflects a common environmentalist (and dark green) belief that time in nature is essential if people are to reconnect with the sources of their being and reharmonize with life on Earth.[25]

Cameron obviously values documentaries and understands that they can help to educate and mobilize the public in positive ways, but he also recognizes that "they're usually watched by people who already understand the problem, as opposed to a piece of global mass entertainment that will reach everybody" (Suozzi 2010). So with *Avatar*, instead of just trying to provide information and provoke "a kind of intellectual reaction," Cameron sought to evoke "a powerful, emotional" response (ibid.). This alone is not enough, Cameron acknowledges, for a film like *Avatar* does not tell people what to do. He does think, however, that such art can precipitate action.

Cameron wanted, of course, to remind audiences about colonial histories wherein one group invades and steals the land or resources from indigenous cultures, "sometimes wiping them out completely, to the point that we don't have many truly indigenous cultures left in this world" (Dunham 2012, 192). For Cameron, this is not merely of historical interest but a source of outrage, as was apparent in his resistance to pressure by the studio to define "unobtanium"—I surmise because he wanted to keep its metaphorical flexibility so that the film's message could be read as relevant to diverse historical and current events. As Cameron put it, "Unobtanium is beaver pelts in French colonial Canada.... It's diamonds in South Africa. It's tea to the nineteenth-century British. It's oil to twentieth-century America. It's just another in a long list of substances that cause one group of people to get into ships and go kick the shit out of another group of people to take what is growing on or buried under their ancestral lands" (Keegan 2009, 253). "We do the same thing with nature—we take what we need and we don't give back, and we've got to start giving back" (Dunham 2012, 192).[26]

Put simply, Cameron's stated goal in *Avatar* was to evoke in audiences "an emotional reaction to how we relate to nature" so that they will "wind up looking at things from the side of the Na'vi, with their deep respect for nature" (193). Cameron hopes that this will promote dramatic change in global consciousness and behaviour: "I'm hoping there will be a continued conversation around *Avatar* and around the needs and wishes that will elevate the consciousness and help us get the things done that need to be done. That's my new mission" (201). Some of his critics, of course, are disparaging of his strategic vision.[27] One can judge Cameron's strategic choices to be ineffective or morally suspect, but it only seems fair to acknowledge that he has thought deeply about how best to communicate ideas dramatically at variance with the most prevalent beliefs and assumptions undergirding contemporary industrial societies.

Cameron's Responses to Criticisms

Cameron has responded directly to a number of the most common criticisms of *Avatar*. To the charge that *Avatar* was extremely expensive and did nothing to challenge the consumerism that drives the destruction of native peoples and environmental systems, Cameron is unapologetic, noting that the film generates profits and in so doing helps many people to make a living (Dunham 2012, 196). But he has acknowledged that consumerism is a key problem, commenting that through our consumer appetites, "market forces cause a continuous expansion of our industrial presence, our extraction industries and so on," which is clearly linked to the destruction of indigenous societies and the habitats upon which they depend (Suozzi 2010). Yet he also speaks passionately of the tragic, global loss of indigenous knowledge and asserts that all of humanity has much to learn from indigenous societies: "The main point is that there is a value-system that they naturally have that has allowed them to live in harmony with nature for a long time and those principles, that wisdom, that spiritual connection to the world, that sense of responsibility to each other, that's the thing that we need to learn. It's a complete reboot of how we see things. I'm not even sure we can do it, but if there is hope, it lies in our ability to have a sea change in our consciousness—to not take more than we give" (ibid.). Cameron has also explicitly rejected the "white messiah" critique, responding to an interviewer, "I don't buy that.... I don't think that any of these indigenous people that see their reality in the film felt that at all." He added that the reaction of the indigenous people has "been overwhelmingly positive" (while acknowledging that he could be unaware of criticisms from such peoples). He then emphasized that the very survival of indigenous people is at stake as "a highly mechanized, industrialised force" destroys their forests. "When all you've got to fight back with is bows and arrows, there has to be intervention from the international community. So I don't care what race the messiahs are, but we all have to be those messiahs, we have to help these people because you can't stop a bulldozer with a bow and arrow."

Of course, in these statements, Cameron expresses an oversimplified view of indigenous cultures and what resistance entails: clearly, not all native peoples and cultures, all the time, live in harmony with nature, let alone with one another (Krech 1999; Harkin and Lewis 2007; Potts and Hayden 2008). Moreover, when such cultures have elected to resist invaders violently, they have often used weapons other than bows and arrows. Nevertheless, Cameron is correct that where indigenous people have secured concessions or (more rarely) territorial integrity in the face of expansionist cultures, allies, even colonial ones, have usually played important roles. Cameron also understands that such allies can come from surprising places, such as anthropologists and biodiversity scientists, who today are generally much more sensitive to the needs and rights of indigenous people than in the past (Suozzi 2010, Taylor 2012). Cameron also appears to be aware that relationships between indigenous peoples and prospective allies are typically bedevilled with mistrust, misperception, and misunderstanding. Still, Cameron believes that by raising awareness and evoking sympathy through the film and by helping to dramatize specific injustices presently unfolding through his high public profile, he can help to give a voice to indigenous leaders. Although Cameron insisted, "I don't want to speak for them," he was obviously pleased that by dramatizing the plight of Amazonian Indians resisting a large dam project in Brazil, he had helped to give them "a bit of a spotlight to speak for themselves" (Suozzi 2010).

The Importance of Allies

Cameron is correct about the importance of allies. Indeed, there are many Earthly examples of *Avatar*'s plot line, wherein someone from a technologically dominant, invading culture defends the invaded culture, sometimes even "going native." Scott Littleton (2011), for example, points to the example of Gonzalo Guerrero in the sixteenth century. Guerrero, a soldier with the invading Spanish conquistadors, joined the Mayan resistance, and, because of his knowledge of Spanish military tactics, helped repel the invaders for a significant period of time. Littleton concludes that the resistance apparently ended shortly after Guerrero was killed, showing that the happy ending of

Avatar in these sorts of stories is "very hard to achieve in real life" (210). But Littleton also accurately notes a number of examples in which anthropologists embraced the cultures they came to study and have done their best to defend them against more powerful, impinging cultures (208–9).

My own work (including with collaborators) has documented cases in which, despite missteps and misunderstandings, activists, scientists, and other concerned people have been able to work sincerely and over the long term with native peoples; through such engagements, mutual learning and respect can develop, sometimes even leading to significant victories (Taylor 1995a, b; 1997a, b). Occasionally, these successes, which have to do with preventing some further or new injustice, are directly related to the concrete solidarity provided by actors who publicize the injustice and resistance to it, forcing changes—through public scrutiny and, sometimes, outrage—to corporate and/or governmental plans (Taylor 1995a; Adamson 2012a). Rob Nixon, who has tried to foster a rapprochement between post-colonial critics and the environmentalists who are often their targets, has spotlighted the importance of writer-activists and media "spectacle" in slowing or arresting the often invisible "slow violence" of environment-degrading imperial histories and profit-driven social systems. According to Nixon (2011), in the absence of spectacle-driven public attention, great injustices are all the more likely to occur and remain unchallenged. In 1995, for example, the Nigerian military executed the Ogoni indigenous-rights activist Ken Saro-Wiwa, who was fighting Shell Oil and government corruption in his people's homeland. Nixon notes how little international attention his case received before the execution, which made the regime think it could get away with killing an eloquent opponent, even though most observers considered the case bogus and the trial unfair.[28] It is just such a "deficit of spectacle," as Joni Adamson (2012a, 145) aptly puts it, that writers and filmmakers of various sorts can help to overcome.

Adamson cites, for example, the way the documentary *Crude: The Real Price of Oil* (2009), along with a number of celebrities and activist attorneys from the United States, contributed to the strategy and public attention that made easier an $18 billion civil judgment against the Chevron Oil Company that was filed on behalf of affected Amazonian Indians.[29] Adamson also discusses the ways in which indigenous activists have seen their own struggles reflected in *Avatar* and have used the film to dramatize their plights and campaigns. She notes, for example, that Cameron has joined the battle against the gigantic Belo Monte Dam in the Brazilian Amazon, which is threatening a number of indigenous tribes there (see Barrionuevo 2010). Working with the environmental justice group Amazon Watch, Cameron spoke out against the dam and helped produce an educational film contending that its construction would violate indigenous rights and critically important rainforest habitats.[30] As Adamson put it when summarizing one of her central contentions: "Blockbuster films and documentaries are playing an increasingly important role in global environmental justice struggles," or as she put it elsewhere, in "indigenous cosmopolitics" (Adamson 2012a, 146; see also Adamson 2013).[31]

Developing cross-cultural and international alliances to protect vulnerable peoples and habitats is difficult, however. Two volumes have focused attention specifically on the difficulties and possibilities of indigenous/non-indigenous alliances (Haig-Brown and Nock 2006; Davis 2010). All involved agree that developing such alliances demands deep commitment and, usually, long-term hard work. As the scholar of indigenous knowledge Leanne Simpson (Alderville First Nation, Canada) puts it in her introduction to the Davis volume, "Those of us involved in the movement for indigenous self-determination and social and environmental justice are well aware that every hard-fought victory has been a direct result of the alliances and relationships of solidarity we have forged, maintained, and nurtured with supporting Indigenous nations, environmental networks, and social justice organizations" (Davis 2010, xiii). Simpson also notes that while "building relationships with our supporters has been a key strategy in our movement for change," despite good intentions, "these relationships do not always come easily. Too often they have been wrought with cross-cultural misunderstandings, poor communication, stereotypes, and racism" (xiii–xiv).[32]

Despite such difficulties, the subsequent reflections in Davis's volume demonstrate the importance of alliances across diverse scales, from global campaigns to pass the United Nations Declaration on the Rights of Indigenous Peoples to local campaigns to protect native territories and lands (Davis 2010).[33] I was struck when reading this work, just as I have been with the generous tone of the indigenous elders and intellectuals on the occasions when my fieldwork has been in or near Native North American territories. In contrast, one rarely hears non-native activists or intellectuals, perhaps especially those immersed in post-colonial discourses, stress the unity of human beings or the responsibility that we have toward "all life," let alone the importance of forgiveness and love, as have the elder and scholar Gkisedtanamoogk and several others (see especially Woodworth 2010; Swamp 2010; Gkisedtanamoogk 2010; Da Silva 2010; and Christian and Freeman 2010).[34]

Moreover, some who have been closely tracking developments within grassroots social/environmental movements perceive a new kind of politics emerging that rejects—or at least seeks to transcend—tense relations between peoples of the Global North and South, and between environmental and social justice activists. Instead, there are those who try to embrace what Isabel Stengers calls "cosmopolitics," and Marisol de la Cadena "multinaturalism," in which nature is understood to have its own value and agency, and dualistic perceptions of a disconnect between the interests of human and other organisms are considered inaccurate and shortsighted (Stengers 2005; De la Cadena 2010).[35]

In a striking passage that draws on Stengers, De la Cadena, Good Fox, Bruno Latour, and others, Adamson (2012a, 347) links the new cosmopolitics to *Avatar*:

> What is astonishing about indigenous groups linking their own regionally specific movements to *Avatar* is not that a blockbuster film is playing in India or the Andes or the Amazon; it is that the "things" that *Avatar* is helping to "make public"...are living systems (mountains, rivers, forests, deserts) that may help inaugurate a politics that is more plural not because the people enacting it are bodies marked by race or ethnicity demanding rights, or by environmentalists representing nature, but because they force into visibility the culture-nature divide that has prevented multiple worlds and species from being recognized as deserving the right to maintain and continue their vital cycles.

The emergence of such a multi-natural, multi-ethnic, trans-national cosmopolitics—which has a religious dimension that the political theorist Dan Deudney and I have discussed as "civil" or "terrapolitan" Earth religion—is indeed coming into view.[36] The most important examples of such cosmopolitics may be found in the Ecuadorian Constitution (passed in 2008) and in Bolivian legislation (passed in 2009). Drawing in part on Andean indigenous spiritualities, in a stunning innovation for nation-states, these nations conferred rights on nature.[37] A long-odds effort to gain United Nations ratification for the "Universal Declaration of the Rights of Mother Earth," which draws on Ecuador's constitution and the Bolivian law, was subsequently proposed by Bolivia's President Evo Morales and has been studied and promoted by the UN's Permanent Forum on Indigenous Issues.[38]

An increasing number of scholars, likewise, seem to be gravitating toward a much more comprehensive anti-colonial perspective, one that rejects not only the domination of one human group over another but also the human domination of other organisms and environmental systems as a whole. This nascent but promising trend promotes a holistic vision that seeks to make visible and precipitate resistance to violations of the right of all living beings to live and flourish (Naess 1973, 1989; Stone 1974; Cullinan 2003; Linzey and Campbell 2009; Latour and Weibel 2005;

Latour 2011a; Apffel-Marglin 2011; Huggan and Tiffin 2010; Nixon 2011; DeLoughrey and Handley 2011).[39]

Truth in the Fiction of *Avatar*'s Cosmogony

Every work of art is subject to interpretation and critique, and I hope that *Avatar and Nature Spirituality* will be valued for provoking the kinds of discussions over issues of the rights of nature and of indigenous peoples that the filmmaker, and even some of those who were ambivalent about the film, had hoped might result. My perception is, however, that most of the critics, even those especially sensitive to and supportive of indigenous sovereignty, have not fully appreciated the extent to which *Avatar* is a true story. An exception to the rule is the progressive British commentator George Monbiot (2010), who, although he is critical of some aspects of the film (and especially the "preposterous" happy ending), nevertheless calls *Avatar* "a profound, insightful, important film" because it spotlights both a long history of ongoing genocidal campaigns against indigenous people that "no one wants to hear, because of the challenge it presents to the way we choose to see ourselves." He concludes that it "speaks of a truth more important—and more dangerous—than those contained in a thousand arthouse movies." I agree.

Although it is a work of fiction, *Avatar* metaphorically presents a generally true cosmogony, or narrative about how the world came to be the way it is. The steady and now intensifying erosion of Earth's biological and cultural diversity has been, first and foremost, the result of a ten thousand–year process that began with the domestication of plant and animal species and the advent of agriculture. Since the lands that agricultures need for expansion are almost always already inhabited, agricultural civilizations are *necessarily* imperial, although not in every phase of expansion violently so. As Steven Stoll (2007, 56) puts it, agrarian societies generate large populations so they must expand if their subsequent generations are "to reproduce the material world of their parents." As such societies expand, they kill or displace through threat or coercion the pre-existing gatherer-hunters, or they convert them into agriculturalists, either by convincing them of benefits (e.g., greater food security), or of the idea that their best chance for survival is to assimilate. Whatever its specific characteristics in different times and places, this process has precipitated the dramatic, global decline of both cultural and biological diversity (Amery 1976; Diamond 1987, 1997; LaDuke 1999; Lockwood and McKinney 2001; Marsh [1864] 1970; Mason 1993; Oelschlaeger 1992; Ponting 2007; Shepard 1992, 1998; Stoll 2007; Wolfe 2006; Williams 2003). This is, moreover, a process saturated with religious significance and legitimation: the now predominant so-called world religions have fuelled and legitimated this process.[40] In the West, for example, forests were seen as a threat to Christian civilization—indeed, as the "last strongholds of pagan worship" (Harrison 1992, 61). But the religious agricultures (agrarian societies) of Asia have been no kinder to indigenous peoples or biologically diverse environmental systems. Thus, the long antipathy of agriculture toward indigenous peoples, even if not universal, has been the general trend and continuing dynamic. (A few of the many recent examples include Barton 2010; Douthat 2010; Beisner, n.d.; and Stewart, n.d.). This antipathy is obvious to anyone who studies how the ongoing deracination of indigenous peoples from their lands continues in those regions of the world only recently reached by agricultural civilizations, which are now all the more destructive, powered by capital, fossil fuels, and industrial machinery.

Avatar presents but one extreme depiction of the everyday reality in which biocultural diversity is threatened by advancing agro-industrial civilizations. It is not didactic: it does not explicitly teach about the diverse ways in which such civilization spreads. It does not explain, for example, the ways in which the "settler colonialism" of virtually all agricultural peoples is violent (if not always obviously so). Nor does it point the finger at who has benefited, whether directly or indirectly (Wolfe 2006). Nevertheless, as Cameron and some of his critics hoped, the film opens the way for discussions of the dynamics that lead to the violation of human rights and the widespread destruction of environmental systems, and it does so by evoking sympathy, if in a metaphorical way, for the many victims of these processes. It can, therefore, provide social and environmental activists with educational openings and recruitment opportunities for their causes.

The Mythic and Political Possibilities of Motion Picture Spectacles

James Cameron has said that in *Avatar*, he aspired to mythic movie making, and myths, of course, orient people to their worlds and shape actions within them. It could well be that the cinematic arts provide the most powerful medium for myth making in the modern world. "Of modern art forms," Adrian Ivakhiv (2013) insightfully writes in *Ecologies of the Moving Image*, "it is cinema—the art of the moving image—that comes closest to depicting reality itself, because reality is always in motion, always in a process of becoming." According to Ivakhiv, film also "provides for the morphogenesis, the coming into form, of worlds." And it is especially important to note that the "spectacle" of cinema is related to its affective power, and that cinema can thus serve an ethical function, to "revivify our relationship to the world."[41] In the sixth chapter of his book, Ivakhiv provides a nuanced reading of *Avatar* that could profitably be read alongside the analyses in this volume. Like many of the critics whom he sympatheti-cally cites, he is not sanguine about the film mobilizing people in the cause of social and environmental justice. But he also suggests that the critics may be too hasty in their judgments, because "a film is not only what hap-pens between the dimming and the turning back up of the lights. It is also what happens in our discussions, dreams, and lives as we work with the images, sounds, and symbols it makes available to us." So while Ivakhiv concurs with some other critics that the film grossly oversimplifies the world's complex political dynamics, he concludes that it also "has pre-sented opportunities for activists to stake their own cases" and, moreover, that "fandom, once triggered, sets off on its own trajectories, which in this case may include those that turn viewers into radical activists."

It is quite clear that the film has not led to massive consciousness change or a new army of indigenous and environmental rights activists. Yet it has not been entirely without its desired impacts, either. Its fruits include not only the attitude shifts that we've documented in this volume but also more tangible results. On 8 February 2011, the Earth Day Network announced what is probably the most concrete activist outcome: the partners involved in the "Avatar Home Tree Initiative" had succeeded in mobilizing over thirty-one thousand individuals in planting over one million trees.[42] And the previous examples of literature and film moving people emotionally and then to action, combined with the examples of modest mobilization following the film documented in this volume, suggests that the film is playing, and probably will continue to play, at least some role in environ-mental mobilization.

It would be best to make neither too much nor too little of the potential power of the arts in general, and cinema in particular, in changing atti-tudes and altering behaviour. After all, social and environmental activists deploy many strategies toward just such an end—mostly they lose and usually their successes are limited and reversible. It is better to see a film like *Avatar* as both *reflecting* broad, if nascent and fragile, cultural shifts and emerging sensitivities, as well as *contributing* to them. Whether one judges such social changes as positive or negative, it will probably remain impossible to determine their future trajectory, given that environmental and social systems are complex and that the decisive variables, feedback loops, and tipping points, if any, are difficult to discern. Far better, then, to understand *Avatar* (including the envisioned sequels) as innovative ethi-cal and spiritual cultural productions that are, as the military officer cited earlier put it, calling people toward the better angels of their natures.

Although I cannot predict the impact of *Avatar*, I do find hopeful many of the typical responses to it, wherein people are moved by its depiction of a beautiful forest and a flourishing forest culture living in respectful reciprocity with the diverse biota of its surround. I am encouraged that some who see it feel outrage at the injustice and destruction wrought by the invaders and joy when the riotous chorus of life arises to repel them. I doubt that most of those who felt such things had the cognitive frames to understand the tragic and long-term histories to which the film alluded. Nor do I think most audience members realize that the battles melodramatically depicted in the film are going on right now, let alone that their own societies, and the ideologies and worldviews that undergird them, are highly complicit in these destructive dynamics. Nor do most audience members know that it is possible to support, if not directly participate in, the resistance to the ongoing reduction of Earth's biocultural complexity. But the film can reinforce such understandings where they exist or can lead people to them where they do not. Activists of all sorts, if not all of the film's critics, have been quick to recognize that *Avatar* has provided them with an unusual opportunity to educate and organize those moved by the film into communities of solidarity and resistance.

I especially find it hopeful that when a film reveals the beauties of Earth's living systems (even if through the artifice of spectacular technology and Earth's metaphorical displacement to another planet) and reminds audience members (or reveals to them) what is being and has been lost, a significant number of viewers are moved and wish there was something they could do to prevent or reverse the losses. Perhaps this suggests the plausibility of the biophilia hypothesis, which was discussed appreciatively by a number of the contributors to this volume. The biophilia hypothesis was originally advanced by Harvard biologist E. O. Wilson and soon afterward, by his protege Steven Kellert and a number of others (Wilson 1984; Kellert and Wilson 1993; Kellert 2007). The basic notion is that there is a universal (if sometimes weak and forgotten) human aesthetic appreciation for biologically diverse and flourishing environmental systems, and this is because we know somehow, unconsciously, from deep down in our genome, that these are the systems in which we flourish. In short, we appreciate natural beauty not just because our cultures shape our aesthetics, even though they certainly do, but because the appreciation of wild nature is an adaptive evolutionary trait. This theory, if correct, would help to explain why the aesthetic appreciation of nature is part of the emotional repertoire of our species. And if this is the case, it may be that the power of many artistic productions, including *Avatar*, is to be found in the diverse, religion-resembling ways that they express and evoke such feelings.

I began my effort to understand the significance of *Avatar* by wondering if it was another example of the increasing influence and cultural traction of what I have called "dark green religion." If it does exemplify such spirituality, I wanted to know whether it was a salutary or dangerous form of it. Clearly, some critics have judged it harshly. Like many other academicians, had I made the film, I would have anticipated and avoided some of these criticisms. That is easy to say, of course, as I have neither the talent nor the experience or vision to make such a film. It is clear that Cameron is unsurpassed in his ability to draw millions to his films, which evoke strong emotions and sometimes even inspire critical reflection and action. Whatever the critics may say, *Avatar* may be more promising as a means for revisioning our relations to nature and understanding the injustices that accompany its destruction than not only a thousand art house films but also university courses, radical political commentaries, and scholarly books. Nevertheless, *Avatar* did not emerge from a vacuum, so whatever genius lies behind it is not that of one man. Rather, it is a reflection of the increasing global awareness of the value of both biological and cultural diversity and of the ways in which all of today's dominant civilizations continue to erode them. At the same time, it also reflects diverse new ways in which people today express and promote reverence for life. *Avatar*, as well as much of the reaction to it, suggests that a gestalt change in consciousness may indeed be emerging. How extensive and effective this will be remains to be seen... perhaps even in the forthcoming *Avatar* sequels and their reception.

Notes

1 See "Resisting the Green Dragon" at http://www.resistingthegreendragon.com/, Cornwall Alliance for the Stewardship of Creation at http://www.Cornwall Alliance.org, and, especially, Beisner (n.d.) and Wanliss (2011).

2 See "*Avatar* Movie Is Evil," an undated critique at http://www.jesus-is-savior.com/ Evils%20in%20America/Hellivision/avatar_is_evil.htm.

3 A paper by University of California, Santa Cruz, sociologist Bernard Daly Zaleha, "'Our Only Heaven': Nature Veneration, Quest Religion, and Pro-Environment Behavior" (2013), which he kindly shared with me and my students during a National Endowment for the Humanities Seminar in July 2011, provides an excellent review of research showing that in America and Europe, where we have the best data, panentheistic and other nature-venerating religions are on the rise, even within Christian churches, and that orthodox Christian monotheism is in modest but significant decline. The fears of Christian conservatives about slippage in their preferred forms of the faith appear to be borne out by existing quantitative data. See also Zaleha (2008, 2010).

4 His post was made on 15 January 2010 and, while signed with his name and rank, his screen name was "JUDGEBIANCHINI." His comments and the fascinating and diverse reactions to *Avatar* were posted at the Military Times Forum, http://www.militarytimes.com/forum/archive/index.php/t-1584779.html, but have since been removed.

5 Some of this text had disappeared on 5 April 2012, as it had over three hundred comments in response to it.

6 "*Avatar* Made Me Want to Throw Up," 19 December 2009, http://forums.anandtech .com/showthread.php?t=2034216.

7 For a good overview of the diversity of post-colonial thinking about *Avatar*, see Thomas (2010).

8 Literary scholar and post-colonial theorist Anthony Carrigan, who read a draft of this article, pointed out, citing Žižek (1991, 34–35) that this antipathy has been longstanding for Žižek.

9 My account here is based on decades-long research and fieldwork within radical environmental subcultures, including since the release of *Avatar*.

10 This reharmonization is often seen as involving the collapse possibly precipitated by insurrection of authoritarian and ecologically unsustainable industrial agricultures; see Zerzan (1994) and Jensen (2006a, b).

11 See http://johnzerzan.net/radio/.

12 Adrian Ivakhiv (2013) provides a nuanced review of the critiques of the film, including more details on the contending views of the film expressed by anthropologists.

13 One of the anonymous reviewers of this manuscript noted that here I was disagreeing with Chris Klassen's article in this volume and wondered why, then, I included it in the volume. Klassen defined *misogyny* in the most literal way, as hatred of women, and I did not find compelling her contention that the deaths of Augustine and Chacon evidence misogyny. Given this definition, I also doubt her assertion that misogyny is "nearly universal," even if it is all too common. But it would violate my expressed intention to promote engagement and debate about the film to exclude views with which I disagree.

14 Anthony Carrigan (personal communication, 12 May 2012) is probably correct that some gender commentators would probably complain that by creating characters that mirror masculine traits, Cameron does little to disrupt assumptions about conventional gender roles. I have not found such critiques published, however, and I think, moreover, that there is more complexity to Cameron's characters than such a criticism would acknowledge.

15 For a similar argument and many other scathing and sardonic criticisms of the film, see John Clark (as Cafard 2010). Clark concludes that *Avatar* in no way promotes resistance to the "global system of domination" and in fact, "no message will have a salutary effect in the real world, if that message is transmitted through the dominant media."

16 For similar views on the constructive possibilities presented by the film, see Latour (2011a) and Clifford (2011).

17 All Good Fox quotes are from this essay, which I highly recommend.

18 Rachelle Gould and her collaborators (this volume) made a similar point about analogies.

19 Several of the earlier articles in this volume noted that Sully is as much if not more saved than saviour in the film; a different argument against the "white messiah" charge is that Eywa, "the planetary mind," is actually the saviour (Pilkington 2011, 39). Pilkington, moreover, argues that those who consider the film racist are willfully misreading the film's plot and particularly the events in the final battle, con-

cluding, "Alas, not everyone who went to see Avatar left his or her expectations and prejudices behind" (68).

20 Bresette, an Ojibwe activist and enrolled member of the Loon clan of the Red Cliff Band of Lake Superior Chippewa, was a co-founder of the Wisconsin Green Party, and an ardent opponent to mining in his homeland (present-day Wisconsin). The Indian-environmentalist alliance, which had significant successes during the 1990s, is detailed in Whaley and Bresette (1994); see also Gedicks (1993, 1995). McIntosh recalls Bresette saying, as part of the ceremony, "We must all learn to be indigenous now" (Williams, Roberts, and McIntosh 2011, 426; cf. McIntosh 1998).

21 Bresette's was not the only Native American voice expressing such a view. In a way that reminds me of Bresette's welcoming ceremony, William Woodworth (Raweno:Kwas, of Mohawk heritage) wrote: "The Hotinonshon:ni prophecy of the gathering of peoples from the four directions under the White Pine Tree of Peace appears to be coming to fruition. The time has come for Indigenous peoples to share their ancient responsibilities to welcome and host visitors to their home-lands" (Woodworth 2010, 25).

22 The kind of language he used at the Golden Globe Awards ceremony (quoted in the prologue to this volume and found at http://www.accesshollywood.com/james -camerons-avatar-wins-big-at-golden-globes_article_27831) is common for Cameron. Similarly, he told his biographer: "All life on Earth is connected...but our indus-trial society...will inevitably lead to a severe degradation of biodiversity and ultimately to a serious blowback effect against humanity" (quoted in Keegan 2009, 254).

23 See, for example, his Earth Day speech in April 2010 at http://www.youtube.com/ watch?v=YDHkO5-Hf78, and the video introduction at the "*Avatar* Home Tree Initiative" website, http://www.avatarmovie.com/hometree/. Cameron attributed the success of the film to increasing eco-social consciousness, while also noting the strong resistance to such understandings.

24 Cameron has "sworn off agnosticism," labelling it "cowardly atheism," according to biographer Rebecca Keegan, who recorded Cameron as adding, "I've come to the position that in the complete absence of any supporting data whatsoever for the persistence of the individual in some spiritual form, it is necessary to operate under the provisional conclusion that there is no afterlife and then be ready to amend that if I find it otherwise" (quoted in Keegan 2009, 8).

25 Louv himself recognized Cameron's affinity with such a view by writing an open letter to him that was published in *Psychology Today*, appealing to Cameron for help in creating a mass back-to-nature movement (Louv 2010). Louv was hardly the first to express the views that made him a well-known environmental writer; for those who beat him to the argument, see Shepard (1982) and Nabhan and Trimble (1994).

26 Cameron has long sought to include socially important messages in his films, criti-cizing class divisions in Titanic, for example (Cameron and Dunham 2011).

27 Cameron made another statement that those who want to force reparations on those who have benefited from past injustices would find objectionable: he contended that one of the great things about science fiction is that it can make us seriously "look at the human condition" without causing the kind of defensiveness that comes when charges and blame is directly assigned. As Cameron put it in an interview, science fiction "can hold up a mirror to all of us without pushing specific buttons of your

worse than—this guy's worse than this guy, you see what I mean? Science fiction doesn't really predict the future, that's not what it's there for. It's there to hold a mirror up to the present and look at the human condition, sometimes from the outside" (Cameron and Dunham 2011, 193).

28 Anthony Carrigan (personal communication 12 May 2012) astutely observed when reviewing this point in the chapter that there is an important level of complexity here that the film does not choose to engage due to the decision to stage its colonial encounter as a moment of relatively new contact. In so many places today, one of the most enduring legacies of colonialism has been the establishment of governments co-opted by ruling class and/or military elites that work against the interests of a wider if often characteristically fractured public sphere. In short, part of the film's more romanticized approach is to give primacy to colonial contact struggles over the even messier and intractable neocolonial realities that are much closer to the problems faced by most oppressed groups today globally.

  While I agree with the facts expressed in his statement, I doubt that a film more focused in a complex way on the contemporary world would have drawn a mass audience. In my judgment, *Avatar* provides a unique opportunity for scholars and activists to build on the understandings and empathies that the film arouses. There is a temptation among intellectuals to want a theatrical filmmaker to make the documentary they would have made, but I think it is wiser to welcome the efforts of such artists, for these are not just matters of the head and sophisticated analyses—they are matters of the heart.

29 Chevron's appeal of the judgment was rejected in January 2012; see "Ecuador Appeals Court Rules against Chevron in Oil Case," BBC News, 4 January 2012, http://www.bbc.co.uk/news/world-latin-america-16404268.

30 See "Stop the Belo Monte Monster Dam" at http://amazonwatch.org/work/belo-monte-dam, and the video "A Message from Pandora," 27 August 2010, at http://amazonwatch.org/news/2011/0907-message-from-pandora, in which Cameron shows not only that he has worked hard to understand the issues, but also that he has—as far as can be seen—attempted to work in respectful solidarity with the indigenous people and social activists whom he met there.

31 Despite these protests, Brazil's Supreme Court overturned lower court rulings suspending the dam's construction in August 2012, but the battle has continued at the site. Although hundreds of fishers and indigenous people have occupied the site, halting construction for weeks at a time, as this volume goes to the press in the spring of 2013, it appears that the Brazilian government is likely to succeed in building the dam (Associated Press 2012, Hance 2012).

32 For a similar statement by the volume's editor, see Davis (2010, 4). Simpson is of Michi Saagiik Nishnaabeg ancestry, is a member of Alderville First Nation, and has published these books on indigenous movements: see Simpson (2008, 2011b) and Ladner and Simpson (2010).

33 See especially part 2, 55–210, "From the Front Lines," which "documents concrete examples of alliance-building," including the "successes, tensions, and complexities" (Davis 2010, 8). Thomas (2010) mentions several post-colonial theorists who have also stressed the importance of alliances.

34 I wonder if "decolonizing" one's mind can include incorporating these sorts of perspectives from indigenous peoples. In 1994, Edward Said described environ-

mentalism as "the indulgence of spoiled tree huggers who lack a proper cause." It is no wonder, therefore, that so many of his progeny have had antipathy toward environmentalists and have failed to see that protecting environmental systems is critical to human well-being as well as the rest of the living world; for this quotation, see Nixon (2011, 332n69) and the related text (250–55).

35 Latour (2011a) has also used the term *multinaturalism*; I do not know who coined it.

36 For a discussion of an emerging "civil earth religion," see Deudney (1995, 1996, 1998), in which he coined the term *terrapolitan*, and Taylor (2010a, 180–99; 2010b).

37 Joni Adamson (personal communication, 24 July 2012), who kindly reviewed this manuscript, commented at this point that these groups were not foregrounding spirituality or ethnicity, for fear of being dismissed as "superstitious," but instead were emphasizing rights—first civil, then non-human. She also noted that they seek a broad coalition based on these rights, regardless of whether individuals practise traditional religion. For more of her views in this regard, see Adamson (2012b).

38 Catherine Eade, "'Mother Earth' to Be Given Same Rights as Humans under UN Plan," *Mail Online*, 12 April 2011, http://www.dailymail.co.uk/news/article -1376244/South-American-countrys-treaty-giving-Mother-Earth-rights-citizens .html. See also the "Study on the Need to Recognize and Respect the Rights of Mother Earth," Permanent Forum on Indigenous Issues of the United Nations, 15 January 2010, at http://www.un.org/ga/search/view_doc.asp?symbol=E/C.19/2010/4.

39 See also the website of the Global Alliance for the Rights of Nature, http://therights ofnature.org/founding-meeting/, and the sources listed there.

40 As Robert Harrison (1992, ix) put it in his study of forests, which applies equally to other wildlands, "The governing institutions of the West—religion, law, family, city—originally established themselves in opposition to the forests, which in this respect have been, from the beginning, the first and last victims of civic expansion." For further discussion, see Taylor (2012).

41 These passages are from the book's foreword. Because I read this excellent book before final proofs, I could not provide pagination, nor am I certain there will be no changes during production, but I cite the manuscript with the generous permission of Professor Ivakhiv.

42 See "Avatar Home Tree Initiative Plants over 1 Million!" Earth Day Network, http:// www.earthday.org/gallery/avatar-home-tree-initiative-plants-over-1-million.

References

AbdelRahim, Layla. 2009. "Avatar: An Anarcho-Primitivist Picture of the History of the World." *Works by Layla AbdelRahim*, 23 December. http://layla.miltsov .org/avatar-an-anarcho-primitivist-picture-of-the-history-of-the-world/.

———. 2010. "Response to Critiques of Avatar That Accuse It of Scientism and Racism." *Works by Layla AbdelRahim*. http://layla.miltsov.org/ response-to-critiques-of-avatar-that-accuse-it-of-scientism-and-racism/.

Adamson, Joni. 2012a. "Indigenous Literatures, Multinaturalism, and *Avatar*: The Emergence of Indigenous Cosmopolitics." *American Literary History* 24(1):143–62.

———. 2012b. "'¡Todos Somos Indios!': Revolutionary Imagination, Alternative Modernity, and Transnational Organizing in the Work of Silko, Tamez, and Anzaldúa." *Journal of Transnational American Studies* 4(1): 1–26.

———. 2013. "Source of Life: Avatar, Amazonia, and an Ecology of Selves." In *Material Ecocriticism*, edited by Serenella Iovion and Serpil Oppermann. Bloomington: University of Indiana Press.

Amery, Carl. 1976. *Natur als Politik: Die ökologische Chance des Menschen* [Nature as politics: The ecological opportunity of humankind]. Reinbek bei Hamburg: Rowohlt.

Apffel-Marglin, Frédérique. 2011. *Subversive Spiritualities: How Rituals Enact the World*. Oxford Ritual Studies Series. Oxford: Oxford University Press.

Associated Press. 2010. "James Cameron's 'Avatar' Wins Big at Golden Globes." Access Hollywood, 17 January. http://www.accesshollywood.com/ james-camerons-avatar-wins-big-at-golden-globes_article_27831.

———. 2012. "Brazil: Court Allows Dam Construction to Resume." *The New York Times*, 28 August 2012. http://www.nytimes.com/2012/08/29/world/ americas/court-allows-dam-construction-to-resume-in-brazil.html?_r=0.

Barrionuevo, Alexei. 2010. "Tribes of Amazon Find an Ally Out of 'Avatar.'" *New York Times*, 10 April. http://www.nytimes.com/2010/04/11/world/ americas/11brazil.html.

Barton, Adriana. 2010. "Eco-Spirituality: Perhaps the Vatican Should Be Worried about Nature Worship." *Globe and Mail*, 25 January. http://www.theglobe andmail.com/life/eco-spirituality-perhaps-the-vatican-should-be-worried -about-nature-worship/article1443672/.

Beisner, E. Calvin. N.d. "The Competing World Views of Environmentalism and Christianity." Cornwall Alliance for the Stewardship of Creation. http://www.cornwallalliance.org/articles/read/the-competing-world-views -of-environmentalism-and-christianity/.

Boaz, David. 2010. "The Right Has 'Avatar' Wrong." *Los Angeles Times*, 26 January. http://articles.latimes.com/2010/jan/26/opinion/la-oe-boaz26-2010jan26.

Cafard, Max. 2010. "Intergalactic Blues: Fantasy and Ideology in *Avatar*." *Psychic Swamp: The Surregional Review*. http://issuu.com/stephanz/docs/ psychic_swamp__1.

Cameron, James. 1994. *Avatar*. Scriptment. http://sfy.ru/?script=avatar.

Christian, Dorothy, and Victoria Freeman. 2010. "The History of Friendship, or Some Thoughts on Becoming Allies." In Davis, *Alliances*, 376–90.

Clifford, James. 2011. "Response to Orin Starn: 'Here Come the Anthros Again: The Strange Marriage of Anthropology and Native America.'" *Cultural Anthropology* 26(2): 218–24.

"Corps Official: *Avatar* 'Sophomoric.'" 2010. *Military Times*, 8 January. http:// www.militarytimes.com/news/2010/01/marine_avatar_010810w/.

Cullinan, Cormac. 2003. *Wild Law: A Manifesto for Earth Justice*. Totnes, UK: Green.

Da Silva, Judy. 2010. "Grassy Narrows: Advocate for Mother Earth and Its Inhabitants." In Davis, *Alliances*, 69–76.

Davis, Lynne. 2010. *Alliances: Re/Envisioning Indigenous–Non-Indigenous Relationships*. Toronto: University of Toronto Press.

De la Cadena, Marisol. 2010. "Indigenous Cosmopolitics in the Andes: Conceptual Reflections beyond 'Politics.'" *Cultural Anthropology* 25(2): 334–70.

DeLoughrey, Elizabeth M., and George B. Handley. 2011. *Postcolonial Ecologies: Literatures of the Environment*. New York: Oxford University Press.

Deudney, Daniel. 1995. "In Search of Gaian Politics: Earth Religion's Challenge to Modern Western Civilization." In Taylor, *Ecological Resistance Movements*, 282–99.

———. 1996. "Ground Identity: Nature, Place, and Space in Nationalism." In *The Return of Culture and Identity in IR Theory*, edited by Yosef Lapid and Friedrich Kratochwil, 129–45. Boulder, CO: Lynne Rienner.

———. 1998. "Global Village Sovereignty: Intergenerational Sovereign Publics, Federal-Republican Earth Constitutions, and Planetary Identities." In *The Greening of Sovereignty in World Politics*, edited by Karen Litfin, 299–325. Cambridge: MIT Press.

Diamond, Jared. 1987. "The Worst Mistake in the History of the Human Race." *Discover*, May.

———. 1997. *Guns, Germs, and Steel: The Fates of Human Societies*. New York: Norton.

Douthat, Ross. 2010. "Heaven and Nature." *New York Times*, 20 December. http://www.nytimes.com/2009/12/21/opinion/21douthat1.html.

Dunham, Brent, ed. 2012. *James Cameron: Interviews*. Conversations with Filmmakers Series. Jackson: University Press of Mississippi.

Gedicks, Al. 1993. *The New Resource Wars: Native and Environmentalist Struggles against Multinational Corporations*. Boston: South End Press.

———. 1995. "International Native Resistance to the New Resource Wars." In Taylor, *Ecological Resistance Movements*, 89–108.

Gkisedtanamoogk. 2010. "Patients Finding Our Way Despite Modernity." In Davis, *Alliances*, 42–53.

Good Fox, Julia. 2010. "Avatars to the Left of Me, Pandora to the Right: An Indigenous Woman Considers James Cameron's *Avatar*." *Good Fox: Culture, Politics, Indian Country*, 21 January. http://juliagoodfox.com/avatar/.

Haig-Brown, Celia, and David A. Nock. 2006. *With Good Intentions: Euro-Canadian and Aboriginal Relations in Colonial Canada*. Vancouver: University of British Columbia Press.

Hance, Jeremy. "Indigenous People Re-Occupy Belo Monte Construction Site." *Mongabay.com*, 9 October 2012. http://news.mongabay.com/2012/1009-hance-belo-monte-reoccupation.html.

Harkin, Michael Eugene, and David Rich Lewis. 2007. *Native Americans and the Environment: Perspectives on the Ecological Indian*. Lincoln: University of Nebraska Press.

Harrison, Robert Pogue. 1992. *Forests: The Shadow of Civilization*. Chicago: University of Chicago Press.

Heise, Ursula K. 2008. *Sense of Place and Sense of Planet: The Environmental Imagination of the Global.* Oxford: Oxford University Press.

Huggan, Graham, and Helen Tiffin. 2010. *Postcolonial Ecocriticism: Literature, Animals, Environment.* London: Routledge.

Ivakhiv, Adrian J. 2013. *Ecologies of the Moving Image: Cinema, Affect, Nature.* Waterloo, ON: Wilfrid Laurier University Press.

James, John, and Tom Ute. 2011. "'I See You': Colonial Narratives and the Act of Seeing in *Avatar.*" In *The Films of James Cameron: Critical Essays*, edited by Matthew Kapell and Stephen McVeigh, 186–99. Jefferson, NC: McFarland.

Jensen, Derrick. 2006a. *The Problem of Civilization.* Vol. 1 of *Endgame.* New York: Seven Stories Press.

———. 2006b. *Resistance.* Vol. 2 of *Endgame.* New York: Seven Stories Press.

Justice, Daniel Heath. 2010. "James Cameron's *Avatar*: Missed Opportunities." *First Peoples: New Directions in Indigenous Studies*, 20 January. http://www.firstpeoplesnewdirections.org/blog/?p=169.

Keegan, Rebecca. 2009. *The Futurist: The Life and Films of James Cameron.* New York: Crown.

Kellert, Stephen R. 2007. "The Biophilia Hypothesis." *Journal for the Study of Religion, Nature, and Culture* 1(1): 25–37.

Kellert, Stephen R., and Edward O. Wilson, eds. 1993. *The Biophilia Hypothesis.* Washington, DC: Island Press.

Krech, Shepard III. 1999. *The Ecological Indian: Myth and History.* New York: Norton.

Ladner, Kiera L., and Leanne Simpson. 2010. *This Is an Honour Song: Twenty Years since the Blockades.* Winnipeg: Arbeiter Ring.

LaDuke, Winona. 1999. *All Our Relations: Native Struggles for Land and Life.* Boston: South End Press.

Latour, Bruno. 2011a. "An Attempt at a 'Compositionist Manifesto.'" *New Literary History* 41: 471–90.

———. 2011b. "Waiting for Gaia: Composing the Common World through Arts and Politics." A lecture at the French Institute, London, November. http://www.bruno-latour.fr/sites/default/files/124-GAIA-LONDON-SPEAP_0.pdf.

Latour, Bruno, and Peter Weibel, eds. 2005, *Making Things Public: Atmospheres of Democracy.* Cambridge, MA: MIT Press; Karlsruhe, Germany: ZKM/Center for Art and Media.

Linde, Harold. 2010. "Is *Avatar* Radical Environmental Propaganda?" *Mother Nature Network*, 4 January. http://www.mnn.com/technology/research-innovations/blogs/is-avatar-radical-environmental-propaganda.

Linzey, Thomas, and Anneke Campbell. 2009. *Be the Change: How to Get What You Want in Your Community.* Salt Lake City: Gibbs Smith.

Littleton, Scott C. 2011. "Gonzalo Guerrero and the Maya Resistance to the Spanish Conquistadors: A Sixteenth-Century 'Avatar' of *Avatar.*" In *The Films of James Cameron: Critical Essays*, edited by Matthew Kapell and Stephen McVeigh, 200–215. Jefferson, NC: McFarland.

Lockwood, Julie L., and Michael L. McKinney. 2001. *Biotic Homogenization*. New York: Springer.

Louv, Richard. 2005. *Last Child in the Woods: Saving Our Children from Nature-Deficit Disorder*. Chapel Hill, NC: Algonquin Books.

———. 2010. "An Open Letter to James Cameron." *Psychology Today*, 24 January. http://www.psychologytoday.com/blog/people-in-nature/201001/open-letter-james-cameron.

Marlowe, Ann. 2009. "The Most Neo-Con Movie Ever Made: *Avatar*'s Deeply Conservative, Pro-American Message." *Forbes*, 23 December. http://www.forbes.com/2009/12/23/avatar-neo-con-military-opinions-contributors-ann-marlowe.html.

Marsh, George Perkins. (1864) 1970. *The Earth as Modified by Human Action*. New York: Scribner, Armstrong. Reprint, New York: Arno.

Mason, Jim. 1993. *An Unnatural Order: Uncovering the Roots of Our Domination of Nature and Each Other*. New York: Simon and Schuster.

McIntosh, Alastair. 1998. "The Gal-Gael Peoples of Scotland: On Tradition Re-Bearing, Recovery of Place and Making Identity Anew." In *Nature Religion Today: Paganism in the Modern World*, edited by Joanne Pearson, Richard H. Robins, and Geoffrey Samuel, 180–202. Edinburgh: Edinburgh University Press.

McVeigh, Stephen, and Matthew Kapell. 2011. "Surveying James Cameron's Reluctant Political Commentaries: 1984–2009." In *The Films of James Cameron: Critical Essays*, edited by Matthew Kapell and Stephen McVeigh, 15–43. Jefferson, NC: McFarland.

Monbiot, George. 2010. "Mawkish, Maybe. But *Avatar* Is a Profound, Insightful, Important Film." *The Guardian*, 11 January. http://www.guardian.co.uk/commentisfree/cifamerica/2010/jan/11/mawkish-maybe-avatar-profound-important.

Nabhan, Gary Paul, and Stephen Trimble. 1994. *The Geography of Childhood: Why Children Need Wild Places*. Boston: Beacon Press.

Naess, Arne. 1973. "The Shallow and the Deep, Long-Range Ecology Movement: A Summary." *Inquiry* 16: 95–100.

———. 1989. *Ecology, Community and Lifestyle*. Translated by David Rothenberg. Cambridge: Cambridge University Press.

Nixon, Rob. 2011. *Slow Violence and the Environmentalism of the Poor*. Cambridge, MA: Harvard University Press.

Oelschlaeger, Max. 1992. *The Wilderness Condition: Essays on Environment and Civilization*. San Francisco: Sierra Club Books.

Pilkington, Ace G. 2011 "Fighting the History Wars on the Big Screen: From *The Terminator* to *Avatar*." In *The Films of James Cameron: Critical Essays*, edited by Matthew Wilhelm Kapell and Stephen McVeigh, 44–71. Jefferson, NC: McFarland.

Ponting, Clive. 2007. *A New Green History of the World: The Environment and the Collapse of Great Civilizations*. Rev. ed. New York: Penguin.

Potts, Malcolm, and Thomas Hayden. 2008. *Sex and War: How Biology Explains Warfare and Terrorism and Offers a Path to a Safer World*. Dallas, TX: BenBella.

Rizzo, Allesandra. 2010. "Vatican Slams 'Avatar.'" *Huffington Post*, 12 January. http://www.huffingtonpost.com/2010/01/12/vatican-slams-avatar-prom_n _419949.html.

Shepard, Paul. 1982. *Nature and Madness*. San Francisco: Sierra Club Books.

———. 1992. "A Post-Historic Primitivism." In *The Wilderness Condition: Essays on Environment and Civilization*, edited by Max Oelschlaeger, 40–89. San Francisco: Island Press and Sierra Club Books.

———. 1998. *Coming Home to the Pleistocene*. San Francisco: Island Press.

Simpson, Audra. 2011. "Settlement's Secret." *Cultural Anthropology* 26(2):205–17.

Simpson, Leanne. 2008. *Lighting the Eighth Fire: The Liberation, Resurgence, and Protection of Indigenous Nations*. Winnipeg: Arbeiter Ring.

———. 2011b. *Dancing on Our Turtle's Back: Stories of Nishnaabeg Re-Creation, Resurgence and a New Emergence*. Winnipeg: Arbeiter Ring.

Starn, Orin. 2011. "Here Come the Anthros Again: The Strange Marriage of Anthropology and Native America." *Cultural Anthropology* 26(2): 179–204.

Stengers, Isabelle. 2005. "The Cosmopolitical Proposal." In *Making Things Public: Atmospheres of Democracy*, edited by Bruno Latour and Peter Weibel, 994–1004. Cambridge: MIT Press; Karlsruhe, Germany: ZKM/Center for Art and Media.

Stewart, David J. N.d. "*Avatar* Movie Is Evil." *Jesus-is-savior.com*. http://www.jesus-is-savior.com/Evils in America/Hellivision/avatar_is_evil.htm.

Stoll, Steven. 2007. "Farm against Forest." In *American Wilderness: A New History*, edited by Michael L. Lewis, 55–72. Oxford: Oxford University Press.

Stone, Christopher D. 1974. *Should Trees Have Standing?* Los Altos, CA: William Kaufmann.

Suozzi, Marguerite A. 2010. "Q&A: It's a Complete Reboot of How We See Things." *Inter Press Service*, 28 April. http://ipsnews.net/news.asp?idnews =51222.

Swamp, Jake. 2010. "Kanikonriio: Power of a Good Mind." In Davis, *Alliances*, 19–24.

Taylor, Bron, ed. 1995a. *Ecological Resistance Movements: The Global Emergence of Radical and Popular Environmentalism*. Albany: State University of New York Press.

———. 1995b. "Resacralizing Earth: Pagan Environmentalism and the Restoration of Turtle Island." In *American Sacred Space*, edited by David Chidester and Edward T. Linenthal, 97–151. Bloomington: Indiana University Press.

———. 1997a. "Earthen Spirituality or Cultural Genocide: Radical Environmentalism's Appropriation of Native American Spirituality." *Religion* 17(2): 183–215.

———. 1997b. "Earth First! Fights Back." *Terra Nova* 2(2): 29–43.

———. 2005. *The Encyclopedia of Religion and Nature*. London: Continuum International.

————. 2010. *Dark Green Religion: Nature Spirituality and the Planetary Future.* Berkeley: University of California Press.

————. 2012. "Wilderness, Spirituality and Biodiversity in North America: Tracing an Environmental History from Occidental Roots to Earth Day." In *Wilderness in Mythology and Religion: Approaching Religious Spatialities, Cosmologies, and Ideas of Wild Nature,* edited by Laura Feldt, 293–324. Berlin: De Gruyter.

Tocqueville, Alexis de. (1835/1840] 1969. *Democracy in America.* Translated by George Lawrence. 2 vols. New York: Anchor Books.

Treese, Jack L. 2010. "A Veteran Speaks: 'Avatar' Demeans Our Military." *Breitbart,* 11 January. http://www.breitbart.com/Big-Hollywood/2010/01/11/A -Veteran-Speaks--Avatar-Demeans-Our-Military.

Wanliss, James. 2011. *Resisting the Green Dragon: Dominion or Death.* Burke, VA: Cornwall Alliance.

Whaley, Rick, and Walter Bresette. 1994. *Walleye Warriors: An Effective Alliance against Racism and for the Earth.* Philadelphia, PA: New Society.

Wilhelm, Maria, and Dirk Mathison. 2009a. *James Cameron's* Avatar: *An Activist Survival Guide.* New York: HarperCollins.

————. 2009b. *James Cameron's* Avatar: *The Movie Scrapbook.* New York: HarperCollins.

Williams, Lewis, Rose Alene Roberts, and Alastair McIntosh. 2011. *Radical Human Ecology: Intercultural and Indigenous Approaches.* Burlington, VT: Ashgate.

Williams, Michael. 2003. *Deforesting the Earth: From Prehistory to Global Crisis.* Chicago: University of Chicago Press.

Wilson, Edward O. 1984. *Biophilia.* Cambridge, MA: Harvard University Press.

Wolfe, Patrick. 2006. "Settler Colonialism and the Elimination of the Native." *Journal of Genocide Research* 8(4): 387–409.

Woodworth, William Raweno:Kwas. 2010. "Iroquoian Condolence Practiced on Civic Scale." In Davis, *Alliances,* 25–41.

Worster, Donald. 2008. *A Passion for Nature: The Life of John Muir.* Oxford: Oxford University Press.

Zaleha, Bernard Daley. 2008. "'The Only Paradise We Ever Need': An Investigation into Pantheism's Sacred Geography in the Writings of Edward Abbey, Thomas Berry, and Matthew Fox, and a Preliminary Survey of Signs of Emerging Pantheism in American Culture." Master's thesis, University of Florida, Gainesville.

————. 2010. "Nature and Nature Religion." In *Encyclopedia of Religion in America,* edited by Charles H. Lippy and Peter W. Williams, 1527–33. Washington, DC: CQ Press.

————. 2013. "'Our Only Heaven': Nature Veneration, Quest Religion, and Pro-Environmental Behavior," *Journal for the Study of Religion, Nature and Culture* 7(2).

Zerzan, John. 1994. *Future Primitive.* Columbia, MO: CAL Press.

Žižek, Slavoj. 1991. *Looking Awry: An Introduction to Jacques Lacan through Popular Culture.* Cambridge: MIT Press.

———. 2010a. "Return of the Natives." *New Statesman,* 4 March. http://www.newstatesman.com/film/2010/03/avatar-reality-love-couple-sex.

———. 2010b. "Slavoj Žižek on Ecology as Religion." *YouTube.* http://www.youtube.com/watch?v=lQbIqNd5D90.

Afterword: Considering the Legacies of *Avatar*

DANIEL HEATH JUSTICE

Comprehending Pandora

As the diverse contributors to this collection make clear, the cultural phenomenon of *Avatar* has more than one legacy, more than a single story to tell, more than one audience to interpret its multiple layers of significance and controversy. It is, as editor Bron Taylor notes in his prologue, not unlike the Rorschach inkblot, upon which viewers impose their own meanings through their particular lenses and experiences. Taylor offers this apt observation: "The filmmaker and the film have been labelled pro-civilization and anti-civilization, pro-science and anti-science, un-American and too American, anti-Marine and pro-Marine, racist and anti-racist, anti-Indigenous and pro-Indigenous, woman-respecting and misogynistic, leftist and neo-conservative, progressive and reactionary, activist and self-absorbed. And, of course, there have been religious labels: pagan, atheistic, theistic, pantheistic, panentheistic, and animistic." It is probably still too early to know how lasting and influential the Na'vi and their verdant world of Pandora might be in popular culture, especially in the industrialized West, but there's little doubt that the film has captured something in the imaginations of millions of viewers, something that scholars and critics are still struggling to understand. Is the movie a harbinger of a worldwide green awakening that affirms our engagement with the living biosphere on which we depend? Does it speak to a growing dissatisfaction with the ecocidal material practices of the dominant world religions, especially the anthropocentric Abrahamic faiths? Is it simply an example of narcissistic liberal hypocrisy that requires globalized capitalism to facilitate its feel-good critique of that same system? Or is it a deeply felt ethical response to the industrial and commercial devastations of our planet and the loss of diversity, habitat, and healthy relationship between the various participants in that system? Is it an indictment of imperialism or a product of it? Do Na'vi ways offer something new to imagining a different way of being with the other-than-human world, or do they simply replicate the familiar "noble savage" stereotype, although rendered more palatable in cutting-edge 3-D graphics?

The various voices and perspectives in this volume offer a provocative opportunity to posit how *Avatar*'s environmental concerns impact both our ideas and lived practices—if indeed they do so—and this conversation is an important step in that process. And, as the contributors demonstrate, the film's narrative and spiritual/philosophical concerns are highly contested. That is as it should be. My comments in this afterword-essay take up some of these complicated considerations, especially regarding the film's representation of Indigenous peoples and indigeneity, and offer further questions for fans and critics alike to consider when reflecting on *Avatar*'s ongoing legacies.

The Final Frontier?

I have repeatedly reflected on the film and its consequences, both intended and unintended, especially when someone cites the film as a reference point for their knowledge about Indigenous concerns, which has occurred regularly in professional and personal conversations since *Avatar*'s release in 2009. I am every bit as conflicted about the movie as I was then.[1]

At that time, *Avatar* was a topic of lively conversation for my students and colleagues at my former institution, the University of Toronto, where for a decade I taught Aboriginal literature and Aboriginal studies. (In 2012, I joined the faculty in the First Nations Studies Program and the English Department at the University of British Columbia.) Unlike the case for many viewers, *Avatar* was not our introduction to issues related to Indigenous sovereignty and spirituality, colonization and decolonization, other-than-human kinship, traditional ecological knowledge, and environmental destruction; indeed, most of both the content and context were all too familiar, both in our scholarship and, to varying degrees, in our lived experience. Although my Toronto colleagues and I were a diverse group, we had a number of values that aligned remarkably closely across our differences. After I saw the film, I was curious what other folks in the Indigenous community thought about the movie. Because *Avatar* met some blistering critique online and in print from conservatives and liberals alike, I initially thought that the underlying perspective emerging from these one-on-one and group conversations would be sweeping dismissal, or at least substantial indignation.

That's not how it turned out, not even for me. Our responses ranged from guarded optimism (given that a huge international audience was clearly so engaged with a film that confronted the horrors of colonialism and resource exploitation) to thoughtful frustration. Although *Avatar* was emotionally powerful in so many ways, I wondered: Do we really need yet another story about Indigenous struggle told through a non-Native person's voice and perspective? But to my surprise, no one categorically dismissed the film. On the whole, the overwhelming sense was, "Well, it's flawed, but at least it's getting people talking." That there was so much commentary in the blogosphere on the film's underlying current of "white guilt" indicated to me at the time that *something* was happening with audiences and critics; I thought then that *Avatar* offered a good opportunity to engage an audience on Indigenous issues that might not otherwise have been interested or receptive.

Perhaps it did. Three years later, however, it seems clear that the hoped-for engagement did not have much of a lasting effect on most viewers: rainforests still burn in the Amazon as Indigenous leaders are murdered; activists and community members still try to bring attention to the ongoing toxic effects of bitumen processing in Alberta and the desecration and theft of sacred lands in Hawai'i by extractive and tourist industries; First Nations in British Columbia still fight against oil pipelines in their traditional lands; water wars have erupted in Peru and elsewhere across the world, as hydropolitics become increasingly fraught. The Conservative government of Canada is currently in the process of gutting federal environmental regulations, privileging expediency for extractive industries over both short- and long-term public and ecological health; Republican electoral gains in the United States typically have similar effects. For most viewers, it seems, *Avatar* was an enchanting spectacle, but it hardly seems like the harbinger of a more wide-scale ecological revolution. As demonstrated by the essays in this volume, however, the relationship between art and social change is slippery: for example, Matthew Holtmeier offers a useful cautionary note about too quickly dismissing this potential, identifying what he calls "Na'vi sympathy" as a potential impetus for environmental and Indigenous-rights action, and Taylor reminds us in his epilogue that "the previous examples of literature and film moving people emotionally and then to action...suggests that the film is playing, and probably will continue to play, at least some role in environmental mobilization."[2]

It would be manifestly unfair to expect Cameron's film to carry the burden of worldwide eco-action or spiritual awakening; the problems are too deeply entrenched, too complicated, and too contested to expect that any one counter-narrative would change them. And given his ongoing activism on behalf of Indigenous peoples in the Amazon and consistent commitment to environmental protection, we should be wary of letting reactionary cynicism direct our critical response. Yet it is certainly fair to ask about the influence of the film on actual actions and ideas, small-scale as well as large. Has anything changed as a result of *Avatar*? What kind of change can we expect or hope for? *Can* anything change? And if it can, could *Avatar* be an effective tool in that transformative process? The essays in this collection go a long way toward answering some of these questions, while raising questions and concerns of their own.

Stumbling toward Paradise

To be honest, when I first saw *Avatar*, I fully expected to hate the film; today, I still find my response to be firmly mixed. Before seeing it, I had already heard it referred to as *Dances with Wolves* in outer space. Moreover, the heavy-handed parallels to popular films were readily apparent even in the first half-hour, as humorously lampooned by Randy Szuch in his video mash-up of Disney's *Pocahontas* and *Avatar*, which made the Internet rounds and was even featured on the *Huffington Post* comedy blog.[3] And the plot was not the only concern. The minute I saw Michelle Rodriguez as the tough-talking pilot Trudy Chacon, I expected that her character was going to die—heroically, but die nonetheless. Death, humiliation, or rescue by white men are too-frequent fates of strong Latinas and other women of colour in science fiction films and television. Examples of the former in cinema include Jenette Goldstein's alien-slaughtered Private Vasquez in Cameron's *Aliens*, the exile and punishment of Maria Gonzales (Samantha Morton) in *Code 46*, and C.C.H. Pounder's doomed Bertha in *Robocop 3*; on television, two examples that immediately come to mind are Kendra, the only one of the three major Slayers who actually stays dead in Joss Whedon's *Buffy the Vampire Slayer*, and Michelle Rodriguez (again) as the betrayed and murdered Ana-Lucia Cortez of *Lost*. For all the amazing 3-D effects, *Avatar*'s characters are largely simplistic caricatures, much of the dialogue is leaden and clichéd, and the storyline is surprisingly predictable for a $300 million epic. To my surprise, there was enough in terms of world-building and interest around the Indigenous Na'vi to keep my attention; indeed, I would have liked to have seen much more of the Na'vi and their world and much less of the human invaders.[4]

The film did not annoy me so much as make me sad, largely because it promised to be much more substantial than it actually was. Its successes seem to emphasize the stumbles and missed opportunities even more. In terms of setting, for example, Pandora is a remarkable creation; David Landis Barnhill's comparative analysis of Cameron's action- and violence-driven *Avatar* and Ursula K. Le Guin's Vietnam-era novel *The Word for World Is Forest* provides many important insights, but one of the most significant is the recognition that, while plot and characterization might have suffered in the film, the world of Cameron's imagination differs from Le Guin's setting in its complexity, danger, and "rich...notion of sacred place"—a notion that Barnhill subsequently questions. As further noted, the danger in *The Word for World Is Forest* comes from the invading Terran humans, not from anything to do with the land itself. Pat Munday further explicates the feral beauty of Pandora in his provocative discussion of the hunting ethos of the Na'vi and the spiritual role of predation in the film. For Munday, Pandora is not an Edenic garden for urban nature-lovers to drop by and visit; it is an intricate and often threatening place where death and suffering belong as much as beauty and mystery, and where predators in all their bloody glory serve a function beyond biological necessity. This seems to me more in keeping with the ways in which traditional and rural peoples on Earth often understand nature—you simply cannot survive on the land or in the bush if you do not have profound respect for its capacity to hurt you.

But setting can only offer so much, for all its appeal and costly special effects; ultimately, story and characters matter, too, and this is where I see the film stumbling most egregiously. That Cameron chose the least interesting and most consistently obtuse figure in the film (Jake Sully, a paraplegic ex-Marine, performed by Sam Worthington) to be the point-of-view character is, I think, symptomatic of the most significant failures of *Avatar*: namely, that for all its visual sophistication, the story suffers from low narrative expectations, and it regretfully fulfills them. Complexity and ambiguity are surrendered for expedient moralizing; the possibility of richly realized and multi-dimensional characters is tossed out in favour of stock heroes and villains. Cameron drives home the relevant political concerns with the subtlety of a sledgehammer; the good guys are very good, the bad guys are very, very bad, and there is little overlap between the categories. (Stephen Rust's fascinating essay on *Avatar* as eco-realist melodrama interprets this aspect rather differently and ties it convincingly to the film's marketing and blockbuster status.) The Na'vi are exotic and intriguing, but their narrative function is to serve as the redemptive influence on a disillusioned white guy; they are more interesting than the humans but, ultimately, only to show what qualities the good humans will attain.[5] It is all part of the "white guy goes native" Western film formula—the only real difference is that these whooping, warlike Natives have blue skin and ride oddly limbed alien horses or fly giant bat-beasts.

The implications of these narrative choices—and their participation in a long and unpleasant representational genealogy—are significant. Chris Klassen's incisive critique of the film and its invocation of the "noble savage" is worth considering here. She locates *Avatar* in an oppressive patriarchal lineage in which white masculinity is empowered and even expanded through the efforts of women and Indigenous men, most of whom must die to ensure the white man's savage supremacy.[6] Sully, for all his Na'vi sympathies, is still a settler subject; indeed, although his settler status is obscured through his inhabitation of a pseudo-Na'vi body (pseudo, because the Na'vi are very well aware of the constructed and possessed status of the avatars), he is even *more* dangerous at the end, as Klassen contends: "Just as the myth of the ecologically noble savage requires the death of real Indians, so too Sully's becoming of the Other in *Avatar* requires the death of the Na'vi male leaders. The white male is thus in control of the image of the noble savage. The association with femininity works similarly. Sully's becoming the *ecologically* noble savage, where nature is feminized in the Mother Goddess, requires the death of 'real'—that is, human—women. The male must be able to control the image of femininity." Far from being a real victory, as Klassen argues, the end of the film is actually something far more problematic:

> Even as Sully is attempting to fight against the military powers of the Company, he does so in a way that transforms the Other—those seen as living in harmony with all living beings—into himself, a Marine. Harmony is broken. The warrior is triumphant and as the humans are escorted off the moon, we see Na'vi soldiers, not hunters, lining the way.... And the sacrifices necessary for this victory reinforce a dominant masculinity embodied within this world view. The human women cannot survive to see this "victory." The male Na'vi leaders also must be sacrificed so that this "victory" can allow the white human Marine, Sully, to become the male and masculine triumphant noble savage, the leader of an indigenous people who have become what they originally were positioned against.

Here I depart somewhat from Joy Greenberg's contention that there is much substantive or symbolic difference between Sully in human and avatar form or that his transformation undoes the longer literary genealogy to which he is connected. Although he is presented in a much more exotic skin than his predecessors, there is little to distinguish Sully from other fictional(ized) and converted/adopted settler patriarchs like John

Smith (of *Pocahontas* fame), Natty Bumppo/Hawkeye (from James Fenimore Cooper's *Leatherstocking Tales*, including *The Last of the Mohicans*),
Lieutenant John Dunbar (*Dances with Wolves*), Captain Nathan Algren
(*The Last Samurai*), or the problematic racialized and gendered worlds
they realize. Greenberg's thoughtful analysis of romanticism in the film
(and in environmental religions themselves) I find more convincing, and
it challenges critics to eschew knee-jerk reactions to non-rationalist sentiment when considering the power of emotion to effect engagement and
transformative change.

Easy Outs and Cardboard Characters
Taken together, these issues gesture toward my primary disappointment
with *Avatar*: because the characters and their motivations are so clumsily
handled, because the story is so formulaic, because the imaginary setting
is so unimaginatively derivative of this world, the potential for *actual* critical commentary is diminished. And as a result, the *real* complexities of
colonialism, militarism, reverence for the living world, or environmental
destruction are flattened out and, to some degree, evacuated of substance
and significance. There is nothing of the complexity or ethical self-reflection
evidenced by Michael B. MacDonald's contribution to this volume, wherein
his own participation in a field (ethnomusicology) with a deep colonial history brings with it dangers of "becoming complicit in the very thing *Avatar*
criticizes," while his work with members of living traditional communities
is embedded in relational responsibilities; in reflecting on Britt Istoft's essay
on *Avatar* fandom and the development of a green mythology (not unlike
the final frontier mythology of *Star Trek*), there certainly seems to be more
nuance and provocative narrative experimentation among hard-core fans
of the film than is evidenced by the plot of the film itself.

Nor, indeed, does *Avatar* deal with some of the seemingly more self-evi-
dent issues of representation, such as dis/ability, in spite of Sully's injuries
and their effects on his sense of self. That he ends up not only ambula-
tory but immensely powerful in his Na'vi body at the end of the film is
another narrative cheat. Is it so hard to imagine in a science fiction film
that a paraplegic can be an adventurous hero in his own ways and with his
own body and can do so in a way that does not ultimately require him to
be something other than he is? By lingering on the interpretive surface and
not descending more fully into the emotional and ideological depths, the
film is a journey into a not-so-strange world that neither disorients nor dis-
locates viewer expectations; indeed, it asks very little of its audience aside
from a willingness to be enraptured by its own spectacle. That may be good
for entertainment, but that's not asking for much.

Let us consider the alternative possibilities. What if we grant, for the sake of argument, the proposition that Cameron had decided for a legitimate reason that the main viewpoint character could *not* have been Indigenous: How then might the film have been different, perhaps even more challenging? Sigourney Weaver's character, the scientist/teacher Dr. Grace Augustine, would have been an immeasurably more interesting and complicated choice than Sully, the pouting and resentful soldier/jock.[7] In their thought-provoking contribution to this volume, Jacob von Heland and Sverker Sörlin examine Augustine's struggle as a Na'vi-attuned scientist to "understand and support actions that are both factually accurate and morally correct" through her move from an advocate of ostensibly objective Baconian science to a more open, humble, and intimately relational engagement of Na'vi knowledge and the world views in which such knowledge is embedded.

Although the film offers some muted critique of academic colonialism, the decidedly mixed blessings of Augustine's work as a teacher of human ways to the Na'vi are almost entirely obscured by the contrast between her and the murderous thug Colonel Quaritch (Stephen Lang). Because she is not a sneering, cardboard villain and because, in spite of her bristly personality, she obviously has good intentions, the dangerous legacies of her interference in the world of the Na'vi are ultimately erased, and she remains a hero. Yet many of the devastations visited upon Indigenous cultures have come from well-meaning teachers, preachers, and scholars, many of whom have believed that their actions were for the good of the peoples whose cultures they undermined and even eradicated.

Such shallow attention to motivation does not begin or end with Augustine. Quaritch is despicable and vindictive, almost entirely for the sake of efficient brutality. There is nothing sophisticated about his evil, nor is there anything about him that would elicit audience empathy—he is meant to be simply a murderer, an ecocidal maniac, an all-around monster. But how much more complicated a story might it have been had he been, in some ways at least, a good man of personal integrity who proudly did his duty in spite of the horror he felt at decimating a people and their world? How much of the evil in our contemporary world is created by people whose sole purpose is destruction and devastation? Not as much as is done by those who believe that what they are doing is a good thing or who know something is wrong but feel powerless to resist or conclude that some higher duty compels them to act despite moral qualms. The "interspecies empathy" that Lisa Sideris so compellingly posits in this volume would be immeasurably deepened, and challenged, if it had been explored through such a viewpoint character. Much more could have been done with this, .

as well as with the complications related to the fact that Quaritch and his other fighters worked for a private corporation but that their identities were still shaped by the military honour code of fighting on behalf of God and country. Therein lie the makings of a true tragedy, but one that would be far more unsettling—and un-*settling*—to viewers.

Following that line, what if, instead of the hackneyed convention of a cruel white man assaulting Indigenous peoples on another world, the main character had instead been a world-weary Indigenous warrior from Earth conflicted between his empathy for the Na'vi and his (or her) sense of duty as a soldier? (Given Cherokee actor Wes Studi's exceptional skills as a performer, I wonder what he might have done with a deeper and more interesting Quaritch rather than the largely underdeveloped role of the Na'vi chieftain Eytukan.) Having numerous family members (both Native and non-Native) who have served in the US armed forces and knowing something of their complicated relationships to their military service, I am not willing to simply dismiss them as brutes and bigots, as Cameron seems to have done in *Avatar*; given that American Indians have the highest rate of military service of any other group in the United States and having seen the US flag carried proudly by Native veterans at many powwows and community gatherings, I think it is fair to say that all kinds of people join the military for all kinds of complex, sometimes problematic reasons, mostly because of a mixture of love for their people, nation, and country; a search for adventure in another land; and a hunger for opportunities that are otherwise limited or denied by their current circumstances. None of these motivations are neutral, and none are without their dangers or moral complications, but none are categorically evil, either—people can be sensitized to the beauty and humanity of other cultures through military service, just as they can be turned into xenophobic killers. This is a much more poignant but ultimately less comfortable perspective, one that finds many degrees of good and harm in an entire range of characters, one that indicts the viewer as much as the character. (Taylor's epilogue is worth turning to on this point, as he gives substantial attention to the fascinating and diverse responses of service members to the film.)[8]

There are certainly some impressive moments of depth and narrative brilliance in the film, as when Zoe Saldana's warrior-woman Neytiri saves a stupidly unprepared Sully from being killed by viperwolves, then chastises him for his casual response to the destruction of life his rescue required; the soul-crushing horror of Hometree's destruction and the survivors' disorientation and exile; the adoption ceremony that remakes Sully into a full Na'vi, with both the rights and responsibilities that such a ceremony necessitates; and his subsequent betrayal of the Na'vi and Neytiri's anguished response. The film also, as Taylor argues, gestures toward the possibility of alliance—not simply that of Sully and the Na'vi, but of sensitized settler descendants and Indigenous peoples today. Such "cross-cultural and international" alliances are not easy; indeed, they demand "deep commitment and, usually, long-term hard work." They also require humility (especially on the part of the settler), patience, and generosity, qualities that we might assume are part of Sully's integration into and commitment to the Omaticaya clan.

For all its good intentions, for all its visual spectacle and effecting sentiment (yes, I got teary-eyed a couple of times), *Avatar* is still ultimately a story about "those bad guys who aren't us." Sadly, as we know from example after example in the past, both distant and immediate, the bad guys, all too often, *are* us. It is a comforting lie to believe that those big bad guys with the superweapons or the white hoods and burning crosses are the only ones who do nasty racist things, but it is a lie, nonetheless.

In distancing the audience from any complicity with these evils against our world, the film actually fails to take seriously what would really be required of the audience to effect real and lasting change. The genocide perpetrated against the Na'vi is undeniably evil and despicable, but, contrary to the message of the film, genocide is not enacted only by wicked, bloodthirsty soldiers—mundane, ordinary people participate in all kinds of atrocities at home and abroad, knowingly and unknowingly, every day. There are so many examples of this invidious dynamic: when we insist on cheap chocolate or electronics, for instance, probably providing financial support for forced child labour in the chocolate industry of Cote d'Ivoire or the electronic sweatshops of China and India, while also increasing the ravenous demand for raw materials that further the degradation of the environment, habitat for other beings, and our own water and land; or when we vote for legislation that penalizes immigrants as "illegals" outside the protections of law; or when we consider poor and Indigenous women to have minimal human value or personhood, contributing thereby to a climate of brutalization, rape, and murder, as in Cuidad Juárez on the US–Mexico border or the Highway of Tears in British Columbia; or when we ignore abuse, neglect, or inequity for reasons of discomfort, expedience, or disinterest. In such cases, we minimize the best possibilities of our humanity and give our tacit support to all that is worst and most vicious in our nature. Indeed, as historian Hannah Arendt reminded us, it is usually ordinary people whose actions are most responsible for such horrors, and this is made all the worse because of their seeming banality.[9]

But because no audience member is expected to take the side of the over-the-top Colonel Quaritch or of Parker Selfridge (Giovanni Ribisi), the insipid and cowardly corporate sycophant, audiences can only claim the righteousness of the Na'vi for themselves.[10] In so doing, they—or rather more often, *we*—are exempted from the hard work that actually accompanies the struggles for decolonization, social and environmental justice, and peace. And again, here is where the idea of alliance is a useful corrective to the superficial moral surety of the film, as it requires specifically that hard work to realize the actual possibilities for transformative change. Otherwise, there is no real sense that good intentions, on their own and without deeper commitment to long-lasting relationships and their complexities, can actually be far more destructive to a people (and have much more lasting impacts) than shooting napalm into the Hometree; there is no acknowledgement that people can do terrible things out of a sense of misplaced obligation rather than simply because they are sociopaths.

Ghosts of Indians Future

> In the Great American Indian novel, when it is finally written,
> all of the white people will be Indians and all of the Indians will be ghosts.
> —Sherman Alexie, "How to Write the Great American Indian Novel"[11]

One other important point deserves mention here. Cameron's future Earth is a devastated world, a diseased body quickly hastening toward death; Pandora is Earth's lush and vibrant twin, literally radiating life in myriad manifestations. The Na'vi are presented as exemplars of an embodied nature faith and harmonious co-participants in the complicated processes of life on Pandora; their traditional ecological knowledge is, in large part, responsible for Sully's transformation from wannabe avatar to adopted Na'vi warrior.

But the entire enterprise depends on the profoundly grim assumption that, for Indigenous peoples of Cameron's future Earth, traditional knowledge and lifeways have failed. On Earth, corporations and extractive industries have won the battle. There are no First Peoples in the future, no Indigenous Earthlings in space. Given this underlying assumption, how optimistic can we really be that the victory at the end of the film will be a lasting one? After all, if, after centuries of struggle to maintain lands, languages, relationships, and distinctive ways of being in the world, Indigenous peoples of Earth have lost the struggle, what possible hope is there for a good green future for any of us, whether human or Na'vi?

A more jaded interpretation might be that the only ones who really offer much hope for the future are the Jake Sullys of the world, settler men who are more successful at being Indigenous than the Indigenous people themselves, and upon whom the Indigenous population depends for its ultimate survival. The Na'vi and their animal allies do fight bravely and successfully for their home, but it is a victory that the film renders plausible and possible *only* after Sully brings them together, *only* after he becomes their great war leader, and *only* after he makes his heartfelt appeal to Eywa (an appeal that, incidentally, the *tsahìk*/medicine-woman-to-be Neytiri insists is hopeless, so here, too, he demonstrates his deeper tie to the world than even its most spiritually insightful Na'vi inhabitants). Sully is the catalyst, the shaman, the tactician, and the great *toruk*-wrangler; without him, there is no war, no victory. It is worth recalling, too, that previous Na'vi campaigns against the humans resulted in brutal reprisals by the Corporation, including the death of Neytiri's sister and the closing of Augustine's school; it is only after Sully becomes their alliance-building leader that they actually succeed in driving out the invaders. Whatever the ultimate success of the Na'vi struggle on Pandora might be, the background history of *Avatar* implies that *for the First Peoples of Earth*, the future universe is one of Indigenous failure, not victory, of ghostly hauntings, not lived continuity and struggle.

As Taylor discusses at length in his epilogue, and as I note earlier in this afterword, there are many Indigenous and non-Indigenous viewers for whom the film offers a number of hopeful, even positive, messages about Indigenous resistance and ways of being, traditional ecological knowledge, and the coming together of different peoples through a shared commitment to the green world in which we abide. Thore Bjørnvig suggests a further option, that the film "tries to bridge the fundamentally different world views of progressive outer space religion and environmentalist dark green religion. It does so by returning the spectator, through a highly complex symbolic journey, to the historical point of convergence between the two different world views."

These are all heartening possibilities. Yet having reflected on *Avatar's* approach to indigeneity with a bit more distance, I cannot help but still be ambivalent. For all the film's ostensibly optimistic messages and calls to environmental arms and Indigenous rights, a significant underlying message might nevertheless be one of deep cynicism and hopelessness, at least about the ultimate possibilities of change here on Earth. If this is the case, then the immersive wonder of the film might indeed be simply an escapist fantasy, with the awful realization that there simply is no real escape for us but rather only for future (non-Indigenous) humans, who might at last find wisdom or redemption in a world unburdened by colonial history and settler guilt.

I still believe that, whatever its sincere ambitions and Cameron's clear political and ideological commitments, *Avatar* misses important opportunities to engage the complexities of injustice and more thoughtful relationships with one another and the natural world. The film could have been as profound in substance as in spectacle; it could have asked difficult and unsettling questions of its audience that might not have been as popular or lucrative but would have been more challenging. Instead, it settled on a feel-good, pop progressivism that may hide a cynical centre. Thus, it may also have wasted, or at least diminished, the chance to make a profound difference for more than a sensitive minority of viewers.

And yet . . .

Closing Thoughts

Although Cameron's beautiful, evocative, and deeply flawed epic falls prey to the surprisingly limited ambitions of its characters by exchanging complexity and narrative nuance for heavy-handed and simplistic political evangelism, the film is not his alone, nor is the world of Pandora or its inhabitants. Pandora, it seems, is out of the box; as *Avatar* becomes a locus of spiritual concern for audiences worldwide and a centre of religious devotion for a small subset of that audience, the phenomenon takes on possibilities that extend beyond the talents and limitations of its creator(s).

In Hawai'i the film becomes something different for different audiences; Gould, Ardoin, and Hashimoto provide fascinating documentation of audience response to the film, with particular emphasis on the ways in which Hawaiian audiences draw on the film and its ideological vocabulary in their understanding of local history and contemporary environmental and social justice concerns. Similarly, the appropriation of *Avatar* by opponents to the Alberta oil sands/tar sands as related by Haluza-Delay, Ferber, and Wiebe-Neufeld gives ample evidence of the film's use value to a wide range of viewers. Taylor cites Adrian Ivakhiv on this point as well: "fandom, once triggered, sets off on its own trajectories, which in this case may include those that turn viewers into radical activists." And, as Taylor notes further, consequences are emerging from the film's call to action, including the Avatar Home Tree Initiative which "succeeded in mobilizing over thirty-one thousand individuals in planting over one million trees." In all cases, *Avatar* is more than a science fiction story about intergalactic environmental despoliation and Indigenous struggle; rather, it serves as a common conceptual grounding for the lived experience and social action of human beings in relationship with the land and one another.

What audiences are doing with the film—and the critical conversation taking place here—give me hope that all the hype was not for naught, that there might actually be something deeper that *Avatar*'s messages of ecological kinship are actually achieving, that a more responsible and thoughtful relationship with the other-than-human world with which we abide is not only possible but desired by more than just Indigenous peoples, that the future may be one with Indigenous presence in more than just memory or symbol.

That this film has prompted so many fine scholars to engage the central questions of faith, belonging, and purpose in the world seems to me another important consequence of these challenging questions. If these conversations continue and if the wider community of viewers debate, contest, and claim Pandora's possibilities and provocations (especially when the long-promised sequels/prequels appear), then one legacy of the film is assured. How much that will extend beyond the theoretical to lived practice and relationship is unclear, but the contributors to this volume offer a number of intriguing possibilities. Taylor's words are particularly apt here: "Activists of all sorts, if not all of the film's critics, have been quick to recognize that *Avatar* has provided them with an unusual opportunity to educate and organize those moved by the film into communities of solidarity and resistance." I would hope that such organizations include the careful attention to long-standing relationships and alliances that would make such communities viable in the long term.

While much remains to be considered about the short- and long-term legacies of *Avatar*, what is certain is that these questions matter, to mainstream audiences as well as to critics, and certainly to those on the front lines where biological and cultural diversity are imperilled and eroding further. The challenge now is the next step. What kind of future do we see for ourselves, for our neighbours, for our descendants, for our other-than-human relatives? What kind of ancestors do we hope to be: the ones who made possible a different and more humble way of living in the world, or the ones who gave in to our basest hungers and most thoughtless indulgences? Will we be honoured ancestors, or will future generations curse our names?

The future is our shared challenge. what kind of future that will be is entirely in our hands. But perhaps we need not look to Pandora for salvation. Perhaps we have everything we need right here, right now, in this glorious green world we call home.

Notes

Thanks to Kyle Wyatt, Alice Te Punga Somerville, Domino R. Perez, and Kent Dunn for their thoughts on the film and for helping me work through some of these ideas. And special thanks to Bron Taylor for the invitation to participate in this project and for his patience in awaiting my contribution.

1 This essay is a revised and expanded version of an online essay on the film that I wrote for the blog of *First Peoples: New Directions*, an Indigenous studies co-publishing initiative between four university presses. The original can be accessed at http://www.firstpeoplesnewdirections.org/blog/?p=169.

2 In his fascinating study of the film, in this volume, Holtmeier identifies two impacts on particularly sensitive subsets of viewers. In the first, "post-Pandora depression," the film creates an immersive but transitory dreamworld where the end of the film is associated with an alienating and largely unwelcome awakening. For PPD sufferers, the point is to return to the world of the film and to escape this world. But in the second group, "real-world community-based solutions" rooted in "Na'vi sympathy" spur them to action. He writes of these viewers: "What is unique about the film is that its emotional impact has enlisted 'warriors for the earth' from individuals not previously engaged in green causes, while also...bolstering the resolve of those who are already committed to the environment."

3 Randy Szuch, "Avatar/Pocahontas Mashup," 11 February 2010, http://vimeo .com/9389738; see also "'Avatar' and 'Pocahontas' Get Much Deserved Mashup (Trailer)," *Huffington Post Comedy*, 28 April 2010, http://www.huffingtonpost .com/2010/02/26/avatar-and-pocahontas-get_n_478845.html.

4 This response was heightened when I recently re-watched the film with a Maori friend and colleague, who had managed to avoid seeing the film during its initial run but was game to offer her critical insight as a fellow Indigenous literature scholar during my work on this afterword. As creative writers as well as scholars, we tend to be quite open to a range of storytelling techniques and approaches, but the primary feeling we both took away from the film was a surprising amount of boredom with the plot—there just is not enough depth of narrative or compelling action or relationships throughout most of the film to make it a fully satisfying imaginative journey. That said, the film's evocative world-building and complicated relationship to the history of cinematic representations of indigeneity have provided another kind of critically and intellectually satisfying engagement.

5 Bruce MacLennan's Jungian analysis of the Na'vi as "ideal humans" who "activate our ancestral archetypes" is a well-considered and compelling alternative interpretation, but it focuses specifically on the internal and does not take up the sociopolitical implications of these archetypes or their more problematic distillation as simplistic and often racist stereotypes.

6 In his epilogue, Taylor argues. "The criticism that *Avatar* (and, by implication, Cameron) is misogynist can be quickly dismissed, for it appears to be based on weak, if any, evidence, as well as upon a remarkable ability to ignore evidence to the contrary. Cameron is properly recognized, to provide a counter-argument, for creating powerful heroines, unlike most Hollywood directors." While Cameron's female characters might be better than many in Hollywood cinema and the charge of misogyny may well be extreme, this does not necessarily mean that they escape the bounds of sexist representation; indeed, the empowerment on offer may well be a false one, given the sustained emphasis (and most trenchant criticism) on sexual objectification of the characters, their frequent embrace of masculinist violence, and the not-infrequently negative attitude toward both motherhood and women's bodily integrity. Certainly, the characters of Lt. Ellen Ripley from *Aliens* (Sigourney Weaver), Helen Tasker of *True Lies* (Jamie Lee Curtis), Rose DeWitt Bukater of *Titanic* (Kate Winslet), and Sarah Connor of the *Terminator* franchise (Linda Hamilton) provide some of the most interesting pre-*Avatar* female characters for analysis. There is a wealth of respectable scholarship that asks important

and challenging questions of the representation of women in Cameron's oeuvre, in which Ripley gets the most significant attention. A few examples include Harvey R. Greenburg, "Fembo: *Aliens'* Intentions" (*Journal of Popular Film and Television* 15, no.4, Winter 1988), Constance Penley, "Time Travel, Primal Scene, and the Critical Dystopia" (in *Close Encounters: Film, Feminism, and Science Fiction*, 1991), and Rhona Berenstein, "Mommie Dearest: *Aliens, Rosemary's Baby*, and Mothering" (*Journal of Popular Culture* 24, no. 2, Fall 1990).

7 That Weaver's fine performance is both multi-layered and compelling in spite of the weak script demonstrates once again that she is an extraordinary talent; regrettably, some of her best lines and most interesting characterization never made it into the theatrical release and are available only on the special-edition DVD.

8 Taylor does make the point in his epilogue that Cameron has a long and public history as a strong supporter of the US Marine Corps. The distinction that some military viewers made was between *soldiers* and *mercenaries*, with the former honouring the traditions and ethics of military service and the latter being motivated by profit rather than principle. While this distinction is a significant one, it does not seem very well supported by the film itself, as there is a great deal of bleed between the categories, and when Sully becomes a freedom-fighter in opposition to Quaritch, he does so as a Na'vi warrior, not as a Marine. Colonel Quaritch, on the other hand, remains staunchly embedded in his military persona, so although a mercenary, he nevertheless seems to present as a Marine in ideology.

9 See Hannah Arendt, *Eichmann in Jerusalem: A Report on the Banality of Evil* (1963; reprint, New York: Penguin, 2006). Aside from the subtitle, the term actually appears only in the last paragraph of the book.

10 Actually, as Taylor notes, the reactionary responses of some conservative Christian commentators to the film indicate that some viewers found *no* characters to be redeeming.

11 Sherman Alexie, "How to Write the Great American Indian Novel," in *Native American Songs and Poems: An Anthology*, edited by Brian Swann (Minneola, NY: Dover, 1996), 29.

Contributors

Nicole M. Ardoin is Assistant Professor at Stanford University, with a joint appointment in the School of Education and the Woods Institute for the Environment. Her research focuses on sense of place and environmental behaviour, with an emphasis on geographic scale; the use of social strategies by non-governmental organizations to engage individuals and communities in environmentally related decision making; research and program evaluation in informal activities and settings, including nature-based tourism, museums, and parks; and the impact of "green" buildings and the built environment on environmental attitudes, knowledge, and behaviours. She also serves as an associate editor of the international journal *Environmental Education Research*.
Website: http://www.stanford.edu/~nmardoin

David Landis Barnhill is Director of Environmental Studies and Professor of English at the University of Wisconsin, Oshkosh. His publications include *At Home on the Earth* (1999; an anthology of American nature writing), *Deep Ecology and World Religions* (2001; co-edited with Roger Gottlieb), and a two-volume translation of the Japanese nature poet Bashō (2004–5). Recent articles include "The Spiritual Dimension of North American Nature Writing," "The Social Ecology of Gary Snyder," and "East Asian Influence on Recent North American Nature Writing." His courses have included American nature writing, Japanese nature writing, and bioregionalism.
Website: http://www.uwosh.edu/facstaff/barnhill

Thore Bjørnvig has an M.A. in the history of religions, is an independent scholar, works as a freelance writer, and blogs for the science news sites

videnskab.dk and sciencenordic.com. His research centres on astroculture and intersections among science, religion, and technology as these relate to outer space. His latest research assignment was at Kroppedal Museum, unit of astronomy, where he studied interactions and boundaries between industry and academia in the creation of the Danish Oersted Satellite. Currently, he works on the religious aspects of the NewSpace movement and the history of space toys, the latter mainly focusing on LEGO space themes from 1978 to 1987.
Website: http://thorebjornvig.dk/

Michael P. Ferber is Associate Professor of geography and Co-Director of the Environmental Studies Program at The King's University College in Edmonton, Alberta. His publications include an article on the insider/outsider problem in the geography of religion in the *Annals of the Association of American Geographers* (2006), an article on scale and religion in *The Journal of Critical Realism* (2013), and numerous articles and many encyclopedia articles on religion and the environment.

Rachelle K. Gould expects to complete her Ph.D. from the Emmett Interdisciplinary Program in Environment and Resources at Stanford University at about the time this book is published. Her research aims to facilitate integration of a diversity of ecosystem-related values into land-use decision making. Her dissertation investigates biophysical and social aspects of reforestation in Hawai'i. She is especially interested in cultural ecosystem services, a lens that can be used to understand the intangible human values associated with ecosystems. The goal of this two-pronged approach (ecological and social) is to allow multiple dimensions of value to be incorporated into land-use decision making.
Website: http://www.stanford.edu/~rgould

Joy H. Greenberg completed a Ph.D. in mythological studies at Pacifica Graduate Institute with a theoretical dissertation entitled "Strands: Weaving Mythopoietic Narratives of Place as Environmental Ethics." She also has an M.F.A. in creative writing with a focus in creative non-fiction from California State University, Chico. The memoir that formed the culminating project for her M.F.A., *A Pause in the Rain*, details her marriage to the late Chuck Greenberg, founder and leader of the Grammy Award–winning band Shadowfax (http://www.joyhornergreenberg.com). Her articles have appeared in the *Journal for the Study of Religion, Nature, and Culture* and other periodicals, including *American Vedantist, Spring,* and *Ecopsychology.*

Randolph Haluza-DeLay is Associate Professor of sociology at The King's University College in Edmonton, Alberta. He is a co-editor of the anthology *Speaking for Ourselves: Environmental Justice in Canada* (2009). He has authored over twenty-five journal articles and book chapters focusing on environmental justice and the cultural politics of socially just environmental sustainability, social movements and the Alberta oil sands, and the development of an "ecological habitus." He is a co-editor of *How the World's Religions Are Responding to Climate Change* (forthcoming). Before becoming an academic, he was a mountaineering and wilderness guide. Now, he is an active cross-country skier, community volunteer, and father of two teens.

Jennifer K. Hashimoto earned her B.Sc. in biology with a concentration in cell and molecular biology at the University of Hawai'i at Hilo in 2012, while also pursuing her interest in Hawaiian cultural studies. She was born and raised in Hawai'i and is of Native Hawaiian ancestry. Her biological background and academic studies of Hawaiian culture combine to inform her work and perspectives on society in Hawai'i today. She is pursuing a clinical research career, which will enable her both to keep up with the newest technological innovations in science and to continue to interact with and care for the public. Acquiring a post-baccalaureate position at the National Institute for Allergies and Infectious Diseases (NIAID) within the National Institutes of Health (NIH) has been a priceless experience that has allowed her to pursue her academic and professional goals.

Matthew Holtmeier earned his Ph.D. at the University of St. Andrews, Scotland, in 2013, writing a dissertation titled "The Modern Political Film: Biopolitical Production and Cinematic Subjectivity." His publications include works on global cinema, film philosophy, and the interaction between films and approaches to the environment. He recently successfully funded and launched DeleuzeCinema.com, a collaborative resource on Deleuze's work with cinema, and FramesCinemaJournal.com, a peer-reviewed journal based at the University of St. Andrews. Website: http://www.MatthewHoltmeier.com

Britt Istoft has a Ph.D. in the history of religions from the University of Copenhagen and has worked as an Assistant Professor at the University of Southern Denmark. She is now an independent scholar. Her research areas are religion and popular culture (in particular, fantasy and science fiction), (neo)paganism (in particular, Wiccan movements), and medieval studies (in particular, heresy, gender, and mysticism). She has published on religious minorities (e.g., the medieval Cathars), gender issues (e.g., female mystics and "feminist" heresies in the Middle Ages), and religion and popular culture (e.g., religious innovation in fantasy/sci-fi novels/films/television series and in media fan cultures).

Daniel Heath Justice is Canada Research Chair in Indigenous Literature and Expressive Culture at the University of British Columbia. A Colorado-born Canadian citizen of the Cherokee Nation, he lives with his husband in the traditional, ancestral, and unceded territories of the Musqueam people on the UBC campus in Vancouver, where he is also Chair of the First Nations Studies Program and Associate Professor of First Nations Studies and English. His work includes *Our Fire Survives the Storm: A Cherokee Literary History* (2006), the Indigenous epic fantasy *The Way of Thorn and Thunder: The Kynship Chronicles* (2011), the co-edited anthology *Sovereign Erotics: A Collection of Two-Spirit Literature* (2011), and, with James H. Cox, *The Oxford Handbook of Indigenous American Literature* (forthcoming). Current projects include a cultural history of badgers, an essay collection on why Indigenous literature matters, and a new dark fantasy series. Website: http://www.imagineotherwise.ca.

Chris Klassen is Assistant Professor in Religion and Culture at Wilfrid Laurier University. She is the author of *Storied Selves: Shaping Identity in Feminist Witchcraft* (2008) and the editor of *Feminist Spirituality: The Next Generation* (2009). She is also a co-editor of the *Journal of Religion and Popular Culture*.

Michael B. MacDonald is Assistant Professor of Music at MacEwan University. His work explores the application of critical theory to listening and to the critical pedagogy of music education and eco-critical musicology. As well as contributing to *Walking the Line: Country Music Lyricists and the American Literary Canon* (2012) and the journal *Vis-à-vis: Explorations in Anthropology*, he has been recognized by the University of Guelph as a Distinguished Early Career Scholar and has won the Society for American Music's Cambridge University Press Award for a paper co-authored with Dr. Mary Ingraham. He founded and edits *Sound and Noise*, an online journal and blog.

Bruce MacLennan is Associate Professor of electrical engineering and computer science at the University of Tennessee, Knoxville. He received his B.Sc. (mathematics, honours) from Florida State University in 1968 and his M.Sc.

and Ph.D. (computer science) from Purdue University in 1974 and 1975. Before his current position, he worked for Intel Corporation and served on the computer science faculty of the Naval Postgraduate School. Much of MacLennan's academic research has been directed toward understanding the mind in a way that respects both psychical and physical reality and that attempts to understand their interconnection. Since the mid-1980s, his research has focused on new approaches to artificial intelligence based on neuroscience and informed by phenomenological philosophy and psychology. His research emphasis is basic science: What can AI reveal about the structure of natural intelligence and the relation of mind and matter? Website: http://web.eecs.utk.edu/~mclennan

Pat Munday is Professor of science and technology studies at Montana Tech in Butte, Montana. He teaches courses in technology and society, environmental communication, and semiotics. He is also an environmental activist who works with grassroots groups on Superfund issues in the upper Clark Fork River basin and on endangered species issues. As a four-season outdoors person, he backpacks in the wilderness, fly fishes for trout in the rivers, hunts elk in the mountains, and skis cross country along the Continental Divide near his home. Blog: http://ecorover.blogspot.com

Stephen Rust is a post-doctoral instructor in cinema studies and English at the University of Oregon. His research explores the intersections of media and environmental understandings. Stephen is a co-editor of *Ecocinema Theory and Practice* (2012) and his work has appeared in such journals as *ISLE* and *Jump Cut*. He is also a co-founder and site moderator of the online scholarly community at http://ecomediastudies.org.

Lisa H. Sideris is Associate Professor of religious studies at Indiana University, Bloomington. Her areas of research include environmental ethics, religion and nature, and science and religion, particularly Darwinian theory and evolution controversies. She is the author of *Environmental Ethics, Ecological Theology, and Natural Selection* (2003) and a co-editor with Kathleen Dean Moore of *Rachel Carson: Legacy and Challenge* (2008).

Sverker Sörlin is Professor of environmental history in the Division of History of Science, Technology, and Environment at the Royal Institute of Technology, Stockholm, including its KTH Environmental Humanities Laboratory (http://www.kth.se/abe/om-skolan/organisation/inst/philhist/2.3231/ehl). He is also affiliated with the Stockholm Resilience Centre at

Stockholm University. Among his recent books in English are *Nature's End: History and the Environment*, co-edited with Paul Warde (2009), *Northscapes: History, Technology, and the Making of Northern Environments*, co-edited with Dolly Jorgensen (2012), and *The Future of Nature: Documents of Global Change*, co-edited with Libby Robin and Paul Warde (2013). Website: http://www.kth.se/abe/om-skolan/organisation/inst/philhist/2.3231/personal/sverker-sorlin-1.38487

Bron Taylor is Professor of religion and environmental ethics at the University of Florida, and a Carson Fellow of the Rachel Carson Center for Environment and Society in Munich, Germany, which supported the research published in this volume. Dr. Taylor's research focuses on the emotional and spiritual dimensions of environmental movements, and he has led and participated in a variety of international initiatives promoting the conservation of biological and cultural diversity. His books include *Dark Green Religion: Nature Spirituality and the Planetary Future* (2010), the award-winning *Encyclopedia of Religion and Nature* (2005), and *Ecological Resistance Movements: The Global Emergence of Radical and Popular Environmentalism* (1995). He is also the founder of the International Society for the Study of Religion, Nature, and Culture and the editor of its affiliated *Journal for the Study of Religion, Nature, and Culture*. In his pre-professorial life, he served as an ocean lifeguard and peace officer in the California State Department of Parks and Recreation. Website: http://www.brontaylor.com

Jacob von Heland received his Ph.D. in natural resources management from Stockholm University in 2011. The thesis built on fieldwork on sacred groves in southern Madagascar and combined complex systems ecology, ethnography, and science studies. Partly in response to this book chapter, he now works on a report on ways for cross-scale environmental policy to assess and evaluate sacred sites from a multiple-evidence perspective. This work reviews landscapes in India and is conducted at the Stockholm Resilience Centre, Stockholm University. Jacob is also passionate about film and regularly works as a director in documentary and commercial productions.

Tim Wiebe-Neufeld has been an advocate for creation-care in the Mennonite church for over twenty years. He has been involved in youth and outdoor programs and, for the past decade, has served as co-pastor of First Mennonite Church in Edmonton, Alberta. His Master of Theological Studies from Conrad Grebel University College in Waterloo, Ontario, focused on Mennonite approaches to environmental theology. He is a father, hiker, and hockey player.

Index

Environmental Humanities Series

Environmental thought pursues with renewed urgency the grand concerns of the humanities: who we think we are, how we relate to others, and how we live in the world. Scholarship in the environmental humanities explores these questions by crossing the lines that separate human from animal, social from material, and objects and bodies from techno-ecological networks. Humanistic accounts of political representation and ethical recognition are re-examined in consideration of other species. Social identities are studied in relation to conceptions of the natural, the animal, the bodily, place, space, landscape, risk, and technology, and in relation to the material distribution and contestation of environmental hazards and pleasures.

The Environmental Humanities Series features research that adopts and adapts the methods of the humanities to clarify the cultural meanings associated with environmental debate. The scope of the series is broad. Film, literature, television, Web-based media, visual art, and physical landscape—all are crucial sites for exploring how ecological relationships and identities are lived and imagined. The Environmental Humanities Series publishes scholarly monographs and essay collections in environmental cultural studies, including popular culture, film, media, and visual cultures; environmental literary criticism; cultural geography; environmental philosophy, ethics, and religious studies; and other cross-disciplinary research that probes what it means to be human, animal, and technological in an ecological world.

Gathering research and writing in environmental philosophy, ethics, cultural studies, and literature under a single umbrella, the series aims to make visible the contributions of humanities research to environmental studies, and to foster discussion that challenges and reconceptualizes the humanities.

SERIES EDITOR
Cheryl Lousley, English and Film Studies, Wilfrid Laurier University

EDITORIAL COMMITTEE
Adrian J. Ivakhiv, Environmental Studies, University of Vermont
Catriona Mortimer-Sandilands, Tier 1 CRC in Sustainability and Culture, Environmental Studies, York University
Susie O'Brien, English and Cultural Studies, McMaster University
Laurie Ricou, English, University of British Columbia
Rob Shields, Henry Marshall Tory Chair and Professor, Department of Sociology, University of Alberta

FOR MORE INFORMATION, CONTACT
Lisa Quinn
Acquisitions Editor
Wilfrid Laurier University Press
75 University Avenue West
Waterloo, ON N2L 3C5
(519) 884-0710 ext. 2843
Email: quinn@press.wlu.ca

Books in the Environmental Humanities Series
Published by Wilfrid Laurier University Press

Animal Subjects: An Ethical Reader in a Posthuman World, Jodey Castricano, editor / 2008 / 324 pp. / ISBN 978-0-88920-512-3

Open Wide a Wilderness: Canadian Nature Poems, Nancy Holmes, editor / 2009 / 534 pp. / ISBN 978-1-55458-033-0

Technonatures: Environments, Technologies, Spaces, and Places in the Twenty-first Century, Damian F. White and Chris Wilbert, editors / 2009 / 282 pp. / ISBN 978-1-55458-150-4

Writing in Dust: Reading the Prairie Environmentally, Jenny Kerber / 2010 / 276 pp. / ISBN 978-1-55458-218-1 (hardcover), ISBN 978-1-55458-306-5 (paper)

Ecologies of Affect: Placing Nostalgia, Desire, and Hope, Tonya K. Davidson, Ondine Park, and Rob Shields, editors / 2011 / 360 pp. / illus. / ISBN 978-1-55458-258-7

Ornithologies of Desire: Ecocritical Essays, Avian Poetics, and Don McKay Travis V. Mason / 2013 / 306 pp. / ISBN 978-1-55458-630-1

Ecologies of the Moving Image: Cinema, Affect, Nature, Adrian J. Ivakhiv / 2013 / 432 pp. / ISBN 978-1-55458-905-0

Avatar and Nature Spirituality, Bron Taylor, editor / 2013 / 378 pp. / ISBN 978-1-55458-843-5

Sustaining the West: Cultural Responses to Western Environments, Past and Present, Liza Piper and Lisa Szabo-Jones, editors / forthcoming 2013/ ISBN 978-1-55458-923-4

Found in Alberta: Environmental Themes for Anthropocene, Robert Boschman and Mario Trono, editors / forthcoming 2014 / ISBN 978-1-55458-959-3